The Best American Sports Writing 2005

The Best AMERICAN SPORTS WRITING™ 2005

Edited and with an Introduction
by Mike Lupica

Glenn Stout, *Series Editor*

HOUGHTON MIFFLIN COMPANY
BOSTON • NEW YORK   2005

ISSN: 1056-8034
ISBN-13: 978-0-618-47019-8   ISBN-10: 0-618-47019-0
ISBN-13: 978-0-618-47020-4 (pbk.)   ISBN-10: 0-618-47020-4 (pbk.)

Printed in the United States of America

MP 10 9 8 7 6 5 4 3 2 1

Contents

Foreword

I am often approached with a variation of the same question. "How can I or my wife (or husband, son, daughter, boyfriend, girlfriend, grandson, granddaughter, columnist, feature writer, beat writer, freelancer, publication, etc., etc., etc.) have a story selected to appear in the *Best American Sports Writing?*" There is, of course, a deliciously short answer, after which the speed-reader or the impatient can feel free to skip forward to Mike Lupica's introduction, namely, "Write something memorable and write it well."

For those who have chosen to continue, the number of times I am asked this question tells me that many questioners have already figured this part out. What he or she is really looking for is some kind of edge, some keen insight into the inner workings of the *BASW* home office. They hope I will reveal the secret formula that lifts the as-yet-undiscovered classic-to-be out of the noisy fray. Then, on that cold day in February when the snow blocks my driveway and I settle in with the appropriate beverage to make my final selection of seventy-five stories to package and express to our esteemed guest editor, it will miraculously leap into the forefront of my consciousness and land on top of the heap.

Frankly, after fifteen years of this, I don't have a clue how to respond. That secret formula has never revealed itself to me, which is why I'm in this part of the book instead of further back. As far as I can determine, for a few short days each year my body is taken over by an entirely other being who makes the selections for me, then departs for whatever dark corner it inhabits the rest of the year until the sound of me lugging the late mail in on the Day of Reckoning causes it to stir once more. It's back, awakening from slumber in a kind of circadian emergence, not unlike those damned Asian ladybugs that come from nowhere one day each fall and swarm over my house for a day before disappearing. Where it comes from, where it goes, and how it does its task between doing the dishes, looking after the dogs, plowing the drive, and putting my daughter on the school bus is a mystery. Like the spring, however, I'm damn glad when it finally puts in an appearance.

A friend once offered that perhaps I was inadvertently channeling the souls of sportswriters from earlier epochs. That was an intriguing notion, but on reflection one that I rapidly dismissed. I am in Vermont, after all, and barely that. For all its many charms (see Pam Belluck's story "How to Catch Fish in Vermont"), Alburg is one of only two towns in the lower forty-eight states not contiguous to the rest of the nation. This means that those with *gephydrophobia* (bridge phobia) or *champophobia* (fear of sea monsters inhabiting Lake Champlain, as profiled on the Discovery Channel) have to buy groceries (*épicerie*) in Quebec, and if we ever decide to secede all we have to do is cut the bridges and hope someone notices.

In other words, Alburg is not quite Sedona, or even Ojai. Few sportswriters make the trek up this far when living, so I can't imagine any would do so postmortem. If this kind of spectral visitation is even possible, I think visiting me is pretty far down on the list. Personally, I'd choose to haunt an expatriate with a trust fund living in a resort hotel somewhere in the Caribbean.

A better question to pose might be, "How can I or my wife (husband, son, daughter, boyfriend, girlfriend, grandson, granddaughter, columnist, feature writer, beat writer, freelancer, publication, etc., etc., etc.) not make that slumbering giant rue the annual awakening and dump the submission into the dustbin?" That's a question I can answer, for after fifteen years I have developed some perspective in this area. So listen up.

As writers, we have all been admonished at one time or another to "put yourself in the reader's shoes," or some other piece of clothing. Fine advice. My house is cold, the price of fuel oil high, and the top of my head increasingly barren, so I often wear a hat in midwinter, usually of the knit variety. So feel free to put yourself under my hat.

Now we're getting somewhere. Read along with me for a moment . . . ah, here's a story, I mean a real piece of work, one that leaves a latent retinal image and causes me to envision it in galley form, leading reviewers to gasp with delight and the author to be plucked from the mob and lavished with awards, book deals, and radio talk shows. And then . . .

. . . Take your pick. Since the inception of this series, the deadline has always been February 1. Always will be. While I have always been generous to late arrivals, imagine our dismay (remember, you are wearing my hat) to be reading such a classic tale in late March, then to discover (the horror!) that the author meant for the story to be considered for the book that has just been sent off. In other words, the deadline has been missed, and badly.

This happens more often than you would imagine and makes me throw the hat across the room, where the dogs chew holes in the damn thing. This is a deadline business, but from my side of PO Box 549, Alburg, VT 05440, I receive so many late submissions that I'm amazed anything is ever published on time at all. I suspect that's why so many magazines I receive in June are dated September. Even as I write this in late March, earlier this morning I read a story published last June that should have been sent to me this past January. I suspect there are more to come, for I know a few Red Sox writers still laboring without book contracts, pondering a submission, and dreaming of literary glory. Sorry, but that story about your visit to Granddad's grave last October will have to go undiscovered this time around. You are too late, and there is nothing to be done about it except wait another eighty-six years for cliché-ridden longing to regain poignancy — or else start writing about the Cubs.

In addition to meeting the deadline, each story must have been published in 2005 (for the next edition), in the English language, in either the United States or Canada. For the geographically challenged, Canada, my matriarchal homeland, is a right turn at the end of the driveway. The rest of the United States, where Dad was born, is to the left. English is the language you are reading now. While I support multilingualism on restaurant menus and find Quebec a fine place for groceries, I understand other languages about as well as major league baseball's waiver rule, hence the Can-Am chauvinism of this collection. One need not be a citizen of either nation, although familiarity with the Roman calendar is of assistance in determining the current year.

The only other requirement for a story to be considered for inclusion in *The Best American Sports Writing* is the *BASW* equivalent of a wartime request for name, rank, and serial number. In order to select a story I need to know (a) who wrote it, (b) the name of the publication, and (c) the publication date. Like the deadline and country of origin, this too has remained a constant for fifteen years, but whenever a submission arrives lacking one or more of these critical factors, our hat gets a few extra holes. I could fill a book with stories that might well have made the annual volume except that I didn't know some combination of who wrote them, where, or when, and no database yet exists that can help find me the answers. Someday soon I am going to propose to my editor that we consider a companion volume entitled *The Best American Sports Writing Written by Someone, Published Somewhere, Sometime.* Meanwhile, these submissions are of great help lighting the woodstove.

Other bad strategies, while perhaps less egregious, nonetheless may tilt the gods of this project against you. There are always a few souls who I suspect believe they should be the author of every story in the book, a worthy goal but perhaps not a realistic one. Here's a tip: if you are sending me twenty or thirty stories or more, you may wish to consider publishing your own book. Not only will you receive multiple free copies upon publication that make great, albeit cheesy, Christmas presents, but your name and not mine or that of the guest editor will be on the cover. There are also those submissions that include such items as résumés, curricula vitae, books, sugar cookies, and other extraneous items. These, too, are of great help with the stove, and the dogs appreciate the cookies.

So what does work? Apart from blank checks, not much beyond a complimentary subscription to your publication. This relieves the individual author of innumerable ethical pitfalls and potential embarrassments. I do, however, admit to a soft spot for the suck-up cover letter that praises my literary skill, rough-hewn good looks, social magnetism, genetic legacy, and whatever sports team the writer imagines I secretly favor. Whenever I tire of reading sports writing and feeding the stove, I read these closely and repeatedly.

So there. Like playing mini-golf, placing a story in this collection requires adhering to a very short set of rules easily understood by everyone over the age of five. Don't swing too hard, don't fib on the scorecard, and when you hit the windmill, keep trying.

Works for me.

Every season I read every issue of hundreds of sports and general interest magazines in search of writing that might merit inclusion in *The Best American Sports Writing*. I also contact the sports editors of some three hundred newspapers and hundreds of magazine editors and request their submissions.

I also encourage writers, readers, and all other interested parties to send me stories they've written or read in the past year that they would like to see reprinted in this volume — please feel free to alert me to either your own work or that of someone else.

A story submitted for consideration in *The Best American Sports Writing 2006* should meet the following criteria:

- It must be column-length or longer.
- It must have been published in 2005.
- It must not be a reprint or book excerpt.
- It must be published in the United States or Canada.
- It must be received by February 1, 2006.

All submissions must include the name of the author, the date of publication, and the publication name and address. Photocopies, tear sheets, or clean copies are fine. Readable reductions to 8½ by 11 are preferred. Submissions from online publications must be made in hard copy, and those who submit stories from newspapers should submit the story in hard copy as published. Since newsprint generally suffers in transit, it is best to submit newspaper stories by copying and then mounting them on 8½-by-11 paper, with the appropriate URL attached if the story also appeared online.

There is no limit to the number of submissions either an individual or a publication may make, but please use common sense. Owing to the volume of material I receive, no submission can be returned or acknowledged. I also believe it is inappropriate for me to comment on or critique any individual submission. Publications that want to be absolutely certain their contributions are considered are advised to provide a complimentary subscription to the address listed below. Those that already do so should make sure to extend the subscription.

Please address your submission to:

Glenn Stout
PO Box 549
Alburg, VT 05440

No electronic submissions will be accepted, although stories that only appeared online are eligible. Please send all submissions by U.S. mail — in midwinter I often can't receive UPS or FedEx submissions, and I'm not kidding. In the event a story is selected for publication, your publication will be contacted concerning rights and permissions. Those with questions or comments may contact me at baswed@sover.net.

Copies of previous editions of this book can be ordered through most bookstores or online book dealers. An index of stories that have appeared in this series can be found at glennstout.net.

Thanks again go out to Houghton Mifflin for allowing me to continue to work on such a gratifying project, particularly my editor Susan Canavan, Sarah Gabert, and Larry Cooper. Thanks also to Mike Lupica for his diligence and generosity, the website sports journalists.com for posting submission guidelines, and Siobhan and Saorla for letting me read more than anyone should ever be allowed. And thanks again to the writers whose efforts make the work of this book the best part of my day.

GLENN STOUT
Alburg, Vermont

Introduction

THIS ALL really started for me back in the late 1960s when I was a junior at Bishop Guertin High School, writing about my high school teams for the *Nashua* (New Hampshire) *Telegraph,* getting paid five dollars for the stories once Mike Shalhoup, the editor of the paper, convinced me it was a much better idea to start double-spacing them.

Of course, this was before I had the only kind of job I ever wanted, writing a sports column in New York, which is the job that had me sitting in Fenway Park when Bucky Dent hit his home run against the Red Sox on October 2, 1978. And sitting in Lake Placid the night Herb Brooks's hockey team beat the Russians. And watching Kirk Gibson's ball fly out of Dodger Stadium one World Series night in 1988. It is the job that has given me a front row seat to everything else I have seen, all the way to the Red Sox coming back from three games down to beat the Yankees last fall.

When the ball that Gibson hit went out of the ballpark that night, the great Jack Buck made this unforgettable call: "I don't believe what I just saw."

Nobody believed what they saw in the 2004 American League Championship Series after the Yankees were ahead three games to none. I have always said that, for me, nothing could ever top Mike Eruzione and Jim Craig and what they did in that rink in Lake Placid the night Al Michaels asked if we all believed in miracles. And I still don't think anything ever will. But watching the Red Sox come back that way against the Yankees, no matter which way you were rooting, was pretty good for the silver medal.

I got paid to write about that Olympic team and got paid to write about the Yankees versus the Red Sox. I once told Jimmy Breslin that I liked doing what I was doing so much I would do it for free. Breslin snapped, "This isn't the Lawn Tennis Association. We don't just play for the love of the game." Believe me, the point was well taken. But really, from the time I was a teenager, the only life I ever imagined for myself, at least professionally, was writing about sports.

My dreams about that did not begin with the *Nashua Telegraph*. More than anything, they really began in the 1960s, when I tore through my copy of *Sports Illustrated* as soon as it arrived in our mail on a Friday, wanting to see what Dan Jenkins was writing about college football or golf or even skiing and to read any of the other star writers they had at the time. More than anything else the magazine and its writers were doing in those days, they were expanding the possibilities. And making kids like me want to somehow figure out a way to do what they were doing. For me it started with Jenkins, who I believe did more to invent modern sports writing than anybody alive.

It doesn't mean there weren't tremendous sports columnists in the newspaper business when I was growing up. There were, there are. My friend Bob Ryan, from the *Boston Globe,* is a classic American sports columnist and would have been a star, I believe, in any era. Later in my career I would discover the pure, clear genius of W. C. Heinz, one of the best sports columnists of all time for the old *New York Sun*, and also a storied war correspondent for that paper who traveled across Europe during World War II with his old Remington typewriter and the First Army. In the 1950s, Heinz would come home and write what is still, for my money, the best sports novel ever written, *The Professional.*

Red Smith was another of my heroes, not just because of the way he could write, but because of the elegant way he went the distance in this business, writing like a total star almost until the day he died. He was a giant of talent and grace and made you proud every single day to be in the same business. Over the years more than a few people have asked me why I stayed in sports, knowing there had been opportunities to write a different kind of column in the front of my paper, the *New York Daily News*. I've always had the same answer — that if writing a sports column was good enough for Red Smith to spend his whole life doing it, it's more than good enough for me.

But I didn't start reading Red until I got to Boston College. First came *SI*, just absolutely blowing the doors off everything. Later in my life there'd be a movie I liked a lot, *The Turning Point*, with Anne Bancroft and Shirley MacLaine. It happened to be about ballet. About which I knew nothing. But watching the dancing in that movie, I sure knew this: what Mikhail Baryshnikov was doing was different from everybody else.

The writing in the old *Sports Illustrated*, under the legendary managing editor Andre Laguerre, was like that. It was different. And after it, nothing was the same in sports writing.

It wasn't just a different sports world in those days. There was no Internet, of course, no ESPN.com acting as some sort of huge grazing pasture for everybody in the business, a place for people to go at the start of the day to make up their minds about what they wanted to write and what they wanted to say. There was no sense that guys in the business were sometimes writing for each other instead of the reader. There was no talk radio, the giant weather vane of modern sports opinion, the monster that tries to shape what everybody thinks and has turned so many modern sports sections into printed versions of what the editors are listening to on the radio.

Now, in the modern American sports culture, the town hall is *SportsCenter* on ESPN. It is the one place where fans and players and coaches and managers and general managers and writers and broadcasters can collect every night, the sports version of what the nightly network news used to be on television.

There was none of that in the old days.

In the old days, if you wanted to find out what people in other places were writing about things, you had to do what I did in college — go to the Out-of-Town Newsstand in Harvard Square, which is where I first read one of the great sports sections of all time in the old *New York Post* — the pre-Murdoch version of that paper — with Paul Sann as the editor, a future boss of mine, Ike Gellis, as the sports editor, and writers like Larry Merchant and Vic Ziegel and Paul Zimmerman just laying you out every single day.

One night the Mets pulled out an improbable victory in the bottom of the ninth inning. Even now, almost thirty years later, I can tell you Ziegel's lead:

"The game is never over until the final out, the *Post* has learned."

He made me laugh that day and is still making me laugh as a colleague at the *Daily News.*

In the front of that paper was Pete Hamill, one of the great big-city newspaper columnists of them all.

But in those days, the town hall for everybody who even thought about writing sports for a living was the old *Sports Illustrated.* That was the home office for all the dreamers of the world. In all the years I have known Hamill, he has always had a wonderful expression to describe any talented group of people in any profession, an expression that comes from his deep love and deep knowledge of music. The first time I ever heard him use it was when he was talking about the old Knicks one day, the Knicks of Willis Reed and Walt "Clyde" Frazier and Bill Bradley and Dave DeBusschere.

"It was like the Basie band," Hamill said.

He was a New York kid out of the 1930s and 1940s. So the frame of reference came from there. In my world, my generation, those *SI* writers of the 1960s and 1970s were the Stones. The greatest rock-and-roll band of all time.

And Jenkins was Mick Jagger.

Here is Dan Jenkins writing about a college football game as famous as any ever played, the 10–10 tie between Notre Dame and Michigan State in 1966:

> Old Notre Dame will tie over all. Sing it out, guys. That is not exactly what the march says, of course, but that is how the big game ends every time you replay it. And that is how millions of cranky college football fans will remember it. For 59 minutes in absolutely overwrought East Lansing last week, the brutes of Notre Dame and Michigan State pounded each other into enough mistakes to fill Bubba Smith's uniform — enough to settle a dozen games between lesser teams — but the 10–10 tie that destiny seemed to be demanding had a strange, noble quality to it. And then it did not have that anymore. For the people who saw it under the cold, dreary clouds or on national television, suddenly all it had was this enormous emptiness for which the Irish will be forever blamed.

He was just getting warmed up. I sat next to him at enough big events later on, so I know what it was like. He wrote clean, fast, funny, always nailing everything first time through, and he was packing up his typewriter when the rest of the guys in the room must have felt like they were just getting started. Cigarette on one side, coffee on the other, the coolest one in the room . . .

Forget everything that came before, all of that ferocious thudding in the line that was mostly responsible for five fumbles, four interceptions, 25 other incompletions, a total of 20 rushing plays that either lost yardage or gained none, and forget the few good plays — the big passes. Put the No. 1 team, Notre Dame, on its 30-yard line with time for at least four passes to break the tie. A No. 1 team will try *something*, won't it, to stay that way?

Notre Dame did not. It just let the air out of the ball. . . .

As you can see, this wasn't the beginning of a normal game story, not by a long shot. Oh, it *was* a game story, all right. As usual, Jenkins had the game he was watching down cold. But it was so much more. It was column, for one thing. It had atmosphere, smart-ass reporting, a rock-solid knowledge and love of college football. It also had this: Jenkins. The one guy everybody wanted to read on this game (even if they didn't get to read him until five or six days after the fact), absolutely dropping the hammer on Ara Parseghian and the most famous college football program in the history of the planet. To the point where as soon as copies of *SI* started making their way to the Notre Dame campus in South Bend, Indiana, that week, people started burning them.

All this time later, nearly forty years, I believe that Jenkins's story on that one college football game, one called The Game of the Century, changed sports writing and did more than anything to make his magazine matter even more than it ever had before.

(For the record, because I called him and asked, Jenkins doesn't think it's the best game story he ever wrote for the magazine, and it wasn't, on either college football or pro football or golf. Maybe his own personal classic was the game story after another Game of the Century, the one between Oklahoma and Nebraska in 1971.)

By the way, as long as we're on the subject, please check out the lead from the 1972 British Open, where Jack Nicklaus failed to win the third leg of golf's Grand Slam:

He stood against one of those sand hills, one foot halfway up the rise, a gloved hand braced on his knee, and his head hung downward in monumental despair. He lingered in this pose, with what seemed like all of Scotland surrounding him, with the North Sea gleaming in the background and with the quiet broken only by the awkward, silly, faraway sound of bagpipes rehearsing for the victory ceremony. This was Jack Nicklaus on the last hole of the British Open and another putt had refused to fall. It was Nicklaus in the moment he knew, after a furious

comeback, that he had finally lost the championship and what might
have been the grandest slam in golf. . . .

As good as it gets.
Or got.
I will tell you again: if you were a kid in those days, dreaming
your dreams, this was how you wanted to do it. You wanted to get
on a plane with the greatest portable typewriter ever made, the
Olivetti Lettera — the one in the blue case, black stripe down the
middle — and go find a moment in sports that made you write any-
thing like *that.*
There were other great writers in that magazine, for sure. But
Jenkins was the one.
Forget about baseball cards.
I should have saved those issues of *SI.*

In college I wasn't just going over to Harvard Square to buy the
Post, because I had the *Boston Globe* to read every day, with Ryan,
now my sidekick on *The Sports Reporters*, writing about the Celtics
and Peter Gammons writing about the Red Sox and Bud Collins
writing about Wimbledon and, always, Leigh Montville's brilliant
column. I was writing for three school papers at Boston College
and writing for the *Boston Phoenix* and working nights at the *Globe.*
By that time, what Jenkins and the others had started was making
its way into the sports section. All of a sudden, it was even *more* the
best-written part of the newspaper than ever before. I like to think
that it still is. Because over all the years and all the changes in sports
writing, not all of them good, one thing has not changed:
We all still go looking for the moment.
It is the moment in sports where the day changes, and the game
changes, and you know how you want to tell your story. Notre
Dame running the ball into the line instead of trying to move the
ball down the field against Michigan State. Nicklaus standing there
after one more putt, which would have made all the difference that
day against Lee Trevino, refused to go into the hole.
When that moment doesn't matter to you anymore, you have to
go do something else, whether you are writing for a daily newspaper or a weekly newspaper or a monthly or *SI.* Last October,
when the Red Sox were down those three games to the Yankees in

the American League Championship Series and the Yankees were three outs away from sweeping them, you better believe there was a moment.

The Yankees had Mariano Rivera, the greatest closer in post-season history, maybe all of baseball history, in the game at Fenway Park, and he was going to get three more outs, the way he had all the times before, and the Yankees were going to the World Series.

Only here is what happened next at Fenway Park:

Rivera walked the leadoff man for the Red Sox, Kevin Millar, to start the bottom of the ninth. Dave Roberts ran for Millar and stole second base. And even though not a single living person, not even the truest of true believers for the Red Sox, knew it at the time, those two small moments — walk, stolen base — were the beginning of the end for the New York Yankees in the 2004 American League Championship Series.

Out of those two small moments, the Red Sox began to write the biggest comeback story in the history of sports and end the eighty-six-year drought since their last World Series.

Walk.

Stolen base.

Single by Bill Mueller up the middle.

Game tied.

History being made, even if we didn't know it at the time.

For the writers of the longer pieces in this book — some of them stunning pieces — the moment can be different. Sometimes it is a quote, like a crucial line of dialogue from a movie or book. A scene. An insight that gives both writer and reader a better understanding of the subject.

There was the unforgettable exchange between Joe DiMaggio and Marilyn Monroe in Gay Talese's legendary piece about DiMaggio for *Esquire* magazine. Monroe is just back from entertaining the troops in Korea, and she's telling DiMaggio about it and finally says, "Joe, you never heard such cheering."

"Yes, I have," Joe DiMaggio says.

Talese's brand of magazine writing, about subjects like DiMaggio and Frank Sinatra, has been called New Journalism. I just always thought it was high literature. The DiMaggio piece, in my opinion, stands with any short story ever written. With Irwin Shaw's master-piece "Girls in Their Summer Dresses." Or Hemingway's "A Clean

Well-Lighted Place." Anything. Talese begins the piece with a writer pestering DiMaggio for an interview, one to which Joe D. never consents, and Talese never tells you that the writer is himself. After that, the piece is as graceful as DiMaggio's game had once been. Reading Talese's *Esquire* piece now is as exciting as it was the first time. The best literature always stands up that way.

There was a point in my career when I wrote *The Sporting Life* column for almost ten years in *Esquire,* first for Lee Eisenberg, then for Ed Kosner, and finally for Terry McDonnell, who now is the managing editor of *Sports Illustrated.* It was a great job. I worked for great editors there. But the spirit of that place, always, was Talese. He was the one who had set the bar high for everybody who came after him.

Sports writing, in the newspaper anyway, was so different when I was starting out back in the 1970s. Now I worry that the sports section is losing out to all the cable channels, to all the yelling on television and radio, to the dot-coms. I worry a lot that too many people in our business are willing to run with the crowd, especially when it comes to the big issues. And that original thinking is simply a clever reworking of what somebody thought first in another paper.

With all that, I still believe sports brings out the very best in talented writers, whether they are professional sportswriters or not. I hope you will see that in what I think is a wonderful and diverse collection of work here in this book. I wish more newspaper columns had been submitted. Glenn Stout, who labors so mightily on this book every year, constantly laments that not nearly enough columns are submitted.

But included in these pages is work from some guys who have been favorites of mine for a long time: Bill Reynolds from Providence and Bill Plaschke of the *Los Angeles Times,* a writer who works the space once occupied by the great, great Jim Murray, with his own style and humor. You will see an ambitious column by Richard Sandomir of the *New York Times* in which he writes, more than successfully to my mind, in the amazing voice of Howard Cosell, speaking beautifully to the whole notion of censorship.

There are fish tales in this book, because if your language and your reporting and your words can make me care about fish, then you've done something. There is Katy Vine's piece about the Kilgore Rangerettes, from that fine publication the *Texas Monthly*. And a touching story from Sean Flynn that is more about friendship than golf.

There is a piece on Joe Paterno by an old baseball pitcher named Pat Jordan, whose work I have long admired. And Ira Berkow of the *New York Times*, tracking down Jim Woods, a star high school player from Chicago against whom Berkow had once competed. I mentioned Mark Kram's boxing writing in *SI;* I've included a piece by his son from the *Philadelphia Daily News*, a moving piece about a football player named Rick Lanetti.

And there is Steve Coll's long story from the *Washington Post* about the death of former football player Pat Tillman. Coll, doing what good newspapermen are supposed to do, tells you the truth about things, even when the truth doesn't fit the legend.

There are pieces about race and steroids and rape and illness and hope and loss, all splendidly told. And honoring the spirit of the old *Sports Illustrated*, I have included several pieces from the modern version of the magazine, just because I couldn't leave out any of the ones I read. So there is L. Jon Wertheim's piece about the rise and fall of tennis player Roscoe Tanner, which knocked my eyes out when I read it in the magazine, mostly because I had covered Tanner back in the 1970s when he was one of the best players in this world.

There is Michael Bamberger's superb account of the drug addiction of a pitching prospect named Jeff Allison, the pride of Peabody, Massachusetts. There is Tom Verducci's celebration of Red Sox fans from the magazine's Sportsmen of the Year issue, brilliantly and movingly told. And Gary Smith is in here, with a piece about the Mexican American runners of McFarland High.

There was one night back when I was starting to do television work — before sliding into one of the best seats on television, the chair on the far left on *The Sports Reporters*, first next to Dick Schaap, now John Saunders — when Dan Jenkins told me that no matter what happened with television, I was never to give up my column.

"They respect you if you write," Jenkins said. "The dumber the world gets, the more the words matter."

I hope you think the words in this book matter. Maybe there will be something in here that will inspire some kid who reads it to go chasing after the old dreams. When I was writing this introduction, I told my literary agent, Esther Newberg, about that 1966 Notre Dame–Michigan State game story. Esther represents Jenkins and Carl Hiaasen and Thomas Friedman and Bud Shrake — another alumnus of the old *SI* — and Maureen Dowd and John Feinstein and Tony Kornheiser. So she has an understanding of the business.

Even with that, she said, "How do you guys remember all this stuff?"

Because you just do.

Because the best writing got into my brain and my heart once and never got out. I can tell you the last line Red Smith wrote — "Someday there would be another DiMaggio" — the way I can quote the first line of *Gatsby*. I can tell you about the lead Curry Kirkpatrick wrote once in *SI* about Ilie Nastase, one that began: "Bad is better than good. . . ."

I can quote to you from the column Schaap wrote when his friend Lenny Bruce died, and I can talk to you all day about Breslin's piece from Parkland Memorial Hospital, recounting the death there of John F. Kennedy. I read it in a paperback edition of *The World of Jimmy Breslin*, a copy I still have and always will, even if it is mostly held together by masking tape now.

During the Yankees–Red Sox series last fall, I was as excited to pick up the Boston papers as I had been when I was a kid at Boston College and knew what I wanted to do with the rest of my life.

The words still mattered.

MIKE LUPICA

GARY SMITH

Running for Their Lives

FROM SPORTS ILLUSTRATED

THERE WAS SILENCE when the footrace ended. Then Ayon threw his arms around the coach's wife and cried, "Why did God do this? I don't know why God did this!" and the boys in red and white each staggered off alone to cry.

They had failed the most successful coach in California schoolboy history. They'd failed the elders who'd walked at their heels to the starting line, reminding them that they had to win the state championship for Mr. White. They'd fallen apart on the old man's last day as a coach, they'd spit on his dynasty and ministry both. *Sixth place.*

Mr. White's wife went to dry their tears. But then she and the elders began crying too, and it was hopeless. No high school sports program in California had ever done what theirs had — won nine state titles — but it had been this team's duty to send Mr. White into the sunset with the untouchable number, the fitting number, the perfect number: 10.

One by one, that autumn day a year and a half ago, the Mexican American boys awaited their chance to speak to the white man alone. To say, "I'm sorry, Blanco. I'm sorry for letting you down."

Except one.

Eight months passed. Evening fell on the heat-slugged little town. Laundry sagged from plastic lines like skin from the brown dogs' ribs. Workers, home from a long day of picking grapes, sat inside their stucco box houses as if stoned by the sun. Chickens in their front yards gave up pecking at the bare earth. Not a peep came through the doors of El Cha Cha Cha.

Wait. Something just stirred on the southwest edge of town. A plume of dust, out in the almond groves. A herd of brown boys kicking up powder on a dirt road.

A bicycle nipped at their heels. It accelerated if they slackened and made them raise dust again. It moved up onto their flank to protect them against the farm dogs' fangs. It dropped back to round up stragglers. Jim White thought he had passed the torch to his faithful assistant, Amador Ayon, thought he had retired and begun to fade away. But his town and his wife and his gut hadn't let him, so here he was at sixty-two, weeks before the 2003–04 school year and cross-country season began, sheepdogging his flock through 100 degree heat, chasing state title number ten. Again.

He rose from the seat of the bike and pumped harder, exchanging nods and words as he passed Julio and Baltazar and Octavio and Steven, both Tonys and both Juans, all the boys who'd hoped with all their hearts that the sun wouldn't set on them, that the town's patriarch wouldn't retire during their four years at McFarland High . . . that they wouldn't end up sitting inside those stucco box houses at night for the rest of their lives, dazed by fieldwork and sun.

What were the odds that Ayon or anyone else could take over and keep this magic dust cloud moving? What were the odds that in the annals of California high school sports — all the years chocked with big-city phenoms and rugged valley boys and wealthy suburban programs — the greatest dynasty would be produced by a band of five-and-a-half-foot Mexican Americans at a little high school in a town with no traffic light or movie theater, one of the poorest communities in America? That year after year a blue-eyed man on a bicycle could compel another bunch of teenage campesinos to run eight miles across the fields and orchards where they'd already worked all day harvesting oranges and grapes and almonds and peaches and plums? Every evening? In their *off*-season?

Mr. White tucked his bike behind the front-runner, the fastest one, the unlikeliest leader he'd ever had. The boy who wished that Mr. White had just packed up and left to live his last years in his cabin an hour away in the Sierra Mountains, as he'd planned.

The man and the boy kept pumping their knees. They were both striving for more than number ten, both straining against all the invisible strings that bound them to McFarland. Both struggling to find their way out.

Mr. White drew closer. "Good work, Javi," he murmured.

Javier Medina didn't lift his eyes. He turned his shoulder to his town's legend.

It didn't seem like a hard town to leave. Most people left before realizing they'd ever entered, barreling through the Central Valley three hours north of Los Angeles along Highway 99, a strip of asphalt that separated McFarland's poor West Side from its poorer East Side. The white descendants of the Dust Bowl refugees who had founded the town had no trouble abandoning it in the 1960s and '70s to Mexican immigrants weary of wandering from town to town, crop to crop. McFarland's movie theater became a mortuary, its newspaper was long gone, and all the bars but El Cha Cha Cha were boarded up. The town had two places to go to jail and nine places to go to eat. The population was 9,600 if you didn't count a couple of thousand illegals and the 1,100 behind bars. McFarland was renowned chiefly for its high incidence of cancer, which had afflicted one of Mr. White's nephews and more than twenty other children between the mid-seventies and mid-nineties and scared visiting teams into bringing their own water.

Mr. White loved McFarland.

He arrived in 1964 fresh from college in L.A., took a fifth-grade teaching job, and jumped in with both feet, making sure his yard too had chickens and rabbits scratching at it. He wanted to get to know people. He wanted *small*. He came from a family of missionaries but had fallen in love with sports: here was his chance to merge duty with passion. He began coaching every school and rec team he could, basketball and baseball and football and track, and when little boys knocked on his front door asking if he'd come out to play tag or ball, he'd say *sure*.

So what if the town turned brown before his very eyes? In college he'd chosen a roommate who was half Mexican, half Native American. So what if Mr. White had never been a runner? The local runts he wanted to coach in cross-country hadn't a prayer on a basketball court or a football field — endurance and slow-twitch muscles were their genetic gifts — and for all his compassion, he needed to win. So what if he had to wait seventeen years to get a coaching job at the high school? He'd grown up in a dozen houses in Stockton, moving as swiftly as his father could build a new one and sell the old, and he longed for roots the same way that the weary migrants around him did. Four decades after Jim and Cheryl White arrived in McFarland, the town would be 99.9 percent Mexican, and that — as their three long-since-departed daughters like to say — was only because Mr. and Mrs. White stayed.

Blanco, his runners often called him. English was their second language, one that bedeviled them in the classroom and kept most of them out of college. Most went to the fields when they reached puberty, stooping and snipping, climbing and crawling and duck-walking through irrigation puddles to supplement their parents' pitiful wages. No one could figure it out, how the runners with the shortest legs and the grimmest lives began winning everything once Blanco took over their program, in 1980. He'd joke that it was the town's notorious water or the beans that McFarland's ma-mas served. He persuaded the boys that it was the "voodoo juice" oil he'd give them before races to rub on their aching backs and legs, the cleansing teas and the shakes full of complex carbohy-drates and the gel capsules full of vitamin E and bee pollen that he'd dole out. But the secret was his vast investment of time and heart.

He'd grip the rawhide hands of the boys' fathers and look in their eyes, convince them that something beyond food, clothing, and shelter mattered, that this silly Anglo notion of high school athletics had meaning. He'd fetch their sons in a battered '59 pickup that had been a forest ranger's truck, two lucky lads up front drinking in his stories and sixteen crammed in the back where they could keep an eye on the road through the rotting floorboards. He'd haul them into the foothills to run the orange groves. He'd take them to collect old bottles or newspapers, to sell tamales, to hoe cotton fields — *Mexican golf,* the locals called it — raising funds so they could compete all across California.

He'd take them where their own fathers hadn't the energy or money to take them — bowling lanes and Putt-Putt courses and movie theaters in Bakersfield, a half-hour away — and farther, much farther, to do things many Mexican boys in McFarland had never done. To set eyes on the ocean, to stay in a hotel, to sleep under a white man's roof and sing "Ging Gang Goolie" on a twelve-hour road trip. To camp at Yosemite and run five miles at sunrise to fish for trout at a lake, then run five back to cook it and roast marshmallows over a fire. To fly in an airplane, as the program grew, to run in New York City and Charlotte, even Germany and China. To see that the flat farmland starting at the edge of town didn't go forever, needn't swallow them if they could just master themselves, just do the simplest, hardest thing: lay one sneaker in front of the other again and again.

He never had a son. He had hundreds of sons. He'd take his runners to the doctor, visit their mothers in hospitals and their brothers in jails. He'd help them study, drive them to college, pay their tuition, feed and clothe them, go to court with them and to the wall for them even when, long after graduation, they strayed off the path. "I need you to come back and run with us, buddy," he'd tell fleshy twenty-five-year-olds through prison bars. Cheryl, who'd grown up watching her mother, a minister's wife, do such things for her husband's Church of Christ congregations, showered the boys with homemade cookies and hugs, heart-to-heart lunches, and handwritten notes signed "Mrs. Coach." Mr. White, following the calling of his cousins and uncles, had served as a minister in his church in McFarland; his sister and an uncle had served missions overseas: he knew no other way to run a team.

He rarely raised his voice. He'd stumbled upon the sorcerer's stone of coaching: give so much of yourself that your boys can't bear to let you down. They won the first state cross-country championship held in California, in 1987, and their town gussied them up in foam antlers and had them pull Mr. White through the streets, scrunched in a red Flyer wagon and wearing a Santa hat. They won twenty-two of twenty-four league titles and fifteen sectional championships, beating schools with enrollments seven times as large as theirs. The first fifteen years that California held championships, they won nine, all in Divisions III and IV, but some years they likely would've taken the whole tamale against the megaschools in Divisions I and II as well, if only they'd gotten the chance. They became McFarland's treasure, their ranks swelling each year as graduates circled back to push them and chide them and mentor them, to chorus Mr. White's wisdom to the next wave. They became so much like a family that one day even Javier Medina decided that he wanted in.

> Something takes a part of me.
> Something lost and never seen.
> Every time I start to believe,
> Something's raped and taken from me.

Javier lay in his bedroom, listening to Korn howl the lyrics to "Freak on a Leash." He was in eighth grade. It was 1999. He was teetering. His sister, Corina, had already tumbled into drugs and darkness, tattooing her wrists with SUREÑAS LOCAS — Crazy Southerners, the female subset of a McFarland gang. Their father kept vanishing, into jail for half a year for hitting Corina, or God knows where for months on end after drinking and raging and being thrown out of the house by Javi's mother.

Javi cranked the music — *Sometimes I cannot take this place / Sometimes it's my life I can't taste / Sometimes I cannot feel my face* — and put on his game face. It wasn't easy. His eyelashes were too long, his eyes too soulful, his stack of books too high for punkhood. He yanked on his blue Korn T-shirt, grabbed the notebook that he'd driven a screw into, and headed to school, late again.

He had tried to honor his favorite anarchy-rock band by ducking into the locker room during Mr. White's gym class at McFarland Middle School and sandpapering KORN onto the brand-new lockers. It had nearly gotten him expelled and — as he tried to talk his way out of it — into perhaps deeper trouble still. "*I'm* going to run for Mr. White one day," he'd blurted to the startled vice principal, one of White's assistant coaches and former runners, David Diaz.

Even Mr. White snorted when he heard that one. *Javi?* The smart aleck who'd flunked Mr. White's phys-ed class because he refused to suit up, suddenly grunting out ten half-mile repeats straight uphill at a 2:45 clip? *Yeah, right.* The sulker with the 0.9 grade point average in seventh grade, the school's Snail Award winner for most days tardy, setting his alarm clock for 6:00 A.M. to run along the irrigation canals? *Sure.* The younger brother of Salvador Jr., who had smart-mouthed and drag-assed his way through high school while running for Blanco just a few years before? Mr. White's life's work was retrieval, salvage, salvation, and so, of course, he'd give Javi a shot, but . . .

Javi went home, lay in bed, and, for the third time, read *Banner in the Sky*, a book about a fatherless boy who climbs a mountain that no one believed could be climbed. Javi went outside as darkness fell and lay in the back of his father's pickup truck, staring at the sky while his dad sat in a plastic chair nearby and drank beer in silence.

They couldn't talk. Salvador Sr. spoke Spanish, insistent on remaining Mexican. Javi spoke English, determined to be American. Each was too stubborn to speak the words he knew in the other's tongue. When Salvador, a third-grade dropout who didn't read or write, saw his son disappear behind another book, he'd bark, "Go out and play! You'll hurt your eyes!" He had smuggled himself into the U.S. twice as a teenager, the first time beneath the hood of a pickup truck, the second, for keeps, in a footrace with the border patrol, one of twenty-five desperate men who darted across the desert. Only two had made it. He believed in work, not words, but he wouldn't let Javi work with him in the grape or rose fields, denied him his share of McFarland's bitter drink. "You're too soft," Salvador said. On summer mornings Javi would watch his older brother and the other boys in town climb into pickups and head off for the fields with their fathers; then he'd return to his books and his bedroom.

Salvador crushed his beer can and rattled it into the bucket of empties. Before the *snap* of the day's first pop-top, he'd vacuum and mop the house and wash every dirty dish, and when he went on errands he couldn't pass a stranger stranded on the road without stopping to help. That was the man Javi loved. Some days he would hide his father's beers in a kitchen cabinet. Others, he was so hungry for approval that he'd be the first to his feet to fetch Dad another cold one. Korn was correct: life was pathetically mucked up.

Salvador sipped and stabbed a callused finger at the stars. "Los Siete Osos," he murmured. The Seven Bears. Javi nodded. Salvador pointed and murmured again. "El Camino de San Diego." The Road to San Diego — the swath of stars that Mexicans on foot followed at night on their way to San Diego, America, hope. Javi nodded again. Those constellations, these moments beneath the night sky, were what he and his father had. When adults asked what he'd like to be when he grew up, Javi had begun to say the most astonishing thing for a McFarland boy: an astronomer.

But how could he reach the stars from a town like his? Just one man there had stretched that far: the tall, handsome white man bicycling down the road, herding his family every single day. Something about Mr. White's steadiness, his resolute pursuit of the highest goals, struck Javi even as he defied the man in gym class. Maybe, too, it was the twinkle in Blanco's eyes as he mangled Spanish, the silly dances he'd do, and the pranks he'd play, smuggling cookies into a teacher's purse and then clucking in disbelief over her gluttony, or crooning, "José can you see . . . any bedbugs on me?" to every José in town. Somehow, Blanco was both a remorseless taskmaster and a big, goofy kid — and one of the few gringo teachers who didn't commute from Bakersfield, who'd lived among McFarland's Mexicans for nearly four decades, showing them the surest way out of town . . . but never taking it.

Javi showed up one day at a rec department cross-country practice directed by one of Mr. White's former runners, a proving ground for prospects. *I'm going to show Mr. White something he won't believe,* Javi told himself. He gasped and quit running and had to walk to the finish. But he came back for the next practice and the next, and by the end of eighth grade — *too soft, huh?* — he had run faster than anyone believed a boy with a chip on his shoulder could: a 4:55 mile!

He joined the fleet trying to stay in front of Mr. White's front tire. He muttered an obscenity during a team outing, and Mrs. White walked him off alone and said, "Oh, no, no, no, not in this family." He apologized, and his life began to fall into a groove. "Running bolts my head on," he'd explain. "I know who I am by running. It puts me into reality, so I don't float off into space. I forget my problems. I say, 'I run for McFarland,' and people are like, 'Wowww!' Deep down I want people to think of me as part of something, even though I pretend that none of that matters. Jeez, man, without this program, I'd have no personality, I'd be . . . nothing."

He made his first true friends, a brotherhood of sweat and pain with runners Juan Gonzalez and Steven Cavazos. He loved bumping fists before and after each practice with his teammates and all of Mr. White's former runners, *los veteranos* who still trained with the team and became a battalion of big brothers to Javi. He loved arriving at meets on the bus and watching the other schools' runners' heads swivel and their eyes cloud and lips move: *McFarland's here.* He loved closing ranks for the team prayer and feeling his stomach knot at the sight of taller, wealthier boys on the starting line. "They're all white," a new kid on the team would sometimes say, and Mr. White would reply, "Yep . . . and they're all bigger. But I guarantee you they aren't as tough and don't work as hard as you do. Let's go take them down."

Mr. White was right. State title number eight came in Javi's freshman year, when he ran with the frosh-soph team. *Omniscient* wasn't a word he'd toss around with the guys, but that was the word, he decided, for Mr. White. *Just follow him,* Javi told himself, *and good things will happen.* He followed Mr. White across the country, felt the thunder of Niagara Falls on a running trip, looked *down* on a cloud from atop the Golden Gate Bridge, saw water at Lake Tahoe that was bluer than any in a dream . . . and began to fix his eyes on college *somewhere else.* He scratched his way to number-five varsity runner in his sophomore year on a team that, midway through the season, clawed all the way to the number-one ranking in the nation among small schools and to number four overall. Anyone who came to the races could see that Javi wasn't too soft to work in the fields, could see his grit as he rubbed out opponents in the last quarter-mile . . . anyone at all. But his father never came.

"Oh, how your father brags of your achievements to his relatives," Javi's mother, Sylvia, would tell her son. But never a word from Salvador to Javi, even when his sophomore season ended with the ultimate ascent, up the ladder with his teammates as their names were painted in white letters on the ninth black silhouette of California on the school gym's outer wall, the display that opponents gaped at when they visited cross-country's Mecca.

Of course, the Snail still crept in late for some practices, skipped some, and moped through others. Javi still was a boy missing something, one who could get lost searching for it in the spaces inside his head. He remembered to get his eyebrow and ear pierced and his hair dyed blond, but he forgot to bring his running gear to a meet. An excellent idea, he thought it was, to sign the Whites' guest book JAVI BAD A** in gangsta graffiti bubble lettering. Then he had to Wite-Out the words to remove the red from Mr. and Mrs. White's eyes. That was Javi. Ten years from now, a *veterano* wondered aloud, would Javi be in astrophysics . . . or in jail?

Mr. White was the weight that could tip the balance. Javi would do almost anything to please that man. He'd set up tables and sell concessions at rec department races to raise funds for the McFarland program, slice fruit for the peewee runners, and act as their rabbit to improve their times. His grade point average rocketed to 3.5 his first semester in high school, then to 4.0, then 4.17. He affixed the watch Mr. White gave him to his bedroom wall — he couldn't risk wearing it on his wrist. He taped Mr. White's photograph amid the pictures of planets that orbited his room.

One day late in his sophomore year, the planets moved, the solar system shifted. Javi heard the rumor: *Mr. White's leaving.*

How do you leave a place where you've taught and coached and loved for thirty-eight years? How do you tell a couple of dozen Mexican boys that it's time to give your children's children what you didn't have time to give your own children: *you*. How do you tell teenagers what you owe your wife after four decades of flying out the door at dawn and trudging back in as she falls asleep? How do you explain to field hands' sons that you've worked so many years that your annual retirement pay would total 96 percent of what you'd get if you kept working . . . that you're human, not a saint?

You don't. You don't explain. You don't call a team meeting and make a big wet fuss over this being your last year and how much they've all meant to you. Not when you're Mr. White, and your life leans on actions rather than words. Not when the words might stick in your throat. You just take aside your trusty disciple Ayon and tell him that you're going to start pulling back and letting him emerge as the leader during this transition year, because that's your goal: to pass the torch without extinguishing the flame.

The rumor festered. The family gathered, as always, at Mr. White's home for their evening runs that summer of 2002. Javi peered at the dark windows of Blanco's weather-beaten stucco box house. Where was he? Off in Texas or Long Beach visiting his daughters, Ayon would say. Off at his new cabin up in the mountains, building the wraparound deck of his wife's dreams. He'll be back to coach this year, don't worry about what happens after that, and c'mon, now, guys, let's pick it up. Javi slogged toward the almond groves. Who had sat all the boys down beneath the orange trees and, in the dulcet voice of a pastor, reminded them over and over how important it was, every day, to show up? Who had said he'd *always* be there for them?

Every time I start to believe . . .

Somehow it didn't seem so urgent anymore to throw one foot in front of the other. Somehow, as summer ground on and no one knew when to expect the coach, it no longer seemed imperative to show up. Mr. White would act as if nothing was wrong, no big deal, when he did appear, full of pleasantries and wisecracks — as unaware of the effect on Javi of his looming departure, it seemed, as Javi's dad had appeared to be all those times he'd left.

But Javi couldn't confront Mr. White any more than he could his father, and so he began to do things that seemed to have nothing to do with the hurt. He began staying up late, emptying a few beer cans of his own, and drifting into practice late because he was walking a girl home from school, kissing off Mr. White's age-old warning that nothing would pull a butterfly back to the caterpillar pile faster than a girlfriend. He didn't need Mr. White's voodoo juice before races anymore. He'd hear the other runners beg Mr. White to change his mind about retiring, but Javi wouldn't do it. *If someone wants to leave,* he kept thinking, *then I don't need him.* It wasn't easy being the one who saw through the armor of the town's white knight. But Javi had gone it alone before, and dammit, his second father wasn't going to lay a finger on the wound left by his first.

The Whites felt him slipping through their fingers but kept giving him another chance. They were old pros at this, at rescuing runners who'd dropped out or impregnated girlfriends or slept on plastic lounge chairs because their parents couldn't afford a bed. But Javi was different from the other lost boys, more intelligent, more sensitive, more perplexing . . . always just out of Mr. White's reach. His long eyelashes would flutter and his face contort for a half-minute before he'd reply to the simplest query, agonizing over how much to drop his guard.

Mrs. White took him out to lunch for one of her heart-to-hearts, but only one heart was put on the table. Mr. White went to Javi's house to talk to Javi's father but couldn't penetrate the beer and language barriers. He tried teasing Javi back into the fold, then tightening the screws. "Look, everyone, we have a new kid running with us today," he'd say when Javi showed up after a few days' absence. "Got your brain on today, Javi?" None of it worked, none of it could, because Javi was waiting for the man to show his feelings, not his needle.

More than for their town or their school, the boys had always run for Mr. White, a tie so strong that it bordered on dependency. Now that rope began to unravel. The team split into cliques. The boys yo-yoed. One day they would speed up, at *los veteranos'* insistence: it was Blanco's final year! The next they'd crawl: it was Blanco's final year. Yet by sheer force of habit McFarland ran well enough, as the state championships approached, to be favored to win number ten — and a fourth straight crown.

Javi, who had become the team's number-two runner, could see it in *los veteranos'* eyes: he'd be marked in his town forever if he failed. It jabbed at his sleep like the bedsprings coming through his mattress. The day before the state meet, Mr. White opened the *Bakersfield Californian*'s sports page and shuddered. *What?*

"We realize that second place is just not going to happen," said Javi in the article. "We're going to win, and that's it. We're not competing against other teams. We're competing against ourselves and trying to get a personal record." Javi had turned his terror inside out.

Ayon pulled the boy aside, aghast. "No McFarland runner," he growled, "has ever been as blunt as you." Silence filled the team van on the ride to Fresno that gloomy Saturday. Thirty former McFarland runners awaited the boys at Woodward Park, reminding them of their obligation to Blanco even as they braced at the starting line. The gun sounded, and the alumni took off as if it were their race, crunching through the dead leaves outside the ropes to keep a bead on the boys.

It was too much cargo to bear. Javi crossed the line in 16:41, twenty-three seconds slower than his best time on the five-kilometer course he'd run so many times. McFarland's top five runners ran their worst races of the year, and the team's sixth-place finish was its worst ever in a state meet. The boys were still weeping into their mashed potatoes at a buffet an hour later, still sobbing when they stumbled out of the van back in McFarland. Javi went straight to his bedroom and wouldn't come out.

The boys walked into the team banquet two months later as if they weren't good enough for the tuxedos Mr. White had rented for them. Blanco apologized to the town, took the blame for what happened, and couldn't beat his tears to the end of his farewell speech. Javi didn't cry, as his mother and the others did. Javi never saw Mr. White give his speech. He'd turned his chair to face the other way.

Sixth place sat in Mr. White's gut like a pit from one of his backyard nectarines. Retirement tasted like the pesticide on a summer breeze. Instead of pride over all the migrants' sons he'd transformed into teachers and administrators and coaches, uneasiness settled over him as he gazed at the mementos of his coaching career. All his life he'd played to win, even if it meant bumping the Ping-Pong table in midrally, pinning down an opponent's arm as he went up for a rebound, or wreaking havoc as a flag football coach by instructing one of his players to *almost* leave the field during a mass substitution, then streak up the sideline unnoticed to snag a touchdown pass.

What, he kept asking himself, had gone so wrong on his final day? Forty-two years earlier his varsity basketball coach had burned him at Magic Valley Christian College in Idaho, banishing him to the jayvee for his defiance of a decree that students attend no other church but the one on campus. He'd *never* do such a thing when he became a coach, he'd vowed — he'd bend over backward to be fair to his kids. But maybe, in his final year, he'd violated his golden rule. Maybe he'd cheated his runners by his absences from summer practice, the furnace in which his teams were always forged.

His wife smelled his uneasiness, and she wasn't so sure that she was ready to retire as Mrs. Coach. Cheryl approached the school board president, Linda Genel, and told her that she'd had a dream in which her husband got the thing he'd been giving boys for decades — a second chance. The idea caught fire with the school board, and a contract was cobbled together that would permit Mr. White to receive his retirement pay yet be kept on as a full-time substitute gym teacher at the middle school for one more semester, so he could sing his swan song again with the boys of McFarland High. Mr. White agreed. All the runners seemed thrilled.

Except one.

Javi spiraled down . . . down . . . down. It was so easy, in a town plagued by gang violence and drug problems, to end up with your mug on a pickle jar on the counter at the Chevron station, soliciting donations to pay your burial expenses. But when the gunfire hit Javi's family last spring, it was his twenty-two-year-old cousin,

Ruben Juarez Jr., who died, and it was Ruben himself who pulled the trigger rather than surrender to police and face a third conviction that likely would've sent him to prison for life. Javi froze. He had grown up playing tag in the dark with Ruben. He stopped eating and studying, cut classes and track practices, piled up detentions, and flunked history. He shut himself in his bedroom and let the confusion in his house howl around him.

"Go see Mr. White," begged his mother.

"I can't," muttered Javi.

"Why not?" asked his brother, Salvador.

"He doesn't care about us anymore," said Javi.

He entered a five-kilometer road race in June and, before Mr. White's disbelieving eyes, crawled to the finish in twenty-one minutes. This was his next leader, his fastest returning senior, the one that Blanco's season of redemption would hinge on? Maybe, Mr. White and *los veteranos* began to suspect, working the fields — which Javi had never done — was more important than any of them had realized. Maybe the fields were what had burned the *will* into their runners all those years, and there was just no way this boy who read books could ever muster it. "Not bad, Javi, only five girls beat you," Mr. White fumed after the race. "Were you waiting for somebody, or just counting the flowers? What's a McFarland runner doing back there? You need to step it up. You need to *wake* up."

Ayon could see it coming, another slap to his hero's face, and could bear it no more. He invited Javi to a Chinese restaurant, waited until he lifted his fork over his beef and broccoli, and then cut loose, freezing that fork in midair for five minutes. "If you can't cut it, I don't care if you're a senior!" Ayon hissed. "You won't be on this team! What happened last year *can't* happen again. You've got to be a leader!"

Who's to say just when or why a boy begins to become a man? Maybe the death of his cousin finally cried out its counterpoint to Javi: *Don't waste your life. It's too precious.* Javi made a promise to God that he wouldn't waste it. Maybe it was seeing Mr. White show up on July 1 for the summer's first evening run, and every night after that, and the words Mr. White spoke to him after one evening run. "I know how you felt last year," he said. "But I'm going to be here for you this year, every day. I'm going to give everything I've got, and I'm hoping you're going to give everything too." Javi still harbored doubts, still wondered if Mr. White was returning out of obligation rather than desire. But he stopped brooding and decided to give the coach that second chance, becoming resolute in his evening training, adding six-mile runs three mornings a week, hitting the weights in the afternoons, and running in a wet vest in the pool. He wrote down his teammates' phone numbers to make sure they'd show up too.

Mr. White assessed his squad: a young one, teeming with promising freshmen and sophomores but lacking a single junior and crying out for leadership from the three seniors — Javi, Steven, and Juan, introverts all. A state title? A tall task.

"We're going to low-key everything," declared Mr. White. "I want to enter the state meet under cover."

"We're not going to talk about doing it for Mr. White this year," Javi said. "We'll just see what happens." But privately he set three lofty goals: a sub-sixteen-minute five-kilometer; a top ten state ranking for McFarland among all schools, regardless of size; and state championship number ten.

Two days before the season's first meet, gunfire erupted again, and two of Mr. White's former runners dropped. José Velasco, a pal of Javi's brother, died in a drive-by gang murder, and José's brother Aurelio survived a bullet in the neck. The Whites went to the Velascos' house on the double, still distraught over the stabbing death of another former runner just weeks earlier. Javi felt as if he were going to throw up. At night he stayed home, warned by his brother that retaliation was in the air and that more bullets might soon be too.

Three weeks later, at the Bell-Jeff Invitational in L.A., Javi led his team to a sweeping 2–3–7–8–10–11 finish as McFarland thrashed fifty-eight schools — thirty-three of them from higher divisions — to gain the number-two overall ranking in the state. Their cover was blown. They were in the headlines.

Then came trouble. Freshman phenom Julio Olvera fell hard for a girl, tumbled all the way into the caterpillar pile, then inflamed a nerve in his hip and ended up having to run for a month in a swimming pool. Juan Gonzalez hurt his knee and was finished, for all intents and purposes, for the season. Now McFarland was down to two seniors and a slew of raw freshmen and sophomores. Ninth-grader Baltazar Topete, the number-five varsity runner, informed

Mr. White that he'd be retiring when Mr. White did because all this pain was pointless without him, and Cheryl kept asking, "Are you sure you want to leave, Jim? Are you sure you're ready?" until the old coach, too, began to wonder whether the torch could ever be passed.

Javi, too, had begun feeling the gravitational pull of a poor Mexican American town. None of Javi's senior friends spoke of moving on, as if the next phase were a betrayal. "Go to college wherever you want," his father said when he learned that Javi was applying to UCLA, UC Santa Barbara, UC San Diego, and San Diego State. "We just won't visit you." It was a leathery Mexican fieldworker's way of saying, "I'm going to miss you, it hurts to think of you going away," but how was Javi, for all the reading he did, ever to read that deep between the lines?

Somehow everything was connected. Somehow McFarland's pack mentality and Javi's own fear of pulling away clutched at him even when it was time to leave everyone behind in a meet. Week after week he led his team across the finish line, but his times remained a half-minute slower than his goal. "Kindergarten times," he snorted. "I'm holding back, running *with* people and not grinding them up. I'm looking for someone to go with, like Steve or Juan, someone I *know*."

And yet, barely realizing it, he'd begun imploring his teammates with the same words that Mr. White had once used on him: he was becoming a leader. Mr. White saw it one day in practice when he instructed his boys to cover a four-and-a-half-mile steep uphill climb in 33:30. "No, we're not gonna run 33:30 like Mr. White said, we're gonna run it in 31:30," he heard Javi tell them, and then he watched Javi stay with the trailers, talk them through their pain, and sheepdog every one of them home in 31:30. "He's just a different kid this year," Mr. White told people. "He's fantastic. He doesn't have that sad face anymore. He's talking, encouraging all the other kids, and working his butt off."

The town bid its formal farewell to Mr. White at midseason. It draped banners for each of the championship years over the hoods of nine shiny new pickup trucks, filled them with runners, past and present, and enthroned Mr. and Mrs. White in a red Porsche at the front of the procession, waving regally while horns honked as if every virgin in town had just been married off. Then everyone sat down to celebrate a life, and Mr. White knew in his bones that he had to leave, this time for good.

In the second-to-last meet of the year, Javi's breakthrough race came at last, a blazing 16:07. "I actually believed in myself," he marveled. "It's peculiar. The fastest race I've ever run felt the easiest."

But there was no time to revel. Every day, every race, was little more than a prelude to what really mattered, the state championships two days after Thanksgiving. A countdown to take two of Mr. White's final day.

Word went out to the vets. Don't spook the boys this time. Don't even mention that it's Mr. White's adios. No need even to show up in Fresno, matter of fact. Mum's the word, men. No Churchill from Blanco. Just another stroll in the park.

The old Javi reared his head. He showed up for McFarland's final practice a half-hour late, well after stretching time, when team meetings were held and the leader might be expected to talk from the heart.

He slept in his mother's bed on the eve of the race, a night of freedom from his bedsprings, but still he tossed and turned for hours. A 16:01 or better would place him among the top ten runners in McFarland's storied history and might pull the freshmen and the sophomores into the 16:30-to-16:45 range required to topple their more experienced foes. A loss, and Javi might go down as the runner who smothered *both* of Mr. White's last hurrahs. It wouldn't be easy, not with the team's leading freshman, Olvera, barely recovered from his hip injury, and not with Carmel and Oak Park, the other two favorites in Division IV, coming in loaded with seniors.

Mr. White and his boys each dropped to one knee and prayed, the runners' white shorts and singlets stark against their brown skin and against Woodward Park's blaze of autumn oranges and yellows and reds. They all locked arms, and their eyes began to mist — exactly what Mr. White had been determined to avoid — as Juan Gonzalez stammered out how much he loved them all and how sorry he was that, because of his knee, he couldn't go to war with them. They walked to the starting line, where 184 other boys in other colors waited to take them down. Javi looked back. There, for the first time, stood his father.

The boys tapped fists. Mr. White and Ayon watched in silence. The gun sounded, and the two men hurried through the mass of spectators and across the creek to catch the boys at the first mile marker. Javi flew by it in 4:52, among the top ten, and his six teammates all managed 5:07 or better . . . not bad, not bad. Blanco's eyes clouded at the second mile marker — they'd bogged down too much in the hills! — then he bolted toward the finish to rally the final kick of his coaching life.

Six runners funneled through the chute, then Javi — he'd done his job, or near enough, with a 16:10 and seventh place, the second-fastest five-kilometer of his life. He whirled at the finish line and squinted, waiting to glimpse the next flash of white breaking from the tree line . . . and waiting . . . and waiting, hope vanishing with every tick of the clock. Finally, at 16:51, they began to arrive, each nearly a half-minute too slow, gasping their apologies to Javi.

He reeled away, no time to think, and wrapped his arms around his father and pulled him to his chest.

No one cried after Mr. White's last race. Blanco wouldn't let them, moving from runner to runner to let each one know that third place, behind Carmel and Oak Park, was no disgrace. "You couldn't do it all," he told Javi.

Javi looked up at his coach in a mournful daze. "Are you doing okay, Mr. White?"

"I'm doing fine, Javi."

It was all over, and now Javi entered no-man's-land, waiting to see if his dream of studying astronomy and running in college would come true. Waiting to find out if he'd really do it, really walk away and reach the other side of the almonds and oranges and grapes, or if this season was the peak of his life, as it had been for so many other runners, and now he'd struggle the way they had when there was no Mr. White to run for.

No, he sensed. A boy couldn't *walk* away from McFarland, he had to run, and so he got up the next morning and ran six miles, and a few days later he upped it to eight, sometimes even ten, as if the season had never ended. "If I don't stop," he said, "I'll keep going."

The team's last night together came at their banquet seven weeks ago. Javi wouldn't go to the podium, just couldn't do it, to express the team's feelings about Mr. White, leaving that to Juan. But Javi hung on every sentence from Mr. White, and when tears streamed down the coach's cheeks and he croaked, "I felt like I deserted the boys a little last year," the words went inside Javi and melted one more layer of ice.

"It felt like a victory, no, not a victory . . . a breakthrough," Javi said. "Something more than 'good job,' because we've heard plenty of 'good jobs.' Something from his heart. I know I should've been more understanding of him. I know I lost a relationship with a good man. And so as I was leaving I told him . . . uh . . . 'I just *hope* you won't be a stranger and I won't be a stranger. I hope I see you more often,' and Mr. White said, 'Yeah,' and . . . and it's not anything big, but I gave him a hug. I know it sounds like something small, but I'd never done it before, and for me it felt *big*. Maybe it wasn't as big for him as it was for me, but I . . . I was just trying to tell him something."

Mr. White got it. He walked away feeling wonderful about Javi and the deep shelf of talent he was leaving behind, vowing to the boys that he'd be back to watch them run, then drying his eyes and heading for his mountain cabin with Mrs. Coach.

And Javi? He lies in bed at night now staring at the planets on the wall, wondering if he'll ever sort the whole thing out. He had reached none of his three goals — not the state title, not the top ten ranking, not the sub-sixteen five-kilometer — but his final season had given him something else, fruits he hadn't even thought to reach for. In those last two races he'd finally learned to run without the McFarland pack: he'd become a *racer.* And up on his wall hung that hug with his father, a picture splashed across five columns of the *Bakersfield Californian* that brought tears to his dad's eyes and kept bringing him back into Javi's room to peer at it in the moonlight while his son slept. And in Javi's heart hung that other hug, with that other man, that moment when at last he didn't run.

Phat Chants

FROM THE LOS ANGELES TIMES

THE COMPTON HIGH softball players huddle at the front of graffiti-scarred bleachers, jeering fans over their shoulders, two hours of dusty humiliation in their face.

They can't win; in ten games they have been outscored, 175–2.

They can't bat; their one official hit this season was a three-foot bunt.

They can't catch; during home games, players chase fly balls amid cars that occasionally barrel through the outfield weeds.

They began the season wearing white T-shirts with numbers scrawled on the back in Sharpie pen. They will end it having begged for balls, with borrowed bats, and with some of their gloves stolen.

Their administration has forgotten them, some of their classmates curse them, their sympathetic opponents purposely make outs for them.

But, girl, can they chant.

Through every flailing batter, with every dropped fly ball, through every name on the roster, they chant.

> Ten is her number!
> Abby is her name!
> She is the reason!
> We're gonna win this game!

On a recent warm afternoon, in the second inning, the umpires warned that they were on the verge of canceling Compton's game against visiting Long Beach Poly.

Because of cold.

Once again, the Compton girls had been frozen out by their administration. No school officials were there to watch the game, a violation of high school rules.

"We have to get somebody over here or they're going to make us stop playing," Coach Sean Corrigan shouted into a cell phone.

A policeman strolled past. He would suffice. He asked if the Compton girls had any cold water.

He was pointed toward a crusty water fountain with a warm trickle. "I ain't drinking out of that," the cop said, walking away. It figured.

From the moment they gathered last fall, faceless girls playing boring softball in a community enamored of its boys and their basketballs, this has been a team shunned.

"You know what I really respect most about our girls?" Corrigan asked. "Knowing what they must go through every day, just to play. I greatly respect them for even showing up."

Corrigan, twenty-three, a history teacher with no previous softball coaching experience, was given the job because nobody else would do it.

The eighteen-player team, following a legacy of isolation and embarrassment, hardly knew the rules.

What countless other softball players in Title IX–bolstered fields across the country take for granted, these Compton girls quickly understood as precious.

Like home plate.

The school did not supply their scrubby home field with home plate until opening day. Until then, they used an old glove.

Or, like bases.

For several months, Compton ran around bases they had purchased at Target, except for second base, which was, well, another glove.

"It stinks, pretty much," said Abby Molina, a senior catcher. "We knew right away the school didn't care about the softball team."

Bats? They used two rusted slabs of aluminum, one so old it quickly broke, and when was the last time you heard of that happening?

Balls? At first, it was strictly BYOB — bring your own balls — until the school supplied some on opening day. But they were the wrong kind, and umpires wouldn't allow them in games.

Then there were the uniforms.

For the first four games, the girls did not have official uniforms, the old ones having been stolen and the school claiming that the new order had been botched by the vendor.

Remember earlier this spring when the city of Compton held a huge celebration for its three championship basketball teams? Complete with music, lunch, and helicopter rides for the players?

Around that time, the Compton softball team was playing in those white T-shirts with Sharpie numbers.

"We had to bend our backs and draw on the numbers right before the first game, with all the girls from the other team looking at us while wearing their brand-new uniforms," junior outfielder Margarita Landeros said. "That's when I wanted to quit."

Nobody quit.

Everyone chants.

> Anna is a friend of mine!
> She can rip it anytime!
> Rip, nah-nah-nah-nah!
> Rip, nah-nah-nah-nah!

During a home game against Long Beach Jordan, as the margin widened, the leaders behaved oddly.

Every inning, it seemed, at least one Jordan girl would be called out for leaving the base too early. As the score crept toward the eventual 24–1 victory by Jordan, the mental mistakes increased.

Did they not know the rules? Were they not listening?

"Oh no, they were listening," said Carter Kendrick, Jordan's coach. "I *told* my girls to leave the base early. I *told* them to make outs."

Ever since Poly took full measure of Compton with a 42–0 victory early in the season, every opponent — including Poly — has backed off.

"To come in here and see this," Kendrick said, shaking his head. "I really feel for those girls."

Visitors to Compton see more than just the humiliation of a sports team, they see the failure of a system.

Every promise made more than three decades ago by the passage of Title IX has seemingly been broken here, left to die like the gophers that once littered the outfield.

Yep, during preseason practices, the girls would jog around the poisoned animal carcasses until they were finally cleared away on opening day.

"Now *that* was no fun," Landeros said.

Next to a well-manicured, fence-enclosed, regulation boys' field, visitors here see a weed-stubbed piece of dirt that doubles as the girls' field.

There are no outfield fences, so cars headed for the boys' field cut across the dying grass during games.

This may be the only baseball or softball diamond in the United States where an outfielder was recently nearly injured by a flying hubcap.

It's no safer in the dugouts because, well, there are no dugouts. The Compton girls sit in the stands, which means they share bleachers with a few students who sometimes show up to curse and jeer.

In some schools, coaches require that their students attend games. Here, Corrigan banned two students when their heckling became too distracting.

The "fans" mock the coach's instructions, laugh at the players, even hide their gloves between innings.

"That's why we all huddle down on the first bleacher, to try to block everybody out," Landeros said. "But they're so close, you have to listen to them, and it's hard."

Of course, when they take the field, it's even harder.

Against Poly last week, someone commented that one of the Poly stars was a strangely awkward left-handed hitter.

"Um, she's not a left-handed hitter," Corrigan said. "She's batting from the wrong side on purpose. A lot of them are. They don't want to make the score worse."

Maxine Kemp, a thirty-nine-year employee of Compton High and current girls' athletic director, doesn't understand the fuss about her softball team.

"I'm telling you, it's not that bad," she said.

Kemp said that times were tough throughout the school, and that softball was simply a victim of its lack of popularity.

"We don't bring in a lot of money out there," she said. "It's not a big revenue sport. It's not a paying sport like football and basketball."

Corrigan said that he'd told Kemp that this attitude, this failure to spread funding equally, was in violation of Title IX.

"That's when she told me, 'If this is illegal, then we've been illegal for years,'" Corrigan said.

Kemp denied making that statement.

"I never said anything about something being illegal," she said. "The truth is, we do our best, but we just don't have the money for everything."

Asked about a failure to supply something as simple as home plate, she said she didn't see the problem.

"The way I see it, you can practice drill steps without a band," she said. "I don't care if they don't have a base out there, that doesn't mean they can't play."

Asked about the uniforms, she blamed the supplier.

"The company that was supposed to get us the uniforms never did, and I'm very upset about that," she said.

Asked about the difference between the boys' and girls' facilities, she attributed it to fund-raising.

"We give the girls attention," she said. "The only problem is, the boys do more hustling. The boys have car washes, fund-raisers, do things that put themselves into tournaments."

The softball team, however, bought candy at Costco and sold it in school to help pay for gloves and uniform bags.

Corrigan said that he has yet to receive funding from the school for his team.

Responded Kemp, "Last year, we outfitted three entire softball teams, spent more than $3,000 on it, and not a stitch of it could be found this year. I'm thrilled we were even able to buy those uniforms again."

Kemp has been to one game, the opener, during which she supervised the repair of a protective fence in front of the bleachers, even as the game was being played.

"I feel for the girls, but I'm not a sorry person," she said, shifting the focus to Corrigan. "He told us he was a softball coach. If you are a softball coach, you have to show them things, do whatever you can do."

Corrigan, who arrived here from Colorado as part of the Teach For America program, has done things he never dreamed he would be doing.

He never dreamed he would have to teach his girls the difference between a ball and a strike.

He never dreamed that, upon getting one of the first hits in the first practice, the batter would run directly to third base.

He had no idea his team would give up an average of 17.5 runs a game while still not understanding the difference between a tag play and a force play.

"It's been a challenge," he said. "It's been like, 'Okay, this is home plate.'"

Or, at least, a glove pretending to be home plate.

But Corrigan also never dreamed that during some of the most heartache-filled months of his life, he would fall in love.

With the spirit of girls who kept showing up. With the integrity of a team that never lost hope.

With words like these, from Margarita Landeros, the outfielder who has the top grade point average in the junior class.

"I know I am getting embarrassed out there," she said. "But if it takes me being embarrassed to learn something about myself, then I will be embarrassed."

And so they learn, about failure, frustration, fortitude, somehow pushing a bright sunflower up through three months' accumulation of gravel.

"They are amazing," Corrigan said.

Watch this team for a couple of games and your ears deceive your eyes.

Strikeouts? The girls cheer the swing. Errors? The girls cheer the effort.

When one of their inexperienced pitchers turns fast-pitch into slow-pitch? They holler for her as though she were Nolan Ryan.

The girls laughed about their T-shirt uniforms by calling them "throwbacks."

They have countered the fools in the stands by filling their area with balloons, with songs, with those constant chants, with unfettered joy.

This spring, they will finish last in every sort of standings.

But next year, if Landeros continues to lead the class, they will be at the top of her valedictorian address.

"No one at the school cares about girls' sports," she said softly. "No administrator has ever given us one word of encouragement. But in my speech, I will talk about this season. I will talk about this team. This special team."

Fatal Errors

FROM THE SAN DIEGO UNION-TRIBUNE

MONTANA. That's where he was going.

Ken Caminiti was getting out of a Houston jail, getting out of the sleeveless orange jumpsuit, getting out of town. He was going to pack his things and load them in his truck and start driving north on Interstate 45. He was going to Montana.

The idea was to get as far away as possible from temptation and convenience and familiarity, from the people he'd met in jails and rehab centers who he couldn't say no to and who were, in the words of one of his attorneys, "leeching" off him. Driving his cars. Living in his house. Stealing his baseball memorabilia. Offering him cocaine. Dragging him back, again and again and again, into an abyss he so desperately tried to claw out of.

Jail hadn't worked. Halfway houses hadn't worked. Interventions from friends and family hadn't worked. Too many stints at rehab centers to count hadn't worked, not in Arizona, not in New Mexico, not in Texas, not in New York.

Montana, he was convinced, would.

"He'd bought some land up there," says Rick Licht, the agent and close friend of the former Padres third baseman who retired from baseball in 2001. "He was going to stay in a cabin and hunt and fish and relax and work on his sobriety. He'd go to some AA meetings. He'd just get away from everything and everyone."

Caminiti kept calling Licht collect from the jail in his final days, telling him how bored he was, telling him how he couldn't wait to get out and get on the road. He wanted to know how soon Licht was coming to Montana to go bow hunting with him. Licht joked that the biggest thing he'd ever killed in his life was a spider.

The hearing date in Judge William Harmon's courtroom was October 5. Caminiti had been found in a Houston motel three years earlier with a crack pipe fashioned out of a Coke can and was placed on three years' probation with the stipulation that he'd submit to regular drug tests. Caminiti kept failing them — one test, two tests, three, then four — and kept landing back in jail. One time he went for four and a half months. This time, he'd been there since September 10.

One option was to continue the probation but in a new long-term rehabilitation program supervised by the Texas court system. The other option was to terminate his probation, have the felony stamped on his record, and face up to two years in jail.

Against the advice of his attorney and probation officer, Caminiti chose the latter, knowing he already had served six months in jail and knowing that, as a first-time felon, he likely would be released based on time served. He appeared before Harmon on October 5. He was sentenced to the minimum — 180 days in jail — and given credit for 189 served. By the evening, he was a free man.

"I was in the holding cell with him that day," says Terry Yates, one of his attorneys. "He looked good, he sounded good, his eyes were clear. He said he was hitting his knees every day, which was Ken's way of saying he was praying a lot. He seemed really committed this time. Everyone seemed to think he had his head on his shoulders."

Caminiti changed out of the orange jumpsuit, went to a gym with friends and worked out, ate dinner with friends, spent the night at a friend's house. The plan was to pack up his things, load up his truck, and start driving.

The next day, he disappeared.

That was Wednesday. On Sunday night, Licht's phone rang at his Los Angeles home. Someone was calling to tell him there was a dead man in a New York hospital who was thought to be Ken Caminiti.

New York? Caminiti was supposed to be on his way to Montana. Licht figured there must be some mistake, that maybe someone stole Caminiti's wallet and ended up dead, that maybe it was a case of identity theft. He gave a description of the man who won three Gold Gloves and played in three All-Star Games and in 1996 was the National League MVP — forty-one years old, six feet, 215 pounds, muscular build, the bushy goatee, the penetrating blue eyes that could bore holes through a wall, the tattoos of his three daughters' names on his chest.

A few minutes later, Licht's phone rang again.

"It's him."

Cordoy Lane is a nice street with trees and sidewalks and middle-class houses. It is in suburban San Jose but, really, it could be anywhere.

Lee and Yvonne Caminiti worked in the aerospace industry. They had two sons, Glenn and Kenny, and a daughter, Carrie. They had a pool. They had good neighbors. The local schools and a park were within walking distance. They had a nice life.

At one end of Cordoy Lane is a streetlight. One summer afternoon, Kenny and the neighborhood kids were doing what kids did in the days before video games and 120 cable TV stations. They were outside playing, figuring out new ways to entertain themselves. They were standing under the streetlight, tossing a fat, old, rubbery softball up at it.

The other kids weren't having much success. Kenny, twelve at the time, had seen enough. He picked up the softball, walked to the opposite end of Cordoy Lane, and fired a laser at the streetlight. The ball smashed into the fixture, swinging open its cover and shattering the lens.

It stayed that way for darn near twenty years, the cover dangling on one hinge, the light still functional but damaged — a constant reminder of his athletic prowess and a chilling metaphor for what would become a shattered life. So talented, and so destructive.

"Anything you gave him," says Jim Wagster, who was there the day Kenny broke the streetlight, "he could do it."

There's the story about the unicycle that one of the neighborhood kids got for Christmas. No one could ride it. No one could so much as get on it, even with a person on either side holding him up. Then Kenny walked by, climbed on the unicycle on his first try, and rode it down Cordoy Lane.

Randy Warren moved into the neighborhood when he was seven. Kenny was the first kid he met.

"What I remember was a kid who liked to play sports and liked to push the limits a little bit," says Warren, who now runs a bread store in Arlington, Texas. "Whatever you did, he could top you with ease.

He had no fear. He would try anything. You didn't even have to dare him. He'd get an idea and just try it."

Yvonne Caminiti has told the story of how Kenny, at age two and a half, decided he was Batman and tried to "fly" down the stairs. When the diving board in the backyard pool wasn't daring enough, he dived off the roof. There was a nearby reservoir where teenagers would summon the courage to jump off rocks into the water. The bravest went off a ledge about thirty feet high. Kenny showed up one day, climbed up to the next highest ledge — maybe thirty-five or forty feet — and calmly jumped. Did a double flip.

He would play football, basketball, and baseball for the Leigh High Longhorns. He was a defensive back in football and was good enough to play in a northern California high school all-star game, but a neck injury and a 160-pound physique derailed his dreams.

There were no such limitations in baseball. In his first varsity game, as a sophomore shortstop with a mop of hair spilling out of his batting helmet, he went 5-for-5.

He was a likable enough teammate, except for one thing.

"He was the one guy you didn't want to warm up with because he threw so hard," says Jim Evans, the Longhorns' second baseman. "It didn't even look like he was trying to throw hard. It just hurt when you caught it."

Caminiti went from Leigh to San Jose City College and then on to San Jose State, the all-American kid living the all-American life. Nancy Smith, his sweetheart since ninth grade, went to San Jose State as well, acquiring the nickname Nectar Nancy because she was "so sweet." They got engaged. He joined Sigma Alpha Epsilon fraternity. Major league scouts began showing up at his games and marveling at the arm that broke the streetlight on Cordoy Lane.

He partied, sure. He could be wild. But ask his childhood friends about his extracurricular habits and the response is the same: It was the early '80s. Who didn't party?

"I've seen a lot of people with worse party habits in college turn out a lot better," says Bryan Grauss, a San Jose State football player who joined Sigma Alpha Epsilon fraternity with Caminiti and shared an apartment with him. "Let's just leave it at that."

What people noticed more was his demeanor. His cars were loud; his personality was not. He was quiet, shy, unassuming, humble, caring to a fault — the rare breed of star who doesn't know it.

"He was just Kenny," Grauss says. "I don't think he realized how good a person he was. He always strived to be liked by people. It's hard to put that in the right context because he wasn't a person in need of attention. But he was always trying to gain acceptance of people. Once you were Kenny's friend, you were his friend for life."

In spring of 1984, the Houston Astros selected him in the third round of the amateur draft. Caminiti signed a contract, got a modest bonus, and immediately went to the local car lot.

"I'll never forget it," Grauss says, "driving around San Jose in that white hot rod truck with Kenny, holding on for dear life."

The wild ride, it turned out, was only just beginning.

Legacy.com is a site that hosts Internet guest books for people who have died. There is one for Caminiti. In a matter of days, it had hundreds of posts.

They are from all over, from Magnolia, Texas; from Fort Gordon, Georgia; from Waldorf, North Dakota; from Dardanelle, Arkansas; from Winnsboro, Louisiana; from Manalapan, New Jersey; from Poway and Coronado and Encinitas. The overwhelming majority, notably, from women.

During his four glorious seasons with the Padres, the club's marketing engine fashioned an image of its chiseled third baseman as the rugged individual on a Harley, as John Wayne in a ball cap. The hunk who could hit a curveball. Before a game once, Caminiti was videotaped warming up with his shirt off; it became a staple on Qualcomm Stadium's video screen. At the Padres' spring training facility in Arizona, the club put up a divider in the locker area to keep female employees from sneaking a peak from nearby offices. The Cammy curtain, they called it.

He was no longer Kenny, the shy kid from Cordoy Lane. He was Cammy now.

He was the rookie who went 2-for-3 with a home run and a triple in his first major league game. He was the third baseman who knocked down a ground ball and gunned down the runner from his rear end. He was the switch-hitter who would hit home runs from both sides of the plate in the same game ten times, including three times in four days in 1995.

He was the gamer who yanked an IV out of his arm, wolfed down a Snickers bar, and wobbled onto the field to hit two home runs against the Mets. The guy who won the '96 National League MVP while not being able to lift his left arm over his head, the guts of the Padres' run to the '98 World Series.

When it was his turn to bat, one of the songs the Qualcomm Stadium speakers blared was, "Where have all the cowboys gone?" People ate it up.

In a 1997 interview with Channel 4 San Diego, Caminiti was asked if there was anything in particular fans should know about him. He chuckled and said: "The less they know about me, the better."

He was only half-kidding.

Caminiti wasn't anything like he seemed.

"You looked at him, he looked mean. He played the game mean," says Craig Biggio, who rose through the Astros farm system with him. "Off the field he was a teddy bear, even though he had that (goatee) and he looked like a big, nasty guy. If you needed a dollar and he had a dollar in his pocket, if that was the last dollar he was ever going to make, he'd give it to you and not ask for it back."

He married Nancy. They had three daughters. They built a sprawling home in the upscale community of Pecan Grove Plantation outside Houston. They had a cocker spaniel named Bailey. He'd take a break from working on his cars (his '55 Chevy once took second in a national vintage car show), load the neighborhood kids into his SUV, and take them to the movies.

He also owned show dogs. Not pit bulls or Great Danes, but fluffy little things, with fur over their eyes, petit bassets griffons vendéens. Two, Charmaine and Yoyo, won ribbons in the prestigious Westminster Kennel Club show in New York.

He patiently signed autographs and posed for photos before games. He heard a Padres fan had cancer and needed money to pay for the treatment, so he donated one of his motorcycles to be auctioned off. After the 1998 season, he turned down an offer from Detroit to sign with Houston for $25 million less — just so he could be closer to his girls.

Caminiti wasn't anything like he seemed.

He was also legendary for partying with the same intensity that he played. For emptying hotel minibars, for finishing a game and immediately popping double or triple the dosage of prescription painkillers, for washing them down with a large cup of vodka with a splash of orange juice, for carrying on into the wee hours of the morning.

One Houston sportswriter tells about the time he flew from St. Louis to Houston with Caminiti. Caminiti, he says, ordered twenty mini bottles of booze in the two-hour flight, drinking most and stuffing the rest in his carry-on.

"There would be times he would be up all night and on cocaine and alcohol and not sleep, and then the next day he'd go out and play a perfect game," says one longtime friend who spoke on the condition of anonymity. "Many, many times that happened. I don't know how he did it."

His parents have said they suspected something was amiss as far back as the late '80s. Caminiti later admitted he "rebelled . . . rebelled hard" and eventually told them to get lost. They were estranged for several years. He was an adult now. He could handle himself.

After the '93 season, Caminiti convinced himself he would stop. That he could stop.

He was strict. No more alcohol. No more painkillers.

"I lasted about twenty days," he said later. "I went to a wedding."

At the urging of teammates Biggio and Jeff Bagwell, he reluctantly agreed to enroll in a sixteen-day rehabilitation program. He reconciled with his parents. He sobered up, conceding in an interview with Channel 4 San Diego: "I wanted to fit in, be a part of the crowd. I just took it to an extra level."

Sobriety suited Caminiti well. He made his first All-Star team the following year, his first with the Padres.

But the injuries and the urgings were too much. This time, Caminiti turned not to alcohol or narcotics but steroids, later admitting he crossed the border into Tijuana and purchased a bottle of injectable testosterone.

The idea was that the steroids would hasten the healing of his injured shoulder. That was June 1996. He quickly swelled to 230 pounds, 70 above what he weighed in high school. He had never hit more than 26 home runs in a season; in the last three months he hit 29. He had never received so much as a single MVP vote in his career; in November, he was named National League MVP.

He was invited to ESPN's ESPYs at New York's Radio City Music

Hall and received two awards. He thanked his wife and daughters. Then he went to the lobby and asked the bartender to mix him a vodka drink and make it look like ice water.

He was going to have only one.

"I drank about a hundred of them," he later told a reporter. After three years of relative sobriety, he had climbed to the higher ledge above the reservoir again and jumped off.

His body continued to break down with increased regularity — the result, some believe, of overdoing the steroids and putting undue strain on his joints — and he relapsed into his old regimen of painkillers and booze and cocaine. He hid it for a few years, until he woke up on Labor Day weekend 2000 in his bedroom. His wife, father, and personal trainer were there too.

He initially resisted the intervention, ultimately agreeing to spend a month at the Smithers Institute in Manhattan. He followed that with ninety AA meetings in ninety days and gave his career one final shot, starting the season with the Texas Rangers and finishing it with the Atlanta Braves.

In late September 2001, the Braves played a three-game series at the Florida Marlins. An old friend, Katie Waite, went to dinner with him.

"He was as clean as could be," Waite says. "But he was so edgy. When I mentioned something, he snapped at me. He was in a lot of pain and I offered him some Advil and he wouldn't take it. I had a glass of wine with dinner, and he just had water."

At 1:35 P.M. on November 14, 2001, Houston police pulled over a 2000 white Mercedes. A man named Lamont Palmer was alone driving the $100,000 sedan. The problem: it was registered to Kenneth Gene Caminiti.

Palmer explained that Caminiti had given him permission to drive it, that they could ask Caminiti himself if they didn't believe him. Caminiti, Palmer told them, was just a couple exits up Houston's Southwest Freeway in room 2025 of the Ramada Limited Motel.

Room 2025 is at the end of a long, low-ceilinged corridor on the second floor. According to the Harris County Sheriff's report, officers could smell crack cocaine as they approached the end of the hallway. They knocked on the door of number 2025, a nineteen-year-old woman named LaToya Bowman opened it, and the crack stench nearly overwhelmed them.

The officers entered the room and found Cedric Palmer, a five-foot-eleven, 290-pound man with a long criminal record, lying on one of the beds. They also noticed the bathroom door closing.

"Deputy Worley immediately walked to the door and discovered a white male . . . standing in the bathroom," the report says. "Deputy Worley looked down and observed a used crack pipe lying in the white bathroom sink in plain view."

The white male: Ken Caminiti.

Officers found a Coca-Cola can and plastic water bottle converted into crack pipes, a spoon with cocaine residue, a book of matches, and a 9mm handgun under one of the beds.

"Also observed on the table," the report says, "was a black Gucci wallet which was checked and was found to have numerous cards issued to Kenneth Caminiti. Deputy Patberg observed that the wallet held no U.S. currency but did observe that the wallet contained a heavy trace of white powder substance where the U.S. currency would go. The white powder substance field-tested positive for cocaine."

The kid from Cordoy Lane had hit rock bottom. Or so everyone thought.

The three were charged with possessing less than a gram of a controlled substance. All three would plead guilty. The twenty-three-year-old Palmer, as a prior felon, was sentenced to eight months. Bowman and Caminiti, as first-time offenders, were placed on probation.

Both, however, ended up in jail as well. Bowman stopped reporting to her probation officer, was tracked down, and did eight months. Caminiti failed a mandatory drug test for cocaine in January 2003 and spent four months in a state jail located in, appropriately enough, Humble, Texas.

"You think it's never going to happen to you, you think you'll never be locked up and never be put away," Caminiti later said at a speaking engagement as part of National Alcohol and Drug Abuse Recovery Month. "That was a real eye-opener for me, walking down the corridors in prison and having people walk up and say, 'Hey, Caminiti, sign my crack pipe.'"

Daniel "Gus" Gerard nods when he hears the story. He was

Caminiti's primary drug counselor. He once had been so hooked on cocaine that it nearly killed him. He understands.

Gerard, fifty-one, played seven seasons in basketball's ABA and NBA. It wasn't until 1993, after "a moment of clarity" following a failed suicide attempt, that he sobered up for good. For the past seven years, he has been the director of The Next Step, a substance-abuse recovery provider in the Houston area.

Gerard was hopeful for Caminiti. He also was realistic, knowing the very traits that made Caminiti $38 million in fifteen seasons on the field and the compassionate soul off it would make him an unlikely candidate to achieve full sobriety. Knowing Caminiti would be his own worst enemy.

Lower back pain, upper back pain, pulled hamstrings, strained abdominal muscles, torn rotator cuffs, torn calf muscles, torn biceps tendons, torn tendon sheaths in his wrist — Caminiti played through them all. A toenail was hurting him so much before a game, the story goes, he ripped it off with a pair of pliers, wrapped up the toe, and laced up his cleats.

"As professional athletes," Gerard says, "we're programmed to never give in and always fight. To achieve recovery you have to give in, you have to surrender totally."

There was something else. Caminiti once asked Gerard how guys in The Next Step program were getting to their daily sobriety meetings, and Gerard explained that most were either taking city buses or riding in the center's broken-down station wagon. Caminiti bought them a fifteen-passenger van.

"He was a savior," Gerard says. "He wanted to save people. But he spent more time trying to save other people than saving himself. You have to be really selfish. You have to worry about yourself and only yourself.

"Being in jail was really humbling for him. When he got out, he was really gung-ho on recovery. He spoke to kids. He spoke to church groups. But then he got overconfident in his sobriety. He didn't have to be in our (halfway house) facility anymore. He was out on his own. Then he started inviting people into his life who put him in high-risk situations because they were still using drugs.

"Your mind starts telling you that you don't have to go to as many meetings. You tell yourself that you can hang around these people. But you can't. You just can't. It doesn't work that way."

So the downward spiral continued. His marriage was falling apart and he was living by himself. He'd sober up, declare himself cured, invite some down-and-out buddy he met in rehab to stay in his house, and toss him the keys to one of his six cars. Then he'd slip, fail another test, and wind up back in jail or a halfway house.

"I'd get a call from Ken," says Kent Schaeffer, one of his attorneys. "He'd tell me, 'You better send someone over to my house.' The last time he went to jail, I had to recover his wallet, his watch, his memorabilia, his cars. I sent someone out there to change the locks and had two or three people escorted off the property. It was like a flophouse with people he went to jail with, or met in rehab or halfway houses . . .

"He was just ripe to be taken advantage of. For someone like Ken, it's not supposed to end up that way. But he just couldn't say no to people."

He couldn't say no to Maria.

Her name is Maria Romero. They met in 2000 during Caminiti's monthlong drug rehabilitation at the Smithers Institute. She called him Bugga. He gave her an e-mail address of dqlol, for "drama queen laughing out loud."

Romero, thirty-four, has three children and has not been married. She says she was Caminiti's fiancée.

"I don't think nobody out there knows Ken like I knew him," Romero says. "He was the real Ken with me. Ken was really closed. He would swallow (emotions). But he opened up around me."

"Every time her name came up, it seemed like there was a problem," Schaeffer says. "A lot of times, toxic mates are a more compelling addiction than drugs. She just had some sort of control over him."

Caminiti showed up late in Arizona this spring to work as a Padres instructor. He had bruises on his face. Schaeffer and Licht say he told them Maria had hit him and that he didn't fight back. Romero denies it.

In May, the Texas court documents indicate a "no-contact" order with Romero was added to the terms of Caminiti's probation. Romero was living with him at the time.

"It was determined by myself and the judge that she was a person he should not be associated with because of incidents we had in the past with her," says Tracy Burns, Caminiti's supervising probation officer. "I personally kicked her out of the house at his request."

What kinds of incidents?

"I can only say that she was involved in all of his relapses with cocaine," Burns says.

Romero denies that and says she only recently learned of the no-contact order.

"My baby's dead and there's nothing that will bring him back," Romero says from Tampa, Florida, where she lives. "I don't care what anyone says. The truth is, we loved each other to death."

The day after he was freed from a Houston jail for the last time, he went to the airport, his associates later learned, to catch a flight to Tampa. To see Maria.

From there, the two flew to New York. By Sunday evening, Caminiti was dead.

What exactly transpired in New York remains fuzzy. Caminiti reportedly went there to counsel Romero's eldest son because he had been caught with drugs. Then they were at Maria's mother's house for a birthday party.

Then he was calling Rob Silva, Romero's ex-boyfriend and the father of the troubled teen, at 4:30 A.M. and making a $1,000 cash withdrawal from his American Express account. By that morning they were walking around the Hunts Point area of the Bronx, notorious for being a haven for drugs. They ended up at the Seneca Avenue apartment with Angel Gonzalez, like Silva a convicted drug felon who had spent time in jail with him.

A few years earlier, the entire block had been boarded up.

"But there'd be people lined up, ten deep, all the time," says a fireman who works in a station down the street from the Seneca Avenue apartment. "There was a small hole in the wall and they'd reach in with their money and pull out whatever drug they wanted."

This was where Caminiti died October 10, where the streetlight finally went dark. Preliminary reports cited a heart attack as cause of death, but medical examiners are awaiting results from toxicology tests.

A memorial service was held in Houston five days later. Dozens of pro baseball players attended. Padres owner John Moores chartered a jet to fly in a contingent of San Diego players and staff.

Hundreds of others were packed into the large church — family, friends, business associates, pew after pew filled with upstanding citizens who had known and loved him.

Above the altar hung a screen with a huge picture of Caminiti from several years earlier. His blue eyes sparkling. A broad smile behind the goatee. Happy. Content. Sober.

It was a Caminiti no one in the church knew in his final years. He still had money, according to his agent, but his relationships with family and close friends had deteriorated. He stayed away from pro ballparks. He was separated from Nancy in 2000; the divorce was finalized in December 2002, granting her primary custody of the girls plus 55 percent of his Major League Baseball pension.

"The criminal justice system criminalizes drug offenders and puts them in handcuffs and puts them in an orange jumpsuit and puts them in front of the cameras," says Yates, a Caminiti attorney. "They dehumanize them. They embarrass them in front of their family and friends.

"That really causes a loss of self-esteem. Maybe what happened in Ken's case is he became comfortable and identified with people in his same situation, felt like they didn't look down on him. Maybe that's why he continued to run with these people."

Jasper VanSolinge, the husband of Caminiti's sister, delivered a eulogy on behalf of the family. He spoke about the wonderful qualities that endeared Caminiti to so many people, about the uncanny ability to play through pain that endeared him to so many teammates. He also spoke about how Caminiti wasn't the same person in recent years, how "the more we reached out to him, the more he stepped back."

VanSolinge flipped through yellow note pages as he read his eulogy. He reached the bottom of the last page, took a deep breath, and said:

"We will always love you, Ken. We will miss you forever. And now we, too, will have to play through the pain."

Schaeffer remembers going to lunch with Caminiti in recent years.

"People would look at him, would recognize him," Schaeffer says, "and he'd say, 'Yeah, but they're looking at me as being a crackhead.' I'd say, 'No, that's not the case. People admire you.' And he'd say, 'No, they don't.'"

His last game was with the Atlanta Braves in the first round of the 2001 playoffs. He was left off the roster for the National League Championship Series, and he was released shortly after the season. A week later, he was found in the bathroom of the Ramada Limited with a crack pipe.

He wouldn't set foot in a major league ballpark for nearly two years. Until September 28, 2003, for the final baseball game at Qualcomm Stadium.

It took some convincing to get him there. Moores and Licht flew to Houston and took Caminiti to dinner that summer, trying to explain how much he meant to San Diego fans, how he was the only Padre ever to win the MVP, how he almost single-handedly saved baseball in the city and helped get the new ballpark built.

He was reluctant. He had just been released from jail after failing another drug test. He was embarrassed, shamed, humiliated. He was convinced baseball wouldn't forgive him for his 2002 steroid confession in *Sports Illustrated* in which he claimed "at least half" of major leaguers were using them.

He said yes finally, under the condition that Nancy and the girls wouldn't go with him; he didn't want his girls, Licht says, to hear him get booed. Then he missed his flight to San Diego. He caught the next one but was sick the entire way. He arrived and said he had changed his mind.

But they got him to the Q. After showing a highlight reel of him between innings, the stadium video board cut to a live shot of Caminiti in Moores' private box. The Q roared again, and at that moment it finally hit the gruff third baseman. *People admire you.* Caminiti stood up, waved, and tapped his heart. His eyes welled with tears.

"He was quivering," Licht says. "He grabbed the back of my neck so hard I thought my head was going to pop off. It was like a vise. I think he was trying to gain his composure. It was a really emotional moment."

After postgame festivities on the field, Caminiti went into the manager's office and reminisced with Bruce Bochy and some of his old teammates. Licht wandered outside, watching the stadium crew break down the field.

He noticed a groundskeeper digging up third base for the last time. He walked over, told him he was Caminiti's agent, and asked if he could have the base. The groundskeeper politely told him he didn't have the authority to give it away.

As Licht was walking back to the dugout, he heard the groundskeeper calling to him. He was holding out third base.

"You give this base to Ken Caminiti," the groundskeeper told Licht. "You tell him he was the best third baseman I ever saw."

MICHAEL LEWIS

The Eli Experiment

FROM THE NEW YORK TIMES MAGAZINE

I. Eli's Joke

The day after Eli Manning was named the starting quarterback of
the New York Giants, in mid-November, his father called him about
tickets. Of course, Eli didn't call home with the news right away; his
news, to him, was never newsworthy. Archie Manning, once an NFL
quarterback himself, learned of his son's midseason promotion
from an ESPN reporter. The next day he had Eli on the phone.

"How did practice go today?" he asked. From Eli's end of the
phone came only silence. A long silence — six, maybe seven seconds.

In those long seconds Archie could have written the headlines
across the nation: "Eli Manning, Named Starter, Skips Practice." If
a life as young as Eli Manning's could be said to have a theme, this
was one of them: his ability to cause other people to worry about
him. "Everyone's always worrying about Eli," says his old friend
Merrick Egan, "and he doesn't need it." "I think where it starts,"
says his oldest friend, James Montgomery, "is that Eli kind of likes
to toy with his dad." When Eli was a star quarterback at the University of Mississippi, Montgomery recalls, Archie would drive up from
his home in New Orleans to see his son play at the school where he
once filled the same role himself. Ole Miss fans still speak of these
visits as a Roman Catholic might speak of a trip by the pope. There
are streets in Oxford, Mississippi, named for Archie Manning, halls
devoted to his memory, ballads written and actually sung to com-
memorate Archie Manning. The speed limit on the Ole Miss cam-

pus is Archie's old number, 18. Archie played games in the late 1960s that they still talk about.

Yet so far as anyone could tell, Eli hadn't read his Scripture — hadn't even bothered to skim the Cliff Notes. Archie can recall Eli wanting to discuss his legendary performances only once: "When he called me after he got to Ole Miss and said he came across my stats in the media guide, and that they weren't very good." If he was only feigning indifference to his father's achievements, he did it well. His two older brothers, Cooper and Peyton (who is the quarterback of the Indianapolis Colts and was the league MVP last year) obsessed mightily over their father's playing days. They watched old tapes, peppered Archie with questions, dragged him out into the back yard to throw the football. But Eli never exhibited even a faint curiosity about what his father had done and seemingly knew nothing about it.

On these visits to Oxford, Archie would always go by Eli's apartment, just to check up on things. "Being the rather tidy person he is," Montgomery recalls, "Archie would just kind of subconsciously start to clean up Eli's apartment. You know, organize the magazines, straighten out all the papers and pens on Eli's desk." And what Eli would do, just for kicks, is quietly follow his dad around the place and reverse the process. Dropping the same magazines back onto the floor, messing up the same papers, etc. "The funny part was," Montgomery says, "his dad would clean the same magazines up about two or three times before finally noticing that he'd already done it."

Twenty-three years of this treatment and Archie was little better than his youngest son's lab rat, responding to electric shocks, grabbing for the cheese. To Archie it was possible, just, that his son, the day after he was named the starting quarterback of the New York Giants, forgot to go to practice. To him, Eli himself seemed worried that he might have skipped practice. It was a simple question: how was practice today? He awaited the answer.

"We don't have practice on Tuesday," Eli said finally.

Oh.

Was it one of Eli's private jokes? You never knew. Most of Eli's jokes, like most of Eli's thoughts, were private.

II. Plato's Cave

Q: When did you make the decision to start Eli?
A: Is that important, really? Maybe it was on the couch at 3:00 A.M. this morning, maybe. Maybe that was it.

Throughout the week leading up to Eli Manning's first game as a starter, reporters pestered the Giants coach, Tom Coughlin, about the reason for replacing his quarterback, Kurt Warner, with a rookie. And all week Coughlin treated the question with contempt — and it's hard to imagine that anywhere else in the NFL is there a coach with such a gift for contempt for the sort of questions journalists ask football coaches. But the truth is, when he made his decision, he might well have been on a couch at three in the morning. The previous Sunday the Giants, then 5–3 and still hopeful, were stifled by a bad team, the Arizona Cardinals. Warner was sacked six times, several times on first and second down, by a previously undistinguished Cardinals defensive line. The sports pages the next day — with a couple of interesting exceptions — vilified the Giants' offensive line. How could these bums allow a bunch of mediocrities to sack a former NFL MVP six times in a single game?

Anyone who watched the game on TV might well have come to the same conclusion: these fellows on the Giants line appeared to be perfectly incompetent. Poor Warner was doing all he could. But Coughlin wasn't sure. He went into the office in the wee hours of the morning and studied the game tapes. The general manager, Ernie Accorsi, was already there when Coughlin arrived; he had spent the night on the maroon leatherette sofa in his office. At a decent hour, Coughlin found Accorsi and asked, "Have you seen the tape?" Coughlin had timed every pass play — all thirty-seven of them — and discovered that thirty times Warner held the ball for 3.8 seconds or more. (Depending on how many steps the quarterback drops back to pass, 1.2 to 3 seconds is considered the norm.) Often Giants receivers were open and Warner wasn't seeing them. The quarterback was more to blame for the sacks than the people assigned to protect him. And one thing Coughlin had noticed in practice about Eli Manning was that, unlike most rookie quarterbacks, he made decisions quickly and got the ball away before the defense could kill him.

And so, on November 21, 2004, against the Atlanta Falcons, the fans are expecting, if not the full answer, then at least the beginning of a response to a big question: is Eli Manning worth it? To get Eli, who was actually drafted by the San Diego Chargers, the Giants handed him a contract worth as much as $54 million and gave the Chargers two future draft picks. (Peyton Manning received a $48 million contract when he signed with the Colts.) Giants fans are understandably worried that the kid might be overpaid. But because Eli Manning is the son of one legendary quarterback and the brother of another, the question they want to ask is more personal than usual. Yeah, he had a great college career, but did this kid get here on his own merits, or is he the NFL's first legacy admission? Did Ernie Accorsi — who was sitting up there in his glass box at Giants Stadium, tense as a snare drum, not wanting to speak to anyone — see something others missed? Or did he just commit the biggest blunder in the history of the NFL draft?

The Giants players pretend that nothing special is happening, but they fool no one. If Eli Manning is a bust, their team is in trouble, for many years. Ernie Accorsi is in trouble. Tom Coughlin is in trouble. A lot of careers are suddenly on the line.

When an expensive rookie quarterback takes the field, he inevitably finds himself on the receiving end of skepticism. It's hard to think of another job at which applicants who seem so well qualified fail so spectacularly. Todd Marinovich, Tim Couch, Heath Shuler, Cade McNown, Akili Smith, Rick Mirer, Andre Ware, Art Schlichter, Jim Druckenmiller, Ryan Leaf: the NFL draft is regularly punctuated by college quarterbacks selected in the first round who then flop in the pros. At no other position in pro football is so much money flushed down the drain. As the sums pile up, you can't help wondering: what do these people who work in the NFL actually know about the ingredients of a great quarterback? They know that it helps to be tall. They know that it's important to have a strong and accurate arm. They suspect that it's important to be able to run a bit — at least well enough to avoid taking direct shots from the monsters coming after you. They know that it helps not to be stupid, though there is no agreement exactly what mental traits are the most important. A gift for geometry? For spatial relations? For making choices under duress?

And while it's hard to see how to fix the problem, it's not hard to see why it exists. Players of other positions face nothing like the quarterback's adjustment — an outstanding college lineman or receiver is likely to prove, at the very least, useful in the professional game. The quarterback experiences the most dramatic change because he is at the receiving end of the game's complexity. The pro game, every year, becomes more complicated, and as it does, the difference between it and the college game widens. (There are natural limits to how complicated college football can become. Players are allowed to practice only twenty hours a week, for a start.) When Archie Manning joined the New Orleans Saints, he recalls, "teams had maybe nine different coverages" — defensive alignments — "and maybe six blitz packages. They'd take into each game maybe four coverages and three blitzes. Against the Falcons, Eli will see that in the *first series*."

When Archie played, the same eleven men came out to play defense, no matter the situation. When Eli plays, the Falcons will deploy nineteen different players on defense, in an essentially infinite array of configurations — making it far more difficult to know which of his receivers enjoys a natural advantage, or which pass rusher is most likely to kill him. Over the course of the game, the rookie quarterback will see, in effect, endless change on the other side of the ball. Throw in the greater speed of the pro players — in the time the typical college quarterback has made up his mind what to do with the ball, the pro quarterback has been crushed under six hundred pounds of man meat — and you have, for a rookie, big problems.

But maybe the biggest change in the life of the NFL quarterback is in the cost of picking the wrong one. When Archie Manning signed with the New Orleans Saints in 1971 — the second overall pick in the NFL draft that year — he was offered what was then an outlandish contract for a quarterback: $410,000 for five years. His rookie salary was $30,000. The combined value of the rookie contracts of his two sons is more than $100 million. And so when Eli Manning started a game for the first time, with his father on hand in an end-zone seat, there was something fairly new to football in the air — not just a competitive thrill; there was a financial frisson. For the price of a $65 ticket, a Giants fan might have the chance to see, in effect, $50 million piled up in the middle of the field and set on fire. Fox Sports had its full roster of thirteen cameras at work: on platforms behind the end zone, on carts racing along the side-lines, on stands in the stadium's corners. A robot camera hovered over the field, suspended by wires.

The people, and the cameras, will follow every move Eli Manning makes. They will come away feeling as if they have achieved a fairly exact accounting of what Eli Manning did as a quarterback. And that is an interesting thing: an exact accounting is exactly what is not possible.

The millions of people watching the game on television — the beneficiaries of thirteen camera angles and endless commentary from smart people, many of whom played the game — in a way have it the worst. The man who oversees the cameras, Richie Zyontz of Fox Sports, explains that "the guys who work the cameras are trying to make a nice picture. The risk is always that it's too tight." Focusing on what grips a television audience — facial expressions, violence, emotion, pretty women — the camera will miss the sub-tleties of the game: the missed blocks, the badly run pass routes.

The naked eye, no matter how well trained, isn't much better. From the chaos on the field it isn't always obvious, even to official scorekeepers, who did what. The *Indianapolis Star* recently pub-lished an article showing that the statistics compiled by the Colts coaching staff — from the tapes of the games — were alarmingly different from the official records kept during the season. The scorekeepers, for instance, credited the Colts linebacker Cato June with fifty-nine solo tackles and fifteen assists; from tapes the Colts coaches know that Cato June had forty-nine solo tackles and forty assists. If the human eye can miss something as central to the action as a tackle, how can it be expected to comprehend the dozens of things that occur away from the ball? Statistics — the answer in other sports — don't help all that much. Football statistics do not capture the performance of individual football players as cleanly as, say, baseball statistics capture the performance of individual baseball players. No player ever does anything on a football field that isn't dependent on some other player. The individual achieve-ments of football players are often, in effect, hidden in plain sight.

But here's the other interesting thing: this hidden game can be seen, though not by the average viewer. Shot unceremoniously from two pillboxes on the stadium's upper rim, the videotape made by the Giants coaching staff frames all twenty-two players on the field. The view the coaches want is the view from the cheapest seat in the house. "When former coaches get into the broadcast booth, that's the first thing they want to see, the all-twenty-two, the eye in the sky," Zyontz says. The coaches want to see that shot because they know it is the only shot that will enable them to figure out who did what — and assign credit and blame — on any given football play.

"After a game," Coughlin says, "you obviously know what happened. But a lot of times you don't know why it happened." If even the coach, who, during a game, is privy to overhead still photos of the action and countless conversations with players, doesn't understand who did what, what hope is there for a mere spectator? In some strange way, until you see the tape, you haven't seen the game.

Giants Stadium, on this afternoon of Eli Manning's debut, is Plato's Cave. The millions of people watching the game are inside the cave, staring at shadows on the wall. The shadows are distortions of the reality outside the cave, treated, erroneously, as the thing itself. No matter how he plays, some part of Eli Manning's game, like his personality, will remain hidden from public understanding. It may be a trivial part; it may be the telling part — the point is that no one can know for sure if the Giants have given their money to the right guy.

III. The $54 Million Crapshoot

The droop of his shoulders, the hangdog look, the soft and gentle face, the tendency to greet every question with a blank expression and a high-pitched note of uncertainty ("Ummmmm") — everything about Eli Manning's outward appearance suggests indecision and youth. "If I was a cop and I saw him out driving a car, I'd pull him over," says Shaun O'Hara, the Giants regular center. His picture has for months graced billboards around New York City, but Eli has been able to walk the length of the fancy part of Fifth

Avenue with his mother — untucked red alligator shirt, unpressed chinos, and sneakers without socks — without once being recognized. By nature he is very private, but what he's withholding from the public is unclear. "I'm Eli's oldest friend," James Montgomery says, "and I don't think I've ever had a serious conversation with him. The last time he called we spent fifteen minutes trying to figure out the last song in *Teen Wolf.*"

The only thing that distinguishes Eli Manning, outwardly, from a slightly shy twenty-three-year-old recent college graduate unsure of what he wants to do with the rest of his life is the way he plays quarterback. He offers new hope to introverts everywhere; such characters don't normally land in such exalted positions of leadership. This may be because conventional leadership skills are necessary for the role. But it may also be a matter of false selection. There aren't many introverts playing quarterback in the NFL for the same reason that, until recently, there were not many blacks playing NFL quarterback: they never get the chance. Shy, quiet kids aren't tapped by their Pop Warner coaches to play the position — unless, of course their fathers were famous NFL quarterbacks. The biggest unseen edge that Eli possesses may be that he is expected to excel at the position. Because of this he will be given more time than most to do it.

In the nine weeks of the season leading up to his first start, Eli rode the bench and watched Kurt Warner play. Still, Coughlin kept him as busy as if he were actually on the field. The people in the video department would run off clips, organized by theme, of the NFL's top quarterbacks — Chad Pennington, Donovan McNabb, Tom Brady and, of course, Peyton Manning. And so every week Eli found himself watching and rewatching themed tape of his older brother: Peyton's footwork, Peyton's two-minute drills, Peyton's long pass plays. One afternoon in early November, I sat with Eli and watched a reel — it was edited to isolate the "red zone," the turf within twenty yards of the opposing team's end zone. "A lot of good decision making is just eliminating what receiver you're not looking at," Eli said, as he reached for the tape. His goal in life seems to be to not make a big deal of anything; or, rather, he makes a big deal about not making a deal. On the surface, he is a passive creature. By all accounts, he cooperates with his elders, is polite even when he doesn't need to be, and hasn't a mean bone in his body.

But at his core there is a truculence. He insists on detaching himself from the life story that was, in a way, written for him at birth.

When he talks about being an NFL quarterback, his chief concern seems to be minimizing the drama of it all: "A lot of it is knowing who should be open. It's a process of elimination that starts even before you take the snap. A lot of it just comes naturally. It's hard to teach someone how to feel pressure, for example. You aren't really thinking about moving around in the pocket. You just kind of have to have a feeling for it."

Into the machine Eli punched the tape and onto the screen popped his brother, trying to punch the ball into the end zone against the Tennessee Titans. Immediately you saw that Peyton's style of play, at least before the play began, was unlike that of any other NFL quarterback's, an overwrought sequence of waving and pointing and hollering more commonly associated with conducting a high school marching band than a pro football team. Opposing players scream at Peyton to shut up; writers suggest the NFL reduce the time between plays so that Peyton has fewer seconds to turn the line of scrimmage into a soliloquy. "A lot of that's for show," Eli said. "Here, look." Peyton was waving and hollering and pointing again; it looked as if he was designing something very, very complicated. Then he handed the ball off to a halfback, who ran straight ahead for the touchdown. Eli chuckled. "All that noise and it was just a running play."

He has watched his antic brother a million times. "Have you seen anything you hadn't noticed before from watching him?" I asked. Eli thought about it. "He complains a lot," he said finally. "Here. . . ." He rewound the tape and then ran one of the previous plays in slow motion. Peyton stuck the ball into a running back's hands, and the running back hurled himself onto a pile. But Eli still had his finger on Peyton, who receded into the distance at the top of the screen. When the back failed to score, Peyton threw up his hands and marched around in a huff. "He does that a lot," Eli said.

Archie and Olivia Manning raised their sons to be well-educated members of New Orleans' upper middle class — nice boys, good people. Archie never intended for them to make careers in football, and he made a big deal of steering as far from their ambitions as he could and still remain intimately involved in their lives. Whatever he contributed to his children's success, he contributed inadvertently. Archie had a phobia that someone might mistake him for one of those Little League dads whose idea of fatherhood is to holler at the umps. ("I've never been embarrassed by my dad," says Cooper Manning, a New Orleans investment analyst whose own promising football career ended for medical reasons. "Not a single time.") He actually made a point of not learning all the bewildering changes to the pro game since he quit playing, in 1985, so that his sons would be more reluctant to engage him in conversation about football, as opposed to something else. And when the Mannings went looking for a school, they picked the one most likely to leave their children with something else to talk about. The Isidore Newman School (my alma mater) isn't, to put it kindly, a football school. Perhaps more effectively than any secondary school in a hundred-mile radius, it is capable of taking the raw material for an All-Pro quarterback and turning it into a high-priced lawyer.

A father agnostic about his sons' football careers, a school ill suited to encouraging them, a society, the New Orleans upper middle class, from which a member is about as likely to matriculate into professional football as into, say, Cosa Nostra: how did this combination of forces yield not one but two pro quarterbacks, both top picks in the NFL draft? In countless ways, small and large, Peyton has explained his own case: he refused not to play in the NFL. Eli wasn't like that. He was detached; he had no obvious internal drama; if you didn't look extremely closely, you might even say he was indifferent. Even as he became perhaps the best high school quarterback in the country, he never let on that football was critically important to him. He couldn't remember his father playing; he didn't bother to sit down and watch the old tapes. "Elway and Marino were Peyton's heroes," Cooper recalls. "Peyton could probably have named every player in the NFL. I don't know if Eli could name a hero. I don't know if Eli could have named a player in the NFL. With Eli, it's all very internal. You have to dig a bit to see how it all works." To which Eli replies, "I'm not the guy who runs down the field with his finger up in the air like I just saved the world."

When Eli Manning submitted his brain to the NFL for inspection, he relaxed his pretense that nothing much was going on inside of it. The NFL actually requires that prospects take an intelligence test — which is, of course, surprising to everyone outside the NFL. As Charlie Wonderlic, the CEO of Wonderlic Inc., which creates the NFL's intelligence tests, puts it, "Why in the world would you want to know how smart a football player is?" But you do want to know, especially when that player is a quarterback. The Wonderlic Personnel Test, given to all prospects, is identical to the test given to more than two million corporate employees each year. It consists of fifty questions. The taker is given twelve minutes to answer as many as he can. Here is one of the easier questions:

> FAMILIAR is the opposite of 1) friendly, 2) old, 3) strange, 4) aloof, 5) different.

And here is a hard one:

> In printing an article of 24,000 words, a printer decides to use two sizes of type. Using the larger type, a printed page contains 900 words. Using the smaller type, a page contains 1,200 words. The article is allotted 21 full pages in a magazine. How many pages must be in the smaller type?

The test has been used by NFL teams for decades, but the emphasis placed on it has grown with the complexity of the game. (Archie Manning recalls, during his senior year, some guy affiliated with a pro team turning up at Ole Miss and handing out an intelligence test. "We all took it sitting on stools in the locker room, with no one watching us," he says. "Two of the tackles cheated off each other.") Teams use it to weed out players whose minds are simply inadequate to the task. The rule of thumb — on offense at least — is that the closer you are to the ball, the smarter you need to be. (Centers are the only players who routinely test as highly as quarterbacks.) The average test score for lawyers is 30 and for janitors is 15. The average test score for halfbacks, the lowest-scoring players, is 15, and for quarterbacks is 25. The head of scouting for the Giants, Jerry Reese, says, "If a quarterback's score comes in under 25, we worry; otherwise we don't pay that much attention to it." Eli Manning scored a 39, putting him in the ninety-ninth percentile of last year's two and a half million Wonderlic test takers. His brother Cooper (he was laughing as he spoke) said, "I think the only guy who scored higher than Eli was a punter from Harvard who didn't make a team." (Actually, Pat McInally, the Harvard punter who scored a perfect 50, did make it onto the Cincinnati Bengals.) Eli

Manning's score was so high that when I mentioned it to Charlie Wonderlic, he suggested I recheck my facts and said, "There's not a job on the planet that requires a person to score at that level."

But Eli Manning may be the only person in the history of the Wonderlic who can score a 39 and not recall his score. Wandering down a hallway in the Giants front office one day I asked him how he did on the test. "Ummmmm — I think I got a 41 or a 42 out of 50."

"How did Peyton do?" I asked.

"Ummmmmmmm — I don't think he did as well, maybe low 30s." Then he smiled and said, "I think Peyton might have been above average."

By all the tests that NFL scouts use to measure college quarterbacks, Eli Manning compared favorably to his famous older brother. And yet the decision to take him with the first pick, and pay him great sums of money, was nevertheless regarded by many inside the NFL as fantastically risky. A few general managers, and coaches, would have refused to make it. When the quarterbacks arrived at the 2003 NFL combine — where the teams put the most highly touted prospects through their paces — the coach of the Carolina Panthers, John Fox, simply walked out. He took a principled stand against spending money and draft picks on a quarterback. No NFL coach will say this, but a few actually build their teams on the principle that the quarterback need not be especially gifted, because he doesn't need to be terribly important. You don't need a god out there; you don't need Joe Montana or John Elway or Peyton Manning. All you need is one very smart coaching staff and a quarterback who won't mess up their intricate plans. Spend less of your money on a quarterback and you have more to spend on the people around him. Ask them to do more, and the quarterback to do less.

The coaches who approach the game this way — Fox, Brian Billick of Baltimore, Bill Cowher of Pittsburgh, Bill Parcells of Dallas, Bill Belichick of New England — define one end of the NFL's managerial spectrum: the end that argues that it's never worth the risk to pay a fortune to a quarterback unproved in the pros. Ernie Accorsi might well define the other. "There is no other position in team sports as important as the quarterback," he says. "A great quarterback, unlike a great running back, cannot be stopped. And if you have a great one, you're never out of it. He walks on the bus and the whole team sees him and thinks, We have a chance." The problem, from Accorsi's point of view, is finding the great quarterback.

IV. The Magic

It was absurd: a sixty-one-year-old New Yorker hustling down to Mississippi on a fall weekend in 2002, just to watch a twenty-one-year-old junior quarterback in the flesh. In the NFL, sixty-one isn't old; it's ancient. Just about everyone who was in the NFL when Accorsi took his first job, in 1970, was gone. He'd retire soon; the long-term future of the New York Giants was of no practical consequence to him. But he'd seen something he couldn't ignore — a tape of an Ole Miss game. And what he'd seen in the Ole Miss quarterback, Eli Manning, got his blood racing in a way it hadn't in years. He wanted to see him play. He could have watched him plenty on television, but Accorsi had grown almost hostile to the way that football games have come to be televised. "You can't even see what's on the field, and you can't see the formations," he said. "The camera is all over the place. On the sidelines. In the stands. On the coaches' faces. I had no idea what Paul Brown and Vince Lombardi looked like because all you saw back then was the games."

He wanted to see what he wanted to see — every move Eli Manning makes — and he wanted to see "how he responds to the pressure of the game — how he responds to the crowd." He arrived early to the field, to watch Manning warm up. He couldn't tell from the tape the strength of Eli Manning's arm; and he couldn't tell from warm-ups either. It was as if Eli were trying not to show what he had. Did that mean he didn't have it? Accorsi couldn't tell. He found his seat, not in the press box, where he wanted to sit, but out on the ice-cold photographers' deck. The opposing team, Auburn, was stacked with NFL prospects. Ole Miss had maybe two, and one was Eli Manning. Accorsi watched as Auburn sprinted ahead, 14–0.

On a couple of occasions, Manning threw long. Running to his right, he drilled a pass, across his body, to the left side of the field maybe fifty-five yards. His arm was stronger than Ernie dared to imagine: the kid had a cannon, possibly stronger than his brother's arm. And then something happened: Accorsi felt it before he saw the scoreboard change. Manning was, improbably, keeping Ole Miss in the game; he was finding a way to win. Ole Miss had simply given up trying to run the football — at one point Auburn had outgained them on the ground, 230 yards to 10. And yet even without a ground game they were moving the ball through the air. Pass after beautiful pass found its mark. Eli Manning was doing the riskiest thing a quarterback can do, and everything about this game merely increased that risk. The pass rushers were always a split second from killing him; the defensive backs were all bigger and faster than his receivers; and, because Ole Miss had no running game, everyone in the stadium expected a pass. And yet he seemed to have a special ability to cope with risk. Accorsi — growing more and more excited — pulled out his notebook. In a later report, he wrote:

> Rallied his team from 14–3 halftime deficit basically all by himself. Led them on two successive third-quarter drives to go ahead 17–16, the first touchdown on a streak down the left sideline where he just dropped the ball (about 40 yards) over the receiver's right shoulder for the touchdown . . . called the touchdown pass (a quick 12-yard slant) that put them ahead at the line of scrimmage himself.

At one point late in the third quarter, Ole Miss found itself on the Auburn fifteen-yard line. The rush came so hard that it knocked Manning down as he took the snap. The Auburn line just hurled the entire Ole Miss line backward, and Manning went over like a bowling pin at the back of the stack. The play looked to be over; but a split end was running a fade to the corner of the end zone. As Eli fell, with his rear end maybe two inches off the ground, he threw the ball. A perfect spiral up and into the outstretched hands of the wideout that would have been yet another score if the astonished Auburn cornerback hadn't stuck out his hand at the last moment and deflected the ball.

This kid wasn't like any Accorsi had seen — not in a long time. He was tall — six-foot-four at least. He could throw the ball plenty far. He was decisive. He was poised — ridiculously so. He had exquisite feel for the game. But that sterile checklist didn't begin to capture what caused Accorsi to feel the way he did. "Forget all about the measurables," he says. "When you're trying to find the difference between the great quarterback and the good quarterback, you have to feel it. The intangibles." In his thirty-two years in pro football, Ernie Accorsi had a chance to draft this sort of talent once: John Elway. As the general manager of the Baltimore Colts, in 1983, he chose Elway with the first pick of the draft — only to hear Elway say he'd rather play professional baseball than play football in Baltimore, forcing a trade to Denver. Accorsi quit in frustration; as he put it, "If I'm going to lose my job, it's going to be over this, not some right guard." And now here was this kid, a junior at a school that hadn't won anything, whom he had a shot of drafting. He wrote in his notebook:

> He has a feel in the pocket. In one case a linebacker coming off the blind side edge had him measured and he was going to get mashed. At first, I didn't think he felt it but he held it to the last split second, threw a completion and got hammered. Just got up and went back to the huddle. . . .
>
>   I know it's just one look. . . . But if I had to make the decision this morning, I would move up to take him. They are rare, as we know.

And here was where Ernie Accorsi, sitting on the cold photographers' deck, reached back behind him to feel a distant memory. Suddenly it is December 28, 1958, all over again. He's seventeen years old and his father has sprung for a trip from their home in Hershey, Pennsylvania, to Palm Beach, Florida. The Accorsis aren't poor, but they aren't rich either. A trip to Florida is an indulgence; Ernie's supposed to feel grateful, and he knows it. But he doesn't; he feels frustrated. The next afternoon, which his father has planned to spend on the golf course with his son, the Baltimore Colts will play the New York Giants for the NFL championship. The game will be televised nationally. His first love — the first love of every kid he knows; after all, this is 1958 — is baseball. But he's becoming more and more interested in football; more specifically, he's following the Colts; more specifically still, he's becoming obsessed with the Colts' quarterback, Johnny Unitas. Johnny Unitas isn't like any player of any sport Ernie has ever seen. Unitas has this rare ability to make the game conform to his will; every other player just seems to be an extra in Unitas's drama. Ernie wants to see that drama, played for high stakes.

And so, three days after Christmas, his father has created a conflict in young Ernie's heart. The second half will be played at exactly the same time father and son are meant to be on the Palm Beach golf course. But there's no way to tell his father that he wants to spend the high moment of this expensive vacation watching TV. Ernie resigns himself to playing the unhappiest nine holes of golf of his life. Arriving at the ninth green, he spies a shack and the glow of the television inside it. He shouts to the caddies inside, "Who won the game?" Back comes the answer, "They're still playing!" Ernie drops his clubs and runs into the shack, and sees the final plays of the NFL's very first sudden-death overtime game — a game that is now referred to, with little argument, as the greatest game ever played.

The score is tied, and in overtime. Unitas has taken the Colts down the field to the Giants eight-yard line. He gives the ball to halfback Alan Ameche, who takes it to the seven. Then Unitas does something only Johnny Unitas would dream of doing: he throws a pass into the flat, sideways across the entire field. His team is within field goal range — and a field goal will end the game, and give it to the Colts — and yet he throws the kind of pass that is most likely of all to be intercepted and, if intercepted, run back for a touchdown. For no obvious reason, he risks the entire game. Colts end Jim Mutscheller catches the pass, and should score, but slips across the frozen field and out of bounds at the one-yard line. This play was, in football circles, "controversial." After the game a reporter asked Unitas how he could do such a thing in such a situation: wasn't he worried he'd be intercepted? "When you know what you're doing," Unitas said, "you don't get intercepted."

The next play he comes to the line of scrimmage. Everyone in the place assumes he'll run left to move the ball in front of the goal posts for a field goal. The Giants have stacked their defense accordingly. Unitas raises his hands, as if he thinks he can quiet the enemy crowd, and calls a new play. Alan Ameche runs untouched over the empty right side and into the end zone.

It didn't matter that Accorsi missed the second half of the game. He can, and will, watch it later, on tape. Hundreds of times. In 1970, Accorsi will get his first job in pro football, as the press guy for the Colts. Johnny Unitas will still be the quarterback; within a few years, Accorsi will become perhaps Unitas's closest friend in the organization. For the next thirty years, as Accorsi rises to run the Colts, then the Browns and finally the Giants, he will telephone Unitas every December 28 and say, "John, you know what today is?" And Unitas will never know, because that is Unitas's job — to shrug off as mere trivia one of the greatest clutch performances in football history. When Unitas dies, Accorsi will carry his coffin to the grave.

In his defining trait, Eli Manning reminds Ernie Accorsi of Johnny Unitas. Accorsi has never spoken to Manning; he has never even shaken the young man's hand. He doesn't know him as a person, only as a quarterback. But as he watched him very nearly beat a vastly superior opponent, Accorsi scribbled in his diary: "Has the quality that you can't define, call it magic."

V. The Eye in the Sky

> Q: Do you sense that it was a little premature to make the quarterback change?
>
> A: No, not at all. That's not my sense at all, and it wasn't yours either. Short memories.

Three games was all it took for the press to ask Coach Coughlin if he wasn't, perhaps, a fool for bringing in a rookie quarterback. In his debut against the Falcons, Manning showed flashes of brilliance and nearly led the team to an upset victory. He was sacked just once; he moved the offense against one of the NFL's better defenses. In the second half, he threw his first touchdown pass, to the Giants tight end Jeremy Shockey. But in his second game, against an even better Philadelphia team, he definitely looked overpaid.

Accorsi wasn't about to attribute much significance to that. The best quarterbacks often play poorly in their first starts. "Unitas's first pass was intercepted," he said. Elway's debut was no more auspicious. "Elway came out and lined up under the guard. The center had to shout at him, 'Hey, John, I'm over here.'" And, as everyone knows, Peyton Manning's team, in his first season, went 3–13. All Accorsi would say about Eli Manning was, "Thank God he showed us he's human."

Before the third game, against the Washington Redskins, Accorsi agreed to watch tape with me afterward and dissect Manning's performance. Monday morning, I found Accorsi in his office at Giants Stadium with an expression on his face somewhere between apologetic and disturbed, like a man standing on the side of the Jersey Turnpike who has just caused a ten-car pileup. Against a team with a 3–8 record, a team that hadn't scored more than eighteen points in a game all season, the Giants lost 31–7. They ran forty-one plays to the Redskins' sixty-eight. Manning was, at best, unimpressive: twelve completed passes in twenty-five attempts for a mere 113 yards. When his receivers were open, his throws were off target. He looked like a different quarterback from the one who had played against the Falcons.

On one play, Giants receiver Ike Hilliard got open running an out pattern. As I watched Hilliard come free for the first time in two games, I thought back to a training scrimmage I witnessed at the Giants' camp in upstate New York one afternoon in August. Eli Manning dropped back to pass, while a cluster of three Giants receivers streaked downfield together like jets in formation — it's called a bunch-three route. At the last moment, Ike Hilliard peeled away and cut toward the corner of the end zone — and fooled no one. A cornerback and a safety stayed on him, step for step. Improbably, the ball appeared over Hilliard's shoulder and dropped into his arms for a touchdown. There was exactly one football-size place to put the ball so that Hilliard, and no one else, might catch it. On the way back to the huddle, Hilliard asked every defender he passed, "Did you see him drop it in there?" When he passed by the coaches pacing on the sideline, someone shouted at Hilliard, "Great job, Ike." Hilliard shook his head and said, "I didn't do nothing."

And now, facing what appeared to be a much easier throw, Manning just missed him. The ball sailed right over Hilliard's head.

About the only nice thing a fan might say about his performance was that the team around him appeared so outclassed that whatever Eli Manning did could scarcely matter at all. Hardly anybody said it, however; the fans were already screaming that the Giants were sacrificing their season for the sake of getting playing time for their expensive rookie. What I hoped Accorsi could explain, using the evidence of the game tape, was how can you tell the difference between the struggles of a promising rookie quarterback and the struggles of a terminally hopeless rookie quarterback? But he declined. "I'm sorry," he said, as I walked into his office. "I can't do the tape thing. I don't have the stomach for it."

Later that day I did get him on the phone. He'd spent the intervening few hours watching the tape, over and over. And his mood had changed. "If you look at the tape," he said, "the guys are all covered. He didn't have anyone to throw it to. They took the run away from us, the whole game was on his shoulders, but he didn't have any help. Our receivers weren't getting open." Another cheering thing was clear: Manning made very few bad decisions. Once, on third and long, with all of his downfield receivers covered, he had running back Tiki Barber open in the flat. If he had seen him, Barber might have gotten the first down — but you never know. "That's one of the things he'll learn to do as he matures. He'll learn to look for his release man." A couple of the balls that appeared to be underthrown were actually tipped by the defense. And that throw to Hilliard — he was hit as he made it.

"It's easy to rationalize this," Accorsi said. "It's easy to talk yourself into thinking it wasn't as bad as it was. But I'm not that way. He got the ball to the only people he could get the ball to. A quarterback with less poise would have been out there throwing interceptions. He was playing within himself. He was making smart, crisp throws. We just didn't give him any help." This actually wasn't all that different from Archie's reaction to his son's first few games. "Too many people talk about quarterbacks like they're golfers," Archie said. "You can only do as much as your team lets you do." Manning, at least in Accorsi's eyes, was the same guy he saw down at Ole Miss two years before. He faced one of the best pass rushes in the NFL and was sacked only once — mainly because he got the ball away so quickly. "Look, you'd like to see the magic faster," Accorsi said. "But I think he did all he could. People will laugh at that. But I'll invite them to watch the tape."

But since he didn't invite me to watch the tape, all I had to go on was the game. The first three quarters I watched from the end-zone pillbox where the Giants video staff operates "the eye in the sky." The last quarter, I walked along the Giants sideline, on the field. It must be a little different in every stadium, but in the Redskins' stadium, the first thing you notice is the strong smell of trampled grass. It's pungent and makes you realize that you aren't in a clean place — an antiseptic television stage set — but a real place, with dirt. But right after that you see that everything and everyone — from the hash marks on the field to the painted Redskins cheerleaders — has been designed to be seen from a great distance. The players themselves are remote beings. In baseball and basketball, the players pick out faces in the crowd. Football players remain essentially detached from the ninety thousand people staring down on them. The fans are just one great noise machine, to be turned on and off by the home team.

The game itself, up close, is a mess. The formations, the elegant strategy, the athleticism — when you're right next to it, it's all chaos. The ball goes up in the air any distance at all and the only way you can deduce what has become of it is by the reaction of the crowd. When Eli Manning drops back to pass, if you're standing a few yards away on the sidelines, you have no sense of him doing something so considered as making a decision. The monsters charging at him from every direction are in his face so quickly that you flinch and stifle the urge to scream, "Watch out!" There is no way, you think, that he can possibly evaluate which of these beasts is most likely to get to him first, and so which of them he should take the trouble to evade. At that moment any sensible person in Manning's shoes would flee. Or, perhaps, collapse to the ground and beg for mercy. Yet he is expected to wait . . . wait . . . wait . . . until the microsecond before he is crushed. He's like a man who has pulled the pin from a grenade and is refusing to throw it.

But here's what's odd: not only must he remain undisturbed by the live grenade in his hands, he must also retain, in his mind's eye, the detached view of the man sitting in the pillbox on the rim of the stadium. The quarterback alone must weld together these two radically different points of view — the big picture and the granular details. For there is no way to react intelligently, in real time, to the chaos; you need to be able to envision its pattern before it takes shape. You have to, in short, guess. A lot. Every time Eli Manning drops back and makes a decision, he's just guessing. His guesses produce uneven results, but he is shockingly good at not making the worst ones. God may know — though I doubt it — if

Eli Manning will one day be a star in the NFL. But if there was the slightest hint of uncertainty or discomfort in the rookie, I didn't see it. The only unpleasant emotion he conveyed — and it was very slight, in view of the circumstances — was frustration. The one emotional trait he shares with his older brother is maybe the most important: success is his equilibrium state. He expects it.

The most revealing play of the game occurred after everyone stopped watching. Down 31–7, the Giants got the ball back with twenty-two seconds left to play. Instead of taking a knee and heading for the showers, Manning dropped back to pass. The Redskins, still high on the novel experience of actually beating someone, blitzed eight men. Manning found his tight end, Jeremy Shockey, for nine yards across the middle, to midfield. With six seconds left and the clock ticking, Manning ran over to the official and called timeout. From any other point of view except for his — and the Giants' long-term future — stopping the clock was deeply annoying. The game was over. The news media — along with Accorsi and the rest of the Giants management — had streamed down to the interview rooms. The Redskins cheerleaders, freezing in their leather micro-shorts, were hurrying to pack up. Most of the ninety thousand fans were gone, and the few who remained booed. But Tom Coughlin wanted Eli Manning to see as much as he could of this very good NFL defense. He wanted Eli to make one more decision, and throw one last pass against the Redskins blitz — incomplete, as it happened. It was the game within the game — the education of Eli Manning.

MARK FAINARU-WADA

Dreams, Steroids, Death — A Ballplayer's Downfall

FROM THE SAN FRANCISCO CHRONICLE

FOR YEARS, the message had been clear to Rob Garibaldi, a kid with major league tools but minor league size: get bigger. Fast.

Garibaldi heard it from the coach/nutritional supplement salesman who started him on legal weight-gaining substances at age sixteen.

He heard it from University of Southern California trainers who handed him two shopping bags of supplements on a recruiting visit and told him he needed to put on twenty pounds.

He heard it from pro scouts who said he just didn't quite fit the physical profile they were looking for in big league baseball.

Garibaldi's response was to use steroids, and his parents and his psychiatrist say it was the extensive use of those drugs that led the once-vibrant young man down an increasingly troubled path that ended in a derailed baseball career, depression, and months of emotional turmoil before he ultimately committed suicide at the age of twenty-four.

His friends and family say Garibaldi, a former star high school outfielder in Petaluma, was simply following behavior he was seeing everywhere — from the college ball fields where he competed to professional stadiums where superstars like Barry Bonds and Mark McGwire clouted home runs regularly.

His father, Ray Garibaldi, says he learned of his son's steroid use just months before Rob shot himself. He confronted Rob and demanded to know what drugs he was using. The son erupted, choking his father and yelling:

"I'm on steroids, what do you think? Who do you think I am? I'm a baseball player, baseball players take steroids. How do you think Bonds hits all his home runs? How do you think all these guys do all this stuff? You think they do it from just working out normal?"

His mother, Denise Garibaldi, said she heard the same kinds of explanations.

"In his mind, he felt like all the guys were getting away with this," she said. "Cheating and doing this is part of what's going on every day, and it was required. This was what you had to do to be a ball-player.

"He said that in order to make it into that caliber, you had to do steroids. And if Barry Bonds is doing it, Mark McGwire was doing it, then skinny little old him for sure had to be doing it."

The Garibaldis said Bonds was one of Rob's idols growing up, and Denise, a clinical psychologist, believed that was a factor. "As far as he was concerned, Bonds gave him permission to use," she said.

As all this was unfolding in the Garibaldi household, federal authorities in the Bay Area were launching an investigation that would ultimately result in indictments involving the distribution of steroids and other performance-enhancing drugs to some of the world's greatest athletes — and turn public attention to the influence that drug cheating by sports stars might have on the nation's youth.

The *Chronicle* reported this month on the grand jury testimony of two baseball stars who were among the most prominent clients of BALCO, the Burlingame laboratory at the center of the sports doping scandal.

Bonds, who set baseball's single season home run record with seventy-three in 2001 and has publicly denied using steroids, told the grand jury that he used a clear substance and a cream provided by a friend who is now accused of distributing BALCO drugs, but that he never thought they were steroids. New York Yankees slugger Jason Giambi testified that he used steroids and also injected human growth hormone.

After the *Chronicle* reported on the testimony, U.S. Surgeon General Richard Carmona told the Associated Press that the problem of steroid use was "less a moral and ethical issue than it is a public health issue. If youngsters are seeing their role models practicing this kind of behavior and it seems acceptable, then we need to do something about that because it is a health risk."

Psychological Impact

In the early morning of October 1, 2002, sitting in a car just around the block from his parents' home, Rob Garibaldi finally put an end to what had been a tumultuous period plagued by depression, rage, and delusional behavior, using a .357 Magnum he had stolen the day before.

For a year and a half, the Garibaldis grieved privately, trying to make sense of their son's dramatic downward spiral. Then, in early March of this year, they saw the parents of a Texas high school baseball player named Taylor Hooton describing on national television how their son had hanged himself as a result of steroid use. The Garibaldis found it hauntingly familiar, and soon began to tell Rob's story to high school students, national television audiences, and state legislators who had taken up the cause in the wake of the BALCO scandal.

As the Garibaldis now realize, Rob's steroid use dated all the way back to the summer of 1997, when he was eighteen years old and had just been honored as a prep All-American at Casa Grande High School. That places him in a population of steroid users for whom parents, lawmakers, coaches, and experts are most concerned: teenagers.

An annual study by the University of Michigan indicates that steroid use among all students in eighth through twelfth grades rose yearly throughout the 1990s, an indication that many kids recognized the drugs could benefit not only athletes but boys and girls simply seeking the body beautiful.

The most recent Michigan study, from last year, showed a decline in some areas but still reported that 3.5 percent of twelfth-graders acknowledged they had used steroids at some point and 2.1 percent admitted to using in the past year. Other studies have indicated use among teens anywhere from 3 to 11 percent.

Steroids enable athletes to work out harder and build up muscle. But in addition to potential physical dangers such as liver damage and heart disease, experts say, steroid use can create psychological trauma.

Dr. Harrison Pope, the director of the biological psychiatry laboratory at McLean Hospital/Harvard Medical School, said in a telephone interview that in addition to the aggressive behavior often linked with steroid use, the withdrawal from using can lead to depression and, in extreme cases, suicide.

Garibaldi's concerns about his body and the use of steroids weren't the only issues he struggled with. Since age twenty-two, he had been taking antidepressants that have since been said to increase suicidal tendencies in children. He also had a learning disability that led him to take Provigil, a drug prescribed to help cope with the effects of attention deficit hyperactivity disorder. And there were periods of marijuana use and drinking that coincided with his taking some of the drugs, friends and family members say.

He also told his psychiatrist he was adjusting his prescribed medications on his own so as not to decrease the effects of the steroids.

Still, Garibaldi's psychiatrist, Dr. Brent Cox, said a series of rage incidents and other emotional issues coincided precisely with three separate, ten-week periods of steroid use that Garibaldi described during sessions. Similarly, excessive bouts of depression fell in line with periods when he had stopped using the drugs, Cox said.

Ray and Denise Garibaldi said their own extensive research convinced them steroids were the ultimate culprit in Rob's emotional demise.

Garibaldi went from being a young man universally described as outgoing and well adjusted to an entirely foreign figure to his friends and family.

"The behavior seemed to come back pretty reliably when he was using anabolic steroids and disappear when he stopped," said Cox, the psychiatrist, who spoke with the family's permission. "There was really a dramatic transformation in this guy. There was a really edgy, irritable quality when he was using steroids, like he was just ready to jump across the room and throttle you."

The Artificial Path

Rob Garibaldi's biggest problem was that he was too little. So he ultimately set out to bulk up in a way that all the weight lifting and nutritional supplementation couldn't help.

"This wasn't an adolescent kid who was looking for beach muscle or whatnot," said P. J. Poiani, who was one of Garibaldi's closest high school friends and who said he was with him when he took steroids for the first time. "This was a kid who every hope and dream he had was surrounded by baseball. And you do whatever it takes."

He was never going to be big enough — not like his father, a bear of a man who said he was a pretty good baseball player before an injury shortened his playing days, or his older brother Ray Jr., now six-foot-two and 200 pounds. From the time he was a five-foot-nine, 125-pound sophomore playing on Casa Grande's varsity squad, Rob had been trying to pump up.

It was then that Garibaldi began to lift weights and receive nutritional supplements, first from Rob Bruno, a salesman at a supplement company who coached Garibaldi on a traveling all-star team, and later from Casa Grande assistant coach Paul Maytorena.

When he left high school in 1997, after three years of lifting weights and ingesting an array of weight- and muscle-gaining supplements that included some legal but controversial substances, Rob was five-foot-eleven, 150 pounds — bigger, but not nearly big enough, he felt.

The supplements he took, his father said, included creatine and androstenedione, known as Andro, the steroid precursor Mark McGwire admitted to using when he hit seventy home runs in 1998. Creatine had become a popular supplement among athletes and gym rats, although there were warnings about its potential dangers, including possible cancer risks.

"What I say now and what I hope I said then is that you need to get stronger, not bigger," said Maytorena, who said he has a degree in exercise science from Sonoma State. Maytorena said he monitored Garibaldi's use of the supplements and provided his parents with information about the substances.

Bruno, who said he was a power-lifter for years, said he gave Garibaldi only a basic weight-gaining supplement distributed by his company and not creatine, but Ray Garibaldi said his son did receive creatine from the coach.

"Obviously, we're going to tell a kid what they need to do in regard to getting bigger and stronger," said Bruno. He said he told Garibaldi what he told many other youngsters, to use supplements as a complement to a solid weight-training program because, "If you're going to be a great athlete, you need to be strong."

Garibaldi later would tell his parents that taking steroids was essentially an extension of taking these supplements.

In the summer after Garibaldi's high school graduation, in preparation for beginning school and a baseball career at the College of San Mateo, Garibaldi decided he needed some artificial assistance with his weight-training program.

"He called me up one day and said he wanted to get bigger, wanted to get stronger," said Brian Seibel, one of Garibaldi's closest friends. "He thought steroids were the way to do it."

Garibaldi had heard Mexico was an easy place to buy steroids — which are illegal to buy or use without a doctor's prescription — so he and Seibel told their respective parents they were going camping, hopped in Garibaldi's car, and headed south. They stopped in San Diego, slept in the car overnight, then drove into Tijuana the next morning.

Seibel thinks Garibaldi knew going in that he wanted to get Sustanon, a substance the Web site steroid.com describes as a "very popular steroid" that is a "mixture of four different testosterones which, based on the well-timed composition, have a synergistic effect." The teenagers walked into the first pharmacy they came upon, and Garibaldi was directed to a doctor's office around the corner. There, he gave the doctor some cash, Seibel said, then returned with a prescription.

Garibaldi hid the steroids behind a car stereo speaker as he and Seibel drove back across the border.

"We were in Mexico I would say probably even less than an hour," recalled Seibel, who said he only went along for the trip and never had any interest in using steroids.

The whole transaction cost about $250 to $300.

Athletes typically take steroids for a period of weeks, called a cycle; upon returning home, Garibaldi began his first cycle. The stuff from Mexico, Poiani said, had everything he needed — syringes, needles, and steroids — and so, with Poiani watching, Garibaldi injected himself in the buttocks for the first of what would be many times.

"I mean, Rob always talked about how he was scared of needles in terms of the doctor, so it was kind of comical in some ways," Poiani said. "He was kind of laughing about just how scared he was, but he just did it. And then it got easier."

Garibaldi completed an eight-week cycle that summer, according to Poiani, and the results showed. Poiani thought his pal gained eight to ten pounds.

Garibaldi eventually abandoned his plan to attend and play ball at San Mateo. Instead, he lived at home most of that first year out of high school and helped his old high school coach, Bob Leslie, who had mouth cancer and would die that June.

At that same time, Poiani said, Garibaldi was working out a lot — and taking another cycle of Sustanon.

"He took a *long* cycle," Poiani said. "Because I remember at the time being a friend thinking, 'What the hell are you doing?' I think people usually take six- to ten-week cycles. I think he was into something like fourteen weeks or something crazy."

Cycles are designed to optimize the effectiveness of the drugs and minimize side effects, with users being "on" for a number of weeks and then "off" for a similar period of time.

"He blew up at that point, I mean for his standards," Poiani said.

One year later, after enrolling at Santa Rosa Junior College in the fall of 1998, the now-five-foot-eleven, 165-pound Garibaldi put together one of the most prolific seasons in school history. He hit .459 with fourteen home runs and seventy-seven runs batted in, earning him state Community College Player of the Year honors.

The performance was good enough to earn him a scholarship to USC, which had one of the nation's top Division I baseball programs. It was also good enough to get Garibaldi selected by the New York Yankees during the June 1999 major league draft, though not until the forty-first round.

"They have their body types and all that," Garibaldi told the *Press Democrat* of Santa Rosa. "I'm not quite big enough."

Garibaldi chose the scholarship to USC, the top college choice of his parents, who were particularly comforted by the school's strong program to help kids with learning disabilities. During a recruiting visit to USC in October, while Ray and Denise met with an academic counselor, Rob took a tour of the training facilities.

He emerged loaded down with containers of supplements, including creatine.

"They said I have to put on twenty pounds," Rob, who had just turned twenty-two, told his parents.

Garibaldi started at USC in January 2000, and he immediately had an impact. He hit .329 with eight home runs and forty-four runs batted in to help the Trojans reach the College World Series. *Baseball America* placed him among the top one hundred college players going into the 2001 season.

"When they went to the World Series, he said, 'All of my dreams have come true,'" his mother recalled. "Being on that field meant everything to him. It was right after that that it all went askew."

Losing Control at USC

First came news that Garibaldi was having academic troubles.

So rather than spend the summer playing ball in the Cape Cod League, as planned, he returned home and took classes to ensure he would be eligible the next season. He became depressed, mostly because of the academic struggles, girlfriend troubles, and the transition from the high of the College World Series to the low of not even being able to play ball at all. His mom suggested he see Cox, a psychiatrist colleague of hers.

Cox ultimately prescribed the antidepressant Effexor, and the drug seemed to work well. Not long before returning to USC, Garibaldi told Cox his time back home represented "the best summer I ever had," according to the psychiatrist's records. Cox knew nothing about his steroid use.

In September, Garibaldi began a ten-week cycle of Deca Durabolin, which steroid.com describes as "the most widespread and most commonly used injectable steroid." His parents visited USC one month later, and Denise said Rob pulled her aside at one point to show her how he had taken a baseball bat to his dresser.

Garibaldi told his mom he was in trouble: he had failed a midterm, was sleeping excessively, and wasn't really sure the antidepressants were helping at all.

Pope, the Harvard psychiatrist with expertise in steroid use, said various studies have supported the notion of "'roid rage" — with users exhibiting irritability, aggressiveness, and sometimes violence, along with a disregard for the consequences.

Pope also cited problems associated with steroid withdrawal, particularly when a person abruptly stops using rather than cycles off the drugs by lowering the dosage in the final weeks. Among the symptoms are depression, disinterest, excessive sleeping, loss of appetite, and, in extreme cases, suicidal behavior.

A week after Garibaldi showed his mom the battered dresser, the Garibaldis received a call from USC's head baseball coach, Mike Gillespie. Rob had slept through practice.

None of this made sense to Ray and Denise. Their once confident, outgoing, successful, and responsible kid was now falling apart. Garibaldi later told friends and family that he was getting teased a lot at USC both about his size and his learning disability. He told his family and friends that Gillespie called him stupid.

Garibaldi made his first admission to Cox about his use of steroids during a phone session the following May, when he said he was in the midst of a ten-week cycle of Deca.

Garibaldi also told Cox he had reduced his dosage of Effexor and intended to stop taking the drug altogether because he wanted to take steroids free of any interactions with other "mind-altering agents" that he was being prescribed, according to Cox's records.

Cox said he advised Garibaldi to stop using steroids, but Garibaldi said that he wanted to gain ten to fifteen pounds. He said he was getting the Deca from a source who was providing the same drug to several Oakland A's players. The A's declined comment.

"The irony is, he is telling me all this with the mind-set of a warrior," Cox said. "He was like a warrior going into battle, and he had to go through this sacrifice in order to sculpt his body into the perfect specimen."

Apparently nobody but Cox — who as Garibaldi's psychiatrist couldn't tell anyone — knew about the steroid use.

Things continued to deteriorate in the spring of 2001. There were repeated clashes with Gillespie, and Rob's behavior became increasingly erratic. His parents say they later were told by one of Rob's roommates that the other players who were living with him had begun locking their doors out of fear.

Finally, just weeks before USC was set to make another College World Series appearance in June 2001, Gillespie kicked Garibaldi off the team and took away his scholarship.

Garibaldi's allegations about his life at USC and treatment by his coach and teammates are not news to officials there.

"The best response from us would be that all these allegations that we've heard before, we've maintained are not true, and we

have even maintained that we are prepared to file a defamation suit," said a USC spokesman.

The Final Act

Maytorena, Garibaldi's coach and friend since his Casa Grande days, said the young man told him about his steroid use sometime after returning from USC. Maytorena, now head baseball coach at Casa Grande, said he believed Rob was using both Deca and Sustanon at the same time, and he urged him to quit the drugs.

In the fall of 2001, Maytorena helped Garibaldi get lined up with his alma mater, Sonoma State, where he had played for coach John Goelz. Garibaldi seemed to start off relatively well, but his mental well-being quickly deteriorated — to the point that Goelz was having to write practice times on Garibaldi's wrist to make sure the outfielder wasn't late. Denise Garibaldi said she had to become her son's ultra-guardian.

"For the whole semester, I became his superego," she said. "I told him where he had to be at what time. I would write everything down for him. I put Post-Its in his car. I would talk to the teachers myself about what the assignments were."

How much or how often Garibaldi used steroids at Sonoma State is unclear. He would later tell his parents he took just one cycle during this time, beginning in the late spring of 2002. Maytorena said he believed Garibaldi did at least two cycles during his time at Sonoma State.

"He would back up cycles," Maytorena said. "You know, it got to the point where he would go back to back.... The way you gotta use that, you gotta cycle on and off, but he would do it and think that more was better. It got to the point where he thought, 'If I do another cycle, I can gain a little bit more and get a little stronger.'"

Garibaldi also apparently wasn't precise in his use, later telling his mother that he took "about this much" each time he injected, never mentioning an exact dosage.

The last few months of Garibaldi's life were tortured. There were admissions of steroid use, limited as they were. He told his mom first, on a Mother's Day camping trip, and pleaded with her not to tell his father.

She agreed, a decision that later would require her to do considerable repair work on her marriage. Denise said she decided to keep the information from her husband for several reasons: she was fearful how he would react; she believed Rob when he told her this would be his first and only time using and that he was doing it to prepare for the major league draft; she could talk to him freely and openly about the potential dangers of using the drugs; and he told her he would stop if she said his behavior became "too weird."

The major league draft was in June, and Rob saw it as his last chance.

Rob's brother Ray Jr. recalled Rob holed up in his room upstairs on draft day, while Denise remained downstairs panicked about what Rob would do if he wasn't picked.

"He comes out just with this blank look on his face and says, 'I didn't make it,'" Ray Jr. said. "He was totally depressed."

The secret between Rob and Denise ended about a month later when Goelz, the Sonoma State coach, called the Garibaldis to say he had heard Rob was using steroids. Now Ray Garibaldi knew, and he confronted Rob, asking what drugs he was on. Rob erupted and tried to choke his father.

There were further violent outbursts, and Rob even became delusional, prompting Denise to remind him of his promise to stop using steroids if he got too weird. By then, Rob was too far gone. He thought actress Cameron Diaz was going to come watch him play ball and then go on a date with him. He thought he was Jesus Christ. He talked to the television and thought it talked to him.

There were attempts to save Rob — such as a family intervention where he insisted, "I'm not a drug addict, I'm a ballplayer." The Garibaldis got him to try a rehab center. But shortly before his twenty-eight-day stint was scheduled to end, he was asked to leave after assaulting an employee.

Finally, four months after he confided to his mother, Rob stole a gun from a shooting range. About 3:30 the following morning, October 1, 2002, he started to leave the house and was stopped by his father. Rob said he was just going to get some food at Taco Bell and then take a drive — something he often did.

Three hours later, the Petaluma police were at the door, breaking the news that Rob had shot himself. He lived another eighteen hours before dying at a Santa Rosa hospital.

The Garibaldis had been keeping tabs on the mileage of Rob's

car — they took away his use of the car for a time because of his unpredictable behavior — so they know he drove some two hundred miles that morning before returning to Petaluma and parking around the corner from the house.

Ray Jr. likes to believe his baby brother toured all his old baseball haunts — from Little League fields in Foster City to the ballpark at Santa Rosa Junior College where he was better than anyone had ever been.

It was standing-room-only at the eight-hundred-seat church where Rob's funeral was held, befitting the kind of tribute paid to someone who made friends easily and who had once known how to light up a room.

Most of those people wouldn't have recognized the Rob who found himself in the car that October morning, with a gun in his left hand and all hope lost.

For Ray Garibaldi, the bitterness remains palpable, with much of his anger reserved for major league baseball and what he sees as public indifference to steroid use.

"I think it's sickening," the father said. "I think the public looks at baseball players as back in the gladiator days. They are just to entertain and if they want to screw themselves up, so what. But the problem is, no matter what anybody says, they are setting the bar for younger kids. And that bar is getting itself all the way down now to the junior high level."

He and Denise see hope, though, and this is what drives them to tell Rob's story.

The Garibaldis have availed themselves not only to legislators trying to address the steroid and supplement problem, but have begun speaking to high school classes about Rob's life. Heather Campbell teaches a sports medicine class at Casa Grande, and she brought in Ray and Denise last May to provide a human touch to her five-week segment on steroids and nutrition.

At one point, the Garibaldis asked the thirty-plus kids how many of them knew of high school students that have tried or are using steroids. More than twenty raised their hands. These are the people Ray and Denise Garibaldi desperately want to hear Rob's story.

"We are all better for having him in our lives," Denise said. "I think what happened was so tragic, so I want people to know that out of ignorance and trust, all this can happen."

PAM BELLUCK

How to Catch Fish in Vermont

FROM THE NEW YORK TIMES

St. albans bay, vermont — The hunter's prey darted into the shadows, just out of reach of Henry Demar's gun.

"Come on, stand up and be counted," Mr. Demar whispered excitedly. "There was a ripple that came out of the weeds. There's something out there."

Dressed in camouflage, gripping his .357 Magnum, Mr. Demar was primed to shoot. But this time, no such luck. With a flick of its tail, his quarry — a slick silvery fish — was gone.

Fish shooting is a sport in Vermont, and every spring, hunters break out their artillery — high-caliber pistols, shotguns, even AK-47s — and head to the marshes to exercise their right to bear arms against fish.

It is a controversial pastime, and Vermont's fish and wildlife regulators have repeatedly tried to ban it. They call it unsportsmanlike and dangerous, warning that a bullet striking water can ricochet across the water like a skipping stone.

But fish shooting has survived, a cherished tradition for some Vermont families and a novelty to some teenagers and twenty-somethings. Fixated fish hunters climb into trees overhanging the water (some even build "fish blinds" to sit in), sail in small skiffs, or perch on the banks of marshes that lace Lake Champlain, on Vermont's northwest border.

"They call us crazy, I guess, to go sit in a tree and wait for fish to come out," said Dean Paquette, sixty-six, as he struggled to describe the fish-shooting rush. "It's something that once you've done it . . ."

Mr. Paquette, a retired locomotive engineer, has passed fish shooting on to his children and grandchildren, including his daughter, Nicki, a nurse.

"You have to be a good shot," said Ms. Paquette, thirty-one, who started shooting at age six. "It's a challenge. I think that's why people do it."

Her eighty-seven-year-old great-uncle, Earl Picard, is so enthusiastic that, against the better judgment of his relatives, he frequently drives seventy-five miles from his home in Newport to Lake Champlain. Mr. Picard still climbs trees, although "most of the trees that I used to climb in are gone," he said. "You can sit up there in the sun and the birds will come and perch on your hat and look you in the eye."

There is art, or at least science, to shooting fish, aficionados say, and it has nothing to do with a barrel. Most fish hunters do not want to shoot the actual fish, because then "you can't really eat them," Ms. Paquette said. "They just kind of shatter."

Instead, said Mr. Demar, "you try to shoot just in front of the fish's nose or head." The bullet torpedoes to the bottom and creates "enough concussion that it breaks the fish's air bladder and it floats to the surface."

Often the target is a female fish come to spawn in shallow water, accompanied by several male acolytes who might also be killed, or stunned, by the concussion.

"If you shoot a high-powered rifle, you can get a big mare and six or seven little bucks," Mr. Paquette said.

Permitted from March 25 to May 25, only on Lake Champlain, fish shooting has probably existed for a century. It also used to be legal in New York, which borders the huge apostrophe-shaped lake.

Virginia used to have several fish-shooting areas, said Alan Weaver, a fish biologist with the Virginia Department of Game and Inland Fisheries. Now, Mr. Weaver said, the only place is the Clinch River in remote Scott County, where, six weeks a year, people can shoot bottom-feeders like "quill-back suckers and red-horse suckers." Virginia is the only other state where fish shooting is still legal, Vermont officials said.

In 1969, fish and wildlife officials in New York and Vermont banned fish shooting. But Vermonters were loath to sever the primal link between fish and firearm, so in 1970, the Legislature not only reinstated the sport, it also added fish like carp and shad to the target list, bringing the number to ten.

Since then, there have been several efforts to halt fish shooting. But they have been stopped by noisy objections from a small but dedicated bunch.

Advocates crossed the state in a near-blizzard to one public hearing in the late 1980s, recalled John Hall, a spokesman for Vermont's Department of Fish and Wildlife. In 1994, fish-shooters "outnumbered the people who spoke against it by about four to one," said Brian Chipman, a state fisheries biologist.

State officials say shooters' claims that theirs is a fading tradition that will die out on its own have not proved true.

"We even think that some of the publicizing of this issue through efforts to pass laws against it has brought it more into the forefront," Mr. Chipman said.

The issue is apparently touchy enough that Howard Dean, governor from 1991 to 2003, "has no interest in going on the record on that subject," said Walker Waugh, a spokesman.

Hunters like Mr. Demar, forty-five, joined recently by his half brother, Calvin Rushford, fifty-six, and Calvin's nine-year-old grandson, Cody, say they make sure that their bullets hit the water no more than ten feet from where they stand. That way, said Mr. Rushford, who like Mr. Demar is a disabled former construction worker, "you'll have no problem because the bullet won't ricochet."

Indeed, state officials say they know of no gunshot injuries from the sport. Bob Sampson, who allows occasional fish shooting on his marsh, remembers only one.

"I think he got shot in the stomach area," Mr. Sampson said of a shooting that he believes took place about forty years ago.

Most hunters say the worst they have seen is people falling out of trees into frigid water. Mr. Demar said his brother Peter once "shot, lost control, and did a nose dive." "He was purple when he come up out of the water," Mr. Demar said.

But Gordon Marcelle, a Vermont game warden who shot fish as a teenager, said every hunter safety course taught that shooting at water was "one of the cardinal sins."

State officials also say that fish shooting disturbs nesting birds and that killing spawning females could endanger the northern pike population (although so far there is no evidence it has).

Worst of all, state officials say, many shooters do not retrieve all the fish they kill. They leave behind fish they cannot find or do not want to wade after and fish that exceed the state's five-pike-a-day limit or fall under the twenty-inch minimum length for northern pike. Mr. Marcelle recently found eighteen dead fish left to rot.

Two dead fish recently greeted Mr. Demar and his companions at the marsh, a species he called mudfish. There were some frolicking muskrats, chickadees in the ash and willow trees, plus shell casings from an eight-millimeter Mauser. ("Oh, that's made for blowing them out of the water," Mr. Rushford said.)

There were not, however, enough live fish to shoot. So Mr. Demar tested his gun on a log in the water, and spray shot up.

"I got a little water on my sunglasses," he said sheepishly. "That's the thing about pickerel shooting. Afterward, you have to turn away, or you get sprayed in the face."

THOMAS McGUANE

Seeing Snook

FROM SPORTS ILLUSTRATED

I STARTED FISHING around Boca Grande as a boy. My father brought me here when I was eleven years old to fish for tarpon: I caught my first one in Boca Grande Pass. For years my father and brother fished here with a redheaded guide who died from the complications of skin cancer. My father and his friends, all clients of the redheaded guide, came to pay their last respects. The old guide was laid out in the living room of his small clapboard house, surrounded by family and friends. In the middle of it all, supported by her sisters, was his grief-stricken widow. When my father and his friends walked in, she looked up blearily, adjusted her focus, and cried, "There's the sonsabitches that killed my husband!" My father and his pals, in coats and Countess Mara ties, clutching Dobbs hats, made humble obeisance until escape was possible. "I thought those crackers would jump us," my father commented in a grave voice as his group headed for the Pink Elephant bar for an eye-opener.

You reach a point at which you have to view your life through the things you've spent so much time doing. The alternative is a perilous feeling of waste. Cancer and gulag survivors alike treasure their experiences for reasons best known to them. The rest of us have logged more platitudinous days, and it takes an effort to assign their place and value. I've spent as much of my life fishing as decency allowed, and sometimes I don't let even that get in my way. Especially when it comes to snook.

Snook remind me of brown trout — something in their covert

nature, their eccentric choices in safe harbors, their sensitivity that seems designed to humiliate the angler when less dramatic options would get the job done. In short, snook are sleazy.

They are also hard to see, hard to hook, hard to land, and, because they are so good to eat, hard to release. But release them we do. Cold weather reduces them to torpor, colder weather kills them. When they're at the threshold of death, a translucent window appears in the top of their heads. Sometimes, when a snook follows your fly, then takes, you notice a quick roll up on its side, as though the fish were bringing the target in for close vision. The snook refusal has a quality of its own: a long cross-eyed follow, then a turn off. Snook just leave when suspicious, or change their swimming rhythm. They can also crash bait as well as jacks or bonito. There is something touching about snook, their funny-faced striving, their sneakiness, their lazy travel turning into serious speed. Their heedless jumps fill us with aesthetic merriment.

The truth is, I have always had trouble catching them and felt that this was something I was going to have to work harder at. I decided to fish with a guide at least once a week, and I called on Austin Lowder, who guides here in the winter and in Montana, where he's from, in the summer. I'd heard he was effective but very demanding, and I thought I could stand a little embarrassment, as long as I learned something. I soon confirmed that Austin is not the guide for the angler who is comfortable with his bad habits or who has lost the ability to learn. As we approached a group of redfish our first day together — brick-colored tails turning slowly, a pink, wavering shape below the surface, grubbing out baby blue crabs — I adjusted my stance to face them and cast. The tails disappeared, and I had no targets. "Don't move your feet," Austin grunted, and we looked for some new fish.

There was a single fish tailing at the edge of the mangroves. In the branches above him, a dozen wood storks watched my performance. This would take a long cast. As I began, Austin's cell phone rang in his pocket. I made the throw but a loop caught under my shoe. Fish gone. I heard Austin say to the caller, "Just missed a fish. Guy with tennis shoes."

If you fish away from your home waters, guides are an excellent investment, although, after a pleasant day together, they will describe

you to the other guides as a complete idiot. There are two kinds of
clients, the meek and the proud. The former are happy to be in-
sulted and abused, the latter regard guides as indentured servants.
I'm a mixture of the two. I can accept a certain amount of abuse if
I'm learning something; then indignation sets in and I become dis-
agreeable. Austin's belief that a successful day on the water consists
of doing a lot of little things right was a useful regimen for me.
Among his assertions: don't move your feet when approaching fish;
don't talk (they can hear you); don't trail a loop in the water; don't
cast overhead unless you're a long way from the fish; watch all low-
flying birds (they spook fish); and so on, in an ever-lengthening
list.

Austin assumes you're trying to get better, but he's a strict instructor. Your first impression from fishing a few days with him is
that you have suddenly acquired attention deficit disorder.

Reaching into my tackle bag for my binoculars to look at a
hooded warbler that had just appeared in the mangroves, I heard
Austin say, "Put them back. You don't need binoculars." He dinged
away at me for days on things like this, and eventually I conformed,
though a few remarkable things stopped us both: a peregrine
power-diving in perfectly still air creating a searing sound of attack;
an immense stork, a jabiru that had drifted away from its Central
American home — from fifty yards away we could hear it crunching crabs with its colossal beak. In any case, back to work.

A big snook lay like a black arrow in the clear water atop an oyster bar that glowed yellow in the afternoon light. I was rigged for
redfish but cast anyway. The fish rushed the fly, took hard, and ran.
I was forced to play him gently to keep from breaking him. After a
heedless jump, he made a run for the mangroves. I had to pull
hard to stop him, and I got away with it. I landed the fish and kept
him alongside long enough to admire the peculiar beauty of a
grown snook — the upward cast of the eyes, the beautiful under-
shot mouth with its sandpaper interior, the boxlike shape of the
body between its ventral fins, the slight greenish cast overall and
the amber fins.

Austin wanted a picture of this fish. "Hold him like a man!" he
commanded.

The next day Austin and I fished together turned out to be when a
stormy northwester was rolling down the Gulf Coast. I assumed

we'd have to cancel, but Austin laughed at the suggestion. We tossed gear into the skiff while the north wind tore through the usually placid bayou, rattling the palms around us. As we got into our foul weather gear, I found it hard to be optimistic. Austin called to Bill, the collector of ramp fees, "I know it's no fishing day! I just want to get paid!"

I hoped this was merely the grim joke it appeared to be, but I was ambivalent about our prospects, and my pessimism increased as Austin powered his Hells Bay skiff over an angry gray chop. After repeated lashings of forty-mile-per-hour cold saltwater, I moved back to the downwind side of the boat. I tried to look where we were going, but I was soon reduced to cowering in the noise of the two-stroke Yamaha, the hammering separations between the seat and my backside, and the sheets of wind-borne seawater.

We ran into a broad bay that narrowed and finally disappeared against a wall of mangrove swamp. Here there was no wind. Clouds scudded overhead, but we were in a place that was quiet as a church, and how very nice it seemed. Austin anchored the boat, and we got out, entered a winding creek much like a prairie trout stream, with a sandbar on one side and an undercut bank on the other. I lost count of all the snook we caught and released.

It wasn't really a story you could tell without ruining your credibility. Angling often requires eluding your fellow anglers and discovering opportunities others don't want, and here is another lesson I'd learned from Austin: go fishing when only a fool leaves his house.

"You know, Austin, I'm thinking of writing about fishing this winter. I learned a lot. I suppose you'll be in it. Might do some good."

"I don't care. I've already got everything I want."

"Well, then let's use a pseudonym for you."

"If you're going to do it, you might as well use my name."

"I was thinking of Captain Marvel."

"Captain Marvel . . . Hey, I like it!"

In the early years that I fished the shallows, we poled our boats from the bow; poler and angler were at the same level. Now the poler — the guide — is on an elevated platform and generally can see much farther than formerly. This should be an advantage to the team, not an opportunity for the guide to humiliate his angler, but this principle is frequently violated by a physiosocial disorder known by its acronym, PIMP — Platform-Induced Moronic Phase-out, and anyone who mounts a poling platform is in jeopardy of contracting it. I've had it several times. Standing up there with the graphite push pole in hand, with all its feeling of thrust and weaponry, you stare down at male-pattern baldness and sunburn and can't help but cry out, "What're you anyway, blind?"

Big snook, nine o'clock, seventy feet going left!"

I looked all over the brown-and-gray-mottled bottom for a gray-and-mottled snook.

"I can't see him."

"He's right there!"

"I don't know where the f—— he is!"

"He's right in front of you! He's right next to that little island!"

"I don't see any little island!"

Austin's shoulders slumped. The push pole knocked against the platform. "He's gone."

"I just couldn't see him."

"He was right next to that little island."

I was getting hot. "*What* little island?"

"It was just this little floating island."

"Show me the little floating island."

Austin laughed, somewhat guiltily I thought. "Forget it," he said.

"I want to see the little floating island."

Austin ruefully poled the boat backward and pointed to a scrap of floating moss perhaps the size of my hand. I let on that it wasn't much of a landmark. I turned back to scan the water ahead.

"Let me offer this," said Austin from behind me in an abraded tone, "*You didn't see the fish.*"

This left me speechless. But I was prepared to admit that I needed to work on seeing. Whether fishing with Austin or fishing alone, I strained to see better, and at the end of the day my eyes were worn out. Later, Austin, perhaps feeling he'd been a bit hard on me, said, "You need a prescription." I knew he wanted me to get glasses. He told me a kindly story about a citrus grower, a lifelong snook man, who had acquired prescription glasses. "Now, when I say nine o'clock, seventy feet" — a reference to my missed snook — "he says, 'Got 'im.'"

*

Seeing fish is the essence of shallow-water angling. Anglers who see fish exceptionally well can fish successfully in less productive water than anglers who don't. Fishermen love equipment and are always looking for mechanical advantages, but there is nothing to compare with learning to see well; if you see well enough, you can walk out in the mud with no boat and catch fish. I wasn't seeing well enough.

Not long ago, in response to a spell of insomnia, I learned some of the principles of meditation, to empty my mind piece by piece. It was like the old game of jacks — cautiously lifting each jack clear of its neighbor until only the empty background remained. I began to use this small skill to see better. Seeing fish well is usually assumed to be the result of concentration, but concentration bears too much of the deliberate — too much willpower and too little intuition about the way wild creatures use surroundings and how they exploit willpower into lies for the credulous predator.

Instead of longing for sleep, I longed to see better. I began to identify the things that kept me from seeing fish — motionless fish, slow-traveling fish, fish concealed in mangrove roots, fish up light, fish in glare, fish in shadows. I continued to scan ahead as the bottom flowed toward me to the gentle lap of the push pole, and when some thought about an unreturned phone call or some e-mail tried to elbow its way in, the old insomniac let it all out the back door. I learned to sail through thoughts as though they were clouds, and this relieved me of direct combat with intrusion. I sailed through clouds and looked into the water.

Before any *real* progress, however, I had another prod from Austin. We were standing on Tarpon Street in front of my little railroad house, the sun glinting off the tin roof, through the grapefruit tree. Leaning on his trailered skiff, Austin pointed down the street. "Read that sign. I think you need a prescription." It was a Realtor's sign with enticements in small print. I read it aloud. He looked confused. "I still think you need a prescription." He got into his truck and drove off.

My wife said to me one evening after Austin and I had fished ten hours in a twenty-mile-per-hour wind, "This fishing you and Austin do just sounds like *work*." It gave me pause. My bones ached, my eyes were red, my tendinitis was aroused. There were no physical benefits — no aerobics, no stretching. It was actually probably bad for anyone who did it. Hemorrhoids, varicose veins, fallen arches come to mind. After a decade or two your dermatologist pleads with you to give it up. You consume a world of fossil fuel trying to get close to nature. A poet says to you, "I ask the fish permission to give herself to me, for I am hungry. I become the fish. The fish becomes me." The twisted sister within says, "I just want to kick fin."

I also have issues with the sun. It raises water temperatures to the point that snook want to come out of their winter hidey-holes and start busting bait. But snook are perhaps better suited to its effects than I. My wife found on the Internet some discounted bedsheets of "thousand-count cotton." I wasn't sure what that is, but they're right smooth, and we were right proud to have them, but by the morning my bleeding lips had ruined them. I moved from 45 SPF to white gobs of zinc oxide and then to a kind of tube sock for my whole head, surmounted by a broad straw sombrero from a saddle shop in Alpine, Texas. I had become a cross between a fool and a leper, staring at tide tables. When I ran the skiff at anything over half speed, the sombrero folded back and I became a child's nightmare of Deputy Dawg, a macabre heat-seeking cartoon of not easily understood motivation.

Mostly, I fished alone.

One of the last days Austin and I fished this spring, we ran down south in Pine Island Sound to a creek with several shallow bays appended to it; left the boat tied to the push pole, which was staked into the soft bottom; and walked a bay that was almost, at this tide, dry land. We stood there silently for a long time, and nothing happened; nothing *could* happen because there was no water for it to happen *in*. The wind rustled the mangroves; egrets came and went. Off by the boat, a group of pelicans had surrounded some bait and would flap forward without taking off to scoop up a meal; tucking their chins to swallow, they looked polite and bashful. However, nothing was going on at all as we gazed at little more than bare ground. I was using all my mind tricks to keep looking and to avoid potential commentary on my eyesight.

The flat began to *moisten*. Austin stood beside me with his unrelenting thousand-yard stare. *What are we staring at?* I wondered. Austin wasn't saying. The tide had turned, and over time the flat flooded, at first with an inch or two; at about half a foot of depth, the snook, lazy pikelike shapes, began to come. They came steadily, and we both caught them in a string of explosive battles. They came in such volume that it became necessary for us to stand back-to-back to manage the onslaught. We lost count of the fish we released, and Austin actually admitted it was the best day he'd ever had. My arm was lead.

I once had an episode of serious depression, and its onset was marked by a loss of interest in fishing. I believe I gave away tackle. I sold cheap my cherished Bogdan reel, which was presented to me thirty years later at a usurious price.

I marvel at people discussing depression, gnawing the topic of their own malaise like dogs on a beef knuckle. My experience of it was a disinclination to speak at all. I had the feeling of being locked in a very small and unpleasant room with no certainty of exit, and I recall thinking that it was the sickest you could possibly be and that my flesh had been changed to plaster. My business at the time was flight from expectations.

It was spring in Montana, and two old friends quite wisely arrived in my yard with a drift boat to take me to the river. I managed to say that I'd go if I didn't have to talk. As I was manifestly off my rocker, they were quick to agree, perhaps relieved at not having to hear my present thoughts. Once gliding silently down the Yellowstone, oars dipping, lines arcing out from either end of the boat, I began for the first time to picture better days, and it proved a turning point. I thought of incessant-angler pal and novelist Richard Brautigan, who relinquished his fly rod as he spooled up for suicide. Fishing, for many, is an indispensable connection to earth and life, and it matters little that the multitude who practice it are incapable of translating its ambiguities to another idiom.

A lingering, cool blow out of the Northeast dropped water temperatures again, spread foam lines across green whitecapped waters, and shrank the broad pallet of local angling geometry to a gerrymandered world of lees around islands and oyster bars. Each jaunt meant donning oilies and the continuous sting of saltwater on sunburned skin.

Mark Phillips — an Alaskan guide — and I went fishing anyway, taking a good spanking as we ran northeast to hide from the wind among the small mangrove keys scattered along the mainland. Mark told me a defining snook story as we poled out of the wind, staring into the water. He had cast to a huge snook, and the fish had followed his fly intently. Just at the moment he hoped for a strike, his cell phone, which he had set on vibration mode and placed on the gunwale, went off, and the buzz put the fish to flight. He threw down his rod, answered the phone, and endured an unpleasant conversation with a despised ex-girlfriend. Another sleazy snook moment.

We caught a couple of small fish, anchored the boat in eight inches of water, and split up to wade, barefoot for maximum stealth. We had seen so many stingrays that I spent half the time watching the bottom in front of me and the remaining half looking for fish. A cluster of juvenile wood storks were scattered on a sandbar not far in front of me, and when I stopped to watch them, a snook blew up bait in the mangroves behind them. I stole over to look, but there was no sign of the fish, and the storks spooked nothing when they flew out over the place I'd hoped to see him.

Then, farther back in a small bay, another blast. This time I was sure I could find the fish because the fish fed in a very shallow corner of mangrove shoots. I crept over without a ripple and looked into every crevice: no fish. So I waded out of the shallow bay and was looking for new water when I noticed a faint wake leaving the area I had just inspected. This time it headed for an isolated clump of mangrove shoots which stood like a small, flooded island away from shore. Back into the bay on tiptoe and expecting only to be fooled again. Standing in perhaps six inches of water, I peered into the mangrove roots and there, nearly perfectly hidden, was my chameleon green snook.

I could only stand motionless and flick the leader into the maze of shoots. It landed a couple of feet from the fish, and as it sank he turned and struck. After several moments of close-range snook pandemonium, I seized him by the lower jaw and the barbless fly fell out. I kept the fish in the water and ran my finger along his topside, feeling the thickness through the shoulders, the rigid upright fins. I then released him, and he swam off with cross-eyed, lazy insouciance. With the tops of the mangroves and wild palms tossing in the wind, the low-tide mud banks plowed up by wild hogs, this one was special.

*

In the end, I occasionally saw fish before Austin saw them. "Good eyes," he even said once. "I didn't see that one." It had been weeks since he'd last told me I needed a prescription.

And then for the rest of the season, with new spring breezes arising in flowering trees, I fished alone, daily. I was catching more fish than I did formerly and getting a bit complacent about how much I'd improved. There was even time to crawl around and peer at the queer, nameless fauna of the shallows. I followed a scarce banded puffer fish, a piggy-looking football with a tiny propeller of a tail that motored him along at such a slow pace that only his spines, or his benign herbivore face, kept him from being chow for some apex predator.

I looked through my binoculars whenever I felt like it. I listened to the conversation of wild pigs, quit fishing to gather oysters, took naps in the skiff, and made more elaborate lunches in the morning, sometimes at the expense of an early start.

There was no doubt about it: I was getting worse.

Making Contact

FROM CHICAGO MAGAZINE

I HAD BEEN LOOKING for Jim Woods, on and off, for years. Long ago, Woods had done the nearly impossible — going straight from high school graduation at Lane Tech, where he was a baseball sensation, to Wrigley Field and the Chicago Cubs, a distance of two miles by bus, but worlds apart. It was 1957; he was seventeen years old.

Growing up in Chicago, I'd played against Woods several times — he was my lone connection to the major leagues, my one degree of separation from the big time. When the trail of his professional career faded away, I tried several avenues to locate him, but came up empty. How could someone who'd enjoyed such early fame — he played briefly with the Phillies, as well — just drop from sight? In August 1986 I wrote about him in my column in the *New York Times*: "Most of us have had some connection, however distant, with someone who reached a particular height," I wrote. "And we followed that person's career, knowing that there but for just a little more talent, a little more speed, a little more power, a little more courage and/or a little more brains, go I."

I concluded: "I think about Woods sometimes, think of the homer he hit off me [in a Pony League game] that may still be going, think of him as my link to the major leagues, and that he realized that boy's dream that so many of us once shared.

"And I wonder: Where have you gone, Jim Woods?"

The last time I'd seen James Jerome "Woody" Woods, as the listing in *The Baseball Encyclopedia* has it, was on a dusty baseball field on a warm late afternoon at Winnemac Park, at Foster and Damen on the North Side of Chicago. It was early June of 1957, and our high school teams were playing against each other in a Chicago Public League game, he pitching brilliantly for Lane Tech, I playing a nominal but sincere first base for Sullivan.

Some three weeks later, both of us were graduated from high school, and I — also seventeen — went to work, that summer before college, collecting garbage for the Fiftieth Ward office of the Department of Streets and Sanitation. Woods, meanwhile, was headed to another part of the city, as I learned from the newspapers: "Cubs Sign Chi School Phenom," read one headline, in *The Sporting News*. Woods didn't just sign a contract; he was going right to Wrigley Field — number 48, in the dugout alongside Ernie Banks and Bob Rush and Dale Long and Turk Lown. In the same league with Willie Mays and Stan Musial and Hank Aaron.

This jump from a high school sandlot to the big leagues was virtually unheard of for the Cubs and had happened only a few other times in baseball history. But Woods was extraordinary. In 1956, in his junior year, he led Lane to the Illinois state high school championship, pitching and winning the semifinal game, striking out eighteen of twenty-one Belleville batters and giving up just one hit. Less than twenty-four hours later he was pitching and winning a complete game against Freeburg, and whacking a triple for good measure. When he wasn't pitching he played third base, knocking down fences as a slugger.

When I was in the batter's box facing him, Woods didn't look much different from any of the rest of the teenage boys on either side of the diamond. In his green-and-gray uniform, he stood about six feet tall, and he appeared to weigh 165 pounds or so. He was a redhead, with high, almost gaunt cheekbones, and, though the bill of his green cap was pulled low, shading his intense eyes, he gave the impression that he'd be as comfortable in a 7-Up ad as he was on the spike-scarred mound at Winnemac Park. A right-hander, he threw hard, to be sure, but he seemed to be standing unfairly closer than the sixty-foot-six-inch regulation distance from the rubber to home plate.

Yet, as fine a pitcher as he was, he was perhaps an even better hitter, batting .444 in his senior year, with a bunch of home runs. The tales about him circulated from word of mouth to newspaper stories to major league front offices. At sixteen, as a third-year high school student, he walloped a home run at Lane Field that sailed through the crossbars on the adjoining football field. (Jerry Krause, the former Bulls general manager and current special baseball scout for the New York Yankees, was a batting practice catcher for Taft High School then, and he recently recalled seeing that blast. "It must have gone 450 feet," said Krause.) Later that summer, in a Colt League World Series championship game held at Comiskey Park, Woods whacked a 370-foot home run (the newspapers reported) into the left-field bleachers.

I had my own dismal experience pitching against Woods. We were fourteen, playing in the Pony League at Thillens Stadium, that small, well-appointed ballpark on the North Side. I was with the Giants; he was with the Red Sox. I threw my customary quasi-fastball customarily over the heart of the plate, and he smashed a line drive toward the third baseman, who flung up his glove in self-defense. The ball rose over the poor fellow's head and kept rising as the left fielder retreated to the high chain-link fence behind him. The ball sailed higher, over the fence, over the canal that ran behind the fence, over the trees that lined the canal, as I recall. Maybe the ball cracked against the building a block away. I don't remember.

After high school, I casually followed Woods's baseball career. He played two games for the Cubs in 1957, appearing as a pinch runner in each, and never played for them again. The Cubs, as it turned out, had decided to rest their fortunes on another promising third baseman, a kid from Seattle named Ron Santo.

Woods had signed a nonbonus contract with the Cubs for $3,999.99. One more penny and, under the major league rules, he would have been a "bonus baby," required to spend two years with the major league team. Under $4,000, and he could be assigned to the minor leagues and — so the theory went — gain valuable playing experience. (With his signing, the Cubs had quietly informed Woods that they'd give him an immediate but brief taste of the big leagues, which, the team's management reasoned, might help him better understand what it would require to make it with the Cubs. They also thought a little media attention on the signing and elevation of a local prep star couldn't hurt from a publicity standpoint.)

After the 1957 season, the Cubs assigned Woods to the minors, where he did reasonably well in places like Burlington, Iowa; Lancaster, Pennsylvania; and Fort Worth, moving up the professional ladder. Then the Cubs traded him to the Phillies, and he played thirty-four games for Philadelphia in 1960 and '61. He hit two home runs in the span of five days in May of 1961. His future obviously looked bright. He was twenty-one years old. But his batting average had suffered in the early season — it was just a little over .200 — and the Phillies sent him back to the minors. (Oddly enough, it was right after he had gone two for four against Milwaukee on May 24 with a single and a home run.) Then James Jerome Woods seemed to fade away. I learned that at age twenty-four, in 1964, he was out of baseball.

Over the years, I thought about the spectacular skill it must take to make the major leagues — and stay there. I wondered how Woods felt about his career: Did he despair that he didn't fulfill his promise? Could this be another of those melancholy tales of the golden boy getting too much too soon?

While I'd never actually talked to him when we competed against each other, he seemed like an easygoing guy, never preening. I knew that his home life hadn't been perfect. In high school, he had lived for a time with his mother and stepfather above Emil's Tavern on the 3400 block of Lincoln Avenue, not far from Wrigley Field. His mother worked as a waitress, and his biological father, Jim Sr., with whom he had only a distant relationship, tended bar in a tavern across the street from the ballpark. I learned later that his stepfather, said to be a difficult man, had been knifed to death in a bar fight.

Over the years, I would occasionally ask about Woods from people who knew him. No one seemed to have an answer. Even after my column on Woods appeared in the *Times*, I heard nothing of his whereabouts. Once, I asked Yosh Kawano, the Cubs' longtime clubhouse man, if he remembered Jim Woods. As everyone else had said, he replied, "Oh, a real nice guy." Then he added, "You know, I saw him a few years ago."

"You did?"

"He was handling luggage at a ticket counter at an airport in Miami," Kawano said.

But the Miami phone books had no listing.

Then, in February of this year, eighteen years after the column, I got a call from a former Lane Tech teammate of Woods's, Bob "Shotgun" Becker, with whom I had been in casual touch. "I found Jim," said Becker. "I told him you'd like to talk with him, and he said, 'Sure, no problem.'"

So I called Jim Woods, and we made arrangements to meet in Turlock, a small California town south of Modesto. His son lived there, and Woods had just bought a three-bedroom house in nearby Keyes. He was retired from the airlines, having been a ticket agent for National, Pan American, and American, and now he drew a livable pension. He'd also been working weekends at a Wal-Mart selling sporting goods, for medical benefits. "When I was asked about my background at Wal-Mart, and told people I played a little baseball, they got all excited," he said. "It was funny. The assistant manager came over, the stock boys came over — everyone came around."

I also mentioned to Woods (I had pointed it out in my column) that I was sure I'd gotten a hit off him in our junior year, when Sullivan played Lane, and he beat us, 8–0, striking out most of our batters. As years went on, I had begun to wonder if I'd only dreamed that little spot of glory. When I remarked on the purported hit to my cousin and former Sullivan teammate, Ian Levin, now a federal judge in Chicago, he told me that he'd collected a hit off Woods in that game too. That virtually confirmed that I'd been dreaming — apparently, everyone who played against him in those days later imagined they'd gotten a hit.

About two weeks later, I flew to California, and Woods, driving a dark-blue Saturn, picked me up in Turlock in front of my hotel. He was wearing, with intended humor, a retro 1957 Cubs cap, with white stripes against the blue background and the big red "C," the style of cap he'd worn in his brief stint with the Cubs. "Good to see you," he said, pleasantly, though I was sure he didn't remember me. He introduced me to his wife, Stella, and we drove to their son's home, where they were staying, since their new house wouldn't be ready for a few weeks.

I looked for the young man I remembered, but didn't quite see him. Woods, of course, had aged, just like the rest of us. He now wore glasses, sported a mustache that was mostly gray, and had put on some twenty pounds since his professional playing days. When he removed his cap, his hair was still red, though a darker shade than in his boyhood. Medication had pretty much controlled his arthritis. And the hip replacement he'd had a few years earlier aided his gait.

Woods was surprised to learn that he had "disappeared." "I just got involved in my life in Florida, and then the same when I moved to California," he said. "I should have kept in touch more with people. But, well, I had a family, and then my son, Jimmy, was a ballplayer, and we followed him wherever he played. He wound up a good left fielder for California State University at Stanislaus, here. I thought he should have been a third baseman, but I didn't want to interfere with the coach. I let it go."

Woods and Stella have been married for twenty-eight years. "She's my third or fourth wife, depending how you look at it," he said, with an easy laugh. He explained that he had married his first wife a second time, in between divorces.

We talked about his baseball career. "I thought that was a huge amount of money the Cubs signed me for — almost $4,000 — like all the money in the world," he said, sitting on a padded chair in the living room, a thoughtful look on his face. "I mean, until then I was getting a dollar a day lunch money from my mother. I went out and bought a '57 Ford Fairlane convertible, and a down payment on a home for my mother.

"I had signed the contract on my own, without anyone advising me, or giving me direction. There were no negotiations with the Cubs. I didn't know about such things. And I didn't consider going to college — maybe that would have been best. But everyone I know says that if they'd been offered to play in the major leagues at seventeen, they would have taken it too.

"It had been my dream to play big league ball, sure," he continued. "And I had a chance to sign with almost every team in the big leagues, but chose the Cubs because I'd always been a Cub fan. Used to go to their games and sit in the bleachers. I'd keep score listening to Cubs games on the radio.

"When I first joined the Cubs, I was amazed, when I walked into the big league clubhouse. You never had to do anything for yourself. People did everything for you. And I saw the center fielder, Jim Bolger, smoking in the clubhouse. I thought athletes didn't smoke. Unbelievable. And in the dugout, that was amazing too.

Bob Scheffing was the manager and he swore at the umpires. I always thought you were supposed to be polite to the umpires."

He remembered during batting practice standing in awe at the power and bat speed of Musial and Aaron and Banks. "Chris," Woods remembered telling his friend Jim Christopher, when they were seventeen, "it's like a magic show."

As for his new teammate Ernie Banks, Woods recalled: "A great guy. He'd try to build my confidence by telling me that I would get a good shot one day. He'd holler on the bench to Scheffing, 'C'mon, put the kid in.'

"In fact, the one time I played in Wrigley Field, with the Phillies, I got as big a thrill as anything out of hearing the old public address announcer, Pat Peiper, say, 'Now batting for Philadelphia, number 30, Jim Woods.' I'd been to a lot of games there with my friends, and now he was announcing me. And all my friends were there."

Woods didn't get a hit in his lone appearance there, but he did lay down a successful sacrifice bunt that Santo fielded and threw for an error that allowed in the run that won the game for Philadelphia. "So I contributed," Woods said with a smile. And Woods recalled playing third in a game in which Willie Mays hit two triples. "I was taught when running the bases to never look where the ball went, but to listen to your coaches for direction. Well, Willie watched the ball all the way. When you're great, you can break the rules."

Woods sat on the bench for much of the month of September, in 1960, after he'd been called up from Indianapolis, the Phillies' Triple A club. Then Gene Mauch, the manager, summoned him before a game against the Dodgers. "You should do well against the pitcher; he's a left-hander," Mauch told Woods, who batted right. The pitcher was Sandy Koufax. Woods admitted to being nervous. "I was so anxious to do well." He struck out twice, before giving way to a pinch hitter. "I had never seen a ball move the way Koufax's ball moved."

He felt he was learning, however, and when he faced Koufax a second time, the following season, he hit the ball hard. "It was in the Los Angeles Coliseum, and I pinch-hit and I crushed one — a real shot — that hit the top of the high screen in left-center, a double," he said. "If the screen hadn't been so high it would've been out of there. I was looking for a fastball, and I got it."

Still, as Billy Williams, who played in Burlington with Woods, said: "You have to hit consistently, and, at third base, you have to hit with power too. I guess Jim didn't do it. But I loved playing with him. I especially remember that he could get down and dirty at third. He'd get everything — diving, sprawling, didn't matter. Had a great arm too. Surprised he didn't go further."

So was Woods. "When I was sent down by the Phillies," he said, "I thought I didn't earn that — I had started to hit, but I guess they had other thoughts."

Gene Mauch, now seventy-eight and living in Rancho Mirage, California, recalled Woods and the reason he didn't stay with the Phillies: "Jim was a young guy with potential, and I thought he needed more instruction. The place for instruction was in the minor leagues."

Wherever he played, Woods seemed to run into bad luck at his position. "There was Santo with the Cubs; there was Richie Allen, who later went to first base, with the Phillies," Woods recalled. "And then I was purchased by the Reds and went to Macon in the Class AA Southern League, and there was a young Cuban, Tony Perez, at third — a future Hall-of-Famer.

"My mother and sister had moved to Miami, and they'd come up to see me play in Macon. But I was spending most of my time on the bench. I was disgusted. Also, by then, I had got married. I was only making about $6,000 a year — $1,500 less than the major league minimum with the Phillies — and decided that I'd come to the end of the road as a ballplayer, even though I was only twenty-four. You only get so many opportunities, and I had gotten mine. I just didn't hit as well as I had to. When I was offered a job with National Airlines for more money, I took it."

Why didn't Woods try making it as a pitcher? "I just never thought about it after I went into pro ball," he said. "When I look back, I'm kinda shocked that no one even suggested that I walk to the mound. But baseball was different in those days — less, what, detailed? Less businesslike? A lot of things were overlooked."

Woods said that, yes, he wishes he'd had a longer career, but he sees himself as having realized a dream, of making the major leagues.

"I think Jimmy's content," said Stella.

"My dad did great, and I'm proud of him," said his son, Jim Woods Jr., a grade school teacher. "But his career was cut short."

"It's been fun for me to have a father who made the big leagues," the son continued. "I went to a Cubs game against the Giants a few years ago at Candlestick Park and called over Billy Williams, then a coach for the Cubs. I told him I was Jim Woods's son. He got this big smile on his face. And he invited me back to the clubhouse to meet some of the other players, and gave me an autographed ball."

"Funny how things work out," said Woods. "If I hadn't left baseball when I did, I might not have moved to California, might not have met Stella; we might not have had Jim. Yeah, things worked out okay. I have few regrets."

One other thing. When I came into his son's home, Woods, who had his scrapbooks out to help me with the story, fished in a box and pulled out a yellowed copy of the *Lane Tech Daily*, a four-page, comic-book-size newspaper, dated Friday, May 4, 1956. (Lane Tech, remarkably for a high school, published a daily on its printing press.) "You have to read this," he said, with a grin.

The sports page, on the back, detailed the Lane-Sullivan game played the day before, in which Woods had pitched his third straight shutout. Down in the eleventh paragraph of the story, there it was: "In the sixth inning after Woods had retired twelve of thirteen batters since the first, Ira Berkow and Ian Levin opened with singles . . ."

No dream. This alone was worth the trip to California.

When I left Woods to return home, I too thought that he'd done well. He seemed happy with his home life and comfortable with himself. As for his baseball career, well, how many guys make the major leagues at all? How many guys live out that boyhood fantasy? And how many guys can say that they cracked a double off Sandy Koufax?

And I recalled that towering home run Jim Woods hit off me in the Thillens Pony League. So he had crushed a pitch off both Sandy Koufax and me. Yes, I thought, yes, I was in very good company.

SEAN FLYNN

The Memorial

FROM GOLF MAGAZINE

THE FIRST HOLE at Cook's Creek Golf Club is a gift, 528 yards rolling straight and wide on a dewy Saturday morning, a long sparkle of water far to the right, a simple par 5. In two decades, it's the loveliest view we've ever had from an opening tee.

I am not encouraged. Nineteen years I've played in this tournament, and nineteen years I have lost this tournament, including a coin-toss tiebreaker back in '94. Year twenty is off to a worse-than-usual start. My hands are trembling — side effect of what my companions are charitably calling food poisoning, which is true only if tequila can be called food.

I'm also missing my lucky shirt, the orange-and-red palm print I filched off Tim our freshman year, the shirt that finally disintegrated to a point beyond acceptable golf attire. And our threesome is up first. I've got first-tee yips.

So I'm relieved when my drive lands in the vicinity of the fairway. Two 3-woods and a wedge later, I'm absolutely stunned: my Top-Flite is less than a yard from the flag. Six-time champion Andy is scrambling for bogey, perpetual bridesmaid Tim is looking at double, and I, the perennial also-ran and occasional rock-bottom finisher, am two level feet from the cup.

Half a minute later, after one glorious hole, I am leading the Matt George Memorial Golf Outing.

If only it was about the golf.

The phone in our dorm room rang before sunrise on May 4, 1984. Tim lumbered off the top bunk with a thud to answer it. He stood by the door in his skivvies, holding the phone to his head, saying nothing, just listening, until he hung up and looked at me and said, "Matt's dead."

There was no emotion in his voice, which was because a kid like Tim — like me, like any of us — had no idea how to process such a thought. We were nineteen and twenty years old, sophomores and juniors at Ohio University in Athens, at an age and in a place where death was so distant as to be irrelevant.

The rest of the memory is fragments. Walking up the hill, maybe six of us, to Matt's apartment. Andy and his girlfriend, Jenny, bringing everyone breakfast from McDonald's. Hearing the first report — a wreck on Interstate 64 in Kentucky — and knowing it couldn't be that simple, knowing that Matt had no business in Kentucky in the middle of the night.

We found out later — I can't remember when — that Matt had bought a Bic lighter at a gas station just off the highway. Then he had soaked himself and his Monte Carlo with gasoline, gotten behind the wheel, and floored it back onto the interstate. He blew himself up just before a curve in the highway.

Matt did not leave a note. He did not say good-bye, and he did not explain. But I like to believe that he waited for the bend in the road, waited for a spot where his car would glide off into an empty field, away from traffic. Twenty years have worn his memory into smooth clichés — he was funny, he was loyal, he was all the things that people say of anyone who dies too young — but I am certain that he was gentle. Matt would have never hurt anyone. Not on purpose.

There was a funeral in the city where Matt and our tight constellation of friends had grown up, a memorial service in the chapel on the college green, and then a more informal service in a bar down an alley that served beer by the bucket. And there was more: a raw, almost physical grief that lingered until each of us either got over it or got used to it.

A year went by and the next spring came. There was a cookout in Matt's honor. Someone suggested a commemorative round on the Ohio University golf course. There were only four or five of us, and it rained like hell, and the whole thing was kind of strange because we'd never played golf with Matt; some of us hadn't even known him all that well. But it seemed a respectably somber way to honor our friend, golf being timeless and all, so we did it again the next year and the next, and that's how it started — Matt's tournament.

*

If Matt hadn't died, the rest of us probably wouldn't still be friends. It wouldn't be deliberate. It would be because Jim moved to Boston and Woody went to California and everyone else went somewhere else. We would have stayed in touch for a few years, and of course we would all have been there when Andy and Jenny got married. But it wouldn't have lasted. The centrifugal force of our lives — our wives and kids and jobs and neighbors — would have slowly pushed us apart until we became people we remembered once knowing. Without Matt, there would be no reason to push back.

Yet even our dead friend wouldn't have been enough without the golf. You couldn't gather so many people in the middle of the country every year just to relive the single most miserable experience of their young lives. Raising a silent, melancholy toast to Matt can be done solo; it happens every May 4 at my house in Swampscott, Massachusetts, and no one notices except my wife.

But a weekend of golf is an event. A tournament is a ritual, a tradition, and people will travel for tradition. We come from San Diego and Chicago and Portland and Boston, and we plan for months in advance, shuffling calendars and business trips until we find a weekend when all of us, or most of us, can get to Columbus, Ohio. It's always in Columbus, which was convenient at first because a handful of us settled there after college, but now Columbus is part of the tradition itself because Andy and Jenny have a huge yard with a horseshoes pit and a hot tub for the post-golf party. Andy and Jenny have always been the responsible ones. In college, they were in charge of our dorm, and they were the first to get married, buy a house, and have kids. Secretly, they're sort of our heroes.

We start on Friday afternoon with an eighteen-hole scramble, then spend the night eating in some chain restaurant and drinking in a strip mall bar. Most years anyway. A twentieth anniversary is a landmark, and it was celebrated as such — in the bars of Athens, Ohio, where most of us hadn't been for more than a decade, some of us closer to two. Athens is ninety minutes southeast of Columbus, but it seemed appropriate that we toast Matt in Tony's Tavern and C I and The Pub, all the places where we used to drink so much more vigorously so many years ago. We almost made it to closing time before Woody, thoroughly reformed into our cold-sober designated driver, hauled us north again.

The next day we play. We take the golf quite seriously, in our own

way. Mark has kept records going back to 1987, and there is a trophy — a plaque in the shape of a ball perched on a tee. The ball's
dimples are brass circles on which the names of the winner and
runner-up are engraved, and it's supposed to be passed around
every year, like the Stanley Cup. But the same three people have
won for the last eleven years, so Mark hasn't bothered with any en-
graving since '97. He brings it to the tournament, but then it goes
back on the wall next to his bathroom in Bay Village, Ohio. No one
has ever complained.

The competition isn't cutthroat. True, we play (basically) by the
Rules, and everyone accuses everyone else of cheating. Mostly,
though, we goof off. We tell jokes. We curse our divots. We repeat
lines from *Caddyshack* because they were funny twenty years ago so
they're still funny now, dammit. In fact, the advantage to butcher-
ing the front nine is that you won't have to hear "Miss it, Noonan,
miss it," on the back nine. Probably.

Then we eat. Years ago, we would tap a keg and drink until dawn
or until we passed out on a couch or the floor. (Years ago, tequila
didn't make my hands tremble in the morning.) Now we put a couple cases on ice but never finish them because we've had a few
beers on the course already. Jenny starts making pots of coffee
around nine o'clock. We play horseshoes in the twilight and sit in
the hot tub because we're sore. We tell jokes. We toast Matt and
pass out awards for longest drive and closest to the pin and runner-
up and winner, and then we sit around a bonfire and toast Matt one
more time.

We got old. It happened gradually, like it's supposed to, but it
happened. The eleven of us — me, Andy, Tim, Mark, Woody, A. J.,
Chuck, Eric, Tom, Jim, and Bill — have been through seven marriages and two divorces. Andy's kids are old enough that we talk to
them as Taylor, Ali, and Jacob instead of talking past them and
thinking of them in the abstract — as Andy's kids.

My hair is apparently gray. Tim's is getting there.

And yet we have not aged. The truth is, we know each other less
as we are than as we remember ourselves. A. J. isn't a successful
graphic designer, and Bill isn't traveling all week and eager to get
home to his wife and daughters when Saturday comes, and Jenny
isn't a teacher and Tim isn't a financial planner with my retirement
(*retirement!*) in his hands. We are aware of those things and we talk

about those things, but we are not, for that weekend, those people. We are nineteen and twenty again, college kids whose friend killed himself and we were lost and hurt and angry and sad until we figured out how to help each other through it.

Yet we are not there to mourn. We come to celebrate because we are young again, because we still make each other laugh, because we share great times that haven't ended yet.

That is Matt's legacy, and Matt's legacy is good.

The 18th hole at Cook's Creek Golf Club is a 444-yard par 4, wide open but uphill most of the way. I'm on in three, sink the putt. Another par to bookend the round. On the first and last holes, I am a scratch golfer. But my 104 strokes on holes 2 through 17 leave me well out of contention. Andy isn't faring much better, leaving Tim our threesome's only hope at 96.

We park our carts on the hill behind the green to watch the other two groups come in. Mark (Matt's Memorial champion '97–'99 and '01–'03) is dressed all in black, a bold but unlucky switch from his traditional bright pink shirt. He putts out for 93, then drives up next to us with Woody and A. J. in tow. We squabble about who sucks more, a competition I win easily.

The last foursome is in wedge range. From that distance, body language alone says Chuck, Tom, and Eric are out of contention. Then there's Jim. He set the tournament record of 79 back in 2000. Always a threat.

His pitch is spectacular. He taps in from a foot and walks off with 90 and the title.

Jim gives us a gallery wave on his way up the hill. We give him mock applause and ask how much he cheated. Not that anyone would care all that much if he did. Twenty years I've played in this tournament, and it has never been about the golf, not really. The clubs and the lost balls, the crooked divots and squashed beer cans are a means to an end.

It has really always been about this: a bunch of guys sitting on the fringe of the 18th green, drinking beer and laughing, believing we're still young and yet grateful that we're all still around to grow older. It's about a friend we lost all those years ago, and the friends we still cling to.

DAVID SHIELDS

The Wound and the Bow

FROM THE BELIEVER

I KNOW THAT Howard Cosell was childishly self-absorbed and pet-
ulant ("It's hard to describe the rage and frustration you feel, both
personally and professionally, when you are vilified in a manner
that would make Richard Nixon look like a beloved humanitarian.
You can't imagine what it does to a person until you've experienced it yourself, especially when you know that the criticism is essentially unfair"); that he would obsess upon, say, the *Des Moines
Register*'s critique of his performance; that too soon after he
achieved prominence the beautiful balance between righteous anger and comic self-importance got lost and he was left only with anger and self-importance; that he once said that he, along with Walter Cronkite and Johnny Carson, was one of the three great men in
the history of American television; that he mercilessly teased his
fellow *Monday Night Football* announcers Frank Gifford and Don
Meredith but pouted whenever they teased him; that he was certain he should have been a network anchor and/or a U.S. senator;
that the very thing he thought needed deflating — the "importance of sports" — he was crucially responsible for inflating; that
after hitching a ride on boxing and football for decades he then
turned around and dismissed them when he no longer needed
them ("The NFL has become a stagnant bore"; "I'm disgusted with
the brutality of boxing"); that, in an attempt to assert his (nonexis-
tent) expertise, he would frequently excoriate any rookie who had
the temerity to commit an egregious error on *Monday Night Football*
(dig the Cosellian diction); that he was a shameless name-dropper
of people he barely knew; that he once said about a black football

player, "That little monkey gets loose," then, regarding the brouhaha that ensued, said, "They're conducting a literary pogrom
against me"; that the *New York Times* sports columnist Red Smith
once said, "I have tried hard to like Howard Cosell, and I have
failed"; that the legendary sportswriter Jimmy Cannon said about
him, "This is a guy who changed his name [from Cohane to
Cosell], put on a toupee, and tried to convince the world he tells it
like it is"; that David Halberstam said that he bullied anyone who
disagreed with him; that he frequently boasted about *Monday Night
Football*, "We're bigger than the game"; that he once told a Senate
subcommittee, "I'm a unique personality who has had more impact
upon sports broadcasting in America than any person who has yet
lived"; that he once wrote, "Who the hell made *Monday Night Football* unlike any other sports program on the air? If you want the
plain truth, I did"; that at the height of his fame, when fans would
come up to him on the street to kibitz or get an autograph, he liked
to turn to whomever he was with and say (seriously? semi-seri-
ously?), "Witness the adulation"; that when Gene Upshaw, the head
of the NFL Players Association, said about Cosell, "His footprints
are in the sand," he corrected the compliment: "My footprints are
cast in stone."

I know all of that and don't really care, because for a very few
years — 1970–74, the first four years it was on the air, when I was in
high school — *Monday Night Football* mattered deeply to me and it
mattered because of Cosell. I haven't watched more than a few
minutes of any *MNF* game since then, and at the time I had no very
coherent sense of its significance, but looking back, I would say it's
not an exaggeration to claim that Howard Cosell changed my life,
maybe even — in at least one sense — saved it. *MNF* was "Mother
Love's traveling freak show" (Meredith's weirdly perfect description), a "happening" (Cosell's revealingly unhip attempt to be
hip); it was the first sports broadcast to feature three sportscasters,
nine cameras, shotgun mics in the stands and up and down and
around the field. Celebrities showed up in the booth: Nixon told
Gifford he wished he had become a sportscaster instead of a politi-
cian; John Lennon told Cosell that he became a troublemaker because people didn't like his face (Cosell's comment afterward: "I
know the feeling"); Cosell stood next to Bo Derek and said with
pitch-perfect, mock-self-pity that here was a classic case of Beauty

and the Beast; Cosell told John Wayne that he was a terrible singer and the Duke agreed; after Cosell interviewed Spiro Agnew, Meredith said that what no one knew was that Agnew was wearing a Howard Cosell wristwatch. This was all cool and droll. It was all finally just showbiz, though. What wasn't was Cosell's relation, as an artist, to his material (I use the terms advisedly): "By standing parallel to the game and owing nothing to it, by demystifying it, by bullying it and not being bullied by it — by regarding the game as primarily an entertainment, though realizing also the social forces that impacted on it — I was able to turn *Monday Night Football* into an Event, and I do mean to use the capital E. Now it is part of American pop culture, and if it sounds like my ego is churning on overdrive for taking the lion's share of credit for it, then I'll take the mane."

I grew up in the sixties and seventies in suburban San Francisco, the son of left-wing Jewish journalist-activists. My mother was the public information officer for one of the first desegregated school districts in California. One day the human relations consultant informed her that the revolution wouldn't occur until white families gave up their houses in the suburbs and moved into the ghetto. My mother tried for the better part of the evening to convince us to put our house up for sale. One Easter weekend at Watts Towers, my mother looked smogward through some latticed wine bottles with a positively religious sparkle in her dark eyes. When cousin Sarah married a black man from Philadelphia, Sarah's mother wasn't able to attend, so my mother substituted and brought the temple down with an a capella finale of "Bridge over Troubled Water." My father held dozens of jobs, but perhaps the one he loved the most was director of the San Mateo poverty program during the late sixties. He sat in a one-room office without central heating and called grocery stores, wanting to know why they didn't honor food stamps; called restaurants, asking if, as the sign in the window proclaimed, they were indeed equal opportunity employers. Sometimes, on weekends, he flew to Sacramento or Washington to request more money for his program. Watts rioted, Detroit burned. My father said, "Please, I'm just doing my job." He got invited to barbecues, weddings, softball games. The salary was $7,500 a year, but I never saw him happier.

No one ever had his or her heart more firmly fixed in the right place than my father and mother, with the possible exception of Howard Cosell. Traveling in a limo through a tough part of Kansas City, he saw two young black men fighting each other, surrounded by a group of young guys cheering for blood. After telling his driver, Peggy, to stop the car, Cosell got out and was instantaneously the ringside announcer: "Now I want you to listen here. It's quite apparent to this observer that the young southpaw doesn't have a jab. And you, my friend, over here, you obviously do not have the stamina to continue. This conflict is halted post-haste." Handshakes, autographs. When Cosell got back in the limo and Peggy expressed her astonishment at what she'd just seen, Cosell leaned back, took a long drag on his cigar, and said, "Pegeroo, just remember one thing: I know who I am." Which, according to himself, was "a man of causes. My entire professional life has been predicated upon making the good fights, the fights that I believe in. And much of the time it was centered around the black athlete. My real fulfillment in broadcasting has always come from crusading journalism, fighting for the rights of people such as Jackie Robinson, Muhammad Ali, and Curt Flood. The greatest influence of my life was Jackie Roosevelt Robinson and [. . . the inevitable name-drop] certainly one of my closest friends." My father rooted for the Dodgers because they were originally from Brooklyn and then moved to Los Angeles, just as he was and had, but we as a clan stayed loyal to them because they hired the first black major league baseball player (Jackie Robinson), retained the first crippled black baseball player (Roy Campanella), and started the highest number of nice-seeming black players (Johnny Roseboro, Jim Gilliam, Tommy Davis, et al.). *New York Post* sportswriter Maury Allen said, "The single most significant issue in the twentieth century was race, and Howard Cosell was unafraid about race." Cosell's access to causes was through black bodies; without Ali, he wouldn't have been semi-dangerous, reviled.

He defended Ali when the fighter refused to serve in Vietnam following his conversion to Islam. When Cosell died, Ali said, "Howard Cosell was a good man and he lived a good life. I can hear Howard now saying, 'Muhammad, you're not the man you used to be ten years ago.'" Ali was referring to Cosell standing up at a prefight press conference and saying to him, "Many people believe you're not the man you used to be ten years ago." Ali replied, "I spoke to your wife, and she said you're not the man you were *two* years ago." Cosell giggled like a schoolboy. Asked once what he stood for, Cosell replied, "I stood for the Constitution, in the case of the U.S. versus Muhammad Ali. What the government did to this man was inhuman and illegal under the Fifth and Fourteenth Amendments. Nobody says a damned word about the professional football players who dodged the draft. But Muhammad was different. He was black and he was boastful. Sportscasters today aren't concerned with causes and issues. Can you see any of those other guys putting their careers on the line for an Ali?" According to Cosell's daughter Jill, he frequently said that if people didn't stand for things, they weren't good for much else.

Music to my parents' Marxist ears. As was this: "The importance that our society attaches to sport is incredible. After all, is football a game or a religion? The people of this country have allowed sports to get completely out of hand." Or this: "The sports world is an ever-spinning spiral of deceit, immorality, absence of ethics, and defiance of the public interest." And this: "There's got to be a voice such as mine somewhere, and I enjoy poking my stick at various issues and passersby." And this: "For myself, I wondered when someone other than me would tell the truth." And this: "What was it all about, Alfie? Was football that important in this country? Was it a moral crime to introduce objective commentary to the transmission of a sports event?" — after he'd been pilloried in Cleveland for saying that Browns running back Leroy Kelly hadn't been a "compelling factor" in the first half of the first *MNF* game (he hadn't). "If so, how did we as a people get this way? In the spoon-fed, *Alice in Wonderland* world of sports broadcasting, the public was not accustomed to hearing its heroes questioned." When, following his eulogy of Bobby Kennedy on his *Speaking of Sports* show, fan after fan called in to complain — "Don't tell me how to live — just give us the scores — that's what you're paid for" — Cosell said, "I began to wonder if that kind of thinking is one of the things that makes us so prone to assassination in this country. Maybe there is such an absence of intellect and sensitivity that only violence is understandable and acceptable." "The 'fan,'" Cosell pointed out, "is a telephone worker, a transit worker, a power company worker, a steelworker, a teacher, whatever. He has never given up the right to strike and often does. When he does, the public is inconvenienced and sometimes the public health and safety are threatened. When a ballplayer strikes, the effect upon the public health and safety is nil. Nor is public convenience disturbed, for that matter. Yet the ballplayer and the owner are called upon to each give up their individual bargaining rights because the 'fan' wants baseball and 'is entitled to get it.'" "I never played the game with advertisers, with my own company, or with the sports operators," Cosell said. "And of course I never played the game as a professional athlete."

This is where it gets complicated, because I was a monomaniacal, five-foot-four-inch, 120-pound freshman basketball player at Aragon High School in San Mateo who, somehow, was supremely confident that he was destined to become a professional athlete.

From kindergarten to tenth grade all I really did was play sports, think about sports, dream about sports. I learned how to read by devouring mini-bios of jock-stars. I learned math by computing players' (and my own) averages. When I was twelve I ran the fifty-yard-dash in six seconds, which caused kids from all over the city to come to my school and race me. During a five-on-five weave drill at a summer basketball camp, the director of the camp, a recently retired professional basketball player, got called over to watch how accurately I could throw passes behind my back; he said he could have used a point guard like me when he was playing, and he bumped me up out of my grade level. I remember once hitting a home run in the bottom of the twelfth inning to win a Little League all-star game and then coming home to lie down in my uniform in the hammock in our back yard, drink lemonade, eat sugar cookies, and measure my accomplishments against the fellows featured in the just-arrived issue of *Sports Illustrated. Christ,* I remember thinking, *how could life possibly get any better than this?*

In junior high I would frequently take the bus crosstown, toss my backpack under my father's desk, and spend the rest of the afternoon playing basketball with black kids. I played in all seasons and instead of other sports. In seventh grade I developed a double-pump jump shot, which in seventh grade was almost unheard of. Rather than shooting on the way up, I tucked my knees, hung in the air for a second, pinwheeled the ball, then shot on the way down. My white friends hated my new move. It seemed tough, man-

nered, teenage, vaguely Negro. The more I shot like this the more
my white friends disliked me, and the more they disliked me the
more I shot like this. At the year-end assembly, I was named "best
athlete," and my mother said that when I went up to accept the trophy, I even walked like a jock. At the time I took this as the ultimate
accolade, though I realize now she meant it as gentle mockery.

Sports and politics have always been, for me, in curiously close conversation, alliance, overlap, competition. None of the kids I played
sports with were Jewish. They called me Buddha Boy (I never quite
understood this moniker — Judaism was as unfathomable to them
as Buddhism?) and Ignatz (my body was small and my ears were
large) and asked me why anyone would want to be Jewish. When
Sandy Koufax refused to pitch during the World Series, I suddenly
felt proud to stay home on Yom Kippur. My father derives his
identity at least as much from Jewish boxers and basketball players
from the thirties and Hank Greenberg as he does from his PS 149
schoolmates Danny Kaye and Phil Silvers.

   In high school I was athletic and thus, to a certain extent, popular. However, I worked unduly hard at it, at sports, with very little
sprezzatura, which made me extremely unpopular among the really
popular, really athletic people. Why? Because I made popularity or
grace look like something less than a pure gift. Only the really popular, really athletic people knew I was unpopular, so I could, for instance, be elected, if I remember correctly, vice president of the
sophomore class and yet be, in a sense, underappreciated.

   Cosell knew the feeling, amplified. "I remember going to school
in the morning," Cosell said in his *Playboy* interview. "A Jewish boy. I
remember having to climb a back fence and run because the kids
from St. Theresa's parish were after me. My drive, in a sense, relates
to being Jewish and living in an age of Hitler. I think these things
create insecurities in you that live forever." As if in proof of these insecurities, he said, "I am the most hated man on the face of the
earth."

   Still, he did have a point. He was voted most disliked sports-
caster of the seventies. One sign at a stadium said WILL ROGERS
NEVER MET HOWARD COSELL. Another sign said HOWARD IS A
HEMORRHOID. A contest was held: the winner got to throw a brick
through a TV set when Cosell was talking. Buddy Hackett told
Johnny Carson, "There are two schools of thought about Howard

Cosell. Some people hate him like poison, and some people just hate him regular."

One Saturday night, two medics carrying a stretcher stormed my family's front door, looking for someone who had supposedly fallen on the front steps. Later that afternoon, a middle-aged man, slightly retarded, tried to deliver a pepperoni pizza. A cop came to investigate a purported robbery. Another ambulance. A florist. An undertaker from central casting. Vehicles from most areas of the service sector were, at one point, parked virtually around the block. I was certain, though I could never prove, that my popular, athletic friends, who always gathered together to watch the proceedings with binoculars in one of their houses at the top of the hill, had orchestrated this traffic all night and into the morning. Every Halloween I cowered in my basement bedroom with the doors locked, lights out, shades down, and listened to the sound of eggs hitting my house.

I had company. "Cosell, the Mouth, why don't you drop dead? There's a bomb in Rich Stadium. It will blow you up at 10:00 P.M., Monday." "If he comes to Green Bay on October 1, I'm going to kill him, and your sheriff's department can't stop me." "You will die now, because your government lies. I will be out in October and will be there to get you and all ABC government cheaters." The death threats always came from smaller, less cosmopolitan towns or cities — Buffalo; Green Bay; Milwaukee; Denver; Deer Lodge, Montana — to residents of which Cosell must have seemed like Sissified Civilization itself.

Every plot needs a villain, as Bill Cosby told Cosell. Cosell says that when they were struggling through the first rehearsal for *MNF,* he reassured Meredith: "The Yankee lawyer and the Texas cornpone, putting each other on. You'll wear the white hat, I'll wear the black hat, and you'll have no problems from the beginning. You're going to come out of this a hero. I know this country. There's nothing this country loves more than a cowboy, especially when he's standing next to a Jew. Middle America will love you. Southern America will love you. And there are at least forty sportswriters in the country who can't wait to get at me. You'll benefit thereby. Don't worry about me, though. Because in the long run it will work for the old coach too." Which it did, at least for a while, for longer than anyone thought possible.

Gifford was the fair-haired Hall-of-Famer. "People always looked for things in me they'd like to see in themselves," Gifford claimed. "I've never known what to think of it." Ah, but he did. "Look at him standing there, girls," Cosell liked to say within earshot of Gifford at meet-and-greets before *MNF* games. "A veritable Greek god. America's most famous football hero. The dream of the American working girl. The single most sexually dynamic man in the chronicle of the male sex." Cosell was up for this jocularity; so, in a way, was Gifford (in his memoir *The Whole Ten Yards*, he gleefully quotes his then-wife Kathie Lee calling him a "love machine").

"Anyone who looked like Ichabod Crane and spoke with a nasal Brooklyn accent didn't exactly fit the sportscaster mold," Gifford said later about Cosell, in retaliation. "On top of that, Howard was Jewish."

"Of course there are critics," Cosell sighed one night on *MNF*. "There will always be critics. 'The dogs bark, but the caravan rolls on.'" Meredith — good ole boy with a slight sideways wit — said, "Woof."

A receiver muffed an easy catch, and Meredith said, "Hey, he should be on *Saturday Night Live with Howard Cosell*," which had tanked after twelve shows. Cosell glowered.

Gifford, Meredith, and Cosell couldn't find anywhere to eat late one night, so the limo pulled into a McDonald's in a slum. Meredith urged Cosell to exit: "Ha'hrd, they want you. It's your constituency. You know, the poor, the downtrodden. You're always talking about them. Shit, Ha'hrd, here they are!"

Once, when the Giants were playing the Cowboys on *MNF*, Cosell said, teasingly, that he wasn't impressed by the play of Meredith's and Gifford's (former) respective teams, and Meredith replied, "At least we have respective teams."

Cosell should have laughed, but he didn't. I should have laughed when my faux friends made fun of me, but I didn't, I couldn't (and so they made more fun of me). Cosell was/I was everything they weren't: Jewish, verbal, performative, engagé, contrarian, pretentious but insecure, despising (adoring) athletics and athletes.

Instead, Cosell would tattle to *MNF* executive producer Roone Arledge: "They're doing it again. The two jocks are out to get me. They're after me again."

Instead, Cosell said to Meredith, "Don't start it because you don't stand a chance. Get into a duel of words with me, and I'll put you away."

Instead, he said about Gifford, "He admired my command of the language, my ability to communicate, and he was shrewd enough not to engage me in a debate. He had to know he couldn't win."

Witness the adulation of words. For Cosell, language was everything, as All-American Heroism was/is for Gifford (this all blew away in a storm when Gifford's marriage and career came undone; we're in Cheever country — the perfect Connecticut house is no bulwark against the crooked timber of humanity) and Texan joie de vivre was/is for Meredith (this too was a crock; Meredith came to despise the "Dandy Don" mask that was his meal ticket). Once, on air, Meredith kissed Cosell on the cheek, pretending to gag on Cosell's toupee. Cosell immediately responded by saying, "I didn't know you . . . cared." The way he paused before saying the word "cared," and the pressure that he put on the word, thrilled me to the bottom of my fifteen-year-old toes. "You're being extremely . . . truculent," he admonished Muhammad Ali once, and, again, it was the way he paused before "truculent" and the extraordinary torque he put on the word so that he seemed to be simultaneously brandishing the word as a weapon and mocking his own sesquipedalianism. In *The Whole Ten Yards*, Gifford, surely leaning more than a little on his cowriter, *Newsweek* television writer Harry Waters, says about Cosell: "His genius lay in turning his liabilities into assets. He gave his voice" — thick New Yawk honk, full of Brooklyn bile — "a dramatic, staccato delivery that grabbed you by the ears." I too wanted to turn my liabilities into strengths. I knew what my liabilities were; only what were my strengths?

I had been aware since I was six or seven that I stuttered, but the problem would come and go; it never seemed that serious or significant. I had successfully hid out from it, or it from me. Now, as a sophomore in high school, with my hormones trembling, my lips were too. In class, I'd sit in back, pretending not to hear when called upon, and when pressed to respond, would produce an answer that I knew was incorrect but was the only word I could say. I devotedly studied the dictionary and thesaurus in the hope I could possess a vocabulary of such immense range that for every word, I'd know half a dozen synonyms and thus always be able to substitute an easy word for an unspeakable one. My sentences became so saturated with approximate verbal equivalents that what I thought often bore almost no relation to what I actually said.

The school's speech therapist was very pretty but not especially my type: a little too cherubic to be truly inspiring. Miss Acker knew I was a basketball player and proved to be surprisingly knowledgeable about the game, so for the first half-hour we talked about how it doesn't matter if a guard is short if he knows how to protect the ball; what a shame it was that the high school had no girls' basketball team; how *A Sense of Where You Are* was good but *Last Loud Roar* was probably even better.

At the time, my particular plague spot happened to be words beginning with vowels. Miss Acker's text, for one reason or another, was riddled with them. I kept opening my mouth and uttering air bubbles, half-human pops of empty repetition. Miss Acker didn't have to play the tape back for me to know it had been the very embodiment of babble, but she did, and then, raising her right eyebrow, asked, "Well?"

I explained that the whirring of the tape recorder and her ostentatious tallying of my errata had made me nervous. The proof I wasn't just one more stutterer was that I could whisper.

"But, Dave," she said, "virtually all stutterers can whisper. You're a stutterer. I want you to admit that fact. It's an important step. Once you acknowledge it, we can get to work on correcting it. When you're a professional basketball player, I don't want to see you giving hesitant interviews at halftime."

The flattery tactic didn't work the second time, not least because she was wrong: as Howard Cosell well knew, the athletic aesthetic always asserts that the ecstasies experienced by the body are beyond the reach of words, whereas to some cerebral people, unfortunately, the primal appeal of a warrior-athlete is incalculable. I'd regularly distinguished myself from the common run of repeaters by the fact that I could whisper; now, informed I was one among millions, I was enraged — at what or whom I didn't quite know, but enraged. I tore down a poster of a seagull and ran out of the room. Having never before confronted myself and found myself in any real way wanting, I returned to her office the next day and began what still — thirty years later — feels like my life: a life limited but also defined by language.

Within a week, Miss Acker got me switched out of Typing into Public Speaking. I suffered predictably, but then I hit on the idea of doing a speech imitating Cosell. This was 1972 — fall, the first month of my sophomore year, the second year of *MNF* — and so I went to school the only way I could on "The Mouth," without the aid of a VCR, which was more than a decade away. I simply watched him and thought about him as much as I could, even more than I had before.

"The Mouth" was a good nickname for him. He was such an insatiably oral guy, talking nonstop and always pouring liquor down his throat and jamming a huge stogie in his mouth. Dick Ebersol, now president of NBC Sports, said about Cosell, "He was defined by what he said, not how he looked or spoke." As with virtually everything Dick Ebersol has ever said, this is exactly wrong. How Cosell looked and how he spoke were everything. With his pasty skin, his stoop-shouldered walk, his ridiculous toupee, his enormous ears and shnoz, he always reminded me of nothing so much as a very verbose and Jewish elephant. The sportswriter Frank Deford's paean to him nicely conveys this quality: "He is not the one with the golden locks [Gifford] or the golden tan [Meredith], but the old one, shaking, sallow, and hunched, with a chin whose purpose is not to exist as a chin but only to fade so that his face may, as the bow of a ship, break the waves and not get in the way of that voice." The things he could do with that voice: the way, every week at halftime on *MNF*, he would extemporize the NFL highlights in that roller-coaster rhetoric of his and, in so doing, "add guts and life to a damned football game," as he said, or as Chet Forte, executive director of *MNF* for years and years, said later, "It's not a damn football game. It's a show. That's what those guys [Gifford and Meredith] never understood. They never appreciated what Howard did. He could make two eighty-five-year-olds playing a game of marbles sound like the most exciting event in the history of sports." He had found a way to be better than what he was reporting on, to bully reality, to make life into language.

After a week of practice, I had my Cosell imitation down. Stutterers typically don't stutter when singing, whispering, acting, or imitating someone else, and I when I did my Cosell imitation, I didn't stutter. I was melodramatically grandiloquent and entertaining in the Cosellian vein. Everyone in the class loved my performance — it ended with the football purportedly landing in and thereby shutting my/Cosell's mouth — and the speech teacher,

Mr. Roshoff, loved it too. For the next three years, he rarely passed me without saying softly, out of the side of his mouth, "HEL-lo, every-BODY, this is HOW-wud Cos-SELL." It was easy to see why my sister and several of her friends had crushes on him. Still, I could imitate Howard Cosell; so what? So could, and did, a lot of other people. Where did that get me exactly?

Toward the end of my sophomore year — Mother's Day actually — I badly broke my left femur and was in traction the entire summer. When the doctor misread the X-ray and removed the body cast too early, I had a pin inserted in my leg and I used a leg brace and crutches my entire junior year. With the jockocracy newly closed to me, I became, nearly overnight, an insanely overzealous chess player, carried along by the aftermath of the Fischer-Spassky World Championship. I got to the point that I dreamt in chess notation, but I was certainly never going to become a chess whiz, and I rationalized to myself that if one could be, as Bobby Fischer was, the best chess player in the world but still a monster and a moron, the game wasn't interesting, and so I abandoned it after several months, then joined the school paper.

By my senior year I had recovered well enough from my broken leg that I was twelfth man on the varsity basketball team and second doubles in tennis, but sports no longer meant much to me. All that physical expression had gone inside; language was my new channel. I suddenly loved reading; I became the editor of the paper; my parents (especially my mother) were thrilled; it was sickening. I spent no more time on my studies than I had before, but now instead of six hours a day playing sports, it was six hours a day working on the paper, writing nearly every article, taking every photograph, attending journalism conferences around the Bay Area, submitting my work to every possible high school journalism competition, submitting the paper and my work (virtually synonymous) for competitions. My bible was *New Journalism*, an anthology of pieces edited by Tom Wolfe, which I read over and over again. I thought I would become a new journalist, à la Hunter Thompson or Joan Didion.

In college, though, writing for the weekly, weakly student magazine, I got in trouble for making stuff up. Also, I was trepidatious — still — about calling people on the phone (I couldn't imitate

Cosell) and so I crabwalked into creative writing courses. I'd become a fiction writer. I'd make stuff up, and that would be okay. The only problem, as I discovered in graduate school, was that compared to other fiction writers, I'm not very interested in making stuff up. I'm much more interested in contemplating the so-called real world, including, alas, the world of sports. I've now written several books of fiction and nonfiction, and to my astonishment and horror, half of them deal more or less explicitly with sports.

In *The Wound and the Bow*, Edmund Wilson analyzes how various writers, such as Dickens, Wharton, and Hemingway, used the central wound of their life as the major material of their art. Throughout her entire childhood, a writer I know worked fiendishly hard in the hope of becoming a professional ballet dancer, entering the Harkness Ballet trainee program at eighteen, but she left after less than a year. It's only right that her first book, published a couple of years ago when she was in her midforties, is a collection of stories set in the world of ballet and her novel-in-progress is told from the point of view of George Balanchine. In *Rocky*, asked what he sees in dowdy Adrian, Rocky says, "She fills gaps." I was a great child-athlete and I just assumed this play-paradise would last forever. It didn't. Writing about it fills gaps.

RICHARD SANDOMIR

Five-Second Delay Can't Mute Old Voice

FROM THE NEW YORK TIMES

HELLO AGAIN, everyone, this is Howard Cosell, speaking of *Monday Night Football* — and the five-second delay instituted with singular imprudence upon the broadcast by those who rose to lead ABC Sports after my untimely passing.

Pointless, irrational, absurd, nitwitted, cockamamie, and, perhaps, unconstitutional.

There is no question that a five-second delay is all of these things.

Once out of my mouth, it was verily my expectation that each word I spoke immediately took residence in the cerebrum of America.

So it is unimaginable to this reporter, who not only battled for free expression for Muhammad Ali but who himself set the bar for public discourse far beyond the puny realm of sports, that my former network — once the domain of the modern Charlemagne, Roone Arledge — should so fear the stray intrusion of foul verbiage that it is postponing by five seconds the dispatch of '*Monday Night Football* to the waiting world.

For as you know, it was yours truly who made *Monday Night Football* what it is today. Not the Danderoo. Not the Giffer. Not Alfalfa Michaels or John Madden. So I know wherefore I speak when the fetid button of censorship stands between the game and the multitudes, many of whom will surely recall how I was the first to inform them of the murder of my friend John Lennon.

I am rendered nearly mute with rage at what might have been excised from the program when I bestrode it like a broadcast Colossus. Perhaps some trembling production hack would have cut out certain lyrics from the Danderoo's singing. Or gone forever might have been the vision of one fan who presented us with the middlemost of his five fingers as his personal commentary on a stupefyingly dull game.

Some might argue that a five-second delay might have provided welcome respite from the uninspired commentary of Fred Williamson in the exhibition season of 1974, yet I shall defend to my death and beyond the Hammer's right to fashion banal analysis in real, not delayed, time. The same goes for one Orenthal James Simpson, the irrepressible Juice of my most vibrant years, who was a dismal failure at *Monday Night* yet such a dear friend to beautiful Emmy and me.

I am cognizant of the reverberations caused by the breast-baring antics of those two popular music scamps, Janet Jackson and Justin Timberlake, during the Super Bowl halftime show earlier this year.

I was surprised but not scandalized at the appearance of young Janet's rightmost mammary gland. Her brief revelation of nudity was the ultimate feat of free speech, but the reaction by the National Football League — a duly adjudicated, illegal monopoly — was as ineffectual as its antitrust strategy was against Al Davis, another scamp who stretched the limits of the league's tolerance.

Before congressional committees — many of which I once testified to, such was my versatility and scholarship — the league apologized for what was not its fault, and stumbled over itself with shame and promises that even a fleeting glance of pulchritude would not be perpetrated again by any of its network partners.

It is doubtlessly true that a palpable fear of future indecency — whether in the form of skin or words — inhabits the sclerotic heart of ABC Sports. In the Arledge era, I was permitted to take any position, without fear or favor, but I was protected against the delayed dissemination of my verbosity.

Had I been told that the very words that made me simultaneously the most loved and most hated sportscaster in America were being held up for inspection, like sirloin before the USDA, I would have resigned and surely been elected to the United States Senate seat that I knew belonged to me, and not Alfonse D'Amato or Daniel Patrick Moynihan.

Already, it seems, the five-second delay is failing as surely as the ski jumper Vinko Bogotaj did as the human symbol of the "agony of defeat" in the introductory montage to *Wide World of Sports*, a program that was never more important than when Muhammad Ali and I were the centers of America's attention.

On Monday night, young Alfalfa related a patently indecent tale about how Minnesota Vikings Coach Mike Tice kept his ever-present pencil in his pants until, one day, the lead "got stuck in his tush."

But it was not bleeped, underscoring the hypocrisy of the delay.

Still, it is with the deepest worries about the future of the sports division that I remade through my courage that I tender my posthumous resignation to ABC Sports. I have told it like it is for too long to stop now. I am now a free agent, much as my great and good friend Curt Flood should have been.

This is Howard Cosell.

PAT JORDAN

The Lion in Late, Late Autumn

FROM THE NEW YORK TIMES MAGAZINE

ZACK MILLS, a twenty-two-year-old quarterback at Penn State University, and Graham Spanier, the elegantly dressed fifty-six-year-old president of the school, are separated by a generation, but both are equally amazed by the youthful vigor of someone who is from another generation altogether, Joseph Vincent Paterno, Penn State's seventy-seven-year-old football coach. Mills says that Paterno can still drop to the floor and perform twenty push-ups and that the coach often takes part in drills with his linemen that result in a bloody nose. "Nobody tries to hit him," Mills says. "But accidents happen. It's funny to see a man his age running around like a kid." Paterno isn't trying to be funny. "I'm young physically, so I can horse around in practice," he says.

Spanier says that Paterno's youthful exuberance is a result of "incredible genes, which is why his black hair only recently began graying." (Back when he was in his sixties, Paterno adamantly denied using Grecian Formula.) Spanier also tells this story, which he does often: "When Joe and I go to parties, I want to leave at midnight, and Joe's saying, 'Doesn't anyone else want to dance?'"

It is because of Paterno's incredible genes, in part, that Spanier recently rewarded him with a new four-year contract that will extend the coach's fifty-four-year career at Penn State to 2008, when Paterno will be eighty-two. "Joe is a treasured resource of this university," Spanier says. "He's a brilliant man, the school's greatest ambassador, the school's best fund-raiser, and a philanthropist who regularly gives back part of his salary to the English department and the library, which is named after him and his wife, Sue. Joe doesn't raise money for football, because it's not about football with Joe."

Paterno is the architect of Penn State's "Grand Experiment," which emphasizes players' moral values, discipline, character, and scholastic achievements over merely winning football games, which Paterno calls a "silly" endeavor. "At Penn State," Spanier says, "losing a game is not as catastrophic as at other universities," where it can cause fans "to be dejected and question the integrity of their program."

Of course — and it's only incidental, according to Spanier — Paterno was also signed up until 2008 because he *does* win football games. He is, in fact, second among active major-college football coaches in victories, behind Bobby Bowden of Florida State. Paterno has been called the greatest college football coach ever, both by his peers (Bowden for one) and in a recent ESPN poll. His record of achievement is phenomenal, considering that Penn State, according to Spanier, has the highest academic admission requirements for athletes of schools in its conference, the Big Ten — and the Big Ten's admission standards "are higher than the NCAA's," Spanier says.

In his thirty-eight years as head coach of the Nittany Lions, Paterno has won 339 games, lost 109, and tied 3. He has had five undefeated teams, has won two national championships, and has been named Coach of the Year four times. He has been a coach for more than half of the football games Penn State has played since 1887, and his reign has spanned 11 U.S. presidents and 742 coaching changes in Division I football.

When Paterno was offered his new extension, he says he debated it: "I took a look at myself. What am I going to do on a beautiful Saturday afternoon without football? Cut grass? I'm not a hunter, golfer, or fisherman. I'm not going to retire to Florida and go nuts. But I think this is the last contract for me." Paterno laughs. "I know, I know, I said it before." What Paterno has said before is that he "didn't want to stay too long" at Penn State. He said that he might retire in '73, '78, '82, '86, and so on, or maybe he would retire when his children graduated from college. (All five of his children have long since graduated from Penn State.) But he didn't retire. Now he says that he signed his latest extension because "I want to get this thing back where it belongs. I can't get out of it like this." What Paterno means is that his last four teams have won only twenty-two games and lost twenty-six. Three of those teams had losing seasons, and last year Penn State was 3–9, Paterno's worst record ever, which is why his contract extension met with criticism from some fans and the media, which claimed that JoePa, as he is known, has stayed on beyond his effectiveness.

Over the last four years, JoePa's teams have been criticized for being sloppily coached (at more than one point in one game he had teams of ten and twelve players on the field), for losing the recruiting wars (he no longer signs the best players even from Pennsylvania), for having a stodgy offense called "grunt 'n' grind" (a reference to his penchant for running his backs off tackle and shunning the pass), for his misguided loyalty to his unimaginative and unquestioning assistant coaches, and finally for starting less talented upperclassmen instead of more talented underclassmen. Chris Korman, last year's sports editor at the *Daily Collegian*, the school paper, says that Paterno has been "the sole person in charge for so long he doesn't know how" to delegate authority to his assistant coaches, a claim that Nick Gancitano, a place-kicker on Penn State's teams from 1982 to 1985, echoes. Gancitano now says that Fran Ganter, a former offensive coordinator, "had his hands tied. He was never given control of the offense or Joe's trust. Joe didn't want to give it up." The former player gave up watching Penn State games and says: "There's no passion there. The team lacks intensity and that comes from the top."

Paterno has also been accused of ducking tough teams he used to play. (Penn State's first three games this season are against Akron, Boston College, and the University of Central Florida, not in a league with old rivals like Miami and Nebraska.) Walt Harris, the football coach at the University of Pittsburgh, was recently quoted in the *Daily Collegian* as saying that the traditional Penn State–Pitt rivalry has been put on ice since Pitt beat Penn State, 12–0, in 2000, and that the two teams won't ever meet again "as long as one man is running the program." For years, Penn State played an independent schedule, but like most independent teams not affiliated with a conference (Notre Dame excepted), it had increasing difficulty filling its schedule in the '80s. So Paterno and the school decided that joining the Big Ten would make for a perfect fit for Penn State, which considers itself (and truly feels like) a midwestern school despite its eastern location. Membership in the Big Ten would also provide financial benefits and the prestige that comes with belonging to a premier football conference. Yet even though Penn State won the Big Ten championship in 1994, its second season in the conference, the team has otherwise been overmatched in the Big Ten. Besides that year, the Nittany Lions have never finished higher than third in the conference, and over the past six years they have finished fifth, fifth, sixth, sixth, fourth, and tied for ninth.

"I look like a Mafia thug," Paterno said in his office. He was pointing to a photograph of himself from the 1950s. He's wearing a double-breasted topcoat that could conceal a Thompson submachine gun. He's a beefy, thick-necked, sullen-looking youth with narrow eyes and pouty lips. He doesn't look much like the JoePa of Penn State. He is leaner these days, except for a slight paunch, and his leanness makes his prominent Italian nose look bigger than it did years ago. His swept-back hair is slightly gray, and his eyes are hidden behind tinted black-rimmed glasses. JoePa dresses Ivy League now. Blue oxford-cloth, button-down shirt, rep tie, navy blazer with brass buttons and baggy khaki slacks: his JoePa uniform of the last forty years.

Like most children of second-generation Italian Americans, Paterno, who was reared in Brooklyn, is not much enamored of the Mafia. "I don't watch *The Sopranos*," he said, "and I walked out on *The Godfather* — making a bunch of bums look like heroes." His mother once told him, "Your grandfather didn't come to America to be an Italian; he came to be an American." Paterno said, "Jeez, my father wouldn't even talk Italian to us."

After Paterno graduated from a Jesuit high school, he went to Brown, where he majored in English and quarterbacked the football team to an 8–1 record as a senior, despite the fact that, according to a local sportswriter, he couldn't run or pass. After graduating in 1950, Paterno became an assistant coach at Penn State. When he telephoned his father to say that he had chosen to be a football coach rather than to go to law school, "he almost hung up on me," Paterno said. Italian American parents of his youth didn't envision careers in sports for their children, but rather the professions of medicine, law, academics.

Penn State, with its quasi–Ivy League pretensions, was the perfect place for Paterno. It was situated in the country, in the middle of the state in a Norman Rockwell little town, State College, that was nestled in a bucolic valley, Happy Valley, and surrounded by protective, lush green mountains. There is something eerie about Happy Valley, with its neat colonial houses, manicured hedges, spotless malls, friendly people. Happy Valley seems like a place out of time, or maybe just out of a movie — *The Stepford Wives*, say, or *Pleasantville*.

Many of Paterno's coaches are from Happy Valley or are Penn State grads. "People graduate and come back here to live," says Jeff Nelson, the athletic department's media adviser. "They get married, have kids, and come back to live in eight years or when they retire." Tim Curley, the athletic director, a trim, youthful-looking man in his fifties, was reared across the street from the old playing field. As a boy, he sold football programs there. "It's a real comfortable place to live," he says. "It's isolated and protected. We have a lot of stability, continuity, and a family atmosphere." Fran Ganter, the former offensive coordinator, says: "My three sisters went here. I played here in '67 and never left." The coordinator in charge of recruiting, Mike McQueary, twenty-nine, says: "I'm a State College kid. I stayed close to home. It's a special place. But I'm biased. I grew up here and went to school here." McQueary has aspirations of one day becoming a head coach, hopefully at Penn State — "but Joe will probably outlive me," he says. This sense of devotion to Happy Valley and its coach is why, according to Steve Swart, the current sports editor of the *Daily Collegian*, "even our boosters don't criticize Joe." The bartender at the Gingerbread Man, downtown, says that after last year's home losses the students who came in to drown their sorrows rarely complained about JoePa.

Paterno sat on a sofa in his office and talked about the only time he ever thought of leaving Penn State, to coach the Patriots in the NFL in 1972. "I debated it," he said in a gravelly whisper, as if to avoid eavesdroppers. "But the college environment is the perfect place for me. I enjoy the academic environment, the talk of politics and literature." Everyone in Happy Valley likes to talk about Paterno's intellectual bent. Spanier says, "Football provides a window to the world for Joe." Paterno says, "I am a little bit of an egghead," which is something he has said often to the news media. There is a book about ancient Greek athletes conspicuously in the center of his desk. He likes to point out that he read the *Aeneid* in Latin in high school (as did every Jesuit-trained boy) and that Virgil has been the most important influence in his life. Intellect was prized in the Paterno family. One aunt was an artist; another was the head of a Romance-language department; an uncle was a lawyer; his father, Angelo, graduated from law school at forty and became the clerk of a Brooklyn court. Angelo encouraged debate around the dinner table. This took with Joe, who, his coaches say, likes a good argument. He also likes to listen to opera while diagramming plays, and he has written op-ed articles for the *New York Times*. He once addressed a faculty club on the relationship between football and the *Aeneid*. He told one recruit that he would give him a scholarship if he read a dozen novels over the summer.

When pressed about his intellectual side, however, Paterno gets embarrassed. "Aw, I'm just a dilettante," he said. "I know a little bit about this and that. But after a couple of drinks I'm an expert."

"Happy Valley is for people with values," says Curley, the athletic director. "But it's not for everyone." Which has been Paterno's problem of late: he has had difficulty recruiting players to Happy Valley who either don't share his "values" — discipline, pride, loyalty, honor — or would prefer to formulate their own. For years, Paterno focused on recruiting the kind of hard-nosed, blue-collar ethnic kid that he had once been himself. But the days of Bronko Nagurski and Andy Robustelli dominating college football have given way to a different kind of college football player: speedy black athletes from small towns in the South, often possessed of an independent streak. And, as Korman, the former sports editor at the *Daily Collegian*, puts it, "Penn State didn't recruit individuals."

Yet recruiting is precisely why a lot of people believe Paterno was given his contract extension. For years, other college coaches were telling recruits "that Joe wouldn't be here long," according to McQueary. "And now they're all gone, and Joe's still here." The consensus is that Paterno was given his extension to reassure recruits, although Korman says he thinks that's a non-issue. "Joe's been retiring since the '80s," he says. "The program draws recruits as much as Joe does. I just think it is more about fund-raising than recruiting."

Paterno likens recruiting to getting married. "I tell them that I'm wooing them, telling them how good I am, but not giving them too much because we've got to have a relationship," he says. "Yeah, we missed some kids. I lost a kid recently who wouldn't even visit us. He told me, 'I respect you, but I know what you're about, and I want a different lifestyle.' He was honest; he didn't waste my time. Some kids are turned off by my tight control. Some I don't recruit because I'm just looking for trouble." He pauses. "Where'd the kid go? Miami."

Paterno's references to troublemakers and Miami inevitably evoke the curious and very public case of Willie Williams, the University of Miami recruit whom Spanier described to me as "a criminal" because of his rap sheet of crimes. (He has been convicted of stealing stereo equipment and has pleaded no contest to setting off a fire extinguisher in a Gainesville hotel and to hugging a woman against her will.) Williams is not Penn State material; he doesn't come from the kind of mold that produces the Stepford players Penn State wants. Williams is a youth with sharp edges that need considerable sanding. In a recent memo circulated throughout the university and printed in the *Miami Herald*, Donna Shalala, the Miami president, wrote: "This young man is not perfect and has made some bad decisions. . . . However, he is young, and his file reveals academic talent as well as the better known athletic ability."

One aspect of that athletic ability is exactly what has been lacking in Penn State players for the last few years: speed. "It's tough to convince the fastest players to come here," says McQueary. "The conference is not known for speed." But today's college football game is all about speed. Even Paterno admits that. "It's a wide-open game today," he says. "The grunt 'n' grind days — four yards and a cloud of dust — are over with." Paterno says that the fastest young players today are usually found in southern high schools and usually end up at southern colleges like Miami, Florida State, and Florida, which are known for speed.

"Florida has not been a recruiting hotbed for us," Ganter says. "We haven't put in the effort. If something comes to us — we're looking for them, but maybe our reputation for a conservative offense doesn't appeal to some kids. In today's game, superior players dictate the outcome of a game. Running backs and wide receivers. The darters and jukers. It's not as much about coaching anymore."

Paterno doesn't like to recruit in the South. He prefers Pennsylvania players who fit the Happy Valley mold and not the Willie Williamses of the South. (Fifty-two of the current team's 115 players are from Pennsylvania.) Also, Paterno has become complacent about recruiting: he seems to be waiting for the best players to come knocking on his door, and even then he might not let them in. When Archie Manning, the former NFL quarterback, pleaded with Paterno to recruit his son Peyton, Paterno declined. When Manning pleaded with Paterno to recruit another son, Eli, a few years later, Paterno again declined. Peyton went to Tennessee and is now a superstar in the NFL; Eli went to Mississippi and was selected by the New York Giants as the first pick in this year's draft. Paterno explained his reason for not recruiting either of the Mannings to a Penn State magazine: "I didn't want to waste my time. I knew they'd play in the South."

JoePa is an icon in Happy Valley. When he walks through campus to the house he has lived in for forty years, he says students stop him to ask him to take a picture with them, although lately, he adds, some students are whispering behind his back, "Why doesn't he quit?" In Happy Valley, fans can find life-size cardboard cutouts of JoePa or coffee mugs with his image and the words "Cup of Joe" on them or golf balls that are guaranteed to go down the middle of the fairway three out of four times, like his running backs. There is even a Peachy Paterno ice cream.

JoePa's image in Happy Valley is that of a paternalistic father confessor (Paterno happens to mean "fatherly" in Italian) or of a strict but beloved headmaster. He is beloved in Happy Valley because, as McQueary puts it, "there is only one constant — Joe Paterno." He dresses conservatively, and so do his teams: unadorned navy jerseys and black high-top football shoes that Paterno thinks make his players look "tough." When Penn State once played in the Orange Bowl and the team was told to wear an orange patch on its jerseys, Paterno and his players refused, because to comply would have marred the austere severity of their traditional jerseys. (When Nike approached Paterno and asked him to let his players wear a swoosh in return for a sizable contribution to the school, however, Paterno agreed.)

As befits his old-fashioned image, Paterno is a frugal man. "My father never owned a house," he says. "My wife and I don't spend money. She still washes and irons my clothes. I'm just not a money guy. I have more money than I can spend." Spanier says that until the 1970s Paterno never even had a contract at Penn State, just a letter appointing him to his position. When the media made an issue of it, Spanier says, he gave Joe his extension "to finalize it. We give Joe raises when Curley and I think it's time, but Joe has never asked for a raise. Most of the time, he just gives it back to the school in philanthropy." (Penn State will not disclose Paterno's salary, saying only that it is comparable to that of other top coaches — some of whom earn in the seven figures.)

At practice and during games, Paterno's image as a coach is less benign. In a Big Ten game against Iowa in 2002, Paterno got so frustrated over a referee's call that went against the Nittany Lions that he uncharacteristically chased down the referee after the game. "I'm pretty much scared of him, although he doesn't come off as a tough guy until you get to know him in practice," Zack Mills, the quarterback, says. "It's got to be his way. Last year there was a lot of screaming in practice. He was frustrated because of our losing, and there was more criticism and pointing fingers at Joe and his staff." Paterno once said he didn't care if his players liked him, and another time, in 1972, when a player collapsed with an asthma attack, Paterno called him a baby. But he has tried to change from that hard-nosed coach over the years. "When I got here, Joe was strictly a dictator until he got the program going," Ganter says. "Now he realizes he can't just say, 'Do it,' but rather, 'Do it because. . . .' He's doing a better job communicating."

Whether or not Paterno is communicating better with his players in practice, no one but his players and coaches will ever know, because all of his practices are conducted in secret. No press. No students. No parents. No boosters. "It's the way we always did it," Ganter says. "I don't know any other way. I visited FSU once and saw fifty kids sitting on a hill watching practice. You don't want anyone seeing someone berate a kid and see it in the paper the next day. I don't look at it as secrecy but as tuning out distractions." This despite the fact that Penn State plays most of its games in front of 100,000 screaming distractions on Saturdays.

"The assistant coaches have a gag order not to talk to the media after Media Day," Swart says. "There's so much going on behind the scenes that 90 percent of what people think is conjecture. There's a constant rumor mill about why Joe does things. You don't see in practice why Joe started a player. Then, when Joe is criticized, he says you didn't see what I saw in practice. But he won't let people see what he sees."

*

JoePa showed me around his office. The photographs of his children and grandchildren. The award from the Sons of Italy in Philadelphia. A plaque from the Anti-Defamation League, which his father worked with at times. "He fought against Pancho Villa, you know."

In person, JoePa seems more like his image than he does the hard-nosed coach in practice. He is relaxed, easygoing, and voluble, even about the criticisms that have been directed at him lately.

"Aw, it's mostly the local press," he said. "I don't read the papers. Maybe I haven't delegated as much as I should have. I give my assistants the chance to come up with plays, and I say yes or no."

McQueary says that Paterno is both hands-on and laissez-faire at the same time. "He definitely doesn't overcoach" during a game, McQueary says. "He says, 'Just get 'em lined up and let 'em make a play.'" Which is a good policy when a coach has superior players. When he doesn't, he has to coach more and let his players freelance less.

Paterno admitted that he was lazy last year, maybe the last few years, which is why he has no thought of retiring. "If I thought I'd done a better job, I'd say, 'You had it,'" he said. "But I'm working harder this year than in the last thirty years. I'm spending more time with the coaches, the kids, looking at tape. I'm working my butt off and paying attention to details. Last year I let things fall through the cracks. Kids got away with things, and I didn't get in their faces in practice when I should have. In my mind, I thought it was coming to an end. So I decided to go back to the way I started. I was an SOB when I started, and I'll end up as an SOB."

JoePa looked at his watch and stood up. He said, "If I do everything I can this year and we're not good, I'll say something's missing." He seemed physically incapable of saying the words, "I'll retire."

He walked me toward the door, chitchatting about one of his trips to Prague in the Czech Republic. He told me what a beautiful city it was. How he was amazed that it was still intact after World War II because the Czechs surrendered before the Germans could bomb their beloved Prague into rubble.

"It just goes to show you," Paterno said. "There's something to be said for learning when not to fight."

DAVID DiBENEDETTO

The Biggest Fish Story
Ever Told

FROM MEN'S JOURNAL

I

EVERY ANGLER is haunted by a certain fish. Mine, a redfish I hooked in the surf off a barrier beach in South Carolina, spooled my reel when I was thirteen years old. I can still vividly recall the steady thumps of its powerful body as it swam seaward and the whine of my reel's drag. The fish stopped briefly on its march to deeper water, tilted its head toward the shallow, sandy bottom, and inadvertently waved its massive tail above the surface. It gave me a second of hope — maybe I had turned it! But the redfish picked up speed again, and in less than a minute I watched the last of my line unwind. My rod, now feeling the full force of the fish, bent deeply and the line snapped, its parting marked by a sound similar to the report of a .22 rifle: *pow.* I dropped to my knees and wept, sure that I had lost the fish of a lifetime.

The wound never heals, but I apply salve by telling my story to other fishermen. They understand. And then they relay their own tales. That's what's happening on a small dock near the Susquehanna Flats of the Upper Chesapeake Bay. Albert McReynolds is telling me about his fish. It swims in his dreams and swallows the sinker of his thoughts. Twenty-two years after he hooked the creature, McReynolds still blames it for his gypsy lifestyle and the lack of anyone he can truly call a friend. In fact, McReynolds claims the fish ruined his and his family's lives. The strange thing is, he actually caught the fish.

II

On September 21, 1982, McReynolds met his buddy Pat Erdman for a night of surf fishing. The first day of fall had arrived in blue-bird fashion, but a nor'easter was now pinwheeling toward the coast. Thirty-five-mile-per-hour winds, eight-to-ten-foot swells, and lashing rain were predicted along the Jersey Shore by midnight. After plumbing a few spots without much luck, the two men pulled up to the Vermont Avenue jetty, at the northern end of Atlantic City's fabled boardwalk. The jetty extends roughly twenty-five yards into the ocean and is made up of a jumble of large granite boulders capped with uneven concrete.

As McReynolds and Erdman watched from the beach, large waves roared over the entire structure with a force strong enough to lift a man off his feet and into the sea. But in the water the two fishermen could see thousands of silver flashes. Schools of mullet were rushing along the length of the jetty, their flanks reflecting the light from the Showboat Casino. McReynolds understood that striped bass had the mullet pinned against the rocks and were gorging on them beneath the cauldron of whitewater.

McReynolds and Erdman pushed out as far onto the jetty as they dared and took root. The wind drove rain into their eyes, and sea spray seeped through their foul-weather gear, soaking their heavy sweatshirts. Each time a particularly large wave broke on the rocks the men were inundated with a flood of whitewater swirling up to their knees. When it receded, dozens of five-inch-long mullet were left flopping on the jetty. After a feeble cast into the maelstrom Erdman hooked the first of many nice stripers.

None of them would compare to the giant that swiped McReynolds's lure, a five-and-a-half-inch black and silver Rebel swimming plug, at 10:00 P.M. The fish opened its mouth just beneath the lure, creating a hole on the sea's surface. "It looked like someone pulled the plug on a bathtub," says McReynolds. Then the fish's head rose above the foam-streaked sea, the lure resting crosswise in its mouth. For a second or two the striper seemed to be "looking dead at us," says Erdman. "It was really strange. Then it just sank straight back, tail first, like a submarine. It was the only striper I've ever seen that didn't turn and run." McReynolds reared back, driving the treble hooks into the fish's mouth. The striper responded by ripping 150 yards of 20-pound test line from his reel. The striped bass fight of the century was on.

The battle began as a one-sided affair. The fish used its enormous size to bully McReynolds and his fairly light tackle. The rod was bent to the handle as the wind blew a haunting whistle across the tight line. More than once McReynolds looked down to see that he had just a few feet of line left on his reel, so he applied as much pressure as he dared, tempting the line to break, and turned the fish. "My back was aching and my forearms were locked," he says. "I was just praying to God that I would get a look at the fish." The struggle raged, each participant giving and taking, for an hour and twenty minutes before the striper finally surfaced on its side. Now McReynolds had to step down into the raging water to recover the beast. It's a tricky endeavor when the weather is calm, requiring the agility of a sandpiper. When the weather is sloppy it can be deadly.

McReynolds brought the fish in close to the rocks, timing his move with the passing swells, swung at it with a small hand gaff, and missed. As he readied for another shot he lost his footing and slid down the slime-coated rocks into the water. When he surfaced the behemoth was floating in front of him. "She was opening her gills, so I stuck my fist under the gill plate, and I bear-hugged her," says McReynolds. "Then Pat came down and dragged me up by the hood of my sweatshirt."

McReynolds literally collapsed on the jetty next to his fish while Erdman shouted congratulations. Then, above the roar of the breaking surf and the howling wind, the striper's sides heaved, and it seemed to exhale in a loud whoosh. Neither of the fishermen had ever heard a fish do anything like that. But it did it again and again. Soon the men were staring wide-eyed at their quarry, not sure they had even caught a fish but possibly a sea monster in the shape of a striper.

III

Reluctant to leave the fish biting, the two men put a blanket over the catch, strapped it to the hood of Erdman's car, and continued fishing. Only as dawn approached did they head over to Corky Campbell's tackle shop for the start of business hours. On the way, a cop pulled them over.

"What's on the hood, guys?" he asked through the window.

"A body," said McReynolds, leaning over from the passenger side.

"Oh, it's you, Albert. Go ahead. Must be a nice fish."

At Campbell's the sun was just casting light on the scene when the fish was carted to the scale. The three men had seen plenty of big striped bass, but nothing like this. Campbell phoned a few witnesses to attend the weighing, and the men waited, sipping coffee and struggling to comprehend the size of the animal in front of them. Once on the scale, the striper blew away all of their estimates. The scale's wildly bouncing arm finally stopped at 78.5 pounds. McReynolds's fish weighed two and a half pounds more than the reigning world record. That fish had been landed a year earlier by an angler using heavy tackle from a boat off Montauk, New York, the mecca of striper fishing. McReynolds landed his fish on light tackle during one of the year's worst nor'easters from a nearly featureless stretch of beach better known for winos and floating syringes.

The tackle shop was just off the highway, and a crowd quickly formed. As word spread, the shop received twenty-five calls an hour, some from as far away as Europe and Australia. "It became a huge party," says McReynolds. "People were pouring cans of Budweiser on my head and lighting cigarettes in my mouth." By the afternoon 1,500 people had visited the shop. Some, like worshipers at the Western Wall, touched the fish reverently. Many speculated about its live weight — its mass immediately after it was removed from the surf. Like a water balloon with a leak, a fish on land loses weight fairly rapidly. Most agreed that the striper would have pushed 82 or 83 pounds if it had been weighed just after it had been caught.

The heaviest striper ever captured reportedly pushed 125 pounds. It was snared in a net near Edenton, North Carolina, in 1891. Another, rumored to weigh 86 pounds, was landed on a rod and reel in 1897. Both specimens, however, lack official documentation. If those estimates are accurate, nothing within even a dozen pounds of the lesser of the pair was officially recorded until a two-year run starting in 1980.

The first of the modern heavyweights to fall was John Baldino's 71-pound striper caught off Norwalk, Connecticut, in July 1980.

Almost exactly a year later, Bob Rocchetta hammered a 76-pounder on a live eel while fishing the rips around Montauk. Tony Stezko's 73-pound striper, hauled from the Cape Cod surf in November 1981, was next. Then came McReynolds's pièce de résistance.

The giant fish were all born in the early 1950s, a period of optimal spawning conditions in the stripers' primary East Coast breeding ground, Chesapeake Bay. "The extraordinary number of fish born in those years meant that there were more chances for a Shaquille O'Neal," says Gary Shepherd, a research biologist with the National Oceanographic and Atmospheric Administration. Fishing pressure in the '50s was also fairly light, meaning those genetic mutants had a clearer shot at reaching maturity. During the late '60s and '70s they were strapping enough to survive the pollution that decimated many of their offspring, and, amid the diminished competition for food, they grew even bigger. By the early '80s, with fishing regulations still lenient, anglers were stacking enormous stripers on docks and beaches like cordwood. But large fish form the backbone of the breeding stock, and as these fish were weeded out so were their contributions of billions of eggs each spring. By the night McReynolds dropped his line into the roiling New Jersey surf, the species was on the verge of collapse. Though he could hardly have known it at the time, it was the high-water mark for a Greatest Generation of fish, the likes of which hadn't been seen in one hundred years, and may never be again.

The party at Campbell's was still rocking when Nelson Bryant from the *New York Times* called to tell McReynolds he could be eligible to win $250,000 in a sweepstakes run by Abu-Garcia, a tackle manufacturer. The rules stated that the first person to catch a world-record striper, salmon, or largemouth bass in 1982 would win. Even Campbell would receive $25,000, for weighing the fish.

A few days later Edward Keating, a sports agent who worked with Dick Butkus and Arnold Palmer, phoned to offer his services. According to McReynolds, there was also a call from a lawyer representing a posh hunting lodge. The owner of the lodge was willing to match the $250,000 in exchange for the skin mount of the fish. Campbell took out a $100,000 insurance policy on the striper and locked it in his bait freezer.

IV

Albert McReynolds was born in 1946 — as it happens, just a few years before his fish. He gravitated to the sea at an early age and, by his own admission, his proclivity toward fishing made him the smelliest kid in class. At seven years old he was selling minnows to bait shops; by nine he was waking at 3:00 A.M. to bait tubs of cod hooks for commercial fishermen before school; at ten he was working on a charter fishing boat, where he once hooked a giant sea turtle. He was offered $500 for the catch and he accepted. By then a pattern had been set: toss a hook in the sea and pull out money. "I've always had a relationship with the sea," says McReynolds. He dropped out of school at age thirteen (without learning to read or write) when a bunk opened on a commercial scallop boat out of New Bedford, Massachusetts. His education would come on the decks of fishing boats and at the hands of old salts'who whiled away hours patching holes in nets. By all accounts he had an otherworldly talent for finding and catching fish.

As McReynolds matured he also found work as an Atlantic City lifeguard and joined the Teamsters, who were building casinos around the fading former resort town. McReynolds eventually married and had three children, but he had the reputation of a hard-partying man. Before the catch the family lived day-to-day, bouncing from one cheap motel to the next, followed by a growing mound of debt. His big striper seemed like a gift from Poseidon himself, but within a few days he was being dogged by those who believed he had lied about its capture.

An anonymous letter had been sent to the International Game Fish Association claiming that McReynolds and Erdman had found the fish floating in the surf. The letter, typed on an Atlantic City postcard, also claimed that McReynolds was under investigation for welfare fraud and had cheated in past fishing contests. Others suggested that he had been given the striper by one of his commercial cohorts who had caught it in a net. Surf fishermen on the Jersey coast who had been out the night of the catch argued that there was no way McReynolds could have set foot on the jetty, much less landed a fish from it. The whole story just seemed, well, fishy.

The investigation included a review of photographs taken at the weigh-in and intense interviews of those close to McReynolds. Though the IGFA didn't require it, McReynolds and Campbell brought the fish to a local radiologist's office to prove it had not been stuffed with extra weight. (Although the fish was certainly a female, the radiology report listed it as "Bert Bass.") Four months later the association certified the catch.

Not long afterward, McReynolds was escorted to New York City in a limousine, and at a lavish awards ceremony at the Explorers Club, amid busts of Admirals Peary and Byrd and a twelve-foot-tall stuffed grizzly, he was presented the $250,000. As he stood on the podium next to a giant cardboard check, with spotlights from news cameras blinding his vision, McReynolds's life seemed on the verge of a major sea change. The fish's worth, including endorsement deals from tackle companies, was estimated at nearly $3,200 a pound. The *Guinness Book of World Records* listed it as the world's most valuable game fish.

McReynolds told the crowd his first purchase would be a "good secondhand car," and he planned to set up a trust fund for his children. But first there was a celebration to be had. The next day McReynolds withdrew $10,000. "We didn't see him for three weeks," says Corky Campbell. "He was buying steaks and chops. It was the biggest party around." He also wrote a check to Pat Erdman for $10,000.

Keating, the sports agent, had agreed to manage the funds and was pursuing endorsement deals. He set his sights on Wheaties. There seemed to be no reason why McReynolds couldn't be the first fisherman to grace a cereal box. For more than a month McReynolds's mug was plastered on magazines and newspapers. The governor of New Jersey sent him a letter of congratulations. In no time he was a regular guest on the sports banquet circuit, rubbing elbows with Joe Dimaggio, Ted Williams, and Burt Reynolds. He was the most famous fisherman in the country.

Wearing the laurel wreath of world-record-holder, however, soon felt more like a crown of thorns to McReynolds. Hate mail from anglers flooded in. "I had people write me saying I had devastated the future of the striped bass, and others still claiming I found the fish dead," says McReynolds. He became mired in squabbles over money. To escape the brouhaha he and his family spent time in Cape Cod, Florida, and Hawaii, but they eventually returned to Atlantic City. There was no warm homecoming. He couldn't even find work. "Everyone acted like I was a rich guy," he says.

Fishing was the only constant in his life, so McReynolds loaded his wife and kids in the car and began an angling odyssey that continues to this day. When I caught up with the family they had just begun to follow the striped bass migration up the coast. It would take them all way to Maine, where they would spend most of the summer and then turn around and follow the fish south. When the stripers stopped at their wintering grounds off North Carolina the family would continue along the coast to Texas, pursuing whatever game fish swam within casting distance of shore. McReynolds's daughter left the backseat when she married a guy from the Midwest, but his wife Karen and two sons, Al Jr., twenty-four, and Tom, twenty-two, still travel with him.

When I met McReynolds he stretched out his hand: "Albert McReynolds, world-record-holder of the striped bass." I had seen only one photo of him and it had been twenty years old. He had not aged gracefully. His body was stooped and he was missing most of his front teeth. Life on the road, I imagined, was not easy.

The family was traveling in a used Chevy Suburban that was loaded with rods and nets; a large bait tank, the type you normally see bolted to the transom of giant sportfishing boats, occupied most of the truck's rear storage space. Like jousting lances, half a dozen rods stretched toward the front seat, and numerous tackle boxes were stashed here and there. The sagging ceiling felt was pinned to the roof with an assortment of thumbtacks, giving the impression that you were looking up at one of those fishing nets that hang from the ceilings of cheap seafood restaurants.

For the McReynoldses, each day is a carbon copy of the one before. The four of them wake in a single hotel room, grab breakfast at the nearest fast-food restaurant, and go fishing. McReynolds says his pension plan from his lifeguard days provides the family with some money; selling bait and winning local tournaments generates a few dollars more. I'd been told by someone who knew him that stopping at churches to beg for money was a third source of income. Al Jr. and Tom claim they enjoy an idyllic lifestyle, but they have never been properly schooled, and life on the move has left them with no friends. It would seem their future is as bleak as their father's.

In the two decades since McReynolds pulled up to Corky Campbell's tackle shop with his fish on the hood, he has seen his fortunes skyrocket and as abruptly spiral into a tailspin. It's the spiral that gets to him. "When you break a world record, your feet leave the ground and you're on cloud nine with your achievement. You don't think people are going to be cruel or nasty or thieves. You're leading with good faith, and you expect them to. It doesn't work out that way. When money enters into it, it changes everything. We have family that refuses us for holidays. People that I thought were my best buddies tell us they have other plans when we visit."

McReynolds went through the last of the more than a quarter of a million dollars from the tackle company and various endorsement deals years ago. As for the other offer of $250,000 from the hunting lodge, McReynolds says it was rescinded after Corky Campbell told him eight months after the catch that he had thrown the fish away because it had freezer burn. McReynolds claims that when he pressed Campbell on the topic a few weeks later, suspicious that his fish had been sold, not tossed in the garbage, Campbell showed him his gun.

Still, even that was less galling to McReynolds than the way he has become a pariah along the Striper Coast. "I was at a bar in Maine once when a guy started talking striped bass. I said, 'Hey, man. I'm the world-record-holder.' He says, 'I know who you are, and you're a goddamn liar. If you open your mouth again I'll break your jaw.' I bowed out politely and left. That stuff happens all the time."

When I asked McReynolds about all those who say it was too rough that night to fish from a jetty, he threw up his hands. "It was rough, and I did get washed off. But the idea that you couldn't fish the jetty is just bullshit. Of course you're not gonna go out where a big mama is gonna break on your head and put you through the rocks. We just went out far enough to cast into the wash behind the waves. It's no big deal if the tidal surge breaks on your knees. I grew up on Vermont Avenue and worked as a lifeguard there. I knew that jetty better than anyone."

He took a deep breath; I could tell it wasn't the first time he had answered the question. "You know," he said, "I was just doing something I loved. I can't read or write, but if I could I'd publish a book called *The Night I Hooked the Devil.*"

V

Corky Campbell has a less sympathetic view of McReynolds's situation. That may have something to do with the fact that McReynolds has sued him numerous times. Ever since Campbell reported that the fish had been ruined by freezer burn McReynolds has insisted he's owed the $100,000 from Campbell's insurance policy. All of the suits have been dismissed.

When I showed up unannounced at Campbell's current place of business, a marine repair shop in Somers Point, New Jersey, his wife told me to leave a card and maybe he would call me back. As I loitered by a rack of antifouling paint, Campbell, dressed in a blue jumpsuit, eventually appeared, holding a large binder. "It's all here. The whole story," he said. "Take as long as you'd like, but I don't have time to talk." The binder contained newspaper clippings of the catch, phone-call logs for McReynolds, contracts with Rebel lures, a copy of the anonymous postcard the IGFA received, the salvo of letters McReynolds's lawyers fired at Campbell, and much, much more. I was reading a copy of a letter from the agent Keating to McReynolds, threatening that their partnership would end if the "impetuous spending" didn't stop, when Campbell came back in the shop and to my surprise asked if I had any questions.

I started with the gun. "Let's just say there's a lot of revisionist history going on here," he said.

"Well, do you think this fish ruined McReynolds's life?" I asked.

"How can you ruin something that doesn't exist? He didn't have a life before this fish. It was an opportunity squandered. Maybe he had the wrong people leading him. But even if he had the right people I'm not sure he could have been led. It's like trying to manage Mike Tyson professionally."

Campbell's reaction was like so many I heard in the course of my reporting: McReynolds was a bum who blew a shot at fame and fortune. But did he? Could he have milked a single fish for a lifetime of opportunity? And if so, why the vitriol? Professional athletes crash harder than McReynolds every year. To this day, no one denies that McReynolds is a great fisherman, which is all he has ever aspired to be.

There is only one thing to do: go see the fish. Although the actual carcass is apparently by now completely decomposed in a New Jersey landfill, four foam mounts were made before Campbell cleaned out his freezer: one for Campbell, one for Rebel Lures, one for McReynolds, and one for the taxidermist. The taxidermist subsequently donated his to the obscure Marine Mammal Stranding Center's Sea Life Museum in Brigantine, New Jersey, where it still hangs. McReynolds donated his to the recently closed Gene's Beach Bar, four blocks away from the museum, to settle a bar tab. (Or so I've been told.)

It was at its perch in the bar that I first laid eyes on the fish. The Beach Bar is a low-slung structure just off the ocean, and the striper was hanging by the door in a backlit glass case. It was like that moment toward the end of *Boogie Nights* when the Mark Wahlberg character finally drops his pants for the camera. I'd heard how big this fish was, but I wasn't prepared for it up close. It struck a classic fish pose, bent in a slight U shape, fins erect, mouth agape. You could have almost stuffed a volleyball in the opening, and its girth, thirty-four inches, was the same as my own waist. Its tail was as wide as a straw broom. Its stripes, bold swaths of black and silver at the front, were mere pixelated dots toward the middle, as if they had been unable to stretch over the fish's entire body. Surrounding the fish were a few faded photos of McReynolds hoisting it up by the gill plate. The striper was nearly as long as McReynolds was tall.

Standing there as patrons filed past, eager to grab a beer, it seemed strange that this fish had been relegated to a dim bar where classic rock blared on the jukebox. The chaos it had created continued to swirl through people's lives twenty-two years later. Now I could understand why. This wasn't just a fish: this was the culmination of thousands of years of evolution, survival instinct, extraordinary genetics, and a whole lot of luck, both very good and very, very bad.

Late that afternoon the wind intensified to twenty-five knots out of the northeast. I decided to drive to the Vermont Avenue jetty, curious to see it in conditions that matched those that McReynolds had braved. From behind a dune I could hear a *whomp* as each wave met the end of the jetty. Two surfers scurried past with the hoods on their sweatshirts cinched tight. They had wisely left their boards on the roof of their truck. On the beach I watched as seven-footers rolled almost the entire length of the jetty, the surf zone a riot of whitewater. It would have been dangerous to drop a line in the foam — but not impossible. As a wave receded I focused my eyes on the approximate spot where two natural forces — fisherman and fish — are said to have met, and, as if played out on an ancient Greek stage with an ominous storm-tossed sea as the backdrop, brought each other down.

ANDREW MILLER

Field of Broken Dreams

FROM THE PITCH

To FIND the best baseball story in Missouri, you must drive roughly six hours southeast from Kauffman Stadium, where a struggling team sheds salary, or three hours south from the home of the St. Louis Cardinals, whose first-place run has galvanized the game's self-described best fans.

After a numbing stretch of highway billboards for historic downtowns and quaint, country-cooking eateries ("home of the throwed rolls" — *thrown* would be too city-slicker), you'll reach Wardell, population 258. There, tastefully appointed trailers, generously spaced among fields of cotton, soybeans, and rice, share rural territory with rusty, corrugated-tin-roof shacks.

And you'll find Wardell's most accomplished resident, onetime major league outfielder Jeff Stone.

Living in a tidy brick house next to the trailer owned by his twin brother, Jerome, Stone hasn't exactly come full circle. That would mean sharing space with fifteen other inhabitants of a four-room house with no running water (the family pumped it by hand), no heat (they chopped trees for fireplace fuel), little furniture, no indoor plumbing (they used an outhouse, checking carefully for snakes), and cracks in the splintered hardwood floor that offered glimpses at the underlying dirt.

Now Stone lives in comfort, thanks to savings from the relatively modest salaries he earned during his eight-year major league career (he never made more than $160,000 a year) and his twelve-hour shifts as an inspector at a steel mill in Blytheville, Arkansas. He has fulfilled the promise he made to himself as a teenager, when he worked ten-hour days chopping cotton for food money and played American Legion baseball at night before coming home to share a bed with four, sometimes five brothers: "I ain't going to live like this."

But it took more than financial security to ensure Stone's peace. For years, he couldn't watch baseball, couldn't keep in touch with his teammates or discuss his playing days with the curious children who waited outside his house to hear about what it was like to play with Pete Rose, Mike Schmidt, Cal Ripken, Ozzie Smith, and Roger Clemens.

"I felt really angry," Stone says in a soft-spoken drawl. "I didn't want anything to do with baseball. This was the only place I could get the game out of my system."

Now, after a significant stretch of silence, Stone is ready to tell his story. He's willing to relive a period of his life dominated by the oppressive frustration of unfulfilled potential and perceived injustice. He has been haunted for years, but he's finally free of the specter.

An elderly desk clerk at a motel in Portageville, fifteen miles north of Wardell, isn't sure why her establishment is called the New Orleans Inn. The decorations strewn across the lobby are vaguely Bayou-themed but offer no additional clues. She is, however, familiar with the entire population of the neighboring city, her hometown.

"Who are you here to see?" she asks. "Jeff and Jerome? I know them. Black boys."

She says it matter-of-factly. It's the same tone of voice that Stone family friend Jeff Baldwin later uses to deliver a Jimmy the Greek–style diatribe about the twins' speed.

"I couldn't believe they were that quick," Baldwin says as he reaches out from his reclining chair and pats Jerome on the back affectionately. "I know you black fellers are quick because you've got all those extra muscles, but you ain't that black."

Such insensitive remarks don't rattle Jerome, a jovial five-foot-six-inch high school coach with an easy smile and a loud laugh. "There was no racism, nothing like that at all," Jerome says as he steers his Ford Explorer out of Baldwin's driveway and onto Wardell's lone thoroughfare. "Around here, everybody knows everybody. Everybody likes everybody," he says as he cruises past a mobile home with a massive Confederate flag covering its windows.

Jeff and Jerome Stone were born in Wardell the day after a

muted Christmas celebration in 1960. They started playing sandlot ball at an early age, tossing each other rocks from the road and hitting them with a broomstick. When they weren't working in the cotton fields, they'd practice for hours, with only a daily can of pork and beans as fuel.

The brothers learned discipline at an early age. Lee and Eliza Stone ran a strict household, sometimes enforcing rules with a belt. Lee had a sixth-grade education, but he knew how to fix the family's pickup truck, which would haul the nine brothers and six sisters to games.

"He had common sense," Jeff says. "They raised us good."

By high school, Jeff was attracting attention as a pitcher with a ninety-mile-an-hour fastball, but his career path changed when two Philadelphia Phillies scouts came to visit. Stopwatches in hand, they saw Jeff and Jerome dash through a plowed cornfield. Both high school juniors were wearing cleats — and blue jeans. Still, they posted times comparable to college sprinters, with Jerome running one second behind his lankier brother.

Players with superhuman speed are much rarer than high-velocity hurlers, so Jeff moved from the pitcher's mound to the outfield, where he could track down anything within an acre. He signed his contract on a family friend's kitchen counter, with his father watching over his shoulder. "Son, I might not be here when you get back," Lee told him. Those were Lee's last words to Jeff, who was playing for a minor league team in Bend, Oregon, when Lee died later that summer.

This type of down-home transaction, a father and son negotiating a modest bonus in a country kitchen, couldn't happen today, even in Wardell. DirecTV satellite dishes protrude from the roofs of even the most humble dwellings. Agents use Internet scouting services to track down promising prospects, regardless of where they are.

"The whole world is more sophisticated now because of the communications media," says Phillies scout Jerry Lafferty. "But we're still looking for athletes like Jeff Stone and developing them. Boy, if I could find another Jeff Stone, that would be great."

Jeff's story serves as inspiration for gifted athletes in small towns throughout the region, from Belton to Boonville to Braggadocio. If someone found Jeff Stone twenty-five years ago, without cell-phone tips or e-mail leads, someone can definitely discover the next Jeff Stone now.

"I want to show kids that you can make it in this area," Jeff says. "I hope I made a big impression."

He made a huge impression on the Phillies within his first few years in the minor league system. He was Player of the Month in August 1981, an All-Star in 1982, and Player of the Year in 1983. He stole more than 90 bases in three consecutive seasons, including a then-record 123. He struck out a lot, but when he made contact, he had a decent chance to make it on base safely, even when he just grounded a lazy roller into a fielder's glove.

The ballparks got bigger, but in Jeff's eyes, the pitches still seemed like chunks of gravel, the base paths stretches of clear-cut farmland.

For a while, he made it look easy in the big leagues too.

In his first major league start, Jeff Stone had three hits in four times at bat, including two triples. In his first twelve games in the big leagues, he had ten multi-hit showings. He hit .362 and stole twenty-seven bases in 1984, his rookie year.

Stone had some difficulty adjusting to the City of Brotherly Love, though. People he encountered on the street were often rude, and the steady symphony of horns, screeches, and clatter tested his nerves. He kept to himself, staying inside his room whenever possible.

But baseball stayed simple, thanks to Phillies manager Paul Owens's minimalist approach.

"Certain players you don't fool with, and Stonie was one of them," Owens told *Sports Illustrated* in 1992. (Owens died in December 2003.) "My advice to Stonie was, 'You see the ball, you hit it and you run.' And he said, 'That makes sense.'"

Prior to the 1985 season, the Phillies printed posters with Stone's face on them, put him on the cover of the team's calendar, and built a public relations campaign announcing the beginning of the "Stone Age."

But it was the Owens era that proved more significant for Stone. When the grandfatherly figure moved into the team's front office, the Phillies replaced him with monotone crank John Felske, whose caustic criticism immediately eroded Stone's confidence.

Suddenly, see-hit-run wasn't good enough at bat, and sprint-to-wherever-it's-hit wouldn't fly in the field. There were strategies and statistics to memorize, pickoff moves and outfield positioning shifts to learn. Even when he was a pitcher back in high school, Stone hadn't worked with signs; Jerome had been his catcher, and the two simply tossed the ball back and forth as if they were at home. But baseball wasn't a primal process anymore. It was a complicated, almost academic pursuit, and Stone wasn't a quick study.

"When they started messing with him, he started thinking," Owens told *Sports Illustrated*. "And he wound up getting so confused, he forgot how to play."

"To be honest, he couldn't absorb a lot of instruction," adds Phillies chairman Bill Giles, who was the team's president at the time. "A lot of other coaches and managers tried to make him more than he was capable of being, and then they decided he didn't have the ability to learn," Giles tells *The Pitch*.

After his auspicious debut, Stone had made several cameo appearances in the pages of national publications. For the most part, writers cast him as an endearingly baffled bumpkin, usually in the form of the tall tales known as "Stonie stories."

For example, during a minor league night game (the location varies by publication), he allegedly asked, "Is this the same moon that shines back home?" Asked once if he wanted a shrimp cocktail before dinner, Stone reportedly replied, "I don't drink." Another time, after a season of winter baseball in Venezuela, someone asked Stone why he wasn't taking his television back to the States. He supposedly responded, "It only gets Spanish stations."

These tales, all of which originated in his first year, endeared him to fans as well as to the press. But they also reinforced for Felske and others within the organization that Stone might be too dim to become a star.

In 1985, he went hitless on opening day and never fully recovered. By the end of opening week, he had become a platoon player, starting only against right-handed pitchers. By the end of the month, he was stuck on the bench.

"No matter what I did, it wasn't good enough," Stone says of this nightmare season. "If Felske had left me alone and left me in the lineup, I would have become the player I should have become."

Stone's inability to shake his slump gnawed at him during sleepless nights in the Voorhees, New Jersey, condo where he stayed during the season. He grew paranoid, wondering if the next strikeout or unsuccessful stolen-base attempt would get him shipped out of town. Sweat soaked his sheets. His insomnia spurred one of the few genuine Stonie stories: on one road trip, teammates advised him to start counting sheep — to which he responded, "They don't have sheep in Pittsburgh."

By midsummer, he was back in Portland, Maine, enduring the epic bus rides that mark minor league life.

As he bounced back and forth from the Phillies to its farm team over the next two seasons, Stone kept quiet. He didn't want to be branded as a less-than-established player with a bad attitude.

"I kept a lot of stuff inside," Stone says now. "I didn't make no waves. I was very naive. That was my downfall. I trusted a lot of people."

Stone reached his lowest point in 1988, when the Phillies traded him to the Baltimore Orioles. The profoundly awful Orioles started 0–21; Stone had one hit in thirty-two at-bats.

Eager to please, Stone overcompensated on the rare occasions he did get a hit. This led to several base-running blunders. He killed a rally in one game by getting thrown out going from first to third on a grounder, a brazen risk even for someone so swift. In another unprecedented display of recklessness, Stone was thrown out once at every base in the same game. He was still sprinting, but it was as if he were in a corn maze.

He headed to that team's minor league affiliate in Rochester, New York, to rehabilitate an injured thumb. He never returned to the big team.

When someone asked then-manager Frank Robinson if Stone had been playing hurt, Robinson replied, "I sure hope so."

"He was a negative person," Stone says today. His earnest expression makes Robinson's cutting comment seem unbearably cruel, like a yank on a friendly puppy's tail.

"When a young player has a stretch at the start of his career like Stone had, the question you ask yourself is whether he is genuinely outstanding or whether he is just an ordinary, regular player who played over his head," says Bill James, baseball writer and historian. "Not often does a young player take one step back after another after another. This was what was unusual about Stone's career."

What makes Stone's tale tragic is the likelihood that he was "genuinely outstanding," that, with proper handling, he could have become an amazing player. His rapid descent shattered a romantic baseball illusion, the notion of a backwoods Johnny B. Goode who could swing a bat like he was ringing a bell even as he gawked in wide-eyed wonder at the world outside the diamond.

In the big leagues, such batter savants have a short shelf life. Teams make adjustments, and ability becomes secondary to adaptation. Here was a player who could still outrun all of his teammates and put wood on every batting-practice offering. He competed with inexhaustible abandon during games, as if he were playing a faster-paced sport. Yet he was unable to translate this talent and hard work into something tangible that could keep him in a starting lineup — or even off the waiver wire. When Baltimore and Texas released him during the same calendar year, Stone's corroding career seemed to have come to an indignant end.

Stone had always been a player with flair. He was a fan favorite in Philadelphia because he'd slide into first base during close-call plays or dive in pursuit of balls that were clearly out of his reach. Both approaches might have hurt the team more than they helped, but spectators can always overlook errors born out of irrepressible effort.

Managers aren't nearly as forgiving.

Giles recalls Felske saying, "[Stone is] a fun player to watch, and he can hit some, but you're not going to win a pennant with him playing."

Up until 1990, Stone hadn't had a chance to prove Felske wrong, because he had suited up for exclusively dismal teams. The Boston Red Sox, a solid contender, picked him up that fall. But though he welcomed the opportunity to play in games that could lead to postseason action, his first impression of the city wasn't promising. While he was checking into his hotel, someone stole his Jeep Cherokee, which was filled with all of his possessions, from the parking lot. His introduction to the Red Sox wasn't much better. For a month, he failed to log an at-bat, appearing as a pinch runner without a single steal.

On September 28, 1990, the Red Sox were tied with the Toronto Blue Jays for first place in the American League East. Playing in front of a national television audience — and its largest home crowd in twelve years — the Sox fumbled a 4–0 lead late in the game, then blew a 5–4 lead in the ninth inning. In the bottom of the ninth inning, with the score tied, the Red Sox loaded the bases with one out.

Up stepped Stone.

Blue Jays closer Tom Henke, a fireball dispenser with thick glasses, stared into the on-deck circle, expecting the inevitable announcement of a pinch hitter. Stone peeked back into the dugout, waiting to see who would take his place during the most meaningful at-bat of his career. Manager Joe Morgan waved him into the batting box.

Stone fouled off the first pitch.

He drilled the next one into the outfield, scoring the season-saving run and triggering a massive ovation.

Finally, Stone was, as *Sports Illustrated* had first dubbed him in 1984, "The Natural." He was Roy Hobbs blasting a shot into the scoreboard.

"I'm on cloud ten," Stone gushed after the game. This became an instant Stonie story, with some sources inflating the quote to "cloud eleven" by the time it ran the next day. The *Boston Globe* offered poetic praise: "Stone is one of the last of the innocents, trying to make a name in this graceless age."

When Boston released the last of the innocents in November and failed to invite him to spring training the next year, Stone was shocked. Red Sox fans were still sending him videotapes of his game-winning heroics. But the team itself had forgotten him, deeming the thirty-one-year-old too old to fit into its future plans. To management, Stone's pennant-race contribution was a fluke, a lucky hit from a legendarily luckless player.

Stone returned to Wardell to wait for a call that never came. He settled into a house he had bought the year before and seldom ventured outside its doors. There was no baseball memorabilia surrounding him; the only reminder of his star-crossed career was persistent fan mail from the still-grateful Red Sox faithful.

Stone was paralyzed with regret and anger.

Coming to terms with involuntary retirement from his dream profession, Stone moved on to his secondary childhood obsession and signed on as a police officer in nearby Caruthersville for $16,500 a year.

The job turned out to be more trying than he'd expected. Unlike placid Wardell, some Pemiscot County towns have pervasive crime problems. A quarter of its residents live below the poverty line. Areas of Hayti, a tiny town ten miles down the highway, look as bleak as city slums. Stone found himself regularly dodging bullets — including sixteen on his last day on duty, when he and his partner were ambushed.

"It's nothing to get shot over," Stone says of his law enforcement efforts. "The best thing about that job? Leaving it."

Stone found a more suitable, if still stressful, occupation in late 1994, when the erstwhile man of steal became a man of steel at the Nucor-Yamato mill in Blytheville, Arkansas. He worked on a loading dock without breaks at the non-union job until he moved up from the shipping department to an inspector position. His twelve-hour shifts saw him coming or going at 3:00 or 4:00 A.M.

But he still wasn't through with baseball.

In 1995, the Phillies' Giles called Stone and asked him to attend spring training as part of the replacement roster the team was assembling in case of a seasonlong strike. He initially declined, but he reconsidered after a conversation with his former coach and hometown mentor, Bob McCulloch. "Give it your best shot," McCulloch had urged one evening. Later that night, McCulloch had a stroke. He died two days later, at age sixty-one.

Stone decided to make the trip to Florida, using his three weeks of paid vacation from the plant. "I wasn't doing it to hurt the players' union," he says. "I was doing it for Bob."

Stone was thirty-four. It had been two years since he'd thrown a ball or swung a bat. The first time he stepped to the plate, he narrowly dodged a pitch that bore in on his head.

"I guess that's 'Welcome back to baseball,'" he grumbled to reporters in the clubhouse after the game. "I shoulda stayed home."

Instead, Stone stayed put and hit well. He kept an anxious eye on labor developments and became uneasy when the replacement players remained active just days before the season was scheduled to start.

"I felt awkward," he recalls. "I wanted them to settle so I wouldn't have to do anything wrong. My baseball days were over. I just wanted a vacation."

While Stone felt a sense of loyalty to the Major League Baseball

Players Association, his Wardell roots prevented him from bemoaning the plight of big-money ballplayers. He never criticized the strikers directly, but he did blast a replacement player who dared to demand a raise.

"I read where that guy was griping about his salary, and that made me mad," Stone told the *Philadelphia Inquirer.* "Guys like that ought to try picking cotton, like I did when I was coming up. See how they like that."

When the regular players returned, Stone was ready to go back to work. "I want to get out of here," he told the *Orlando Sentinel.* "I'm tired of Florida."

No longer did Stone love baseball enough to play it anywhere under any conditions. He declined offers for minor league contracts. It was finally time for him to leave the game behind.

But even back home in Wardell, peace has been hard to find. Stone, forty-three, now walks with a slight limp, the result of a car accident in 2001 — another driver ran the only traffic light in town and hit Stone's Cherokee head-on. Stone suffered a broken hip (it's held together by a corrective metal rod) and a shattered ankle.

And his upper body is scattered with scars, the aftermath of a 2002 argument in which his wife, Linda, stabbed him several times, puncturing his lung.

The two had married just a year earlier. Getting married at age forty-one was "weird," Stone says. "I was so set in my ways."

Stone didn't press charges; he and Linda remain together. "It was a situation that got out of hand, and we both lost our tempers," he says, declining to elaborate on the cause of the argument. "Maybe she went too far. If you love someone, you forgive them."

Stone always seems willing to offer the benefit of the doubt, to assume that even the most outlandish attack might have been justified. He is a trusting, generous man, qualities that don't necessarily serve athletes well in professional sports. Grizzled baseball writers invariably described Stone as "sweet." Even in a harsh piece that criticized Stone's strikebreaker status in 1995, the *Philadelphia Daily News* described him as "one of the most unaffected people on the planet."

"Jeff is really a special memory," Giles tells *The Pitch.* "I've probably met three thousand ballplayers in my life, and there hasn't been any like him. You think about 'loving' and 'sweet' all the time, and it's strange to do that with a man, but that's the way everybody feels about him."

"People thought he was dumb, but he wasn't," Paul Owens told *Sports Illustrated* in 1992. "He was naive, but beautifully naive."

Beautiful naïveté might be an appealing personality trait, but it's a decided disadvantage in a business with scant sentiment. In professional baseball, sometimes there is no buffer zone between achievement and disappointment.

Jerome Stone stands on the pitcher's mound at North Pemiscot High School. He's still in athletic shape, occasional asthmatic wheeze aside, and he delights in bringing his young hurlers back to earth by blasting their best shots during batting practice. It's refreshing to remind locals that he too was once a highly regarded prospect.

"People tell me, 'I played against your brother in high school,'" Jerome says. "I say, 'Dummy, you played against me too, because we're twins.' They remember Jeff, not me. I would get asked ten to fifteen times a day, 'How's your brother?' After a while, you get tired."

Jerome played for four years at Arkansas State. Signed as an undrafted free agent, he played in the Phillies minor league system, then played professionally in Mexico. Unable to communicate with his Spanish-speaking teammates, Jerome would remain completely silent during bus trips that sometimes lasted more than two days. He learned quickly not to drink the local water or take chances on indecipherable menus, lest he again sample cow tongue or an entire fish with head and eyes intact.

"He would call home crying," family friend Bobbette McCulloch recalls. "He would say, 'I can't eat anything, I can't drink anything, I can't talk.'"

He did have plenty of colorful stories about life in the Mexican league upon his return. Team owners who couldn't afford lawn mowers would graze cows in the outfield during the afternoon. "If you dove, you'd get a mouthful of cow doo," he recalls. As for the infield, the grass was so tall that routine ground balls to first base would become inside-the-park home runs because fielders couldn't find the ball. On the bright side, when Jerome hit a home

run, home fans would rush to the side of the dugout to hand him
pesos.

Jerome has coached the Kennett High School baseball team for
the past seven years. He's given to gentle diatribes that involve the
phrase "kids today": "Kids today want to get their high off drugs
and all that kind of stuff. We could get our high off playing ball."

He's also quick with commonsense quips. "Some of them are
afraid to change, because they're afraid they might fail," Jerome
says. "I tell them, 'You're already failing, so try something different.'"

He still loves the game, as evidenced by the baseball-shaped rug
and stool in his living room and by the way he speaks with still-twin-
kling eyes about becoming a minor league coach.

Baseball didn't tease Jerome.

It wasn't supposed to end this way. Jeff Stone had a decent major
league career, with a respectable .277 career average and a tran-
scendent late-inning pressure hit to his credit. But to the excited
observers who watched the bootheel blur streak down the line during his rookie season, he could have been so much more.

Still, if he had become an All-Star or even a Hall-of-Famer, Stone
would have ended up in Wardell when it was all done, just as he did
every offseason.

"It didn't ever leave my blood," he says. "I always knew I was going to come back home when my career was over. When I came
back, I would say, 'I'm just a normal man playing baseball. Ain't no
better than you.' It was easy for me to come back here and adjust
quickly, because I kept that same attitude. I think all players should
think like that."

Many baseball fans share his opinion.

Traditionalists love the purity of an undiscovered, raw, rural
player signing a modest deal on the kitchen counter of a neighbor's farmhouse. And the Royals faithful long for a star with small-
town sensibilities. Someone with Carlos Beltran's talent but without the piranha agent or the mercenary loyalties. Someone who
would stroll down the street and talk to strangers.

JOHN BRANT

Duel in the Sun

FROM RUNNER'S WORLD

IN FRONT of some audiences, Dick Beardsley never even mentions
the 1982 Boston Marathon. In fact, he barely touches upon his
running career at all. When he's delivering one of his regular talks
to a twelve-step group, for instance, he simply begins, "Hi, I'm
Dick, and I'm a drug addict," then launches into the rending story
of his disease and recovery.

When Beardsley finishes speaking, and the people are wiping
away their tears and settling back into their seats after a standing
ovation, then the host might explain how Dick Beardsley is the
fourth-fastest American marathoner of all time, and that his race
with Alberto Salazar at Boston twenty-two years ago remains one of
the signature moments in the history of distance running; perhaps,
in the history of any sport.

But other audiences, such as this one at the Royal Victoria Marathon in Victoria, British Columbia, know all about Beardsley's athletic career, and are eager — even hungry — to relive his legendary "duel in the sun" with Salazar.

There's a considerable amount of preamble first. Beardsley is
not good at leaving things out. He tells the crowd of two hundred
about getting creamed at his first high school football practice,
quitting the team, and turning out for cross-country without knowing quite what it was. "Do they tackle you in cross-country?" he
asked a friend. He explains how he ran his second marathon in a
brand-new pair of running shoes that he didn't want to get dirty by
breaking in, and that he prepared by fasting for four days because
he'd read somewhere that fasting worked in ultramarathons, so he
figured . . .

Beardsley is blessed with the fundamental trait of the born enter-
tainer: a complete lack of self-consciousness. He strides back and
forth in front of the podium, laughing right along with the audience, as delighted as they are by his own buffoonery. His voice —
honking, booming, unabashed — rolls around the conference hall
in overpowering waves. Wearing jeans, a red pullover, and a blue
fleece vest, whip-cord lean and with a lilt to his step, Beardsley
might be mistaken for an athlete in his prime, rather than a man of
forty-eight. You have to sit close to notice the hard miles showing
around his eyes.

The crowd's laughter drowns out the canned rock music blaring
from the expo next door. But when Beardsley shifts gears, traveling
back to Hopkinton, Massachusetts, on the sunny noon of April 19,
1982, the room falls raptly silent.

Which only seems appropriate, because the 1982 Boston Marathon was great theater: two American runners, one a renowned
champion and the other a gutty underdog, going at each other for
just under two hours and nine minutes. Other famous marathons
have featured narrow margins of victory, but their suspense developed late in the race, the product of a furiously closing challenger
or rapidly fading leader. At the '82 Boston, by contrast, Beardsley
and Salazar ran in each other's pocket the entire 26.2 miles, with
no other competitor near them for the final nine miles. They were
so close that, for most of the last half of the race, Beardsley, while in
the lead, monitored Salazar's progress by watching his shadow on
the asphalt.

Neither man broke, and neither, in any meaningful sense, lost.
The race merely came to a thrilling, shattering end, leaving both
runners, in separate and ultimately Pyrrhic ways, the winner. The
drama unfolded in the sport's most storied venue, at the peak of
the first running boom, when the United States produced world-
class marathoners in the profusion that Kenya does today.

"An Epic Duel"; "The Greatest Boston Marathon"; "A Display of
Single-Minded Determination and Indefatigable Spirit"; read the
next day's headlines. Since Beardsley was just twenty-six and Salazar twenty-three, everyone assumed that this would be the start of
a long and glorious rivalry, one that would galvanize the public
and seal American dominance in the marathon through the 1984
Olympics and beyond.

But rather than a beginning, Boston '82 represented a climax.

After that day, neither man ran a marathon as well again. And from that day since, incredibly, only two more of the world's major marathons have been won by a native-bred American man. On that day, 156 runners, virtually every one an American, finished the race in a time of 2:30 or faster. At the 2003 Boston Marathon, by contrast, just twenty-one runners logged 2:30 or better.

So some of the younger members of the audience — including the elite runners who will lead tomorrow's Royal Victoria Marathon — listen to Beardsley's story with a mixture of curiosity, envy, and awe. Others in the crowd, those closer to Beardsley's age, listen on a different frequency. They know the enormous toll that Boston exacted on both Alberto Salazar and Dick Beardsley. If the glory of their marathon bore a heroic quality, so did their suffering afterward.

At Nike corporate headquarters in Beaverton, Oregon, Alberto Salazar descends to the ground-floor café of the Mia Hamm Building for a quick lunch. For the last several years, Nike has employed Salazar as a kind of coach-at-large, chartered to deliver that most endangered of species — The Great American Distance Runner — from the brink of extinction. On this drizzly October Tuesday, Salazar has spent the morning training the professional athletes in Nike's ambitious Oregon Project. This afternoon, he'll supervise the cross-country team at Portland's Central Catholic High School.

Both teams, he reports, are thriving. The Oregon Project's Dan Browne has met the qualifying standard for the 2004 Olympic marathon, and Central Catholic's Galen Rupp should repeat as the state cross-country champion. Meanwhile, other parts of Salazar's life are in similar bloom: his oldest son, Antonio, plays wide receiver for the University of Oregon football team, and his younger son, Alejandro, is a star striker for the University of Portland soccer team.

At forty-six, Salazar appears every bit the proud, happy family man and flourishing professional. His brown eyes are clear, calm, and bright, and his cheeks have lost a marathoner's hollowness. He no longer resembles "the young priest fresh from seminary whose face drives all the housewives to distraction," as one writer described him twenty years ago. Now Salazar looks more like a fit-but-comfortable middle-aged monsignor, a man still true to his religious vocation, but also at ease in the worldly realm of fund-raisers and cocktail parties.

A Japanese visitor approaches and politely asks for an autograph. Salazar graciously complies. "After Boston I was never quite the same," he says, after his fan has departed. "I had a few good races, but everything was difficult. Workouts that I used to fly through became an ordeal. And eventually, of course, I got so sick that I wondered if I'd ever get well."

Salazar's warm smile briefly turns wintry. For a moment, his poise falters and he seems like a traumatized man who, after exhaustive therapy, can finally talk about his past.

"It took me a long time to connect the dots," he says, "and see that the line stretched all the way back to Boston."

Monday, April 19, Patriots Day, broke warm and blue over Boston, perfect for just about anything except running 26.2 miles.

After driving out to the start in Hopkinton, Beardsley and his coach, Bill Squires, avoided the high school gym that served as the staging area for elite athletes. For the last four months, Beardsley had spent all of his waking moments, and some of his sleeping ones, thinking and dreaming about Alberto Salazar. Squires wanted to keep Beardsley as removed from the race excitement as possible.

So they camped out in the house of a town matron. Squires went into his usual patter. "How do, missus, beautiful day, lovely home, let me introduce Dickie Beardsley here from Minnesota. Dickie's a dairy farmer, got hay stuck in his teeth, but don't be fooled. In a few minutes he's gonna run the Boston Marathon, and just between you and me, he's got a shot to win it if he sets his mouth right and does the hubba-hubba on the hills . . ."

While Squires and the grandma yakked, Beardsley stretched, sipped water, made a half-dozen trips to the bathroom, and listened to a Dan Fogelberg tape. He punched ventilation holes in the white painter's cap that Squires had given him to ward off the sun, and tried not to jump out of his skin.

At a quarter to twelve he heard the call for runners. He jogged out to the street, heading for the section at the front of the starting area roped off for elite athletes. But thousands of citizen-athletes stood between him and the starting line. He tried to fight through the crowd but couldn't make any progress.

Beardsley panicked. He felt as if he were caught in one of those sweat-drenched nightmares, in which he was desperately trying to reach a critical destination, but couldn't move. (Decades later, after detox, Beardsley will be haunted by a similar nightmare: He's been in another accident. He's lying on a hospital bed and nurses are hooking him up to an IV drip attached to a huge pouch of Demerol. He tries to scream at the nurse to stop, but not a sound comes out of his mouth.)

So Beardsley reverted to character. He started to make noise. "Hey, let me through! I'm Dick Beardsley, for crying out loud! I gotta get up to the front!"

The other runners, immersed in their last-minute preparations, eyed him coldly. Then someone recognized him, and word rippled through the crowd: "Look out, we got Dick Beardsley here! Make way, Dick's coming through!"

The crowds parted, and Beardsley, his nightmare dissolved into a dream, followed a clear path to the starting line.

Throughout the winter of 1981 and '82, as he had sat in front of the TV in the evenings, Beardsley pounded his thighs with his fists 1,500 times. He had read somewhere that pounding your muscles made them tougher. If he thought it might gain him a few seconds on the downhills, Beardsley would have tried curing his quads in a smokehouse. He knew that the marathon would be decided on the course's three long hills rising between miles 17 and 21. If he had any chance of beating Salazar, he would have to fly down the hills like a bobsled racer, capitalizing on the fact that Salazar outweighed him by twenty pounds. Conceivably, a series of rocketing descents might pummel Salazar's legs to the extent that Beardsley would be able to pull away from him before mile 25. If that plan failed, and the race came down to a kick at the end, then Salazar, with his superior short-range speed, would do the pummeling.

Fifteen hundred punches, each thigh.

Born in Havana but raised in the Boston suburb of Wayland, Alberto Salazar, the world's greatest and most charismatic distance runner, was coming home from Oregon to run his first Boston Marathon. It was one of the most eagerly anticipated sports stories of 1982. He was fit and prepared, he announced to reporters upon arriving at the airport with his wife, Molly. If there were no injuries or unforeseen developments . . . well, the facts were plain: he was the fastest man in the race.

Six months earlier, Salazar had won his second consecutive New York City Marathon in a world-record time of 2:08:13, which had earned him, among other honors, a White House audience with President Ronald Reagan. In March, he had finished second at the

World Cross-Country Championships. And just one week before Boston, he had run a blistering 27:30 in a ten-thousand-meter match race with the great Kenyan runner Henry Rono at the University of Oregon's Hayward Field.

The ten-thousand had been Salazar's idea. He had lined up the appearance money for Rono, who had shown up in Eugene looking fat and blowsy, in the early stages of the alcoholism that would eventually destroy his career. But once the race started, he ran with his trademark ferocity. For twenty-five laps around the historic track, Rono and Salazar belted away at each other. Rono outleaned Salazar at the wire, by the width of his jiggling belly, the wags in the press box joked.

Rono's brilliant victory was essentially ignored. But Salazar's draining, world-class effort, just two seconds off Craig Virgin's American record, raised eyebrows. Occurring only nine days before the Boston Marathon, it violated every code in the sport's training canon.

Salazar didn't care. At the age of sixteen he had determined that he would become the fastest marathoner in the world. Instead of the standard training — laying a foundation of endurance, then adding speedwork — Salazar did the opposite. He first honed his track speed to match that of a Henry Rono, then built his strength so he could maintain that pace over the length of a marathon. His goal was to demolish his competitors, run so far out in front of them that there could be no doubt of his greatness.

"I viewed every marathon as a test of my manhood," he says. "It wasn't enough for me to win the race; I wanted to bury the other guys."

At mile 5, the lead pack passed a pond where a couple was floating around in a canoe, enjoying the beautiful afternoon. Bill Rodgers poked Beardsley. "Hey, Dick, wouldn't you love to be out there right now?" As if they were two young executives commuting into the office, looking out the train window.

Then, a few miles later, Ron Tabb and Dean Matthews threw a rogue surge. It was way too early for a serious ante, but not so early that the contenders could afford to ignore it; they had to burn precious energy reeling in the pair. Beardsley laughed it off, but Salazar was genuinely steamed.

The crowds were huge. Most of the spectators cheered for Salazar, the native son. When Salazar waved at his fans, Beardsley did likewise. He waved and grinned as if this were the Fourth of July parade back home in Rush City, Minnesota, and the folks were cheering for him. Salazar was not amused.

Salazar wasn't finding much of anything amusing. He was booming along in the lead pack, looking strong, yet Beardsley sensed that he wasn't quite in sync. He also noticed that, despite the glaring sun and seventy-degree temperatures, Salazar never drank.

There weren't any official, fully stocked water stations. You had to accept cups of whatever a spectator might offer. As often as he could, Beardsley would grab a cup, pour whatever it contained over his painter's cap, take a swallow, then offer the cup to Salazar. But he always refused it.

On the morning of November 13, 1989, snow was forecast for the dairy-farm belt of central Minnesota. Before the storm arrived, Dick Beardsley, recently retired from his professional running career, needed to milk his cows, store the corn that he'd harvested the day before, and pick the corn remaining in his fields. He rose at a quarter to four, blitzed through milking, skipped breakfast, and went to work loading the harvested corn in a grain elevator.

Like much of the machinery on a family farm, the elevator ran on a device called a power take-off, a revolving steel rod connected to the tractor engine. Normally, Beardsley sat in the driver's seat to engage the device; but today, trying to accomplish several jobs at once, he stood on the slippery tractor drawbar. The engine turned over unexpectedly, catching Beardsley's overalls leg in the power take-off. For a horrified moment, he watched his left leg disappear into the maw of the machine. Then he was caught in a whirlwind.

The shaft of the power take-off curled Beardsley's leg around it like a string around a spool, casting him into a devastating orbit. It crumpled his left leg, and flung his skull against the barn floor with each revolution. Beardsley screamed for help, but his wife, Mary, was in the house, too far away to hear. His head hammered into the floor as if it were a rag doll's. On each revolution he desperately reached for the shut-off lever, but it remained just a few inches beyond his grasp.

Beardsley started to slip away. It was an iron-gray morning, spitting snow, but he saw a brilliant light.

Somehow, the tractor engine died. Beardsley pulled his crushed leg out of the machine and crawled out to the yard, where Mary finally found him. Beardsley was relatively lucky; power take-off accidents kill more farmers than they maim. He came away with a punctured lung, a fractured right wrist, broken ribs, a severe concussion, broken vertebrae, a mangled leg, and a monkey on his back.

That first rush of Demerol in the hospital was unlike anything the straight-arrow, teetotaling Beardsley had ever experienced. He rocketed into another world — one without stress or strain or worry. It was so wonderful that if some higher power told him that he could go back, avoid the accident, but never take Demerol, Beardsley wouldn't hesitate — he would turn down the offer flat.

Past the thirteen-mile mark, and past Wellesley College and its gauntlet of shrieking women, the lead pack melted down to Rodgers, Ed Mendoza, Beardsley, and Salazar.

At age thirty-four, the great Rodgers, four-time winner of the Boston Marathon, had lost a step, and the front-running Mendoza would inevitably fade. The only concern was Beardsley, whom Salazar pegged as a talented journeyman. True, he'd run a few good marathons — a 2:09 at Grandma's in Duluth, the win at London the previous year — but he had no credentials on the track. Beardsley's best 10-K was a full minute and a half slower than his own.

And look at him there in his silly little painter's cap, slurping water from every kid he passed. Beardsley lacked gravitas. So let Beardsley and Squires think they could break him on the hills. Salazar knew they were dreaming. He was faster, tougher, and had prepared more thoroughly. The hills belonged to him.

A few feet away, Beardsley was thinking the same thing. He had spent the winter training in Atlanta, not to escape the northern cold, but because Georgia, unlike Minnesota, had hills approximating Boston's. In early April, he left Georgia to finish preparing in Boston, where he could familiarize himself with the marathon course. Shortly after his arrival, however, a northeaster blew into town, bringing heavy snow and a howling wind. Beardsley was scheduled for a key workout on Heartbreak Hill: up one side and down the other, eight times. Squires looked out the window and told him to forget it.

"Come on, coach. Let's give it a try."

"I don't think I can even get us to Heartbreak, let alone have you run

there." But Squires finally relented. He drove at a creeping pace through the deserted streets, delivering Beardsley to within three miles of Heartbreak.

"For chrissakes, Dickie, look at this snow. Let's go home. You're gonna slip and fall and kill yourself."

"Let me give it a shot, coach."

Beardsley got out of the car and started running toward Heartbreak. He ran gingerly at first, but after a few steps picked up the pace. His footprints cut lonesome notches in the unblemished drifts; the icy wind scorched his eyes. Beardsley closed his eyes, moving on touch and sound and instinct, imagining — knowing — that at this desperate moment, Alberto Salazar was running someplace where it was warm.

He completed eight round trips over Heartbreak, just as planned. At the end of the workout, he quietly reported to Squires that he was ready. The hills belonged to him.

In the weeks and months following the 1982 Boston Marathon, Alberto Salazar's decline was so gradual that it barely seemed like a decline at all. In the summer of 1982 he set two American records on the track, in the five-thousand and ten-thousand-meters. In October, he won his third consecutive New York City Marathon. His time was a few minutes slower than at Boston, but he appeared to be his elegant, imperious self — the finest distance runner of his time.

But privately, Salazar worried. Before Boston he'd relished his workouts, ripping through them with the barest hint of fatigue. He was able to follow hard days and weeks of training with even harder ones; the ceiling for one training cycle became the floor for the next. But after Boston, the workouts yielded less and less pleasure. His legs felt heavy, his breathing shallow. It took him days instead of hours to recover from a maximum effort.

Salazar tried to convince himself that he hadn't blown it at Boston; that despite drinking so little, and running so furiously, he hadn't done himself lasting damage. He scoffed at the media for making such a fuss about his "duel in the sun" with Beardsley.

Throughout 1983, Salazar suffered one heavy cold after another. Deep, racking, bronchitis-style colds, one a month, lining up like winter storm fronts off the coast of Oregon. Consistent high-level training became impossible, and he entered the crucial Olympic year of '84 in dire shape. At the Marathon Trials, he struggled to a 2:12, second-place performance. It earned him a berth in the Games, but for Salazar, finishing second — especially in a race restricted to other Americans — was like finishing last.

He had a chance to redeem himself in Los Angeles, but the colds and malaise continued all summer. On the last night of the Games, it was Carlos Lopes of Portugal who ran into the Coliseum before the world's admiring eyes. Salazar finished an exhausted fifteenth.

Still, he was only twenty-six, with many marathons and Olympics seemingly ahead. But the illness and weakness did not abate. Doctors failed to identify his malady, and Salazar, desperate to fight, remained impotent before an invisible enemy. He experienced insomnia, and went to the Stanford Sleep Clinic. He visited a cardiologist. He underwent surgery. He tried training in Kenya. Nothing worked.

But he stubbornly refused to stop running. Because running was how Salazar defined himself. Running was the means by which he proved his manhood. At the same time, on solitary long runs or during exacting workouts with close friends, the sport provided a shelter, a place to escape the pressure of constantly proving himself. Now, in his physical prime, his only outlet was denied him. He couldn't run, yet he couldn't stop running. Salazar reached the point where the best he could do was cover four or five miles in a crabbed shuffle.

"For much of the last ten years, I hated running," he confessed to a reporter in 1994. "I hated it with a passion. I used to wish for a cataclysmic injury in which I would lose one of my legs. I know that sounds terrible, but if I had lost a leg, then I wouldn't have to torture myself anymore."

Just past mile 17, just before the firehouse at the base of the Braeburn Hill, Rodgers started to fade; just beyond it, Mendoza dropped away. Now it was down to Beardsley and Salazar. Beardsley stepped to the lead he would hold for the next nine miles.

As the hills unreeled, Beardsley launched one gambit after another. He would drive hard for four hundred yards, then back off for two hundred. He'd repeat the cycle two or three times. But after a third fast four-hundred, he'd slow down for only one hundred yards. Then, hoping to catch Salazar flatfooted, he would surge. But Salazar covered every move. He stayed plastered on Beardsley's shoulder, throwing his own combinations. The sun was

behind them, so Beardsley could watch Salazar's shadow on the pavement.
When the shadow began to move forward, Beardsley speeded up just enough
to stay ahead of it. Psychologically, he could not afford to let Salazar take the
lead.

Heartbreak Hill came and went. The two runners remained joined.

By the summer of 1995, Dick Beardsley was taking ninety tablets of Demerol, Percocet, and Valium a day. He photocopied physicians' stationery, forged the prescriptions, and filled them at a dozen pharmacies in and around his home in Detroit Lakes, Minnesota. With meticulous care, Beardsley recorded his drug transactions in a small notebook, disguising the entries as bait purchases for the fishing-guide business he bought after recovering from his farming accident.

When Dick and Mary visited a friend's house for dinner, Beardsley excused himself from the table, went to the bathroom, and rifled his host's medicine cabinet for pain pills. He did the same at the house of his father, who was dying of pancreatic cancer.

Beardsley no longer drank water with the pills; he had trained himself to gulp them down dry, as if they were M&Ms or sunflower seeds. He spent all his waking moments thinking about pills — acquiring them, concealing them — much in the way that, years earlier, in the winter before the 1982 Boston Marathon, he spent all his time thinking about Alberto Salazar.

Amazingly, Beardsley was able to hide his disease, live a double life. Nobody in Detroit Lakes harbored suspicions. He appeared to be the same great guy as always: friendly, generous, outgoing, forthright, not in the least bit pompous despite his past as a world-class athlete. His fishing-guide business was thriving. He had become a popular motivational speaker for youth groups.

At the bait shop, or on a boat with a client, Beardsley never slurred his words or stumbled. He drove with obsessive care. He hid his pills in a secret place in his pickup truck, and floated around in a private, secret cloud that insulated him from all trouble and anxiety. He was a week or two away from dying.

"After I got caught, during detox and treatment, the doctors just shook their heads when they found out how much I was taking," he recalls. "It was enough to kill an elephant. The doctors said that thanks to my running, I had a tremendously rapid metabolism, and an incredibly strong heart. Still, it was only a matter of time until one morning I just wouldn't wake up."

At home in the evenings, Beardsley would often nod off over his supper plate. One night, Mary said to him in frustration, "Do you think you could force yourself to stay awake and watch a video with me tonight?"

Worried that his cover might be fraying, Beardsley willed himself to watch the entire movie. The next day, while returning the video to the rental shop, he decided to surprise Mary with another movie. He spent a long time combing the aisles, studying various titles. Finally he found a film he was sure she would like.

At home, when he delivered the surprise, Mary stared at him. The video he had brought her was the same one they had watched the night before.

After watching the early part of the race on TV, and discovering that an extraordinary contest was in progress — two runners, stripped down to bone and will, relentlessly moving down the streets of their city — the citizens of Boston turned out of their houses to witness the finish. Fathers lifted their children up on their shoulders and told them to pay attention, as an estimated crowd of two million turned out to watch some part of the 1982 Boston Marathon.

Beardsley had come off Heartbreak with Salazar breathing down his neck. The crowd pressed so close there was barely a path to run through. They were screaming so loud he couldn't hear himself think. He couldn't feel his legs. They seemed to belong to somebody else.

Twenty-one miles into the eighty-sixth Boston Marathon, and he was running a stride in front of the great Salazar, who must be hurting too. Because if Salazar wasn't fried, he would have blown past him by now.

Five more miles was unthinkable. Beardsley decided he'd just go one more mile. That would be easy — or at least possible. Stay ahead of Salazar for one more mile. After that — well, he'd think of something.

He couldn't feel his legs. One more mile.

Meanwhile, Salazar was hurting. Shards of pain splintered up from Salazar's left hamstring. Sometime during the last few miles he had stopped sweating. His singlet had stiffened, as if covered in dried blood.

All that mattered now was not losing. That made things simple. He could forget about his time and focus on that single and sovereign goal. He might lose a ten-thousand-meter race to a Henry Rono, but he did not lose mara-

thons, especially to a palooka in a painter's cap. Any moment now Beardsley might blow up and drop away like a disintegrating booster rocket. If he could maintain the pace, then it would simply be a matter of outkicking him.

Alberto Salazar feared no opponent, at least none that he could see.

José Salazar, Alberto's father, was a passionate man. Journalists never tired of writing about José's romantic Cuban background: the fact that he'd been a close friend and fellow revolutionary of Fidel Castro; that he'd grown to hate the Communists and, in exile, had dedicated his life to overthrowing his former comrade.

In 1988, José's church in Wayland hosted a guest from Europe bringing strange but exciting news: six teenagers in the Balkans of Yugoslavia had been visited by an apparition of the Virgin Mary. A devout Catholic well disposed toward saints and miracles, José was fascinated. He undertook his own pilgrimage to the distant town, called Medjugorge. Upon his return home, José started sending Medjugorge literature to Alberto in Oregon. Alberto was the most devout of his four children, but also the one most in need of grace.

After a failed bid to make the 1988 Olympic team, Alberto Salazar had started a business career, owning and operating a popular, eponymous restaurant in Eugene. Despite the fact that he'd grown increasingly distant, surly, and abstracted since his running had declined, he regarded himself as a happy and prosperous man. He didn't need any of his father's Virgin Mary moonshine.

But one day in 1990, Salazar picked up a tract that his father had sent him. Within a few months, he was on a plane to Yugoslavia, embarking on his own pilgrimage. While in Medjugorge, Salazar was interviewed by a local priest. At long last, the former champion acknowledged his pain and emptiness.

He told the priest he was once presented with a wreath of genuine green laurels after winning a marathon. "My father took it with him and preserved it as a memento in a safe place," he said. "Several months later, this beautiful wreath, which marked a great victory, had lost its entire beauty.

"For sport is not simply a discipline," Salazar continued. "Sport can become a compulsion, another god. So long as one depends on it, he forgets everything else. If he loses this god, he has nothing else."

He flew home to the United States, sold his restaurant, moved his family to Portland, and went to work for Nike. A doctor finally determined that his chronic health problems were largely due to his overheating at the '82 Boston Marathon. The doctor prescribed Prozac, which resolved the worst symptoms of the pernicious strain of exercise-induced asthma and lifted Salazar's decade-long depression. At age thirty-four, he resumed training. In May of 1994, Salazar won the fifty-four-mile Comrades Marathon in South Africa. Soon afterward, with nothing left to prove, he retired from competitive distance running, and began to coach.

Dick Beardsley still couldn't feel his legs. Mile 24 had passed, so his one-more-mile scheme seemed to be working.

He kept watching Salazar's shadow. Suddenly, it loomed huge on the asphalt. Beardsley wondered if he was hallucinating. But it was the press bus roaring past to the finish line. The crowds were so thick that the bus had to travel the same line as the runners. As the bus went past, its mirror clipped Beardsley on the shoulder. Beardsley punched the bus in frustration. Then it was gone.

By the twenty-fifth mile, Beardsley didn't need to look for the shadow anymore. They had been running together their whole lives. He felt Salazar's presence more palpably than he did his own ruined legs. My God, he thought, *one more mile*, and I'm going to win this thing.

A half-mile to go. Continuing to move in a disembodied, dreamlike cloud, Beardsley flashed on his father. For his high school graduation present, his father had given him an IOU plane ticket, good one day for a trip to the Boston Marathon. Tears started to well up. Beardsley told himself to cut it out, get into this, attend to business.

Beardsley tried one last surge, but as he bore down, a shout of pain arose from his right hamstring. The leg turned to rubber. You could see the knotted muscle bulging.

Salazar blew past him. This was wrong on every conceivable level.

Then the motorcycle cops roared past, following Salazar, forming a phalanx around the new leader. The motorcycles massed together and for the first time all day, Dick Beardsley lost sight of his opponent.

On the morning of October 1, 1996, Dick Beardsley attempted to fill a forged prescription at the Wal-Mart pharmacy in Detroit Lakes, just as he'd done scores of times over the last few years. The pharmacist was a fishing buddy. They always kidded around when Beardsley came in for his pills. But on this day, the pharmacist wouldn't make eye contact. Beardsley knew right away that he was in trouble. He did not flee, and he did not dissemble. He was booked on felony narcotics charges. His shocking arrest made headlines across the country.

Beardsley avoided a prison sentence, but he hardly escaped punishment. He underwent a long, harrowing detox and treatment that entailed methadone, lengthy stays in psychiatric wards, and rigid adherence to a twelve-step program. Mary and Andy, Dick and Mary's son, stood by him, as did his friends in Detroit Lakes and the national running community. Through excruciating work — and the dispensation of grace — Beardsley regained his health, the trust of his family, his business, his public speaking career, and his sport.

In 2002, he ran five marathons, and six more the following year, with a post-accident personal record of 2:45:58 at the Toronto marathon in October 2003. Each September, he puts on a popular half-marathon in Detroit Lakes. In 2003, the special guest at the race was Beardsley's good friend Alberto Salazar.

Just when Beardsley thought nothing more could possibly go wrong, something did. A moment after losing sight of Salazar with less than a mile to go, he stepped in a pothole. That tore it, he thought; the best he could do now was crawl in. But somehow, instead of worsening the pain, stepping in the pothole stretched out the hamstring, straightening out the knot.

Beardsley started to sprint. He put his head down and pumped his arms. He found another gear. He felt like angels were lifting him up. A hard right turn onto Hereford Street. He caught a glimpse of Salazar, like a glimpse of the pope in a motorcade, twenty yards ahead, then put his head down again.

At the top of the hill there was a hard left turn before the final straightaway. Salazar and the motorcycles made that turn and the crowd at the finish line went wild, screaming in their hometown boy.

Beardsley had to weave his way through the motorcycles. The cops thought he was finished, but here he was back from the dead. They looked pie-faced and astonished as he pushed past them.

Salazar glanced back over his shoulder, also thinking that Beardsley was gone. But instead he was right there, on his shoulder, bearing down on him.

Salazar's eyes grew as big as headlights. He turned to the finish line, the last hundred yards, with Beardsley in hell-hound pursuit.

Up in the TV booth above the finish line, Squires kept screaming, "Dickie! Dickie! Dickie!"

It was all clear to Salazar. There was nothing else to consider but the finish line up ahead, somewhere in that insane jumble of people and police barriers and motorcycles. The fact that he did not lose was as ineluctable as a law of physics.

Hail Mary, full of grace. The pain and the jumble and a dry-ice cold all over. My God, Dick Beardsley was tough, but Alberto Salazar did not lose.

The café at Nike's Mia Hamm Building is just about deserted. Alberto Salazar's quick lunch break has turned into a two-hour retrospective of his life and career — just a few minutes less than it once took him to run a marathon.

Finally, Salazar rises from the table. In the lobby, before riding the elevator up to his office, he says, "At the time of the Boston Marathon, I didn't know Dick very well. And to be honest, for a long time after it, I sort of resented him. Well, that passed, like a lot of my stuff passed." He gives a terse shake of his head.

"Then in 2002, the Boston Marathon brought us back for the twentieth anniversary of our race. We got to know each other. Now, among all the guys I ran with or against, Dick might be the one I feel closest to. I'll pick up the phone every few months and give him a call. I think he and I have a special bond. All that he's gone through . . . I'm not saying I can understand it, but maybe I can come close.

"We both give a lot of talks, to all kinds of groups, all over the country," Salazar continues. "Sooner or later, someone always asks about the '82 Boston. I don't mind — I like talking about it, and so does Dick. That's because we never discuss the race in terms of running a 2:08, or beating the other guy. It took us both a long, long time, but we finally realized that that's not what the marathon is really about. It's not what it's about at all."

"After the race, people came up to me and said, 'Gosh, Dick, if you hadn't had to fight through all those police motorcycles, you might have won,'" Beardsley recalls for his audience at the Victoria Marathon. "But I don't look at it that way. I ran the race of my life,

2:08:53. Alberto happened to run two seconds faster. All I know for certain is that I left everything I had out on that course. I didn't give an inch. Neither did Alberto. The way I look at it, there were two winners that day."

The crowd erupts in applause, as if they were at the finish line at Boston. Beardsley lets the cheers wash over him for a moment, then holds his hands up for quiet.

"Tomorrow, at your marathon, you're going to give it your all," he says. "When it's over, you can look back on a job well done. You'll be able to relax. You'll be finished.

"Well, the race that I'm running now, I can never relax, never be finished," Beardsley goes on. "The day I say that I've got my addiction beat, I'll be in greater danger than when my leg got caught in that power take-off. I can't let that day come. I just celebrated my seventh year of sobriety. These have been the seven hardest, and the seven most wonderful, years of my life. Every morning I feel like I'm getting up to run the Boston Marathon all over again."

A Lethal Catch

FROM THE PHILADELPHIA DAILY NEWS

CLOUDS OF SNOW whipped across his windshield. In clear weather the drive to Williamsport, Pennsylvania, always took Rick Lannetti three hours or so, but he gave himself some extra time that cold December day, leaving his Yardley home in the emerging dawn. The turnpike had become an ever-narrowing lane of slush, the visibility poor and getting worse. But kickoff was not until one o'clock that Saturday, so he took it easy on the gas and even stopped for a cup of coffee. He planned to check into his room, get a nap, and then go to the field early to see his only son, Ricky, the Lycoming College wide receiver and kick returner, who that day would be playing an NCAA Division III quarterfinal against Bridgewater (Virginia). "It was the biggest game of his life," Lannetti would say later. By 9:30 A.M., he was just outside of Williamsport when he received a call on his cell phone.

The voice on the other end belonged to his former wife, Terri.

"Check into your hotel and come to the hospital," she said with a pointed urgency. "Ricky is really sick."

The elder Lannetti figured it was just the flu. He was not overly alarmed because he had spoken to his son on Thursday and already knew that he had not been feeling well. With a shrug, he told himself: "Hey, I guess no ball game for him." It was only when he got to Williamsport Hospital that he became aware of the full weight of what was happening. Ricky had been admitted at 7:00 A.M. in critical condition. His blood pressure had dropped to 98 over 27, and his body temperature was erratic. When Rick showed up in the intensive care unit, he was startled to discover his son with tubes running in and out of his body, traces of dry blood on his lip and around his nose. Wide-eyed, he asked where the blood had come from, only to be told that his son had coughed it up upon entering the emergency room earlier that morning.

What followed that day still seems unreal to Lannetti. He remembers his son looking up at him and asking, "What time am I getting out of here?" The game had been rescheduled for Sunday due to unplayable conditions, and it was just like him to think that he could still hop out of bed and play in it. As each hour passed, his condition worsened despite the assortment of antibiotics that were given to him and the wide range of specialists who hovered over him. When his heart began to weaken, his doctors prepared him to be flown to the cardiac center at Temple University Hospital. His coaches and teammates joined one another in the waiting room, their faces grim, uncertain.

One of the doctors told Rick and Terri that their son would be fine if he got through the day, but conceded that the diagnosis remained unclear.

Lannetti remembers a doctor gravely advising him, *"Something is attacking his body . . ."*

Strikes All Levels

Ricky Lannetti died that evening at 7:36. The autopsy that was performed two days later determined the cause of death to be a *Staphylococcus aureus* pneumonia and associated bacteremia. While it remains unclear exactly how the infection entered his body, it did so with a fury that swept through the twenty-one-year-old Father Judge graduate with unsparing force. A week before he had played in the second round of the NCAA playoffs against East Texas Baptist University, only to come down a few days later with what appeared to be flu symptoms. Sadly, what no one knew until it was far too late was that he had contracted methicillin-resistant *Staphylococcus aureus* (MRSA), a form of staph that is stubbornly resistant to commonly used antibiotics. Calling Lannetti an otherwise "excessively healthy individual," Lycoming County coroner Charles E. Kiessling says, "This is just so tragic . . . They were treating him appropriately, but it just happened so quickly; MRSA just overwhelmed his system."

Kiessling adds, "The issue is *how* it got into his system, whether it was from a puncture in his foot or a sore on his buttock or — and this is what it sounds like — whether it was growing in his lungs."

Staphylococcus is a common form of bacteria that humans can carry on their skin, in their nose, or in the back of their throat without it ever progressing beyond that. Thirty percent of normally healthy people carry it around at any given time, according to Dan Jernigan, medical epidemiologist at the Centers for Disease Control and Prevention in Atlanta. Of somewhat larger concern is MRSA, the emergence of which has been traced to the overuse of antibiotics. While Jernigan points out that it very rarely leads to death and is treatable, he concedes that it can become "a nasty problem" if it enters the bloodstream. Says Jernigan, who is acquainted with the Lannetti case: "Clearly, when the opportunity exists and the conditions are in place, this particular bacteria can cause a severe disease."

Hospitals have been typical havens for MRSA for years, but it has lately emerged in the community at large among generally healthy people. Specifically, it has become an increasing problem in athletic settings at the pro, college, and high school levels. The Centers for Disease Control circulated an advisory on MRSA to every NFL team last August; the organization also is addressing league physicians on the subject at a conference this month. The NCAA and the National Federation of High Schools also issued an alert on skin infections last October. Says Jeff Hogan, head athletic trainer at the University of California, Davis: "People I talk to [across the country], this is something everyone is aware of and has experienced to one degree or another."

Outbreaks of staphylococcus within the last year have occurred largely in close contact sports such as football and wrestling, where, Jernigan says, there are "skin integrity issues, shared equipment, contaminated surfaces, and crowded conditions." In the NFL last year between August and October, seven Miami Dolphins contracted it, three of whom were hospitalized; the club suspected that the bacteria was spread with the locker-room hot tub. Cases also affected teams in Cleveland, New Orleans, and Tampa Bay. Seven players at the University of Southern California were identified with it before the season opener, four of whom were hospitalized; the condition also was diagnosed in six football players and a wrestler at UC Davis. Clusters also have been found at the high school level in San Antonio, where eight players contracted the condition — including one player who was in danger of having an arm amputated; and in Franklin, Wisconsin, where one of the four afflicted players developed what was called an "extreme case." In an interview with the *Milwaukee Journal*, the father of the unidentified seventeen-year-old said: "It got into his joint, then his bone, then spilled into his blood, causing him to become septic . . . This is a wake-up call for everybody."

Ordinarily, it is a process that begins under the radar as a small pimple, scrape, or cut, each of which can become a portal for staph to enter the body. In the case of UC Davis quarterback Ryan Flanigan, it invaded his system when he suffered a turf burn on his right wrist. Within a few weeks, it had spread to his ring finger on that hand in the form of a cut the size of a small bug bite — irritating, yes, but hardly something that would keep him from playing against rival Sacramento State that Saturday in early October. Hogan remembers that the tender area was cleaned and dressed, but that "literally within hours it got worse." Flanigan played the first half, but he was overcome with fever, nausea. The finger began to swell and bleed, the hand to discolor in deepening shades of green and blue. Upon discerning that Flanigan had an MRSA in addition to a second infection, the doctors gave him antibiotics intravenously and orally during his six days in the hospital. Flanigan told the *Sacramento Bee*, "I went from, 'When am I going to play again?' to 'I have just got to get healthy.'"

That Flanigan or others would try to play is exactly what one would expect, especially when presented with such an apparently small condition as a cut. Cleveland Browns linebacker Ben Taylor just shrugged when he spotted a one-inch scratch on the back of his right arm last November, only to be awakened from sleep hours later with what he characterized as flu symptoms. "Joints, knee, muscle, everything was killing me," Taylor told the *Akron Beacon Journal*. "My arm ballooned out." He showed up for the team walk-through the following day, but was driven to Cleveland Clinic with a fever of 103. Two surgeries were performed there during his days in the hospital. Still unsure how the staphylococcus entered his body, Taylor told the newspaper: "It could have been from turf, from being outside on the grass, from the hot tub. A little scratch. It's crazy how things go sometimes."

Quick and aggressive action is the recommended course in dealing with MRSA, which would include two forms of therapy: one is to essentially power-wash the area in surgery; the other is to prescribe cutting-edge antibiotics such as Vancomycin or Zyvox. To get a jump on detecting any problems, Hogan says he has urged the athletes to keep an eye on each other in the locker room for small sores or cuts. Since Flanigan contracted MRSA, Hogan says players have come to him and reported, "I was drying off and somebody said to me, 'Hey, you got something on the back of your neck. What is that?'" Hogan says he also reminds them to be conscious of proper hygiene, such as wearing clean clothes, using soap and water, and drying off with fresh towels. Says Hogan, "Just the normal stuff Mom told you."

What remains unclear is what else could have been done for Ricky Lannetti in the week leading up to his death. The last thing anyone thought was that he would die — not someone so young, so strong. The only thing he was worried about was whether he would be able to play that Saturday. He had only missed one game in his entire career at Lycoming, and that was with a twisted ankle during his sophomore year. He was a hard-nosed, go-until-you-drop player who would always keep his ailments to himself. So whatever he had that was weighing him down physically, he figured it was something that he could just shake off. He presumed that the doctors could just fix him up enough to play, but by that Saturday at the hospital his body was under siege and beyond the help of medicine. Kiessling says, "It was just a case of too little too late."

A Rapid Deterioration

Terri Lannetti had driven up to Williamsport the evening before to beat the snow. With her was Bill Koch, a longtime coach at Father Judge and a friend of the family. The two had spoken to her son off and on through the week and knew he had come down with something. She planned to get him a hotel room that Friday, just to get him out of the dorm so he could get some undisturbed sleep, but her son called her on her cell phone at 9:30. He told her he was exhausted and going to go to sleep, that he would see her the following morning. So she checked into her room at 1:00 A.M., only to be awakened three hours later by the telephone.

It was her son.

He sounded short of breath, weak.

"Mom," he said, "can you come and get me?"

Knowing the younger Lannetti the way Koch and others knew him, it was understandable that he would have downplayed his sickness for as long as he possibly could. "He worked his ass off to play," says Koch, who says Lannetti scored touchdowns at Father Judge in every conceivable manner: rushing, receiving, fumble return, interception return, kickoff return, and punt return. No one else at the school had ever done that. When he moved on to Lycoming, he set school records for catches in a game (sixteen) and in a season (seventy). At five-ten and 185 pounds, he earned All-Middle Atlantic Conference honors as a receiver (first team) and returner (second team). He had five catches in the playoff game the previous weekend against East Texas Baptist, and looked forward to the quarterfinal game against Bridgewater that Saturday with the same stubborn earnestness that underscored whatever he did on the football field. Says Koch with a grim chuckle, "When it came to playing with pain, Ricky could be kind of a knucklehead."

The first faint stirrings that something was wrong began on Monday. Koch remembers speaking to him that day, and Lannetti told him he was not feeling well; he had a cough and runny nose. On Tuesday, tight end Sean Hennigar says Lannetti practiced with the team but became woozy and sat out the final few plays. He began vomiting on Wednesday and saw the school nurse the following day. He received something to settle his stomach. Terri says she then called the head athletic trainer, Frank Neu, who arranged to have him seen by a local physician on Friday. Lannetti had some blood work done and it was initially conjectured that he could have hepatitis. Neu arranged for Lannetti to meet with the team physician at 9:00 A.M. Saturday. When he spoke to Lannetti on Friday evening, Neu says that Ricky told him he was "feeling a little better." Says Neu, "That was when he took a turn for the worse."

That Friday night was simply dreadful. In the dorm room he shared with Hennigar and linebacker Brian Connors, Lannetti was unable to get any sleep whatsoever. He was up and down, feverish. He would stretch out on his bed, then get up again and sit in the chair. Hennigar and Connors offered to take him to the hospital, but Lannetti said no; he had that appointment with the team physician later that morning and still believed he had an outside chance of playing. Only when it became clear that his moaning was keeping both Hennigar and Connors from getting any sleep did he summon his mother, who found him in such a declining state that he could barely walk. Hennigar and Connors had to help him to the car. Seeing him in this condition was particularly upsetting to Hennigar, whose brother Greg had just completed his freshman year as a walk-on at Penn State when he died last May in an automobile accident. Says Hennigar, "All I ever had to do was say the word, and Ricky was there for me."

His mother drove Lannetti back to her hotel. "He laid down on the bed and then said, 'Help me up,'" she says. "And I would help him up, and then he would lay back down again. At one point, he said, 'Just lay here with me.'"

Koch called an assistant coach. "We knew we had to do something," he says. "So I called the assistant coach and he called the trainer, who met us at the football complex. Once he got there, he took a look at Ricky and led us to the hospital."

What happened then passed by in a blur. When Lannetti vomited blood on the floor of the emergency room, his mother remembers someone shouted, "*You have to take him now!*" She remembers feeling his hands and feet; they were cold, clammy. "He was having trouble breathing," she says. "And saying over and over again, 'I am so tired . . . so tired.'" When they hooked him up to a catheter, the bag filled with what Koch remembers as "this brown mass." Doctors only then learned from him that he had not urinated in two days; his kidneys were shutting down. His mother held off calling his father, who she knew was on his way to Williamsport, so he would not "go crazy and have an accident getting here." When he arrived at the hospital at 10:30 A.M., he found his son in ICU with a team of specialists attending to him. With his blood pressure and pulse precariously low, they hooked him up for an EKG, which revealed that his heart was failing. The doctors told Rick and Terri that "we have no idea what we are dealing with, if it is viral or bacterial," but just hoped to stabilize him enough to fly him into Temple. He slipped into unconsciousness at 5:36 P.M. and was declared brain-dead.

Rick sighs as he remembers hearing that. "It was just like it was a dream," he says. "I was waiting for someone to tell me what to do. You are . . . well . . . I had gone up there that day to see a football game and this happened."

Terri invited the players to his bedside to say their final good-byes. "Ricky had a half-smile on his face — this smirk," she says, "as if he had just done something and gotten away with it."

Lycoming and Bridgewater played the following day. Rick, up the whole night, was driven home, finally falling asleep in the backseat. Terri decided to go to the game, if only to show her support for the grief-stricken team. Hennigar scored a touchdown, but remembers the hollow feeling as he crossed the goal line. Bridgewater ended up winning, 13–9. Wherever Terri seemed to look that day, she was reminded of Ricky. Someone had written his number 19 in the snow and his teammates had draped his jersey over their bench. "You know, it was a weird feeling," she says. "It was sort of like he was still there."

Passion for Football

They buried Ricky Lannetti a few days later at Resurrection Cemetery, in Bensalem. In the cold days that followed, his parents have tried to piece their lives back together and come to some understanding of how this could have happened. Both have been off from work since Ricky died — his mother as a Philadelphia police officer, his father as a computer analyst at Verizon. He says he spends hours upon hours each day at the computer looking up other cases where staphylococcus has ended in fatality, but so far has found that it tends to afflict the very young or the very old, not someone as healthy and as athletic as his son. Young death is so utterly preemptive.

His former wife has her ups and downs. "Some days I feel fine, other days not so fine," she says, her eyes welling with tears. "I think about him all day. I wake up thinking about him; I go to bed thinking about him. I still have trouble believing this actually happened. I know he is in a better place."

Rick sighs. "I just want to die," says Lannetti, who had two younger daughters with his ex-wife. "If God had told me forty-six years ago that He would take my only son — twenty-one years old — I would have told God: 'Please, I do not want to go on.' I have no desire to keep on living, but I know my daughters need me, so I try to keep it together."

The hard part is coming to terms with what could have been. Ricky Lannetti would have graduated with a degree in criminal justice and had plans of getting into law enforcement, possibly as a parole officer. He also had a cousin who is in the Secret Service, so looking into that also held some appeal. Rick adds that it would not have been beyond his son to take a shot at pro football, if not with an NFL team then in Europe or with an Arena League organization. "This kid just loved his football," says Lannetti, who began filming the games his son played when he was five years old. He says he now has more than one hundred videotapes piled up in his house, but doubts he will ever watch them again. With voice cracking, he says, "Doing that would be just too sad."

Certain days he goes to the cemetery just to think. The graves of Ricky Lannetti and Greg Hennigar face each other, and Rick has had the idea of connecting them with chalk lines: Lannetti the wide receiver, Hennigar the quarterback. He thinks of them there together and feels better somehow. He imagines them playing catch together as they used to as boys at Father Judge, forever young and running pass patterns by the light of the moon.

LINDA ROBERTSON

"A Great Day for Arab Women"

FROM THE MIAMI HERALD

ATHENS — Robina Muqimyar ran one hundred meters on Friday, a short distance unless you consider how far she has come. Just three years ago, she was not allowed to run at all. She was not allowed to go to school. She was not allowed to aspire to anything, much less the Olympics.

When she crossed the finish line in Athens, it was as if she was showing her countrywomen the way. By churning down the track, with bare arms and head, she was providing a powerful example of Afghanistan's potential.

Muqimyar finished second to last in her heat with a time of 14.14 seconds, the second slowest among the sixty-three entrants, and three seconds slower than the qualifying times of the fastest runners.

But her presence mattered more than her time. She was smiling proof that the damage done by the oppressive Taliban regime is being corrected. The bhurka, and the constraining anonymity it represented, is an awful but receding memory.

"I am really happy and proud," said Muqimyar, who wore a T-shirt and long green tights in her race. "I felt a little scared because all the world was watching me. But during the warm-ups, the other athletes told me they understood the difficulties I have faced to get here, and they encouraged me. In the stadium, I heard a lot of cheering — "Robina! Robina!" — and that made me feel good."

Symbolic Day

It was a symbolic day of victory for Muslim women. Danah Al Nasrallah of Kuwait became the first woman to run in the Olympics for her conservative country. She finished third to last overall in 13.92 — a national record.

Rakia Al Gassra of Bahrain, wearing a head scarf, long sleeves, and pants, was fifth in her heat and almost advanced to the quarterfinals. Alla Jassim of Iraq was fifty-second, just six months after she began training every day — when explosions in Baghdad didn't interfere.

In the stadium stands, coach Neema Suratgar couldn't stop crying tears of joy. She is the one most responsible for reviving women's sports in Afghanistan. Her own Olympic dreams were cut short by the Taliban, but she was able to see the next generation compete without fear of punishment.

"It was a great day for all Arab women around the world who deserve to claim their rights," said Suratgar, thirty-three. "I wanted to be on that track, running fast. But ten years have gone by, and it's too late."

During the Taliban reign, Suratgar was forced to give up her job as a teacher. Her basketball and track teams were disbanded. She was not permitted to go out of the house without her husband by her side and without wearing the head-to-toe bhurka, which reduced her gait to a shuffle.

She felt like a prisoner as her body atrophied. She felt faceless and empty. To keep from going crazy, she used to walk up and down a hill near her home, when the bombing range adjacent to it was not in use. She walked up and down, up and down, the hem of her bhurka dragging in the dirt. It was her stealth workout, an act of defiance and survival.

"I could not run in the bhurka, but I just had to go outside and get my legs going and breathe some fresh air," she said. "If someone stopped me, I would say I was going to visit my grandmother's grave."

One time, when police didn't believe her story, she was put in jail for the day.

But Suratgar refused to let the Taliban defeat her. She conducted her own small rebellion, secretly assembling thirty girls at her house every day for math and reading lessons and a soccer game in the courtyard.

Like the author of *Reading Lolita in Tehran,* she did what she could to keep the brains of her pupils from stagnating.

"It was risky," she said. "The Taliban came to our block and questioned my neighbors, but they did not turn me in."

Afghanistan was banned from the 2000 Olympics by the International Olympic Committee. After the Taliban was ousted by U.S.-led forces in 2002, Suratgar went into Kabul neighborhoods and schools and recruited sixty young women. They began basic training and have met considerable resistance from men and women who do not approve of their independence or their outfits.

Learning to Run

"The women did not even know how to run once they took off the bhurka," she said. "We started out just walking."

Muqimyar and seventeen-year-old Friba Razayee are two of Suratgar's protégés. Razayee, who lost in the first round of judo competition, was told when she took up the sport that no one would marry her. But she did it anyway, reveling in her strength and competitiveness.

"I don't do sport to be famous but because I was angry to hear that women are nothing and can do nothing," she said. "Some Afghans have old minds. I can show them through sport that they are wrong."

After her match, she called her father, who told her that what she had done "was like taking the first step on the moon," she said. "This is only the beginning. We hope the situation in our country will change and change."

The simple act of running, which we take for granted, was once forbidden in the land of the bhurka. That's why Muqimyar raised her arms in triumph Friday.

She wasn't second to last. She was free.

STEVE COLL

Barrage of Bullets Drowned
Out Cries of Comrades

FROM THE WASHINGTON POST

IT ENDED on a stony ridge in fading light. Specialist Pat Tillman lay dying behind a boulder. A young fellow U.S. Army Ranger stretched prone beside him, praying quietly as tracer bullets poured in.

"Cease fire! Friendlies!" Tillman cried out.

Smoke drifted from a signal grenade Tillman had detonated minutes before in a desperate bid to show his platoon members they were shooting the wrong men. The firing had stopped. Tillman had stood up, chattering in relief. Then the machine-gun bursts erupted again.

"I could hear the pain in his voice," recalled the young Ranger days later to Army investigators. Tillman kept calling out that he was a friendly, and he shouted, "I am Pat [expletive] Tillman, damn it!" His comrade recalled: "He said this over and over again until he stopped."

Myths shaped Pat Tillman's reputation, and mystery shrouded his death. A long-haired, fierce-hitting defensive back with the Arizona Cardinals of the National Football League, he turned away a $3.6 million contract after the September 11, 2001, attacks to volunteer for the war on terrorism, ultimately giving his life in combat in Taliban-infested southeastern Afghanistan.

Millions of stunned Americans mourned his death last April 22 and embraced his sacrifice as a rare example of courage and national service. But the full story of how Tillman ended up on that

Afghan ridge and why he died at the hands of his own comrades has never been told.

Dozens of witness statements, e-mails, investigation findings, log-books, maps, and photographs obtained by the *Washington Post* show that Tillman died unnecessarily after botched communications, a mistaken decision to split his platoon over the objections of its leader, and negligent shooting by pumped-up young Rangers — some in their first firefight — who failed to identify their targets as they blasted their way out of a frightening ambush.

The records show Tillman fought bravely and honorably until his last breath. They also show that his superiors exaggerated his actions and invented details as they burnished his legend in public, at the same time suppressing details that might tarnish Tillman's commanders.

Army commanders hurriedly awarded Tillman a posthumous Silver Star for valor and released a nine-paragraph account of his heroism that made no mention of fratricide. A month later the head of the Army's Special Operations Command, Lieutenant General Philip R. Kensinger Jr., called a news conference to disclose in a brief statement that Tillman "probably" died by "friendly fire." Kensinger refused to answer questions.

Friends and family describe Pat Tillman as an American original, a maverick who burned with intensity. He was wild, exuberant, loyal, compassionate, and driven, they say. He bucked convention, devoured books, and debated conspiracy theories. He demanded straight talk about uncomfortable truths.

After his death, the Army that Tillman served did not do the same.

Pat Tillman's decision to trade the celebrity and luxury of pro football for a grunt's life at the bottom of the Ranger chain of command shocked many people, but not those who felt they knew him best.

"There was so much more to him than anyone will ever know," reflected Denver Broncos quarterback Jake Plummer, a teammate at Arizona State University and on the Cardinals, speaking at a memorial service last May. Tillman was "fearless on the field, reckless, tough," yet he was also "thought-provoking. He liked to have deep conversations with a Guinness," and he would walk away from those sessions saying, "I've got to become more of a thinker."

In high school and college, a mane of flaxen hair poured from beneath his football helmet. His muscles rippled in a perfect taper from the neck down. "Dude" was his favorite pronoun; for fun he did handstands on the roof of the family house. He pedaled shirtless on a bicycle to his first pro training camp.

"I play football. It just seems so unimportant compared to everything that has taken place," he told NFL Films after the September 11 attacks. His grandfather had been at Pearl Harbor. "A lot of my family has gone and fought wars, and I really haven't done a damn thing."

He was very close to his younger brother Kevin, then playing minor league baseball for the Cleveland Indians organization. They finished each other's sentences, friends recounted. They enlisted in the U.S. Army Rangers together in the spring of 2002. Less than a year later, they shipped out to Iraq.

In Pat Tillman's first firefight during the initial months of the Iraq war, he watched his lead gunner die within minutes, stepped into his place, and battled steadfastly, said Steve White, a U.S. Navy SEAL on the same mission. "He was thirsty to be the best," White said.

Yet Tillman accepted his ordinary status in the military and rarely talked about himself. One night he confided to White that he had just turned down an NFL team's attempt to sign him to a huge contract and free him from his Army service early.

"I'm going to finish what I started," Tillman said, as White recalled at the May memorial. The next morning Tillman returned to duty and was ordered to cut "about an acre of grass by some nineteen-year-old kid."

The Tillman brothers served together in the "Black Sheep," otherwise known as Second Platoon, A Company, Second Battalion, Seventy-fifth Ranger Regiment. They were elite — special operators transferred from Iraq in the spring to conduct sweep and search missions against the Taliban and al Qaeda remnants in eastern Afghanistan. The Rangers worked with CIA paramilitaries, Afghan allies, and other special forces on grid-by-grid patrols designed to flush out and entrap enemy guerrillas. They moved in small, mobile, lethal units.

On April 13, 2004, the Tillman brothers rolled out with their fellow Black Sheep from a clandestine base near the Pakistan border to begin anti-Taliban patrols with two other Ranger platoons. A

week later the other platoons returned to base. So did the two senior commanding officers of A Company, records show. They left
behind the Second Platoon to carry on operations near Khost, in
Paktia province, a region of broken roads and barren rock canyons
frequented by Osama bin Laden and his allies for many years before the September 11 attacks.

Left in command of the Second Platoon was then-Lieutenant
David A. Uthlaut, a recent graduate of the U.S. Military Academy at
West Point, where he had been named the prestigious first captain
of his class. Now serving as a captain in Iraq, Uthlaut declined to be
interviewed for these articles, but his statements and field communications are among the documents obtained by the *Post.*

Uthlaut's mission, as Army investigators later put it, was to kill or
capture any "anti-coalition members" that he and his men could
find.

The trouble began with a Humvee's broken fuel pump.

A helicopter flew into Paktia with a spare on the night of April
21. But the next morning, the Black Sheeps' mechanic had no luck
with his repair.

Uthlaut ordered his platoon to pull out. He commanded thirty-
four men in nine vehicles, including the busted Humvee. They
towed the broken vehicle with straps because they lacked a proper
tow bar. After several hours on rough dirt-rock roads, the Humvee's front end buckled. It could move no farther. Uthlaut pulled
his men into a tiny village called Margarah to assess options.

It was just after noon. They were in the heart of Taliban country,
and they were stuck.

Uthlaut messaged his regiment's Tactical Operations Center far
away at Bagram, near Kabul. He asked for a helicopter to hoist the
Humvee back to base. No dice, came the reply: there would be no
transport chopper available for at least two or three days.

While Uthlaut tried to develop other ideas, his commanders at
the base squabbled about the delay. According to investigative records, a senior officer in the Rangers' operations center, whose
name is redacted from documents obtained by the *Post*, complained pointedly to A Company's commander, Uthlaut's immediate superior.

"This vehicle problem better not delay us any more," the senior
officer said, as he later recalled in a sworn statement. The Second
Platoon was already twenty-four hours behind schedule, he said. It

was supposed to be conducting clearing operations in a southeast-ern Afghan village called Manah.

By 4:00 P.M. Uthlaut had a solution, he believed. He could hire a local "jinga truck" driver to tow the Humvee out to a nearby road where the Army could move down and pick it up. In this scenario, Uthlaut told his commanders, he had a choice. He could keep his platoon together until the Humvee had been disposed of, then move to Manah. Or, he could divide his platoon in half, with one "serial" handling the vehicle while the other serial moved immedi-ately to the objective.

The A Company commander, under pressure from his superior to get moving, ordered Uthlaut to split his platoon.

Uthlaut objected. "I would recommend sending our whole pla-toon up to the highway and then having us go together to the vil-lages," he wrote in an e-mail to the operations center at 5:03 P.M. With sunset approaching, he wrote, even if he split the platoon, the serial that went to Manah would not be able to carry out search op-erations before dark. And under procedures at the time, he was not supposed to conduct such operations at night.

Uthlaut's commander overruled him. Get half your platoon to Manah right away, he ordered.

But why? Uthlaut asked, as he recalled in a sworn statement. Do you want us to change procedures and conduct sweep operations at night?

No, said the A Company commander.

"So the only reason you want me to split up is so I can get boots on the ground in sector before it gets dark?" an incredulous Uthlaut asked, as he recalled.

Yes, said his commander.

Uthlaut tried "one last-ditch effort," pointing out that he had only one heavy .50-caliber machine gun for the entire platoon. Did that change anything? The commander said it did not.

"At that point I figured I had pushed the envelope far enough and accepted the mission," Uthlaut recalled in the statement.

He pulled his men together hastily and briefed them. Twenty-four hours after its detection, the broken Humvee part had brought them to a difficult spot: they had to divide into two groups quickly and get moving across a darkening, hostile landscape.

Serial 1, led by Uthlaut and including Pat Tillman, would move immediately to Manah.

Serial 2, with the local tow truck hauling the Humvee, would follow, but would soon branch off toward a highway to drop off the vehicle.

Sergeant Greg Baker, a young and slightly built Ranger nearing the end of his enlistment, commanded the heaviest-armed vehicle in Serial 2, just behind the jinga tow truck. Baker's men wielded the .50-caliber machine gun, plus an M-240B machine gun, an M-249 squad automatic weapon, and three M-4 carbines. Baker's truck would do the heaviest shooting if there were any attack. Two of his gunners had never seen combat before.

Baker left the Rangers last spring; he declined to comment for these articles. A second gunner in his vehicle, Trevor Alders, also declined to discuss the incident.

Kevin Tillman was also assigned to Serial 2. He manned an MK19 gun in the trailing vehicle, well behind Baker.

They left Margarah village a little after 6:00 P.M. They had been in the same place for more than five hours, presenting an inviting target for Taliban guerrillas.

Pat Tillman's serial, with Uthlaut in command, soon turned into a steep and narrow canyon, passed through safely, and approached Manah as planned.

Behind them, Serial 2 briefly started down a different road, then stopped. The Afghan tow truck driver said he could not navigate the pitted road. He suggested they turn around and follow the same route that Serial 1 had taken. After Serial 2 passed Manah, the group could circle around to the designated highway. Serial 2's leader, the platoon sergeant, agreed.

There was no radio communication between the two serials about this change in plans.

At 6:34 P.M. Serial 2, with about seventeen Rangers in six vehicles, entered the narrow canyon that Serial 1 had just left.

When he heard the first explosion, the platoon sergeant thought one of his vehicles had struck a land mine or a roadside bomb.

They had been in the canyon only a minute. In his machine gun–laden truck, Greg Baker also thought somebody had hit a mine. He and his men jumped out of their vehicle. Baker looked up at the sheer canyon walls. The canyon was five to ten yards across at its narrowest. "I noticed rocks falling," he recalled in a statement, and "then I saw the second and third mortar rounds hit." He could hear, too, the rattle of enemy small-arms fire.

It was not a bomb — it was an ambush. Baker and his comrades thought they could see their attackers moving high above them. They began to return fire.

They were trapped in the worst possible place: the kill zone of an ambush. The best way to beat a canyon ambush is to flee the kill zone as fast as possible. But Baker and his men had dismounted their vehicles. Worse, when they scrambled back and tried to move, they discovered that the lumbering Afghan tow truck in their serial was stalled, blocking their exit.

Baker "ran up and grabbed" the truck driver and his Afghan interpreter and "threw them in the truck and started to move," as he recalled. He fired up the canyon walls until he ran out of ammunition. Then he jumped from the tow truck, ran back to his vehicle, and reloaded. When the tow truck stopped again, Baker shouted at his own driver to move around it.

Finally freed, Baker's heavily armed Humvee raced out of the ambush canyon, its machine guns pounding fire, its inexperienced shooters coursing with adrenaline.

Ahead of them, parked outside a small village near Manah, David Uthlaut heard an explosion. From his position he "could not see the enemy or make an adequate assessment of the situation," so he ordered his men to move toward the firing.

Uthlaut designated Pat Tillman as one of three fire team leaders and ordered him to join other Rangers "to press the fight," as Uthlaut put it, against an uncertain adversary.

Uthlaut tried to raise Serial 2 on his radio. He wanted to find out where the Rangers were and to tell them where his serial had set up. But he could not get through — the high canyon walls blocked radio signals.

Tillman and other Rangers moved up a rocky north-south ridge that faced the ambush canyon on a roughly perpendicular angle.

The light was dimming. "It was like twilight," one Ranger in the fight recalled. "You couldn't see colors, but you could see silhouettes." Another soldier felt the light was "still pretty good."

A sergeant with Tillman on the ridge recalled he "could actually see the enemy from the high northern ridge line. I could see their muzzle flashes." The presumed Taliban guerrillas were about half a mile away, he estimated.

Tillman approached the sergeant and said "that he saw the enemy on the southern ridge line," as the sergeant recalled. Tillman asked whether he could drop his heavy body armor. "No," the sergeant ordered.

"I didn't think about it at the time, but I think he wanted to assault the southern ridge line," the sergeant recalled.

Instead, on the sergeant's instructions, Tillman moved down the slope with other Rangers and "into a position where he could engage the enemy," the sergeant recalled. With Tillman were a young Ranger and a bearded Afghan militia fighter who was part of the Second Platoon's traveling party.

A Ranger nearby watched Tillman take cover. "I remember not liking his position," he recalled. "I had just seen a red tracer come up over us . . . which immediately struck me as being a M240 tracer . . . At that time the issue of friendly fire began turning over in my mind."

Tillman and his team fired toward the canyon to suppress the ambush. His brother Kevin was in the canyon.

Several of Serial 2's Rangers said later that as they shot their way out of the canyon, they had no idea where their comrades in Serial 1 might be.

"Contact right!" one gunner in Greg Baker's truck remembered hearing as they rolled from the ambush canyon.

As he fired, Baker "noticed muzzle flashes" coming from a ridge to the right of the village they were now approaching. Everyone in his vehicle poured fire at the flashes in a deafening roar.

"I saw a figure holding an AK-47, his muzzle was flashing, he wasn't wearing a helmet, and he was prone," Baker recalled in a statement. "I focused only on him. I got tunnel vision."

Baker was aiming at the bearded Afghan militia soldier in Pat Tillman's fire team. He died in a fusillade from Baker's Humvee.

A gunner in Baker's light truck later guessed they were "only about one hundred meters" from their new targets on the ridge, but they were "driving pretty fast towards them."

Rangers are trained to shoot only after they have clearly identified specific targets as enemy forces. Gunners working together are supposed to follow orders from their vehicle's commander — in this case, Baker. If there is no chance for orderly talk, the gunners are supposed to watch their commander's aim and shoot in the same direction.

As they pulled alongside the ridge, the gunners poured an undisciplined barrage of hundreds of rounds into the area where

Tillman and other members of Serial 1 had taken up positions, Army investigators later concluded. The gunner of the M-2 .50-caliber machine gun in Baker's truck fired every round he had.

The shooters saw only "shapes," a Ranger-appointed investigator wrote, and all of them directed bursts of machine-gun fire "without positively identifying the shapes."

Yet not everyone in Baker's convoy was confused. The driver of Baker's vehicle or the one behind him — the records are not clear — pulled free of the ambush canyon and quickly recognized the parked U.S. Army vehicles of Serial 1 ahead of him.

He looked to his right and saw a bearded Afghan firing an AK-47, "which confused me for a split second," but he then quickly saw the rest of Serial 1 on top of the ridge.

The driver shouted twice: "We have friendlies on top!" Then he screamed "No!" Then he yelled several more times to cease fire, he recalled. "No one heard me."

Up on the ridge, Tillman and Rangers around him began to wave their arms and shout. But they only attracted more fire from Baker's vehicle.

"I saw three to four arms pop up," one of the gunners with Baker recalled. "They did not look like the cease-fire hand-and-arm signal because they were waving side to side." When he and the other gunners spotted the waving arms, their "rate of fire increased."

The young Ranger nearest Tillman on the ridge, whose full name could not be confirmed, saw a Humvee coming down the road. "They made eye contact with us," then began firing, he remembered. Baker's heavily armed vehicle "rolled into our sight and started to unload on top of us. They would work in bursts."

Tillman and nearly a dozen other Rangers on the ridge tried everything they could: they shouted, they waved their arms, and they screamed some more.

"Ranger! Ranger! Cease fire!" one soldier on the ridge remembered shouting.

"But they couldn't hear us," recalled the soldier nearest Tillman. Then Tillman "came up with the idea to let a smoke grenade go." As its thick smoke unfurled, "this stopped the friendly contact for a few moments," the Ranger recalled.

"We thought the battle was over, so we were relieved, getting up and stretching out, and talking with one another."

Suddenly he saw the attacking Humvee move into "a better position to fire on us." He heard a new machine-gun burst and hit the ground, praying, as Pat Tillman fell.

A sergeant farther up the ridge from Tillman fired a flare — an even clearer signal than Tillman's smoke grenade that these were friendly forces.

By now Baker's truck had pulled past the ridge and had come into plain sight of Serial 1's U.S. vehicles. Baker said later that he looked down the road, then back up to the ridge. He saw the flare and identified Rangers even as he continued to shoot at the Afghan he believed to be a Taliban fighter. Finally he began to call for a cease-fire.

In the village behind Tillman's ridge, Uthlaut and his radio operator had been pinned down by the streams of fire pouring from Baker's vehicle. Both were eventually hit by what they assumed was machine-gun fire.

The last of Serial 2's vehicles pulled up in the village. All the firing had stopped.

The platoon sergeant jumped out and began searching for Uthlaut, angry that nobody seemed to know what was happening. He found the lieutenant sitting near a wall of the village, dropped down beside him, and demanded to know what he was doing. "At that point I spotted the blood around his mouth" and realized there were casualties — and that Uthlaut was one of them, wounded but still conscious.

On the ridge the young Ranger nearest Pat Tillman screamed, "Oh my [expletive] God!" again and again, as one of his comrades recalled. The Ranger beside Tillman had been lying flat as Tillman initially called out for a cease-fire, yelling out his name. Then Tillman went silent as the firing continued. Now the young Ranger saw a "river of blood" coming from Tillman's position. He got up, looked at Tillman, and saw that "his head was gone."

"I started screaming . . . I was scared to death and didn't know what to do."

A sergeant on the ridge took charge. He called for a medic, ordered Rangers to stake out a perimeter picket in case Taliban guerrillas attacked again, and opened a radio channel to the Seventy-fifth Ranger Regiment's operations center at Bagram.

Seventeen minutes after Serial 2 had entered the canyon, Second Platoon reported that its forces "were no longer in contact," as a Ranger-appointed investigator later put it. It was not clear then or later who the Afghan attackers spotted by half a dozen Rangers in both serials had been, how many guerrillas there were, or whether any were killed.

Nine minutes later, a regiment log shows, the platoon requested a medevac helicopter and reported two soldiers killed in action. One was the Afghan militia soldier. The other was Pat Tillman, age twenty-seven.

His brother Kevin arrived on the scene in Serial 2's trailing vehicle.

Kevin Tillman declined to be interviewed for these articles and was not asked by Ranger investigators to provide sworn statements. But according to other statements and sources familiar with the investigation, Kevin was initially asked to take up guard duty on the outskirts of the shooting scene.

He learned that his brother was dead only when a platoon mate mentioned it to him casually, according to these sources.

It would take almost five more weeks — after a flag-draped coffin ceremony, a Silver Star award and a news release, and a public memorial attended by Senator John McCain (R-Ariz.), Denver Broncos quarterback Jake Plummer, and newswoman Maria Shriver — for the Rangers or the Army to acknowledge to Kevin Tillman, his family, or the public that Pat Tillman had been killed by his own men.

Just days after Pat Tillman died from friendly fire on a desolate ridge in southeastern Afghanistan, the U.S. Army Special Operations Command released a brief account of his last moments.

The April 30, 2004, statement awarded Tillman a posthumous Silver Star for combat valor and described how a section of his Ranger platoon came under attack.

"He ordered his team to dismount and then maneuvered the Rangers up a hill near the enemy's location," the release said. "As they crested the hill, Tillman directed his team into firing positions and personally provided suppressive fire . . . Tillman's voice was heard issuing commands to take the fight to the enemy forces."

It was a stirring tale and fitting eulogy for the Army's most famous volunteer in the war on terrorism, a charismatic former pro football star whose reticence, courage, and handsome beret-draped face captured for many Americans the best aspects of the country's post-September 11 character.

It was also a distorted and incomplete narrative, according to dozens of internal Army documents obtained by the *Washington Post* that describe Tillman's death by fratricide after a chain of botched communications, a misguided order to divide his platoon over the objection of its leader, and undisciplined firing by fellow Rangers.

The Army's public release made no mention of friendly fire, even though at the time it was issued, investigators in Afghanistan had already taken at least fourteen sworn statements from Tillman's platoon members that made clear the true causes of his death. The statements included a searing account from the Ranger nearest Tillman during the firefight, who quoted him as shouting "Cease fire! Friendlies!" with his last breaths.

Army records show Tillman fought bravely during his final battle. He followed orders, never wavered, and at one stage proposed discarding his heavy body armor, apparently because he wanted to charge a distant ridge occupied by the enemy, an idea his immediate superior rejected, witness statements show.

But the Army's published account not only withheld all evidence of fratricide, but also exaggerated Tillman's role and stripped his actions of their context. Tillman was not one of the senior commanders on the scene — he directed only himself, one other Ranger, and an Afghan militiaman, under supervision from others. And witness statements in the Army's files at the time of the news release describe Tillman's voice ringing out on the battlefield mainly in a desperate effort, joined by other Rangers on his ridge, to warn comrades to stop shooting at their own men.

The Army's April 30 news release was just one episode in a broader Army effort to manage the uncomfortable facts of Pat Tillman's death, according to internal records and interviews.

During several weeks of memorials and commemorations that followed Tillman's death, commanders at his Seventy-fifth Ranger Regiment and their superiors hid the truth about friendly fire from Tillman's brother Kevin, who had fought with Pat in the same platoon, but was not involved in the firing incident and did not know the cause of his brother's death. Commanders also withheld the facts from Tillman's widow, his parents, national politicians, and the public, according to records and interviews with sources involved in the case.

On May 3, Ranger and Army officers joined hundreds of mourners at a public ceremony in San Jose, where Senator McCain, Jake Plummer, and Maria Shriver took the podium to remember Tillman. The visiting officers gave no hint of the evidence investigators had collected in Afghanistan.

In a telephone interview, McCain said: "I think it would have been helpful to have at least their suspicions known" before he spoke publicly about Tillman's death. Even more, he said, "the family deserved some kind of heads-up that there would be questions."

McCain said yesterday that questions raised by Mary Tillman, Pat's mother, about how the Army handled the case led him to meet twice earlier this fall with Army officers and former acting Army secretary Les Brownlee to seek answers. About a month ago, McCain said, Brownlee told him that the Pentagon would reopen its investigation. McCain said that he was not certain about the scope of the new investigation but that he believed it is continuing. A Pentagon official confirmed that an investigation is under way, but Army spokesmen declined to comment further.

When she first learned that friendly fire had taken her son's life, "I was upset about it, but I thought, 'Well, accidents happen,'" Mary Tillman said in a telephone interview yesterday. "Then when I found out that it was because of huge negligence at places along the way — you have time to process that and you really get annoyed."

As memorials and news releases shaped public perceptions in May, Army commanders privately pursued military justice investigations of several low-ranking Rangers who had fired on Tillman's position and officers who issued the ill-fated mission's orders, records show.

Army records show that Colonel James C. Nixon, the Seventy-fifth Ranger Regiment's commander, accepted his chief investigator's findings on the same day, May 8, that he was officially appointed to run the case. A spokesman for U.S. Central Command, or CENTCOM, which is legally responsible for the investigation, declined to respond to a question about the short time frame between the appointment and the findings.

The Army acknowledged only that friendly fire "probably" killed Tillman when Lieutenant General Philip R. Kensinger Jr. made a terse announcement on May 29 at Fort Bragg, North Carolina.

Kensinger declined to answer further questions and offered no details about the investigation, its conclusions, or who might be held accountable.

Army spokesmen said last week that they followed standard policy in delaying and limiting disclosure of fratricide evidence. "All the services do not prematurely disclose any investigation findings until the investigation is complete," said Lieutenant Colonel Hans Bush, chief of public affairs for the Army Special Operations Command at Fort Bragg. The Silver Star narrative released on April 30 came from information provided by Ranger commanders in the field, Bush said.

Kensinger's May 29 announcement that fratricide was probable came from an executive summary supplied by Central Command only the night before, he said. Because Kensinger was unfamiliar with the underlying evidence, he felt he could not answer questions, Bush said.

For its part, Central Command, headquartered at MacDill Air Force Base in Tampa, handled the disclosures "in accordance with [Department of Defense] policies," Lieutenant Commander Nick Balice, a command spokesman, said in an e-mail on Saturday responding to questions. Asked specifically why Central Command withheld any suggestion of fratricide when Army investigators by April 26 had collected at least fourteen witness statements describing the incident, Balice wrote in an e-mail: "The specific details of this incident were not known until the completion of the investigation."

The U.S. military has confronted a series of prominent friendly-fire cases in recent years, in part because hair-trigger technology and increasingly lethal remote-fire weapons can quickly turn relatively small mistakes into deadly tragedies. Yet the military's justice system has few consistent guidelines for such cases, according to specialists in Army law. Decision making about how to mete out justice rests with individual unit commanders who often work in secret, acting as both investigators and judges. Their judgments can vary widely from case to case.

"You can have tremendously divergent outcomes at a very low level of visibility," said Eugene R. Fidell, president of the National Institute of Military Justice and a visiting lecturer at Harvard Law School. "That does not necessarily contribute to public confidence in the administration of justice in the military. Other countries have been moving away" from systems that put field commanders in charge of their own fratricide investigations, he said.

In the Tillman case, those factors were compounded by the victim's extraordinary public profile. Also, Tillman's April 22 death was announced just days before the shocking disclosure of photographs of abuse by U.S. soldiers working as guards in Iraq's Abu Ghraib prison. The photos ignited an international furor and generated widespread questions about discipline and accountability in the Army.

Commemorations of Tillman's courage and sacrifice offered contrasting images of honorable service, undisturbed by questions about possible command or battlefield mistakes.

Whatever the cause, McCain said, "you may have at least a subconscious desire here to portray the situation in the best light, which may not have been totally justified."

Working in private last spring, the Seventy-fifth Ranger Regiment moved quickly to investigate and wrap up the case, Army records show.

Immediately after the incident, platoon members generated after-action statements, and investigators working in Afghanistan gathered logs, documents, and e-mails. The investigators interviewed platoon members and senior officers to reconstruct the chain of events. By early May, the evidence made clear in precise detail how the disaster unfolded.

On patrol in Taliban-infested sectors of Afghanistan's Paktia province, Tillman's "Black Sheep" platoon became bogged down because of a broken Humvee. Lieutenant David Uthlaut, the platoon leader, recommended that his unit stay together, deliver the truck to a nearby road, then complete his mission. He was overruled by a superior officer monitoring his operations from distant Bagram, near Kabul, who ordered Uthlaut to split his platoon, with one section taking care of the Humvee and the other proceeding to a village, where the platoon was to search for enemy guerrillas.

Steep terrain and high canyon walls prevented the two platoon sections from communicating with each other at crucial moments. When one section unexpectedly changed its route and ran into an apparent Taliban ambush while trapped in a deep canyon, the other section from a nearby ridge began firing in support at the ambushers. As the ambushed group broke free from the canyon, machine guns blazing, one heavily armed vehicle mistook an allied Afghan militiaman for the enemy and poured hundreds of rounds at positions occupied by fellow Rangers, killing Pat Tillman and the Afghan.

Investigators had to decide whether low-ranking Rangers who did the shooting had followed their training or had fired so recklessly that they should face military discipline or criminal charges. The investigators also had to decide whether more senior officers whose decisions contributed to the chain of confusion around the incident were liable.

Reporting formally to Colonel Nixon in Bagram on May 8, the case's chief investigator offered nine specific conclusions, which Nixon endorsed, according to the records.

Among them:

- The decision by a Ranger commander to divide Tillman's Second Platoon into two groups, despite the objections of the platoon's leader, "created serious command and control issues" and "contributed to the eventual breakdown in internal Platoon communications." The *Post* could not confirm the name of the officer who issued this command.
- The A Company commander's order to the platoon leader to get "boots on the ground" as his mission objective created a "false sense of urgency" in the platoon, which, "whether intentional or not," led to "a hasty plan." That officer's name also could not be confirmed by the *Post.*
- Sergeant Greg Baker, the lead gunner in the Humvee that poured the heaviest fire on Ranger positions, "failed to maintain his situational awareness" at key moments of the battle and "failed" to direct the firing of the other gunners in his vehicle.
- The other gunners "failed to positively identify their respective targets and exercise good fire discipline . . . Their collective failure to exercise fire discipline, by confirming the identity of their targets, resulted in the shootings of Corporal Tillman."

The chief investigator appeared to reserve his harshest judgments for the lower-ranking Rangers who did the shooting rather than the higher-ranking officers who oversaw the mission. While his judgments about the senior officers focused on process and communication problems, the chief investigator wrote about the failures in Baker's truck:

> While a great deal of discretion should be granted to a leader who is making difficult judgments in the heat of combat, the Command also has a responsibility to hold its leaders accountable when that judgment is so wanton or poor that it places the lives of other men at risk.

General John P. Abizaid, CENTCOM's commander in chief, formally approved the investigation's conclusions on May 28 under an aide's signature and forwarded the report to Special Operations commanders "for evaluation and any action you deem appropriate to incorporate relevant lessons learned."

The field investigation's findings raised another question for Army commanders: were the failures that resulted in Pat Tillman's death serious enough to warrant administrative or criminal charges?

In the military justice system, field officers such as Nixon, commander of the Seventy-fifth Ranger Regiment, can generally decide such matters on their own.

In the end, one member of Tillman's platoon received formal administrative charges, four others — including one officer — were discharged from the Rangers but not from the Army, and two additional officers were reprimanded, Lieutenant Colonel Bush said. He declined to release their names, citing Privacy Act restrictions.

Baker left the Rangers on an honorable discharge when his enlistment ended last spring, while others who were in his truck remain in the Army, said sources involved in the case.

Military commanders have occasionally leveled charges of involuntary manslaughter in high-profile friendly-fire cases, such as one in 2002 when Major Harry Schmidt, an Illinois National Guard pilot, mistakenly bombed Canadian troops in Afghanistan. But in that case and others like it, military prosecutors have found it difficult to make murder charges stick against soldiers making rapid decisions in combat.

And because there is no uniform, openly published military case law about when friendly-fire cases cross the line from accident to crime, commanders are free to interpret that line for themselves.

The list of cases in recent years where manslaughter charges have been brought is "almost arbitrary and capricious," said Charles Gittins, a former Marine who is Schmidt's defense lawyer. Gittins said that senior military officers tend to focus on low-ranking personnel rather than commanders. In Schmidt's case, he said, "every single general and colonel with the exception of Harry's immediate commander has been promoted since the accident." Schmidt, on the other hand, was ultimately fined and banned from flying Air Force jets.

Short of manslaughter, the most common charge leveled in fratricide is dereliction of duty, or what the military code calls "culpable inefficiency" in the performance of duty, according to military law specialists. This violation is defined in the Pentagon's official *Manual for Courts-Martial* as "inefficiency for which there is no reasonable or just excuse."

In judging whether this standard applies to a case such as Tillman's death, prosecutors are supposed to decide whether the accused person exercised "that degree of care which a reasonably prudent person would have exercised under the same or similar circumstances."

Even if a soldier or officer is found guilty under this code, the punishments are limited to demotions, fines, and minor discipline such as extra duty.

Records in the Tillman case do not make clear if Army commanders considered more serious punishments than this against any Rangers or officers, or, if so, why they were apparently rejected.

L. JON WERTHEIM

Outside Looking In

FROM SPORTS ILLUSTRATED

ROCK BOTTOM? That's tough to pinpoint, he says, sighing. So many lows to choose from. Rock bottom might have come when he walked into that Stygian cell in a German prison and realized that for the length of his stay he would be defecating in front of his cellmate. "Man," he says, "that was humiliating." The time he was arrested in front of all those fans at a senior tennis event, that was pretty embarrassing too. And when his father, once his most ardent supporter, turned uncommunicative, that one really stung. No, wait, I've got it, he says. Here's the lowest moment of his odyssey: immediately after he finished serving four months in a maximum-security county jail in Florida on a grand theft charge, he was transferred to a New Jersey jail where he would serve five months for willfully withholding child support. For two weeks he sat on a TransCor bus — think Con Air on the interstate — that zigzagged along the Eastern Seaboard picking up other criminals who were being reassigned from one jail to another. The bus, with no air conditioning, was hotter than hell. At night the convicts either slept in their seats or, if they were lucky, bunked down at a county jail en route. They were allotted three meals a day, but there was a catch: their hands never came out of restraints. Ever try eating McDonald's with your wrists locked at your waist? he asks. It's not real pleasant.

This is what it came to recently for Roscoe Tanner. The tennis star who once shared drinks with Prince Rainier on the French Riviera and dined with the Reagans in the White House was sitting on a bus near an exit ramp, positioning his chin at just the right angle so he could eat a Big Mac and some fries.

*

Roscoe Tanner is not, of course, the first retired athlete to turn his life into a Hieronymus Bosch canvas. But it's hard to imagine a less likely candidate to make an absolute mess of things. Tennis players just don't fall into the abyss — especially not a player born to the manor, with a Stanford diploma, a thick Rolodex of connections, and, if that weren't endowment enough, movie-star looks and boundless reserves of charm.

As Tanner retraces his *via dolorosa*, you have to remind yourself that the eminently likable narrator of this story is also its protagonist, the man who is on probation in three states, has amassed a mountain of debt, and is on tenuous terms with much of his family. By all outward appearances, Tanner conforms to the image of a former tennis star in the second set of middle age. He recently turned fifty-three but could easily pass for a decade younger. He's tan, fit, and blessed by the tonsorial gods with a full thatch of light brown hair. He spends his weekends on a beach haven off the coast of southern California called Balboa Island, where $1 million might get you a three-bedroom cottage. Holding court at a restaurant in late October, he is flanked by an assortment of friends and his blond, younger third wife, Margaret. Tanner speaks enthusiastically of his job as a tennis teacher in Laguna Niguel. Margaret gushes that Roscoe is a "super dad" to her twin teenage daughters from a previous marriage.

During the meal there are occasional hints that something has gone terribly awry. A discussion about politics quickly fades when a member of the dinner party realizes that Tanner, as a convicted felon, might not be able to vote. Tanner passes on the bruschetta, casually mentioning that it reminds him too much of the weight he gained in jail eating little but white bread. When the check arrives, Tanner looks away — he can't cover the tab, so he doesn't even feign reaching for it. After the meal he and Margaret walk to a friend's pad where they are living until Roscoe can come up with the cash to pay the security deposit and first month's rent on an apartment.

But Tanner is delightful company, a funny, self-deprecating man who makes everyone feel comfortable. His voice, a rolling bass with a slight southern twang, is nothing if not smooth. Mistakes, he concedes again and again, have been made. But he's "putting things back together," he's "picking up the pieces," he's "attending church regularly and doing the right thing."

You believe him. You root for him. It takes a conscious effort to consider the possibility that this could all just be the latest in his lengthy history of deceptions.

Lookout Mountain, Tennessee, sounds like the kind of backwater town immortalized in country music ballads. It's not. With a median household income in excess of $100,000, it's one of America's most moneyed enclaves, a suburb of Chattanooga that sits on a promontory from which you can see seven states on a clear day. Even in a community steeped in wealth and status, the Tanners were a distinguished clan. They traced their roots to British royalty. Leonard Roscoe Tanner II, a successful attorney, had studied law at the University of Chicago and was friendly with Tennessee's leading politicians, right up to the governor. He and his wife, Anne, had two daughters and then a son, Leonard Roscoe III, who were raised in a succession of ever-larger homes, the last a doge's palace of more than seven thousand square feet.

Roscoe, as everybody called the boy, wanted for nothing. But neither was he spoiled. Leonard, a stoic father cut from the Atticus Finch mold, was, as we say today, old school. He insisted that his son perform chores and *No, Ma'am* and *Yessir* the adults. Leonard took a particular interest in his son's tennis, analyzing his losses as though they were complex legal issues. In 1966 the teenage Roscoe struggled in his matches and finally summoned the courage to confront the old man at the end of the year. "Dad, leave me to figure tennis out for myself," he said. "If I don't get better, I'll quit. But if I win a national title, you have to buy me a car." Leonard went along with that. Liberated from Dad and all the attendant pressure, Roscoe won *four* national titles in 1967. "My dad didn't get me four cars, though," he says. "I got one. A used white Pontiac Tempest."

Roscoe went to the Baylor School, a semimilitary academy in Chattanooga with a powerhouse tennis team coached at the time by Jerry Evert, Chris's uncle. His teammates included Zan Guerry and Brian Gottfried, both of whom would play professionally. Roscoe was an unassuming kid with no discernible ego. "I honestly can't remember a single thing not normal about him," says Gottfried. "Just a nice kid from a nice family."

In an act that amounted to his late-1960s rebellion, Tanner spurned Tennessee colleges to play for Stanford. The school had a modest tennis program that had seldom beaten UCLA or USC. But its young, upbeat coach, Dick Gould, talked of "building a tradition," and Tanner was seduced. In his first season he made the 1970 NCAA finals in both singles and doubles, and his magnetism helped Gould recruit bright prospects. Stanford would go on to win seventeen NCAA titles and become the dynastic program in college tennis. "There's no question," says Gould, who retired last year, "Roscoe Tanner is the guy who put Stanford tennis on the map."

Tanner turned pro in 1972 and quickly made his presence known, reaching the quarterfinals of the U.S. Open and breaking into the top twenty. His game was built around a left-handed serve that he developed by swinging his racket at falling leaves in the Tennessee woods. Though he was not the biggest of players — six feet and a solid 175 pounds — his serve was pure tracer fire, the product of a low ball toss and blinding racket speed. "Rocket Roscoe" once delivered a ball so hard that it snapped a net cable at the U.S. Open. Playing before racket technology went space-age, Tanner once had his serve clocked at a record 153 miles per hour.

Snapping aces and charging the net, Tanner won the Australian Open in 1977 and, over a twelve-year career, took fourteen other titles and nearly six hundred matches. He played on several U.S. Davis Cup squads, helping the team win the trophy in 1981. His finest hour, however, came at Wimbledon in '79. It was the first year the men's final was televised live in the U.S. — the inaugural *Breakfast at Wimbledon* — and the winsome kid from Tennessee played for the title against Bjorn Borg, the defending champ and eight-to-one favorite. Impeccably dressed, Leonard Tanner watched nervously from the players' box as his son pushed Borg to five sets before losing a classic match.

Roscoe returned to the United States a full-fledged celebrity. "We did more deals for Roscoe than for a lot of guys who won bigger," says Donald Dell, Tanner's agent for much of his career. "Everyone wanted him." Racket, shoe, and clothing endorsements rolled in, but his appeal wasn't limited to tennis products. Tanner appeared in TV commercials for Ivory soap, whose slogan, "99$\frac{44}{100}$% pure," would later seem richly ironic. He was invited to appear on sitcoms and to judge the Miss USA contest. In a 1988 poll asking U.S. female fans to name their favorite male athletes, Tanner ranked fourth. Wayne Gretzky was fifth. Tanner won more than $1.7 million in prize money, but that figure was dwarfed by his off-court income.

Tanner was handsome and had a winning smile. He was polished but not slick, melding Stanford sophistication with southern home-spun modesty. Temperamentally he offered an appealing alternative to the fire of Jimmy Connors and John McEnroe and the ice of Borg. "There was a warmth there," says Sam McCleery, a former racket company executive and an old friend of Tanner's. "Roscoe's personality was a lot like his tennis. What you saw was what you got. He came straight at you, not a lot of spin or angles."

If he wasn't the pledge master of the tennis fraternity, he was a member in good standing. Even today, Tanner's contemporaries invariably use the same phrase — "great guy" — to describe him. And his integrity was considered unimpeachable. "Put it this way," says one former player. "Roscoe was Arthur Ashe's doubles partner, and Roscoe was the straighter arrow of the two."

Tanner's longtime coach, Dennis Ralston, recalls his protégé as attentive and tractable: "Never once did Roscoe question my authority. If he told me something, I knew that I could bank on it."

An injury to his left elbow forced Tanner out of tennis in 1984, but his playing career was winding down anyway. ESPN quickly signed him to comment on televised matches, surely just the beginning of a very successful transition to another phase of life.

"You look at the guy, and he sure seemed to have it made," says McEnroe, another Stanford alum. "Never in my wildest dreams did I see what was coming. Roscoe fooled everyone, I guess."

In retrospect anyway, there were hints that Tanner was more complex than his all-American image suggested. His parents would fly across the country to watch him play at tournaments, and when they arrived he would cruelly ignore them. Ray Moore, one of Tanner's doubles partners, nicknamed him Short Fuse for his sudden, inexplicable explosions during practice, after which he would quickly revert to his good-natured form.

Five years after his retirement from the tour, Tanner ran a senior tennis event in Santa Barbara, California. The weekend was a success except for one thing: Tanner did not pay many of the players. He blamed it on a "sponsor screwup" and promised that the checks were forthcoming. The players had known him for years and took him at his word. The checks did arrive, but some took as long as seven months. Thinking back, former pro Dick Stockton, who played in the event and had first met Tanner in the juniors in 1961, says, "There was always an iffy side to Roscoe, things that didn't quite check out, but nothing serious enough for anyone to care."

Tanner was also, he now admits, a womanizer. He was never one to let his marriages get in the way of a good time. He met his first wife, Nancy Cook, at Stanford. They were married in 1973 and had a daughter, Lauren, in '81. But the marriage was a casualty of Tanner's infidelities — after he told her he wanted out Nancy took a pair of scissors and cut the crotch out of all of Roscoe's pants — and they divorced in '83. Not long after, Tanner met a vivacious nightclub manager in Santa Barbara named Charlotte Brady. They married within a few months, but it was only a matter of time, Tanner says, before he strayed again. "I was a smooth talker," he says. "I was good, really good, at saying whatever the other person wanted to hear."

It was the philandering that would cause the entire tapestry of his life to start unraveling. In 1993 Tanner was in New York City for a senior tennis event when he met Connie Romano, a striking woman from New Jersey. They spent a night together in his Manhattan hotel room. Tanner thought little of it — just another one-night stand on the road. (Romano says they met several times.) Then, a few months later, he got a call at the Sherwood Country Club in Thousand Oaks, California, where he was the director of tennis. It was Romano phoning from New Jersey to say that she was pregnant. Tanner told her he didn't think it was possible.

A few months later the summonses regarding a lawsuit for child support started arriving. Tanner says he called Romano's lawyer to discuss a settlement, but the lawyer was asking for too much money. He consented to take a DNA test, which revealed a 99.5 percent chance that he was the father of Romano's baby, a girl born in 1994. Nevertheless, he denied paternity on grounds that the DNA test was not conclusive enough. "He told me that he had been drugged," says Charlotte Tanner. (Roscoe denies having said this but concedes that he might have claimed he had been inebriated.) "He said that as a celebrity he was a target [of gold diggers], and I believed him." Eager to avoid bad publicity, Tanner finally agreed to a $500,000 out-of-court settlement, which at the time he did not have the means of honoring. (He claims he intended to pay

Romano from $1 million he expected to make on a deal that subsequently fell through.)

When Romano received no check from Tanner and he didn't return her phone calls or respond to her lawyer's threats, she contacted authorities. In March 1997 Tanner was arrested while attending a senior tennis event in Naples, Florida, and charged with failing to appear in a New Jersey court to answer for $40,000 in missed payments to Romano. With Leonard's help, Charlotte came up with the money, and Roscoe was released. He returned to the Naples tournament the next day and, sitting in a lounge, regaled his colleagues with stories of his night in jail. When he took the court, the fans gave him a standing ovation. "Roscoe has such a way with people," says Stockton. "It was inconceivable that this great, down-to-earth guy could have done anything wrong."

Three years earlier Roscoe, Charlotte, and their two daughters — Tamara, then nine years old, and Anne, four — had moved from California to Tennessee. They purchased 130 acres in the woods outside Chattanooga, which they were going to transform into the Tanner Tennis Lodge. The architectural renderings called for 140 hotel rooms, a spa, a lake stocked with fish, and an upscale restaurant. Their dream was to parlay the success of the lodge into a chain of tennis resorts.

In the months after Tanner's '97 arrest, however, plans for the lodge fell behind schedule, and investors pulled out. The bank foreclosed on the property. Tanner's endorsement deals had petered out long ago, as had the lucrative pro-am appearances. In 1998 he filed for bankruptcy. Tanner turned to his pals in the tennis world for loans. "I'd say there were twenty-five guys Roscoe tried to borrow from," says Moore, his old doubles partner. Several players — including Borg, Tanner's opponent in that memorable Wimbledon final — stepped up, lending Tanner a total in excess of $100,000. At least Borg *thought* he was lending the money. When no repayment was made, his representatives pursued Tanner. Finally a deal was brokered: a portion of Tanner's earnings at senior events would be deducted to make good on the debt.

As he sank deeper into debt, Tanner was spinning an ever-widening web of lies to his wife and daughters. He had taken a teaching pro job in Florida and was seldom home. Charlotte says that on Tamara's eleventh birthday, in 1996, Roscoe called to say he couldn't fly home to Tennessee due to work. Charlotte later found credit card receipts indicating that he had been in the Cayman Islands that day.

Charlotte and Roscoe were divorced in December 2000. By that time Roscoe and Margaret Barna had already had a "ceremony of commitment" in Hawaii. (Roscoe paid their bill at the Hilton Waikoloa Village with a check that bounced.) The divorce settlement called for him to pay Charlotte $7,000 a month in child support for Tamara and Anne. The checks seldom came, and when they did they were for far less than the agreed-upon amount. Charlotte filed for bankruptcy in the spring of 2001, and she and her daughters had to live apart for four months; Charlotte's credit rating was so bad that she couldn't rent an apartment. She took to selling Roscoe's tennis hardware to pay bills. The 1977 Australian Open trophy fetched $10,000, less a 15 percent commission. The 1981 Davis Cup trophy went for only $1,900.

In May 2001 Tanner was arrested on court during another senior event, outside Atlanta, because he was delinquent in his payments to Charlotte. He spent a night in jail for "willful criminal contempt of court" and was released after paying $8,000. Two months later another warrant was issued for him on the same charge, though he was not arrested on it.

By then Tanner had vowed to friends that he was "starting a new life." He and Margaret had relocated to Florida's Gulf Coast, where he took a job as tennis pro at the Treasure Island Tennis and Yacht Club, near St. Petersburg. The pay was good, the housing was cheap, and he still believed he could somehow make a go of the Tanner Tennis Villages. He had also been seduced by another beauty with a sleek figure — this one thirty-two feet long.

Tanner ogled the Wellcraft yacht, priced at $39,000, and envisioned himself cruising the gulf with Margaret. In the summer of 2000 he gave the broker, Gene Gammon, a $3,000 deposit, and then he dropped off a check for $35,595 — which, Tanner claims, he expected would clear after a tennis-related deal he was working on in Atlanta came through. The deal didn't pan out. "Here was the big star," says Gammon. "I never thought he couldn't afford it."

Gammon was told by his bank that the check had cleared. He gave Tanner title to *Nora's Cruisin'* and paid the manufacturer. Then he learned that, in fact, his bank had made a mistake. Tanner's check had bounced. When he pursued Tanner, he discovered a problem: Tanner had already used the boat as collateral to secure a $10,000 loan from a joint in a strip mall that charged 10 percent interest per month. Not only was Gammon out the money, but the mall lenders now superseded him as creditors.

Tanner offered to pay Gammon from his ATP pension, which would begin paying him $880 a month in January 2001, the year Tanner would turn fifty. Gammon declined. Then, he says, Tanner showed him a receipt indicating that he had paid the money he owed to court authorities. (Tanner denies this.) When Gammon followed up, he says, he found that the receipt was not authentic. Gammon then learned that Tanner had taken a leave from his job at Treasure Island. Having taken a hit of more than $35,000, Gammon had to sell stocks he owned and was eventually forced to sell his brokerage business.

"The guy came in here with a smile," says Gammon, now a broker for another company, "and he damn near ruined me."

There was one man who could make Roscoe's debts disappear and ease a lot of the heartache he had caused. Leonard Tanner had been devastated when his wife died of a heart attack in 1983. But he soldiered on, remarrying and leaving his law practice to become CEO of a tire company. Through it all he remained a pillar of Chattanooga society and a doting father. In 1990 Roscoe was inducted into a regional tennis hall of fame in Atlanta, and he asked his father to give the presenting speech. Leonard delivered a forty-five-minute filibuster lauding his only son. "Leonard," says Dell, "always thought Roscoe walked on water."

When Roscoe first started to court trouble, Leonard came to the rescue, giving him money and working with Chattanooga lawyers and judges to get him off the hook. But eventually Leonard cut his prodigal son loose. He would put some money in the prison commissary fund so Roscoe could buy a razor or a toothbrush, but that was the extent of his contribution. There were times when Roscoe was so destitute that he could afford neither bail nor a lawyer. He got no help from Pop.

Asked about his father, Roscoe loses his smile, and an awkward silence ensues. "It's tough," he says. "He felt that he bailed me out and it didn't stop the problems, and it was time for me to face things myself."

Leonard is eighty-nine now, and though he recently had to give up his tennis, he still cuts a dignified, lawyerly figure. And he sticks by his decision. "There came a time when I thought maybe I was doing Roscoe a disservice by trying to handle everything," he says. "He made an error. I let him handle the error, and I believe it has worked out. I think the unfortunate things he suffered have worked to his advantage. He's a wonderful boy, you know."

It's a surreal narrative any way you slice it. But it would make a lot more sense if Tanner had an obvious vice. Innumerable athletes have descended into darkness because of drug habits, but Tanner says that though he dabbled in cocaine after retiring from the men's tour, he never had a drug problem — a claim supported even by those who have the biggest bones to pick with him. Other athletes have gambled away their millions, but no one can recall Tanner so much as joining a card game. Greed wasn't his motivation either. The stakes involved in Tanner's schemes were not stunningly high.

Finding plausible explanations for Tanner's behavior has become something of a parlor game in tennis circles. Bill Scanlon, a contemporary of Tanner's on the men's tour, wonders whether Tanner isn't simply a spoiled kid who panicked when the money ran out. Others surmise that there is an alter ego that Tanner successfully suppressed during his playing career. "Maybe it's a *Three Faces of Eve* thing," says Ralston, his old coach. "The Roscoe Tanner I knew not taking care of his kids? That blows me away." Charlotte Tanner thinks that the death of her ex-husband's mother triggered some deep psychological reaction.

Provided a summary of Tanner's behavior, a prominent sports psychologist says without hesitating, "Sounds like a sociopath — definitely some pathology." Tanner says he periodically sought counseling to help him deal with his financial and family problems ("Frankly," he says, "it didn't help") but has never been given a psychological diagnosis.

He has his own thoughts on his case. "My vice was selfishness," he says, "but I had an amazing ability to compartmentalize. Things would be eating at me, so much that I had this recurring dream that my body was filled with worms. But I could block it out. I'd just brush people and problems and responsibilities to the side. That's what tennis players do, right? They block out distractions."

He might be on to something. It's become an article of faith that sports build character, that they teach universal virtues. What if that's not always the case? What if the very traits that make some athletes successful get lost in translation when they are applied to life?

Besides that pump-action serve, Tanner's greatest asset as a player was his consistency. He never went through a prolonged slump. He would lose in the first round one week and then win the next tournament. "When I'd lose, I'd put it out of my mind," he says. "Other guys would lose and analyze what they did wrong. My attitude was, I'll just move on to the next match." When the summonses arrived and the past-due notices came and investors called asking what had happened to their money, Tanner treated them as distractions. Block them out and they'll go away.

Few athletes were more positive than Tanner. "Roscoe didn't see his glass as half full, he saw it as overflowing," says former U.S. Open champion Stan Smith, a contemporary of Tanner's who remains in touch with him. "He had supreme confidence. He always thought he was going to win."

The pie-in-the-sky business ventures? The promises to repay money he didn't have? The loan at 10 percent monthly interest? "It was totally flawed thinking," Tanner says, "but I honestly thought that somehow, some way, I was going to pull it off."

Tanner had the self-absorption that is all but required for success in individual sports. Gould, the Stanford coach, recalls congratulating Tanner on being one of the three best college players in the country. Who are the others, Tanner asked, dumbfounded that he might have equals. "Well, Roscoe," Gould replied, "one of them is that kid at UCLA, Jimmy Connors." Maybe that was the same characteristic that enabled him to enter a kind of moral isolation chamber and cheat on his spouses and abandon his kids and put a boat dealer out of business.

"I don't blame tennis," says Tanner. "I did this to myself. I'm not making excuses. But as an athlete you can get in some habits, and sometimes it takes a sledgehammer to break them."

Gene Gammon, the duped boat dealer, didn't give a damn who Tanner had been in a previous life. He wanted his money. Doggedly he followed Tanner on the Internet, and in the spring of 2003 his name appeared in the box score of a club tennis event in Germany.

Germany? Tanner had hightailed it across the Pond with Marga-

ret and her daughters. (He claims it had nothing to do with his legal and financial problems. "We just wanted a new experience," he
says, "and senior tennis pays better over there.") He coached a
struggling British pro, gave some lessons in France, played for a
club team in Germany. Gammon alerted sportswriters in Europe,
who called authorities in Florida to ask about Tanner's situation
and revealed his whereabouts. Tanner was arrested on an extradition order and taken to a jail in the Black Forest town of Karlsruhe.

He has few fond recollections of his six weeks in a German jail
cell. The food was so vile that he often ate with his eyes closed.
Walls were covered with anti-American graffiti. Inmates were permitted only two showers a week. And he feared that another prisoner would try to make a name for himself by slipping a knife into
the gut of the American.

There was, however, one amenity. The televisions in the cells received more than thirty channels. One Sunday morning Tanner
flipped to a broadcast of the Reverend Robert Schuller's *Hour of
Power.* As Schuller read from Philippians, Tanner found it in his Bible and followed along: *Rejoice in the Lord always. Rejoice, let your gentleness be evident to all! The Lord is near. Don't be anxious about anything,
but in everything by prayer and petition, with thanksgiving, present your requests to the Lord.*

Tanner was rapt. He mulled over the passage and then thought
about the train wreck that was his life. As he later put it to a friend,
"I knew I was tired of going Roscoe's way. I'd either spent, lost, or
signed over all of my money. But that wasn't enough: I had ripped
off friends, innocent acquaintances, and creditors on two continents. I had cheated on two wives and failed miserably as a father."

He knelt beside his bed and prayed. Prayed that he would repent. Prayed that he would find peace. And while he was at it, he
prayed that the Lord would take care of the rash he had had on his
wrist for years. A few days later he took a shower. When he dried
off, he noticed that the rash was gone. A few days after that a guard
told him that he had been extradited to the U.S.

Unable to scrounge up bail money, Tanner spent seventeen
weeks in the rough Pinellas County, Florida, jail, where the inmates, most of them black, jokingly nicknamed him Deejay because he couldn't rap. In November 2003 Tanner pleaded guilty to
grand theft and was sentenced to probation until he makes good
on his debt to Gammon. (The current payment plan calls for Tan-

ner to fork over $102,000 in capital and interest over ten years. To do that, he signed over to Gammon his ATP pension payments beginning in January 2006.) Then he served five months in a county jail in Somerset, New Jersey, for failure to make payments due to Romano. He claims that at times he felt it was good for him to be locked up. He had been reading the Bible and helping other inmates learn to read. He even found something redeeming about his prison job cleaning toilets.

After Tanner was released, on April 19, he stayed with friends and relatives in various places — Washington, D.C., Florida, Georgia — but eventually California beckoned. In the state for court appearances, he shuttled along the corridor between L.A. and San Diego, crashing with assorted friends from Stanford and the tennis caravan — ten days in this vacant guesthouse, a week in that basement. Eventually he crossed paths with Cecil Spearman, a silver-haired former Marine who played tennis at Duke in the 1950s, made a killing in business, and runs three upscale tennis clubs in Orange County. Spearman asked a few dozen members what they'd think if he hired Tanner. The responses were "overwhelmingly positive," he says, so he called Tanner to his office at the Laguna Niguel Racket Club, explained that there would be no second chances, and offered him a job giving lessons at $65 an hour. Tanner jumped at it.

Isn't California where everyone gets a fresh start? And his daughters Lauren, Tamara, and Anne were all living in the L.A. area. Maybe he could reconnect with them.

Slowly, the clouds are lifting. He's worked out some payment plans to start chipping away at his debts, which total more than $400,000. He plans to play doubles in a few upcoming senior events. He's continued reading his Bible and attending church, and he says he's working on his autobiography. He's surrounded himself with an AA-style "accountability team" to make sure he doesn't waver in his resolve. In a series of interviews with *SI*, he is nothing if not contrite about his past. He's begun to repair his relationship with Leonard, whom he calls on the telephone. And he's on good terms again with Lauren, a twenty-two-year-old senior at Vanderbilt. "My dad never had to grow up until age fifty," she says. "If I didn't see a major change, he wouldn't be back in my life."

In October, Margaret arrived with her daughters, vowing to give Roscoe a last shot. Immediately she took over the practical details of his life, making the car payments on their Ford Explorer and seeing that other bills get paid on time.

By all accounts it's worked well. What hacker wouldn't want to take pointers from a serving demon who nearly won Wimbledon? James Dolan, the New York Knicks' owner, recently took five lessons from Tanner. Every week more of his time is booked. "The members think the world of Roscoe," says Spearman. "He's a great guy, a great teacher. Boy, he can really carry on and tell a million stories."

Everyone likes a happy ending. This saga may get one, but we're not there yet. Tanner still hasn't gotten together with Tamara and Anne, who live a few miles from him but remain wounded by Dad's disappearing act and the welter of excuses he gave. Tanner claims that Charlotte is standing between him and his daughters, but she points out that Tamara is in college and not subject to her control. "I still can't figure him out, just leaving us and never coming back," says Tamara, a thoughtful, earnest sophomore at Loyola Marymount, where she got a full ride to play tennis. "Two plus two doesn't equal four with him." Last month Tanner sought a reduction of his alimony and child-support obligation to Tamara and Anne.

What's more, in September, Tanner was arrested at a doughnut shop in Laguna Niguel after missing a scheduled New Jersey court appearance in the Romano matter. (He was released and appeared in court in early September.) "It's always the same thing with that guy," says Bob Lang, a Somerset County, New Jersey, prosecutor. "He agrees to meet obligations, he fails to meet them, and then he disappears."

Nor does Roscoe have a relationship with his ten-year-old daughter by Romano. "He has done so much damage to that girl," says Romano, now an artist living in New Jersey. "She asked him for a photograph because she wanted to draw her father. Nothing. He promised to give her a tennis lesson. Nothing. He promised her a teddy bear. Nothing. As far as I'm concerned, he's a loser."

And if Tanner hasn't been run out from the tennis fraternity, he is on something akin to double secret probation. The unpaid loans from many of his former colleagues are part of it. But opinion in the seniors' locker room really shifted when evidence mounted that Tanner was neglecting his kids. "We like the guy, we want to see him get his life together, but we also want to see him take care of his family," says Stockton, whose wife, Liz, remains friendly with Charlotte Tanner. "The whole thing makes all of us who have known him sick."

Tanner knows that he has a lot of accounting to do, that not all of his debts are financial ones. But he didn't hit rock bottom all at once, and he thinks his climb back will be gradual too. "People always say, 'It's day by day,' but really that's what it is with me. There was so much cloudy thinking, so many decisions that any sane person could see were crazy. I went to a pretty good school. I was supposed to be pretty intelligent. Look at me now: I have no money, no credit. But you know what? I'm happier now than I ever was in my tennis career. When I won the Australian Open, I was happy for about ten minutes. There are not those empty spots now. Do I know where this is all going? No. But I know this: I'm through running."

These days you can catch Tanner in Laguna Niguel, usually on one of the eight courts at Spearman's Tennis Club at Monarch Beach, a swank stucco complex where the air is perfumed by breezes from the nearby Pacific. A sheen of sweat on his forehead, Tanner wields a scarlet Wilson racket and tells housewives, kids, seniors — whoever comes through the door — to bend their knees for that volley or shorten that backswing or follow through by pointing at the target. He's charming and energetic, and if he warms up, he can still crank a 120-mile-per-hour serve.

Late one afternoon in October, as palms cast long shadows across the court, Tanner is giving a private lesson to his prize student, Stefan Simikic, a fifteen-year-old with big-time potential. They play a series of tiebreakers. At one point Tanner grooves a serve that recalls the mop-haired pro from Tennessee. Simikic sticks a return back, and the two players, a Wimbledon finalist and a Wimbledon hopeful, rally for a dozen strokes. Simikic bats the ball to the middle of the court, and Tanner is in prime position to chip and charge. But he dumps an easy forehand into the net.

"You had me right where you wanted me!" the kid says, laughing. Tanner, too, laughs at his error. He picks up the ball, stuffs it in his pocket, and retreats to the baseline to play the next point, at once in plain view and obscured by shadows.

WRIGHT THOMPSON

A Man Who Made Good

FROM THE KANSAS CITY STAR

AMES, IOWA — He sees himself in the man's face. The same confident jaw and youthful smile. But the eyes, his eyes, that's what draws George Trice in, sends him back almost a century.

Many students on the Iowa State campus walk past the statue of former football player Jack Trice, the namesake of their stadium twenty yards away, and feel nothing. Don't even turn to look. Then there's George, a relative of Jack's who grew up in the man's shadow all his life.

George is a junior at ISU now. He couldn't even touch the statue when he first arrived. To him, it felt like staring into his own grave.

"It's like a ghost," he says. "People say, 'You look just like it.'"

Jack Trice was the first black football player in Iowa State history — one of the first on the Great Plains. This was long before the civil rights movement, before Emmett Till, and Medgar Evers, and the Lorraine Motel. Jack's legend has become a distant beacon, his story growing fainter every year, even here in the heartland.

"Everybody holds him to such a high standard because he was on the path to be great," George Trice says. "It was a big challenge for me coming here. I caved under that pressure."

He sits by his cousin's statue. College has been hard for George — six years and counting. But he won't quit; he believes that his family needs someone to complete the journey that was stolen from Jack Trice. George knows his mother wants this so badly; he hears it all the time.

"I was letting him know how important it would be for a Trice to graduate from that college," says Wanda Trice-Elbert, "for a Trice to succeed where Jack tried but didn't."

George looks over at the monolithic field rising to his left, trying, like many in this college town, to understand a story from a different time, to bring form to history, air into the lungs of forgotten injustices. All but a handful of the characters are dead. But their actions over six heartbreaking days in 1923 live, in a weathered file in the Iowa State archives, in faded newspapers, in the hearts of the Trice family.

"Why is my cousin's name on the stadium?" George Trice says. "It was eighty years ago. He was killed because he was black."

Thursday, October 4, 1923

The gunmetal midwestern sky creaked. The hard breaths of a killing frost moved across parts of Iowa, a silent alarm that winter was coming early. The weather folks figured it to be the coldest October in thirteen years.

In Ames, Iowa State College head football coach Sam Willaman ran his team through a final practice. They'd be playing a powerful Minnesota squad in two days, and he had reason to be concerned.

So did Jack Trice, his sophomore lineman from the small town of Hiram, Ohio.

As one of the few black football players in the nation, and one of about twenty black students on the entire campus, Trice knew race was always an issue. He understood his symbolic importance.

Two times his freshman season, opponents had refused to play him. Everyone had heard the latest rumors: Minnesota "asked" Willaman to leave Trice at home. Some even whispered about warnings.

Trice was definitely worried. He wrote a letter to his mother, telling her that he feared the Minnesota game. He never mailed it.

At a pep rally, Willaman addressed the student body, then loaded his boys onto the bus. Twelve miles east lay Nevada, Iowa, and the train station.

As the team crossed the wide boulevards toward downtown, Trice made an unusual request: would the bus stop at his apartment, so he could speak one last time to his new bride, Cora Mae Trice? They'd eloped to Michigan, and their love was still so fresh.

The men came to a halt at the corner of Fifth and Douglas in downtown Ames, a square brick building where the Trices lived on the third floor. Jack bounded up the stairs, giving his wife a hug and a kiss. He dwarfed her, and his impatient teammates and coaches couldn't pull him away.

"Come on, Jack," one of the coaches called, according to a Trice biography written by Steven Jones. "We have to go."

He stayed a few minutes longer, lost in her eyes. An uneasy feeling settled over Cora Mae. Something was amiss. She tried to read Jack's face, to root out whatever was troubling him.

At last, Jack let go. He promised he'd come back to her as soon as he could.

Jack Trice was born a second-generation free man. All four of his grandparents had been slaves, and his father had joined the Army to escape the South, finally settling in Ohio.

As a boy, Jack would ask questions about the scar on his daddy's hand, left over from an arrow wound. He took courage from the story: Indians had surrounded his father's unit, setting fire to the wagons. Green Trice managed to escape.

Education fascinated the elder Trice. After the service, he began first grade at age twenty-six. His tiny classmates used his wide arms as a swing set. He found work for a man named Wallace Ford, and years later, he would purchase the farm where he had labored and quietly saved money. The Trice family was going places.

Jack, called Johnny by his friends, grew up comfortably in insular Hiram. The neighborhood children, all white, included him in their parties. Gaylord Bates, a boyhood friend, wrote in a 1956 letter: "He was as full of fun and practical jokes as anyone else. He could not be accused of any more devilry, and certainly no less, than the rest of us engaged in."

Anna Trice worried about her son. She made him work hard. His friends became accustomed to her voice booming out into the afternoon, signaling a premature end to Jack's play.

She knew the world could be cruel, and also that Jack was naive. He liked to believe the best about people. She had seen the worst.

What she needed was a way to toughen him up, and she settled on Cleveland. Anna would send Jack to live with relatives in the city, hoping to give him a dose of real life.

So after eighth grade, Jack Trice packed his things.

He wasn't sure exactly where he was headed, but he dreamed large.

"I think I understand his personality," says Jones, his biographer. "He was idealistic. He was an overachiever. He was intelligent. Articulate. He always wanted to do big things for people."

Friday, October 5, 1923

The team gathered for dinner at the Curtis Hotel, a twelve-story high-rise in downtown Minneapolis. The place didn't allow blacks in its main dining room.

As the Iowa State team ate, several players noticed that Jack was missing. They argued with management, to no avail. Jack sat alone in his room trying to process everything. He took out a piece of stationery, crowned with a sketching of the hotel's towers.

First, he wrote the date, then began, in tall, cursive letters with bold descenders and ascenders.

> To whom it may concern:
> My thoughts just before the first real college game of my life. The honor of my race, family and self are at stake. Everyone is expecting me to do big things. I will!

He stopped and underlined the word "will" for emphasis. Yes, he was sure that great feats awaited. He put the pen back to the paper.

> My whole body and soul are to be thrown recklessly about the field tomorrow. Every time the ball is snapped I will [again, underlined] be trying to do more than my part. On all defensive plays, I must break through the opponents' line and stop the play in their territory.
> Fight low with your eyes open and toward the play. Watch out for cross bucks and reverse end runs. Be on your toes every minute if you expect to make good.

He signed his name to the letter and tucked it inside his sport coat.

In his head, it was already game time.

Jack Trice became a man in Cleveland. He found glory on the football field, becoming part of the East Technical High School powerhouse. They dominated, with Trice on the line and the fleet Johnny and Norton Behm in the backfield.

School didn't come easy to him, but he worked hard at it. His domineering mother, though thirty miles away, stayed in his head. After graduation, he swallowed his dreams and took his diploma to a construction crew.

Under the summer sun, he worked on the roads outside his little Ohio town, the same roads he once imagined escaping on, riding over the horizon to something better. Now, he watched the cars zoom by, bound for somewhere.

Then Sam Willaman, his old high school coach, found him. Willaman had been offered the job at Iowa State College, and he wanted Jack to come with him. It was a shot to keep playing football, to get that education, to get out of town. In just a generation, a Trice had gone from starting first grade at age twenty-six to packing for college at twenty.

Jack struggled with his admission tests but passed. He chose animal husbandry as a major, planning on going south after college to help sharecroppers.

That first year, he studied, played freshman football, and finished first in the Missouri Valley Conference freshman meet in shot put and second in discus. He had a 90 grade point average, and the freshmen had even beaten the varsity. Fans looked forward to 1923.

On campus, Jack found himself. He worked in the State Gym and a downtown office building as a custodian.

The former got him access to the swimming pool and, at night, he and Cora Mae would go skinny-dipping, according to Betty Armstrong, Cora Mae's daughter from her second marriage, now well past seventy.

Trice mostly kept to himself. Decades later, teammate Harry Schmidt would say, as if this were a good thing, "He didn't speak out much. He kept his place."

His place was in the starting lineup, even if some teams didn't want to play against him. He helped Iowa State coast to a tune-up win at home against Simpson, and he turned his attention to Minnesota.

That would be Jack Trice's chance to show them all.

Saturday, October 6, 1923

The team gathered around Willaman in the locker room. More than ten thousand fans waited outside.

"Boys," he told his players, "I know of two men on this team that I know will fight."

The first was Jack Trice.

In the first half, Minnesota punished Iowa State, taking a 14–10 lead. Back in the locker room, Trice grimaced. He'd lived in the backfield, stopping most runs before they started, but at a cost. He had a broken collarbone, though he didn't know for sure.

"How are you, Jack?" Willaman asked.

"I'm okay," he said, "but my shoulder hurts a little."

In the third quarter, Minnesota lined up in its trademark I formation. Trice saw the play going away from him, off tackle, and he tried a roll block, which is now too dangerous to be legal. He threw himself in front of the wedge, landing on his back.

Tired and injured, Trice couldn't roll over, and the entire Minnesota team ran over him, many piling on. Newspaper reports described a trampling, and on that lonely field, Jack began bleeding internally.

"If Jack had just been able to turn over," said William Thompson, an Omaha doctor and former ISU assistant, in an interview recorded in 1974, "you see, turn over on his stomach."

There are several versions of the play. Many said Trice was stomped on viciously, even bitten. Others deny ill intent.

"Absolutely not," said Schmidt, the teammate who would later become identified with the battle to keep Trice's name off Iowa State's stadium.

The Minnesota president wrote the Iowa State president a letter, saying there had been no piling on.

"Well, if I were prosecuting the case," says Charles Sohn, a college professor who spent decades leading a fight to honor Trice, "I suppose the best I could get out of it was manslaughter. I don't think there was an attempt to murder. I think there was an attempt to injure."

Whatever story you believe, one fact is indisputable. There was one black player on the field that day, and he was in trouble.

"He was badly hurt but tried to get up and wanted to stay in," Johnny Behm told the (Cleveland) *Plain Dealer* in 1979. "We saw he couldn't stand and helped him off the field."

The crowd, slowly understanding that something was horribly wrong, began chanting, "We're sorry, Ames."

Trice was rushed to a hospital a half-block from Northrup Field. Doctors examined the tackle and decided he could travel. They loaded Trice onto a straw mattress in a Pullman car and sent him back to Ames, where he immediately was taken to the student health center, a block from the State Gym where he spent so much time.

At 4:00 P.M., on Sunday, his breathing slowed. He struggled through the night. As the sun rose, thunderstorms hit Iowa. A friend of Jack's told Cora Mae to hurry to the hospital. She found him fading and leaned over his face.

"Hello, darling," she said, sweetly.

He looked up at her but couldn't speak. His lungs were hemorrhaging. His intestines were severely contused. Trice was dying a slow, painful death.

At 3:00 P.M., Cora Mae heard the bells on the campanile ring mournfully, one, two, three. Jack Trice couldn't fight anymore.

"That was October 8, 1923," she would write years later, "and he was gone."

Soon he was forgotten too. His mother died. His friends moved on. Even his beloved Cora Mae remarried.

She never talked about her time with Jack, or showed off the necklace he gave her, so friends thought it strange when she became hysterical about her own son beginning football.

"She was very emotional about a lot of things," says Betty Armstrong, the daughter, "and she didn't want my brother to play. She was so fearful that something would happen to him."

In the State Gym, a plaque honoring Jack, quoting his famous letter, gathered dust. Bird droppings covered it. No one bothered cleaning it. World War II came and went. The atomic bomb. Korea. And no one knew, not even a young Tom Emmerson, who'd grown up in Ames.

In 1957, a student at Iowa State, Emmerson spied something by the spiral staircase in the southwest corner. The words took his breath away: here, under their noses, was a story of sacrifice.

"I'd never heard of him," he says. "No one had, actually. No modern student in the '50s would have recognized the name Jack Trice."

Forty years later, after decades of student protests and pleadings, after the school stubbornly refused since the 1970s to name their new football stadium after Trice, the struggle was rewarded.

The biggest structure on campus was christened Jack Trice Stadium in 1997.

"I think it's part of creating a climate that calls attention to the fact that we've come a long way as a university," says then-president Martin Jischke. "And, more important, as a nation."

During the dedication, with the newly named behemoth reaching skyward behind him, Jischke read the famous letter, bringing some of Jack's teammates to their knees. Time hadn't killed the edge of those words.

He looked out at the crowd, which included friends from long ago and students, some of them now adults, who worked so hard to make this day a reality. Jischke quoted the poet Maya Angelou.

"A great soul never dies," he said. "It brings us together again and again."

Tuesday, October 9, 1923

They canceled class. The story took up much of the front page. Nearly three thousand people gathered around the Memorial Tower for the services. A gray casket, draped in a blanket of cardinal and gold, commanded their attention.

The players set up five-gallon milk cans around campus, and more than $2,000 was raised, enough to pay for the funeral, clear the mortgage Anna Trice had taken on her house for Jack's education, and leave some for the family.

Anna took the Northwest Railroad through Cleveland, and she stared out at the crowd, sharing her loss with the school. One by one, teammates, coaches, and teachers stood to tell stories about her boy. Professor Tolbert McRae sang "Abide with Me" and "Nearer, My God, to Thee."

President Raymond Pearson took out the letter found by the undertaker and read, as Jischke would do years later. Listening to his

words, they never imagined Trice would be forgotten. An editorial
in the *Iowa State Student* summed up the feelings of the campus:

> The crowning tribute must come from the minds and hearts of this col-
> lege . . . Some tribute, some tangible thing, must be set up to the mem-
> ory of Jack Trice. Then all who come into the influence of his memo-
> ries, whatever it may be, will experience the steadfastness of purpose
> which was Jack's.

Anna Trice couldn't tell everyone how she felt. Only later, in a
letter to Pearson, did she ask that her son become a beacon.

"If there is anything in the life of John Trice and his career that
will be an inspiration to the colored students who come to Ames,
he has not lived and died in vain," she wrote. "But, Mr. President,
while I am proud of his honors, he was all I had and I am old and
alone. The future is dreary and lonesome."

When the memorial was over, Anna Trice collected the body of
her only child and went back home.

As students struggled to honor Jack Trice, many of his relatives
struggled a thousand miles away. Most still lived in the Cleveland
neighborhood where Jack first played football.

It was as if Jack's death was a standing eight count, and the family
hadn't yet returned to the fight. George tells of relatives in and out
of jail, of young men and women never chasing a dream, spending
their lives on a street corner.

"It's not just Jack," George Trice says. "It's the legacy of the
Trices."

He would be different.

Unable to pay for college, Wanda Trice-Elbert thought of her
cousin and made a call. The school arranged for the George Washington Carver scholarship, named after the university's most famous grad. The chance to do right by a family done so wrong
couldn't be ignored, and George was Ames-bound. Instead of an
end, the story of Jack Trice had a new beginning.

Oh, George has had false starts — he's on the, ahem, seven-year
plan; he has a young son named George Trice III — but he didn't
quit. The school has used him in videos, even having him take
tours to the statue.

"I can only begin to guess at the pressure he must have felt,"

Jischke says, "being the representative of the family. Finally, one of the Trice family is getting a degree from Iowa State."

George thinks that his diploma, that small piece of paper he'll get next year, will erase it all. With his success, the family can leave their pain in the past, finally fighting low with their eyes toward the play.

"I'm the only one to accomplish anything, even though I have a son and I've been in this town for six years," George says. "I'm back in school now. All my other family . . . we're in the gutter."

With the summer sun heating the sidewalk outside the stadium, he steals a glance at the statue. When his mom comes to Ames, they stop by to remind themselves. When he thinks of leaving, all it takes is one look.

"I owe it to my family," he says. "I can't come to a school where the stadium is named after my cousin, when this statue right here resembles me, and not graduate from here. No matter how long it takes. It's not a question. It's not an option. It's a must-do thing."

He knew it from his first trip to campus, the same year the stadium finally took his cousin's name. As the guest of school officials, with the winter of 1997 settling over the state, he found his seat in Hilton Coliseum for an Iowa State basketball game.

During a break in the action, the PA announcer introduced young George Trice, who smiled, looking just like the statue outside.

Ever think history is boring? Think it's about dusty books, forgotten sacrifices, and faceless characters? Well, you should have been in the gym that night. You'd have seen history coming to life.

A roar began near the top of the coliseum, and seventy-four years after Jack Trice died, after students like these fought for years to honor his memory, applause rolled down the bleachers like thunder.

They stood on their toes, honoring a man who'd made good.

More Than Skin Deep

FROM THE ANDERSON INDEPENDENT-MAIL

COALMONT, TENNESSEE. Color defines so much in life.

On an athletic field, it sets two teams apart. In a church, it's the difference between a wedding and a funeral. On a battlefield, it can separate you from shooting the enemy, or your brother. In this town, color is the difference between acceptance and alienation. It's the line drawn between normal and weird. It's reason enough to hate. At one point in K. T. Mainord's life, he was an alien, a weirdo. He was hated by these townspeople.

All because of color.

To arrive on the Mountain, as they call this place, you wind on two-lanes caked with road salt. You go through "cities" such as Monteagle and Tracy City. You pass the Fiery Gizzard Water Treatment Plant, the Hillbilly Restaurant & Lounge, and, seemingly, more churches than houses.

The Stinger Café comes up on you quick. Probably because it looks nothing like a café. It's a big gray house at the corner of Tennessee Highways 56 and 108. It's called the Stinger because it's modeled to be the hangout for the nearby Grundy County High Yellow Jackets, much like The Max from *Saved by the Bell* or Arnold's Malt Shop from *Happy Days*.

K. T. Mainord, who signed February 4 to play football for the University of South Carolina in the fall, has an entire corner dedicated to him at the Stinger. It's filled with stats, stories, and imposing pictures of him from his high school playing days. And no one this side of Minnesota has looked more imposing in purple and gold. You ask how you'll know K. T. and his mother Linda when you see them.

"Well, I have gray hair, and I'm an older lady," Linda Mainord said. "My son's a big guy and will be driving a green Saturn.

"And he's black. He's the only one in the county."

You chuckle, wondering if that was the right play. She chuckles back. Apparently it was okay.

You step inside the Stinger Café and see, besides a family in the corner with the token shrieking child, you're the only people dining here today. And she was right. You really can't miss them.

If by some chance you walked right by them, the family's story would grab you by the ear, throw you in the chair, and force you to listen.

An Anomaly

Kevin Tyler Mainord is a black man in a place devoid of black men.

Mainord falls into the 0.1 percentile of blacks in Grundy County, Tennessee, which is 98.3 percent white, according to 2000 census statistics. By all accounts, Mainord is the only black male living in the county.

Mainord, who is set to graduate with honors in May, is one of two blacks at the seven-hundred-student county high school. And the other black student, a girl who is in foster care, transferred in this year.

"We're an all-white school," Grundy County High principal Ken Colquette said. "He's the only black kid to go through the entire Grundy County school system, kindergarten to twelfth grade. And that's one-hundred-something years old."

Setting that kind of precedent in a racially charged environment comes, almost predictably, with a fair share of growing pains.

"Being the only African American in the county, he had a huge, huge problem," said K. T.'s brother Russell Mainord, who is white, along with the other five members of the immediate family.

"I know it's probably worse than he'd ever tell anybody. I know people in the community say stuff. I hear it. I sense it. It's a great place to grow up, but it's a difficult place to grow up.

"They're afraid of anything different."

If that's true, then they fear the Mainord family most.

Wrapped Around His Finger

Linda and Lowery Mainord brought K. T. into their home when he was four days old.

Someone asked the Mainords if they'd be willing to watch a baby being given up for adoption until a home could be found. Linda — the mother of five children, four natural and one adopted — said she jumped at the chance. Lowery wasn't so hot on the idea.

"No more foster children," Lowery told his wife. "You get too attached, and I can't afford to adopt any more children."

"He told me he wasn't going to have anything to do with it," Linda said.

Then eight-pound, eight-ounce Kevin Tyler showed up at their door.

"He reached and got him and it was over," Linda Mainord recalled.

It wasn't over without a bit of a fight. K. T.'s birth mother decided she wanted to keep her child after all. She visited for a while, but then the visits got fewer and further between, Linda said. Then she disappeared.

After court proceedings, the Mainords officially adopted K. T., whom the family calls Kevin.

"Kevin has always had a way of wrapping you around his finger," said Linda Mainord, fifty-nine, who is the mother of children ranging in age from forty to eighteen.

She was widowed seven years ago when Lowery's truck skidded off a rain-slicked highway on the way to Signal Mountain Cement, where he'd worked for decades.

That left Linda with the sole responsibility of managing the home and family, among other things.

Linda has worked for more than two years as a housekeeper for Exceptional Enterprises, a company that helps mentally ill adults work and live more normal lives. Additionally, she's taking care of her mother and father, who are both very ill. She said she doesn't know if her dad will live through the weekend.

"It's amazing all that she's gone through," Russell Mainord said. "She's put herself through things you can't ask anyone to go through."

All this when raising a unique child would have been enough to handle.

No Small Potatoes

Once, in elementary school, a child told K. T. to go back where he came from.

"Where's that?" a young K. T. asked.

"Africa," the child said.

"I didn't know how to explain it to him," Linda Mainord said. "He said he wanted to be like my color. He said, 'I want to be like you and Daddy.' I told him. 'Honey, you're a good color. People go and lay in the tanning bed to get to be like you.'"

When K. T. was five, Linda finally made an illustration that bored into K. T.'s head.

While at the grocery store, Linda bought two different kinds of potatoes, red and brown. On the way home from the store, K. T. picked up a red one and asked what it was. His mother told him it was a potato. K. T. argued it wasn't.

"When we got home, I cut a red one in half and a brown one in half," Linda recalled. "I showed him they were both the same on the inside. I said, 'That's just like you and me. We're all the same on the inside.'

"He seemed to do better after that as far as understanding."

Just because he accepted who and what he was didn't mean others had.

Linda estimates he has been in about a fight a year. A wooden cross was driven into the end of the family's driveway when K. T. was four.

In 2001, a series of letters containing death threats were mailed to the home because he was dating a white girl.

"They threatened to burn our house," Russell said. "They threatened to catch him out and make him pay. They threatened to castrate him. They threatened to kill him."

The Mainords sent the letters to the FBI, which investigated and told them their problems should be over. Nothing has happened since.

"Should we move?" Linda asked her husband early in K. T.'s life. "What should we do?"

"We're not going anywhere," Lowery replied. "He's staying with us and the county will have to accept him."

Getting Out

Two days after first getting K. T., Linda and Lowery Mainord loaded their new child in a basket and took him to his first football game. Days after he was born, so was a love affair between that baby and sports.

First, Lowery an avid baseball fan, got his son into the game at age one. Then came football a year later. Linda said she realized he had been given exceptional talents when he played for the "Junior Jackets" football team at age thirteen.

Putting K. T. in the community's eye through sports went a long way toward his gaining acceptance.

"I think that involvement helped more than anything," Russell Mainord said. "I think people are afraid. That's what makes them hate. They feel threatened to some degree by something they don't know. By him being involved, they got to where they knew him and accepted him."

K. T., who is now six-foot-four, 266 pounds, said he began to realize he had a gift when he was a sophomore at Grundy County, playing defensive tackle for the Yellow Jackets.

When he signed earlier this month to play for South Carolina, he became the county's first Division I athlete in sixty years.

"There could have been others before me. They just didn't work at it and gave up too easily," K. T. said. "I didn't want to stick around here all my life and wind up working at the Toyota or Nissan plants.

"I think football's the thing to get me out of here."

Despite playing the bulk of the season with a second-degree shoulder separation, K. T. had 150 tackles (sixteen for a loss) and nine sacks last year in leading Grundy County to the second round of the playoffs.

"He has the grades, the brains, the size, the speed, the strength," said Colquette, who is also the school's football coach. "That's a pretty good combination."

The recruiting process was arduous for K. T., though.

Off the Radar?

Twenty-one schools offered K. T. a scholarship. His favorite from day one was Tennessee, which he grew up rooting for. Volunteer coaches told K. T. when he was a junior that they planned to offer him a scholarship early, so he could play his senior season without having to worry about where to go to school.

K. T. waited for papers from Tennessee, but they never came.

His list thereafter, with the exception of Colorado, included only teams that play Tennessee regularly: Alabama, Auburn, Florida, South Carolina, and Vanderbilt.

Alabama zipped to the top of that list until K. T. went to Tuscaloosa for a visit the weekend of January 17.

He said he decided during a prospect dinner, led by coach Mike Shula, that this wasn't the program for him.

That was affirmed when Alabama coaches sent K. T. home after an incident at an off-campus party.

K. T. said he was dancing with a girl, who dropped her wallet when she was leaving the party. K. T. found the wallet and asked a student what to do with it. The student told him to throw it away. He did, except the girl's checkbook, which he says he kept so no one would use her account.

When the girl returned, K. T. gave back her checkbook but said he didn't know, out of embarrassment, where her wallet was.

"I didn't want to tell her I threw it away," he said.

She assumed K. T. had stolen the wallet and went to get the police. By the time the police arrived, K. T. had retrieved the wallet. No charges were filed against him, Alabama police said.

Tide coaches found out the police had been called and told K. T. he should go home. On the ride back to Coalmont the next day, he contacted USC coach Lou Holtz and told him he was going to be a Gamecock.

"Some people said he did it because he thought everyone would drop him," said Russell Mainord, who is a graduate assistant at USC. "He did it because they stuck by him here. Coach Holtz told him, 'Son, that wouldn't have happened here.'"

New World

In the beginning, you wondered how K. T. Mainord ever made it, how he grew up different in a town where different wasn't good.

You were blown away by the volume of barbs and taunts he faced every day inside supposedly safe schoolroom walls. You were stunned that each year K. T.'s elementary school principal would go into his class and explain to the children that K. T. was not like them, but that was okay and they shouldn't tease him.

They learned. And so did you. Acceptance is no longer a problem. Being too popular is.

K. T. is classified by his mother as something like a social butterfly. He's always flanked by an army of girls, she said.

"One of his teachers told me he has like a harem or something," Linda Mainord said, laughing. "They're standing around carrying his books, rubbing his back, and saying, 'Let me do this for you, let me do that for you.'"

While humorous, everyone wonders how K. T. will adjust to college life, life in a "big city." The incident at Alabama didn't do anything to quell those concerns.

"He just needs to grow up some," said Colquette, who recently gave K. T. in-school suspension for skipping class. "Just like you did. Just like I did. If he does that, he'll make them a fine football player. If not, then he'll be somewhere else."

Undoubtedly, when K. T. arrives in June at USC, he'll be in for a big dose of culture shock.

Richland County, where the state capital is located, is 45.2 percent black.

That means in Columbia there are roughly 150,000 black people, 149,999 more than there are in Grundy County.

Color

The word's primary definition is one we all know. It's the one we learned in elementary school, with a box of crayons and a sheet of paper.

"I don't see color," Linda Mainord said. "I see a person. That's it."

Color has other meanings, though. As a verb, it can be defined as to affect, or to influence.

The Mountain has been shaped by K. T. Mainord's life just by his existing — coexisting, really.

Mom and Dad started the change eighteen years ago by adopting him.

"Looking at it now, knowing what all could have happened," Russell Mainord said, "it was nothing short of heroism."

K. T.'s maturation into a man has finished the transformation of a place that was stuck in the 1950s.

"I think him being there changed the community more than it changed him," Russell Mainord said. "Because people learned to accept."

The Mainord family colored Grundy County.

MICHAEL HALL

The Duke of Dunbar

FROM TEXAS MONTHLY

JEFF MURIEL took the inbounds pass running and fired it to Dominique Williams, who dribbled across half-court with his right hand while he pulled up his sagging shorts with his left. He ran about fifteen feet before drilling a pass to the shirtless Jeremis Smith, the tallest kid on the court at six feet six inches, who took one step, rose from the hardwood floor, and slammed the ball down hard. Onto the back of the rim. The ball flew into the air, bouncing toward the bleachers. Nobody said a word, and play resumed; the only sounds were those of the meaty bouncing of the ball and the incessant squeaking of new sneakers on the floor, which, in the echoey gym, sounded like seabirds.

It was August 18, the first day of school, seventh-period basketball class at Dunbar High School, in Fort Worth, and on the sidelines stood the winningest coach in high school basketball history, a tall, gray-haired man, arms behind his back, a scowl on his face. Robert Hughes's expression hadn't changed in five minutes, though at the missed dunk the scowl seemed to bury deeper into his face. He was older than anyone on the court by five decades and taller than most of them too. He wandered back and forth toward the action under the rims, watching carefully as the boys ran up and down the court. And he remained silent — until someone did something that was, as he might say, knuckleheaded.

"Hold it!" he yelled. Coach Hughes doesn't need a whistle. One of the boys had thrown a weak underhand alley-oop pass to the leaping Jeremis, and the ball had fallen short. Hughes walked over into the middle of the group of ten boys, who had stopped playing.

"In the first place," he said loudly, "if you throw the ball under-hand toward the basket, it's going to fall short and flat. A five-foot guy could get to it." His tone was exasperated, as if he had said this before. He demonstrated, tossing the ball underhand; sure enough, the parabola fell short. "What the hell is that? You don't control the ball as well as when you throw it like you shoot it." He demonstrated again. Same result. "Why would you throw a pass like that? *'Cause you're playing to the damn crowd!* The hell with the crowd! They're not even on the damn floor! Pass the ball the way you shoot the ball!"

The coach turned and strode back to the sideline, and the game resumed. For the next ten minutes Jeremis, the unquestioned leader of the team, who has a tattoo of a basketball in the center of a cross on his right shoulder and another of a wildcat on his left shoulder blade, shot graceful fifteen-foot jumpers, fired perfect passes, and made dunking look as simple as reaching up and turn-ing a faucet. At one point he grabbed a pass near the basket, took a step, and went up in the air on the right side of the backboard but was met up there by an opponent, so he transferred the ball to his left hand and curled it in from the other side of the hoop. Again, nobody said a word.

With five minutes left in the period, Hughes stopped play, and the boys — his probable starting five and second team for the up-coming season — moved to the bleachers, where they sat with an-other group of kids, who had been watching the action. It was time for the old man to speak.

Hughes has the gravitas of an undertaker and the voice of a preacher. Though he is seventy-five, he looks fifteen years younger, a trim and healthy six-foot-six, with white frosting on his eyebrows, hair, and mustache. It was still three months before the team's first game, and the stakes were high in the upcoming season, he told the boys. "You better show me more than Tim Duncan," he said, his voice booming in the otherwise silent gymnasium. "'Cause if you don't, your little boo-tay is *gone.*" The longer he spoke, the more or-nery he sounded. "I'm a hard guy to be around if you don't want to play. Can't everybody play basketball. Can't everybody play basket-ball for me. And I'll be the first guy to admit that. It is tough to play here for four years. I'm a hard guy to get along with. 'Cause I don't say everything is okay. I don't say it's okay to miss free throws. I don't say it's okay to be out of shape. I don't say it's okay to play lousy defense. I don't say it's okay to miss practice. I don't say it's okay to blow off class. So if you're looking for an okay guy, I'm sorry. I'm not an okay guy. I want your butt at practice. I want you working. I want you passing your classes. If you can't do that, this is just not the place for you. 'Cause I don't want to be like every-damn-body else. I don't want to be number five and number six. If you're not here doing your best, you shouldn't be here."

In West Texas, they talk about the Odessa Permian mojo, the foot-ball mania of *Friday Night Lights.* In Dallas and Forth Worth, they talk about the Dunbar mystique, an aura that surrounds a basket-ball team that has dominated the game in the area for more than a quarter-century. The Wildcats, aka the Flying Wildcats, intimidate most teams before they even step onto the court. They score more points per minute than the Dallas Mavericks — 84 per 32-minute game last season, which would translate to 126 points in an NBA-length game — and they play defense like they're angry. Dunbar's games feel like roundball circuses, with nonstop fast breaks, brisk passes, alley-oops, and thundering dunks, and they bring out thou-sands of boisterous fans, more than any other high school basket-ball team in Texas.

Last February 11, Wildcats coach Robert Hughes did something no one in history had ever done before: he won his 1,275th high school basketball game, breaking the record for most all-time victo-ries held by Morgan Wootten, the coach of DeMatha Catholic, in Maryland. The Wildcats set the record in front of a standing-room-only crowd of nearly 7,500 at Texas Christian University's Daniel-Meyer Coliseum. Though the outcome was never in doubt, Hughes never let up on his players. "Use your brains, dammit!" he yelled during a late huddle. After the buzzer sounded, six TV cameras surrounded him, and blue and white streamers poured from the rafters. Hughes was given a trophy at center court; he stood with his arms crossed, looking like he'd rather be anywhere else. He doesn't like ceremony, and he doesn't like talk.

He's old-fashioned that way. Hughes has been coaching for forty-five years, that is, since Eisenhower was president and segregation was the law of the land. And even back then, Hughes's teams were playing fast, showtime basketball, racing up and down the court, passing, lobbing, dunking, and pressing. His players were tossing up alley-oops when Indiana farm boys were still trying to master the pick-and-roll, running like mad and lighting up the scoreboard when other teams were walking the ball up the court and carefully setting up. His style has been almost unbeatable: Hughes has a remarkable .837 winning percentage through forty-five seasons.

His numbers should speak for themselves, but even today, some of his fellow coaches dismiss Hughes's success. Some say he's simply blessed with great athletes and that if they had his players, they'd win a lot of games too. But Dunbar's kids aren't superkids: the Wildcats football team this year was only 4–7. Most teens who play basketball for Hughes are of average height, with only a couple of guys every year over six-feet-three. And Hughes has sent only one player to the NBA, Charles Smith, who was drafted in 1997 by the Miami Heat but is currently playing in Italy. Others grumble that Hughes's teams play undisciplined, run-and-gun, playground ball. The truth is, the Wildcats know when to run (always) and when to gun (when they have a high-percentage shot). His guards are trained to look first to the big man in the low post, near the basket; if that option is closed, they pass, looking for holes elsewhere in the defense. All his players are coached to space themselves properly, to keep moving, to shoot only smart shots. (Hughes likes dunks because they are just about the highest-percentage shot you can get.) The other half of Dunbar basketball is playing aggressive defense: crashing the boards for rebounds and pressing the other team, causing turnovers, or stealing the ball and speeding down the court for a quick two points.

The Wildcat system is about timing and teamwork. The players practice their game over and over, as if learning scales on an instrument, so ultimately they won't have to think about what they're doing. This work ethic, Hughes told me, is what makes Dunbar different: "It's because we work so dang hard. There's an intensity at our practices. Players know 'If I can't handle this, I'm going home to Mama.'" Hughes is a disciplinarian in an age of great permissiveness, a man who quotes Frank Sinatra to kids who quote 50 Cent. During games, he almost never talks to the officials; he saves his wrath for his players, either yelling at them or just pointing and hooking his finger, which means someone is going to the bench. The kids may look away when he yells, but they listen. More than anything, kids want to win, and more than anyone, Hughes knows winning. "There's something about looking to the sideline and knowing Robert Hughes is going to put you in a position to win," says Dallas sportscaster Dale Hansen, a longtime observer of Metroplex basketball. "He gives you about a seven-point lead coming out of the locker room."

Last March, Hughes's Dunbar squad capped off the record-breaking season by winning the state 4A championship in front of a crowd of 16,258 at the Frank Erwin Center, in Austin. Dunbar finished the season 37–1, giving Hughes a grand total of 1,282 wins. (By comparison, Dean Smith, the winningest college coach, has 879.) There was talk in the newspapers that with the record and the title, Hughes had the perfect ending to a storybook career. But he didn't see it that way. He had three returning starters. There were games to win. So in the forty-sixth summer before his forty-sixth season, he was standing on the sidelines and watching children the ages of his grandchildren play a game he learned on dirt courts during the Depression. For the next few months, as I watched him get his Wildcats ready for their first game, on November 18 versus 5A DeSoto High School, the only team to beat them last season (and the eventual 5A champs), I wondered: How many more games? One? A hundred? How many wins would be enough to satisfy the man who's won more games than anyone?

On September 27, the Wildcats and forty-seven other area teams went to Colleyville and Grapevine schools for a daylong tournament, or shoot-out. Teams will play several of these in the fall, though according to University Interscholastic League (UIL) rules, their coaches can only observe their kids until the season officially begins, in late October. Hughes sat in the bleachers with a yellow pad, watching his team play and taking notes. He wasn't the only one interested in the Wildcats; whereas the typical turnout at most of the shoot-out's other games was a couple dozen, for Dunbar's games there were more than a hundred, including a handful of middle-aged coaches holding clipboards.

In its first game, Dunbar, wearing gray-and-blue uniforms, played Nacogdoches High School. Jeremis swatted the opening tip to Jared Watley, who dribbled twice and passed to Dominique, who laid the ball in. With five seconds gone it was already 2–0. Almost immediately Dunbar began harassing the Nacogdoches ball handlers, who panicked and began double-dribbling and throwing the ball away. Dunbar scored at will and at halftime led 44–24. I asked Hughes how he thought the team was doing. "Let's see," he said, "one, two, three, four . . . nine turnovers. You shouldn't have nine in a game. To tell the truth, if I was over there, there'd be hell to pay." Hughes had drawn a chart, with points, rebounds, and turnovers. And he was writing notes to himself about what each player was doing badly. "You don't see many other coaches taking notes at these shoot-outs," says Mike Kunstadt, whose TexasHoops.com, a statewide scouting service, organized this one. "They usually just show up to watch their teams and visit with friends."

In the second half, Hughes, sitting by himself in the stands, watched, increasingly frustrated, as his guards hogged the ball. "Pass it," he mumbled, as Naterian Roberts, subbing for the injured Jeff Muriel, dribbled out front, with a man on him, moving up and back, up and back. "Pass it." Up and back, up and back. *"Pass it!"* Naterian finally drove and threw an underhand lob pass to Jeremis. It was blocked. "There you go with that underhand pass again," muttered Hughes. He is fond of saying, "I don't want thirty-one flavors. Give me plain vanilla." His players are constantly struggling with doing what they want to do and what Hughes wants them to do. Watching this dynamic unfold is part of the fun of watching the Wildcats play. Dunbar eventually won the game 73–47, but the coach wasn't happy. "I give them a low C," he told me. "Too many mistakes, nineteen turnovers; nineteen turnovers will get your butt beat. Also, the other team got too many rebounds and second shots. There was too much listening to the grandstand. We lost our concentration."

Between games at Colleyville, hundreds of kids, parents, and coaches wandered around the school's three gyms. Everywhere Hughes went, a coach or a player would hail him and say hello. One coach, who hadn't seen Hughes in a while, said, "Congratulations. Things are going well for you. You look good, too." Hughes thanked him, talked briefly, and walked on. He is part of the coaching fraternity and also separate from it. Despite his loud presence on the court, off it he is quiet, even introverted. He spends his rare free time reading westerns. Hughes doesn't smoke or drink, and he goes to church every Sunday. He's still married to the same woman after all these years. He is from a different generation, as his players joke, a dinosaur.

In game two, as Hughes scouted other teams in other gyms, Dunbar easily dispatched an all-white team from Flower Mound. But their third game, against an all-black Seagoville team whose star center, six-foot-ten LaMarcus Aldridge, is considered by *The Sporting News* to be the best player in the state, was the marquee matchup of the tournament. The duel quickly proved to be one-sided, with Jeremis dunking and hitting from the outside while the Wildcats' press rattled the Seagoville squad. Dunbar was ahead by twenty when, with the last few seconds ticking down, Jared took a rebound and made a behind-the-back pass to Naterian, who dribbled several times before seeing Jeremis break for the basket. He threw up a perfect lob pass, which Jeremis grabbed in flight and slammed through the net as time ran out. Sitting in the stands, his notepad in his lap, Coach Hughes, in spite of himself, was pleased. "I think we did a pretty good job," he said later. This is just about the highest praise he will ever give.

You might expect certain things of the winningest coach in American high school basketball history. A bigger office, for example. Hughes shares his small, cluttered cinder-block space with his three assistants: Charles Hickman, who played for Hughes from 1987 to 1989; Wendell Ivory, who was a Wildcat from 1985 to 1988; and Leondas Rambo, who has been Hughes's assistant coach since 1974. Trophies stand willy-nilly — on the file cabinet, the microwave, and the floor. On the wall are several prints of Indians, including one of Geronimo. On the door are taped-up newspaper stories about Dunbar players who have gone on to bigger things: Charles Smith; Demetric Shaw, who played at Kent State and then in the United States Basketball League; Gary Collier, now retired after playing in Europe; Anthony Burks, who played at TCU and is now in the computer business.

One afternoon in September, wearing slacks, a white shirt, and royal-blue sneakers, Hughes sat in this cramped office behind a small desk. "People say, 'You stress winning too much,'" he told me. "Well, if you don't like it, get a visa and move. Winning, being successful, being the best, is as American as apple pie. Not apple strudel, but apple pie. It's not about the right to be mediocre or average. A lot of guys are mediocre or average because nobody pushed them to be great."

Robert Hughes, all-American, was born on May 15, 1928, in Bristow, Oklahoma, and raised on a farm in Sepulpa, a little town near Tulsa. His parents farmed cotton and corn, and his mother was part Creek Indian. Young Robert had one sister and six brothers, and when they weren't doing farmwork, they were playing basketball. Robert learned to play on dirt courts at age eight and didn't play in a gym until he went to high school. By his senior year, he was a forward playing the low post. He joined the Army and was recruited for a special unit that just played basketball in tournaments in the Far East; it was the first integrated team Hughes had played on.

When he got out, Texas Southern University offered him a basketball scholarship to play under coach Edward Adams. "We ran like the wind," Hughes remembers. "And worked hard." Adams would be Hughes's biggest influence. "I was a finesse guy, a shooter, but I played everywhere — guard, low post, wing. That's why I ride my players to be good at everything." Playing at a tournament in Memphis in 1955, he met Jacquelyne Johnson, who was from Tulsa and who was also part Creek Indian. They later married and had four kids. That same year he was drafted by the Boston Celtics, but he had just torn his Achilles tendon, and he gave up playing. He returned to Oklahoma and went to the University of Tulsa, which had recently opened itself up to blacks, graduating in 1957. Landing a job as a mechanic at Douglas Aircraft and making good money, Hughes was content until Adams called, asking if he had considered coaching. Hughes said he wasn't interested, but Adams persisted and got him a job at I. M. Terrell High School, in Fort Worth.

At the time, if you were a black kid in or near Fort Worth, you went to Terrell, no matter if you lived across the street from a white school or in Weatherford, thirty miles away. There were a few public school buses, but most of Terrell's three thousand students got there by walking, getting a ride, or taking public transportation. Never mind that segregation had been ruled unconstitutional by the U.S. Supreme Court in 1954. In the beginning, *Brown* desegregated the country's schools in name only, and states like Texas found ways to drag their feet.

Under Hughes, Terrell dominated black basketball in Fort Worth. In 1963 the team won its first Prairie View Interscholastic League title (the organization for black high schools), then two more, in 1965 and 1967. Terrell played the style Hughes had learned from Adams: run, pass, lob, dunk, press, crash the boards. Some called it hully-gully ball, or playground ball. "We were playing today's game back in the sixties," says Wayne Lewis, a guard on two of those championship teams. "We were doing the alley-oop lob pass to six-foot-two guys in 1964. Every fourth or fifth trip down the floor was a dunk."

When the UIL finally began integrating, in 1967, Terrell started playing white teams, many of which were befuddled by the frantic offense and stifling defense. The referees, too, seemed unwilling to accept the Terrell brand of basketball. "We weren't prepared for the officiating," Hughes says about those days. "It was blatant. We were playing basketball, but these other teams were playing full-contact karate. The refs would call us for three-second violations, offensive goaltending, carrying the ball. There's not much you can do." Hughes didn't protest the calls, refusing to give the officials the opportunity to call him for technical fouls.

Hughes rode his players harder then than he does now, practicing almost every day, all year long, demanding perfection. "My biggest problem," he recalls, "was to keep from smiling when I was in this serious mode. I realized I've got to be stone-faced when dealing with players." He was a harsh disciplinarian, using a paddle that he called "the board of education." "He never hit you in a way that you thought was him trying to hurt you," says James Cash, who played for Terrell from 1963 to 1965. "It was used mostly on freshmen and sophomores, in a kind of a socialization process, getting you to perform as a team. But if the man you were guarding in practice scored a lay-up, he would say to you, 'Come by me,' or, 'Bring it by me,' and you'd go to the sideline and he'd give you the board of education."

Some of the Terrell players had no father, and the churchgoing, nonsmoking, teetotaling Hughes became a surrogate. He was hyper-responsible, picking the boys up at five-thirty or six in the morning and driving them to Terrell for morning practice, then, when the afternoon practice was finished, driving them home again. When they played out of town, he shepherded them over a network of friendly roads and stopped at restaurants he knew would accept a bunch of black adults and kids. They didn't always sidestep the ugliness, though. Lewis remembers a trip to Texarkana in 1963. "We stopped at a Sonic to get something to eat," he told me. "The waitresses wouldn't serve us. We just sat there while they skated by our cars."

Terrell was closed in 1973, and Hughes took his record of 373–84 into the job market. Black coaches weren't exactly in demand for college jobs, and even at the high school level, they were given poor choices. Initially, Hughes was offered only an assistant coaching job at a local high school. He declined. He was eventually offered the head job at Dunbar, an all-black school a block from his house in the Stop Six neighborhood in southeast Fort Worth. (It got its name from being near the sixth stop on the old Dallas-Fort Worth rail line.) Dunbar High hadn't had a winning season since it opened, in 1953, and in Hughes's first year, many of the upperclassmen quit. They couldn't abide the practices — before and after school and on Saturday mornings. Hughes played the season with mostly freshmen and sophomores and went 12–12. "It was probably my best coaching job," he says now. By 1976 Hughes had led Dunbar to the state playoffs.

Dunbar was finally integrated in 1980, and as the decade progressed, although the Wildcats won a lot of games and district titles, Hughes developed a rep for not winning the big one. By 1993 Dunbar had been to the Final Four nine times and lost three championship games. But that year, with the high-scoring duo of Charles Smith and Anthony Burks, the Wildcats won their first UIL title, sweetening a season in which Hughes also won his 1,000th game.

After a drought in the late nineties (Hughes had his first losing season in 1999), Dunbar returned to the semifinals in 2001 and won it all last year. By the end of the season, Hughes and the Wildcats were the biggest high school sports story in the state, and he had finally gotten some of the recognition that had long eluded him. "It doesn't make up for all the wrongs I've been through," said Hughes. "But, like Frank Sinatra said, 'It was a very good year' — all forty-five of them." But what is it, I asked, that drives you to do it again in year 46? "The same thing that drove me last year," he replied. "I'm probably your ultimate competitor. I'd miss walking into the hostile gymnasium. I'd miss the preparation, developing players to fit a position you know you need to fill to be successful."

But what are you trying to prove? "It's not so much to prove anything. I am a competitor. That's what I do. My engine runs at the maximum. It has always run at the maximum. To cut it off and say that's it — I don't think so."

And what happens to the engine when you finally do retire? "That's going to be a problem."

On October 27, three weeks before their opening game, the Wildcats held their first official practice. The session was most notable for the appearance of assistant coach Rambo, who was beginning his thirtieth year with Hughes. As Hughes slowly walked one side of the court, scowling, hands behind his back, Rambo, much shorter and with a prodigious Afro, walked the other, mirroring him, hands behind his back, looking for all the world like Sancho Panza to Hughes's Don Quixote. Rambo is the friendly face, the intermediary with the parents, the good cop. "The scowling," he told me later about his boss, "is just to let the player know, 'I'm not satisfied, and we've worked on it so much. Either you're refusing to do it, or I'm not getting through to you.'"

The practice began with drills up and down the court — fast breaks, passing, lay-ups. But soon Hughes had the first team playing the second, back and forth, back and forth. "We learn by repetition," he told me. "Whether it's your ABCs or counting to one hundred or playing our set offense. It becomes automatic after you've been doing it for three or four years." The truth is, the reason the team looks so good is that they've been playing almost all year long. They took two weeks off after the state tournament and then, in April, the preseason started for the returning varsity, with weightlifting, conditioning, and workouts at the Martin Luther King Jr. Community Center, five blocks from the school. By the summer they were practicing four days a week — the starting five playing together as a team, usually about three hours a day — plus they played thirty games in tournaments and shoot-outs. The Dunbar off-season head coach is ex-Terrell star Wayne Lewis. His assistants are Derrick Daniels, who played for Dunbar from 1985 to 1987; Vernon Newton, who played for Dunbar from 1981 to 1983; and Otis Evans, who did the same from 1988 to 1991. "We're prep fanatics," says Lewis, who stays in almost daily contact with his mentor. "I know what he wants, what he looks for, what he asks for from his players."

The boys continued practicing after school started in the fall, plus they played in several preseason shoot-outs. Players on the Dunbar first team get to know each other's strengths and weaknesses — who can jump how high, who can shoot from where, who can dribble through what kind of a press — far better and far sooner than those on other high school teams, only a few of which set up operations like Dunbar's. So by the first official day of practice, while other teams were still trying to figure out who would get which uniform, Dunbar was already in pretty good shape.

Except, in Hughes's mind, for one guy. That afternoon he was particularly dissatisfied with Chris Evans, a tall, muscular forward who is the only starter who wasn't on the varsity last year. "In some ways, Chris is the most important player out there," Hughes told me. And so he's harder on him than on the others. When Chris made a shot in the paint, Hughes yelled, "You were in there too long!" When a pass flew off one of Chris's hands, Hughes yelled, "Who fumbles more balls than anyone here? Now, why would you try to catch it with one hand? You can't catch it with two!" A player has to have a thick skin to play for Coach Hughes. He almost never tells his kids they're playing well, and this, one assumes, is the burden of pushing them to be great. But sometimes Hughes's stone face softens and it looks like he's smiling. When he does this, it seems like he's thinking what anyone in his right mind would be thinking: man, these kids are good.

In the Stop Six neighborhood, basketball — or more specifically, Dunbar basketball — is life. Here they talk about the shots Derrick Daniels made in the mid-eighties, the moves Charles Smith made in the mid-nineties, and the dunks Jeremis Smith made last week. The neighborhood kids hang out and shoot hoops at the King Center, and it is here that young boys, eight and nine years old, get their first sense of what Dunbar basketball is all about when they come to learn to play or just to watch the local heroes in the varsity practice. It's at the center that many current Wildcats heard about the Coach, the old man, the guy who yelled at you but made you better. Jared Watley still remembers being in the sixth grade and coming to the center to watch his big brother practice. His father had played for Hughes too, so Jared had heard the stories. "I wanted to play for Dunbar from then on," he says.

Hughes's legend hangs over Stop Six the way Vince Lombardi's does over Green Bay. Like that old-school taskmaster, Hughes has always been seen as a father figure here, and one reason is, he takes care of his own, and he does it, as Sinatra might have said, his way. For example, on October 6, Jeremis, Jeff, and reserve guard Marcus Samuels were arrested for stealing $105 worth of DVDs and CDs from a local Target. Hughes was furious and treated them the way he's always treated his players. "If you step over the line in this program," he told me, "there's a penalty. You're going to have to pay for it. Those three guys are going to be running so much they'll feel like they're on an Olympic marathon team." Some wanted him to kick them off the team, but Hughes was unmoved. "I don't want to get in a debate. It's like some countries — if you steal a biscuit, they cut your arm off. What we do has worked for thirty years. We can handle Dunbar. We can handle our problems here."

Hughes hates talk; he only reluctantly spoke about the shoplifting incident. Like any other stern, no-nonsense guy who reads westerns in his spare time, he's a man of deeds. And as his former players will tell you, it's not important what he says about loyalty or discipline, hard work or responsibility; former Baylor University coach Dave Bliss used to talk about all those things too. "It's one thing to just be a disciplinarian without setting high standards," says James Cash, who went on from Terrell to become the first black player in the Southwest Conference, at TCU in 1965, and who eventually became a senior associate dean of the Harvard Business School. "That wasn't Coach Hughes. I wouldn't be what I am today without him and the lessons he taught. Not because he *told* me I was supposed to act this way but because of the ways he acted. This guy would not let anybody throw him off."

Once, when Cash was in his second year at TCU, he called Hughes after a bad night in Mobile, Alabama, when the refs kept whistling him for no cause, trying to make a black teenager lose his cool. It was 1967, the first year Terrell was playing white teams, and Hughes told Cash about his own experiences with blatantly bad calls. Cash remembers, "He was very angry, but he ended up laughing. He said, 'And they think this is going to break me?' He taught me to stay focused on the task at hand, not to get distracted because people didn't like me for the color of my skin or something else. There was no chance anything thrown at me at TCU would throw me off my stride."

Cash comes back every year to watch the Wildcats play. Many of Hughes's ex-players return, sometimes practicing with the current team, sometimes just going to the games. Dunbar, they all say, is a family; this is home. Mostly they come to see the old man, the one who pushed them so hard, sometimes too hard; the loner who preaches a team game; the man who hates showboating yet loves winning, who hates the drawing of attention to oneself yet whose team thrives on it; the man who suffered the humiliations of Jim Crow yet puts his kids through the hell of Bob Hughes; the man who uses discipline and hard work to help kids play a game to perfection. The man determined to prove one more time that you are better than number five or number six. You're not like every-damn-body else. And neither is he.

The day of the big game, November 18, was like any other; Hughes saw to that. There was no pep rally at the school, even though this was the first game of the season in a quest to be repeat champs and even though it was a match against DeSoto, the only team to beat Dunbar last year. "We don't do pep rallies," Hughes had told me. The players held their own rally just before the game, in the hallway at the Wilkerson-Greines Activity Center. Led by Jeremis, who had just signed a letter of intent to play at Georgia Tech, they clapped, jumped, and chanted "Whoop! Yeah!" for a minute or so while six thousand fans waited. Rambo put his fingers in his ears, and Hughes stood patiently to the side, head down. He wore a blue blazer, slacks, dress shoes, and a shirt and tie.

With Hughes standing on the sidelines of the Robert Hughes Court (it was renamed last year), Dunbar jumped out to a quick 7–0 lead. The first substitution came after Chris Evans threw the ball away — straight into Hughes's arms. Shaking his head in disgust, Hughes marched straight to his bench, pointed at Naterian, and sat Chris down. After a thundering dunk by Jeremis and a withering fast break, Dunbar led 20–8.

And then it all fell apart. DeSoto started pressing, and Dunbar started turning the ball over. DeSoto began hitting three-pointers, and Dunbar seemed powerless to stop them. All of a sudden DeSoto was doing everything Dunbar was known for — crisp passing, smart shooting, aggressive pressing — and the Flying Wildcats looked like house tabbies. At halftime DeSoto was up 40–39. In the second half Dunbar kept trying to get the ball in to Jeremis, and he kept getting fouled, but he was making only about half of his free throws. Dunbar had no spark, no snap, and Hughes was furious, calling players over and yelling at them or benching them. Nothing seemed to work.

With three minutes left, DeSoto had a three-point lead and the ball; they went into a slowdown offense, passing back and forth, waiting for Dunbar to try to make a steal. With forty-seven seconds left, Dunbar fouled, and the teams traded free throws for the next forty seconds. Then, with seven ticks left on the clock and his team down by three, Jeremis made an inbounds pass and was handed it back. He frantically dribbled half the length of the court through a crowd of defenders to a spot thirty-five feet from the basket, where, with two seconds remaining, he leaped, leaned, and launched an off-balance shot.

The ball curved through the air in a perfect arc and snapped right through the basket. The gym erupted. Dunbar had tied the game, sending it to overtime, yet Hughes stood as he had been standing the whole game. Impassively. Furious. And though the Wildcats controlled the overtime period, they continued to turn the ball over and miss open shots. Worst of all, they weren't hitting their free throws. With eighteen seconds left and a comfortable five-point lead, Hughes was out on the floor yelling at Jeff, who was about to shoot two more free throws. He hit only one. Hughes's expression didn't change as the buzzer sounded, and he walked off the court alone, looking down and fuming.

The players waited in the locker room, enveloped in a sense of dread. They had just beaten the defending 5A champs in a revenge match they had been looking forward to for a year. Yet it felt like somebody had died. Or was about to. Hughes walked in. "A word to the wise," he said, measuring his syllables. "If I was you, I wouldn't say a thing. I wouldn't talk to anybody." After a pause, he added, "We missed enough free throws to last a season." He seemed ready to go on but stopped, as if there were too many sins to enumerate. He walked out.

The DeSoto win was number 1,283, and more would follow. But for Hughes, it would not be enough, nor would it ever be.

MICHAEL BAMBERGER

The Pride of Peabody

FROM SPORTS ILLUSTRATED

THE REGULARS at Champions Pub in downtown Peabody, Massachusetts, all grew up in town, and they all say it in the same rapid-fire way: *Peebadee*, one syllable just about. *Peebadee High*. Home of *The Tannas*. There was a time, the regulars will tell you proudly, when Peabody was the leather-tanning capital of the *world*, but then the work went overseas and the factories were converted into low-income apartments, and now all that is left is the school nickname, the Tanners, and the descendants of the last generation of Peabody leather workers, who are old or dead. You can tell the descendants by their working-class Greater Boston accents and their Old World surnames, anchored with consonants, names from Greece and Italy and Poland and Portugal.

There's Ed Nizwantowski — Coach Niz — who's been the football and baseball coach at Peabody High forever. There's James Leontakianakos — Jimmy Leon — who brought Jeff Allison to the hospital the night last summer when the greatest pitcher in Peabody history nearly died. Outsiders in Peabody, wayward tourists in stiff Red Sox hats trying to find the witch trial reenactments in neighboring Salem, they might as well be wearing a sign. The battalions of professional baseball scouts who came to Peabody in the spring of 2003 to clock Jeff Allison's ninety-five-mile-per-hour fastball and to try to take the measure of the kid, they never had a chance. Peabody's not easy on outsiders.

Coach Niz, one of the best athletes ever to come out of Peabody High, is a regular at Champions. Even with all the bad stuff going on in his life — the drug problems of Allison, the Florida Marlins' number-one draft pick in 2003; the same sort of troubles with his own hockey-playing son, whose addiction has left Coach Niz with serious money woes — he can still sit in a cramped booth at Champions, surrounded by his buddies, his chin over a glass of Mich Ultra, and talk about the good times. The other day he and his sidekick, Terry Lee (fellow member of the class of '64, retired cop, assistant Tanners football and baseball coach), were reliving highlights from Jeff Allison's senior season.

NIZ: Remember the Medford coach? He's, like, "I can't tell you how to hit this guy. Just swing. If you get a hit, you can say you got a hit off a future major leaguer."

LEE: How 'bout the Somerville game, when he struck out the twenty?

NIZ: Unfrickinbelievable.

LEE: Kids were getting high-fives for hitting foul balls.

NIZ: That umpire, when he called that third strike a ball?

LEE: Oh, man, did you have it goin'.

NIZ: And Jeff says, "Don't worry — I'll take care of him on this one." Ninety-eight miles an hour!

LEE: The scouts all staring at their radar guns.

NIZ: Kid was a warrior.

LEE: Between the lines, yeah.

NIZ: Yeah.

Even Ed Nizwantowski, the insider's insider in Peabody, did not know that his star pitcher was getting high on the prescription opiate OxyContin, an intensely powerful painkiller five times stronger than the more commonly prescribed Vicodin, all through his senior baseball season. Jeff Allison was striking out two batters per inning. He was allowing nothing — no earned runs — game after game. Scouts were saying he'd be a top ten pick in the major leagues' June 2003 amateur draft. Agents were circling. College coaches were praying, but they had no chance.

Jeff Allison was in *Baseball America* all the time, the best high school pitcher in the country. The talk was that his signing bonus would be well north of $2 million, that he'd be in the majors in a couple-three years, that he'd make everyone forget about Jeff Juden, a first-round pick out of Salem High in '89, whose big league pitching career turned out to be a series of dashed hopes.

Jeff Allison was going to come out of Peabody, out of the little rental house on the dead-end street he shared with his mother and sister, and make Peabody famous and proud again. How could he be a doper?

Coach Niz thought he knew what to look for. He was an expert on the subject, to tell you the truth. In Peabody nobody confused OC with a Thursday night teen drama on Fox. The town was rife with the drug. One of Nizwantowski's former football players, a suspected OxyContin user, had died of a heroin overdose. Another former Tanners football player had been arrested for murder in an incident involving an OC stash and is awaiting trial. The starting second baseman on Allison's team, the son of the school superintendent in Salem, had recently gone through a drug rehab program for OxyContin addiction. (Talk-radio host Rush Limbaugh has done the same.) An outstanding former Tanners place-kicker went through college getting stoned on OxyContin three times a day, then went through hell to get straight, and the only way he gets by now is that one-day-at-a-time mantra.

Then there's Brad Nizwantowski, the middle child of the three Niz kids, graced with athletic skill, as likable as his father is charismatic, as chatty as his mom. Hockey got him to the University of Massachusetts at Amherst. OxyContin addiction, and the desperate rage it fueled, got him to the Hampshire County House of Correction.

Like his father before him, Brad Nizwantowski excelled at baseball, football, and hockey. His parents sent him to a nearby boarding school, Cushing Academy, because they feared that had he gone to Peabody High, other parents and athletes might harass Coach Niz about giving preferential treatment to his son. At Cushing, Brad was a captain of the baseball, football, and hockey teams. He started using OxyContin regularly in his sophomore year at UMass, where he was on a hockey scholarship.

His college days came to an end in December 2001, during his junior year, when Brad, strung out and depressed, talked his way into the apartment of an old girlfriend, locked the woman and himself in her bedroom, pointed a kitchen knife to his stomach, and yelled repeatedly, "I'm gonna kill myself!" He was arrested by Amherst police and convicted, in February 2003, of kidnapping and assault with a dangerous weapon. He spent six months of a

one-year sentence in the Hampshire jail and is now out on probation. Any failed drug test could send him back to jail. His parents
live in fear of that possibility.

After the arrest and before the trial Brad was home in Peabody,
and the full extent of his drug addiction became obvious. The father and son battled constantly. The tension between Patty and her
husband over what went wrong, and why, hung over their every
meal. Each could see lines of despair in the other's face. (Ironi-
cally, when Coach Niz was prescribed OxyContin after major back
surgery in December of '01 — he was left with a dozen metal rods
and plates in his back — the innocent-looking green pills hung in a
small plastic bottle around his neck like a stopwatch.) Trying to
help their middle child (their oldest, Paul, is a custodian at Peabody High), Niz and Patty have twice remortgaged their house and
have spent $45,000 on lawyers, psychologists, therapists, doctors,
and antidepressants. Until he went to jail, the kid had been getting
high daily, often stealing from his parents to pay for drugs. He was
unable to stop himself. The things Brad once loved, hockey, baseball, football, his family, now meant nothing to him.

Brad, when he's straight, is a pleasure. (He's been off OC for
eight months now; his craving for the drug has been eliminated by
a Naltrexone pellet inserted under the skin in his right arm. His
parents pay $400 every eight weeks for a new pellet.) But before,
when he was lusting for drugs in the middle of the night, he was a
wholly different person. One night Coach Niz heard Brad smash-
ing the vinyl siding of the house with a hockey stick. The coach had
had enough.

"Get away from this house!" he yelled at his son. He tried to
shove Brad off the front doorstep.

"Let me in!" Brad screamed. He swung his hockey stick like a
baseball bat and came within a foot of slashing his father's face with
the curved blade.

The next day the father had to go out and face Peabody, walk the
school's hallways and fields as he always had, with his 1960s jock's
strut, as if everything were fine. He was the coach, the gym teacher,
a fixture. He had to deal with the scouts and the college coaches
calling about Jeff Allison. He had to be Coach Niz. Then he'd
come home, and he and Patty would face their broken lives.

*

The scouts sent to Peabody did not want to find a problem with Jeff Allison. When they heard him be disrespectful to his mother — *"I'll come home when I wanna come home!"* — they dismissed it. He took the standard fill-in-the-dots Major League Baseball Scouting Bureau psychological test, and it raised no red flags. (Allison told his teammates the test was "a joke.") The Pittsburgh Pirates, with the eighth pick in 2003, had a doctor test the flexibility and overall health and strength of Allison's pitching arm. He was given an MRI. Allison is tall, strong, and lanky. He was not one to lift weights and has almost never thrown more than 100 pitches in a game (although he threw 153 in his final high school pitching appearance, a must-win playoff game). All the test results were off-the-charts good; Allison had one of the most flexible arms the Pirates had ever seen. Word spread around baseball quickly. Only a few of the scouts talked to Coach Niz, and then only briefly. He offered little more than the stock answer: "He's not a bad kid." (That passes for praise in Peabody, where the typical response to "How you doin'?" is "Not too bad.") Had they caught up with him at Champions, they might have learned more, though maybe not. Peabody's not easy on outsiders.

The visiting baseball men saw Allison's cocky, aggressive behavior on the mound and loved it. Only when they saw similar qualities in his father did they get nervous. They heard Bob Allison make noise about his son's going to the University of Arizona, where he had been offered a full scholarship. They wondered if the father might make his son hold out for an outrageously high signing bonus. The number $2.5 million was bandied about. Jeff Allison didn't know it, but his stock was starting to fall.

"He was a difficult kid to get to know," says Charlie Sullivan, the New England amateur scout for the Pirates. "He had a real intense competitiveness, he had that cockiness. But watching the kid interact with his father — there was no happiness there. That made you worry. You try to get to know a kid, his parents, the girlfriend. But with Allison, we couldn't. For the industry not to have known [about Allison's drug problems], well, we all should have done a better job." Other scouts say almost the exact same thing.

Noreen Allison, Jeff's mother, is often in her small house near downtown Peabody. Brad's mother, Patty, calls her on the phone regularly. Patty Nizwantowski is a schoolteacher with a master's degree. Noreen has been divorced from Jeff's dad for sixteen years, and she isn't working now. (In the past she's worked with mentally disabled adults, which kept food on the table and her son in the batting cages.) What the two mothers share is Peabody, sports — and a nervous system jangled by having a drug addict in the house.

"It's not an easy thing to say, 'My son is a drug addict,'" Patty recalls telling Noreen not long ago. It took her years to be able to say it about her own son. A drug addict, in her view, is a drug addict whether he is in recovery, as Brad is, or not.

"Yeah, I know."

"Maybe we should go to a meeting together." Patty was referring to free counseling sessions, modeled on AA meetings, for relatives of drug addicts.

"Yeah, we should do that."

But they never did.

Noreen is well known in town. Back when she was Noreen Riccardi she was a tomboy jock at Salem High, class of '66, and a star on the girls' basketball team. Later she appeared on a Boston TV bowling show, *Candlepins for Cash.* She watched all of Jeff's games, including his summer games on elite teams, often sitting in the top row of the stands, avoiding the scouts and the reporters. (Coach Niz can't recall seeing Jeff's father at any games before Jeff's senior year.) Sometimes, when Jeff was on the mound, Noreen would point to her right biceps as if it were her son's and say quietly, "Million-dollar arm." People smiled. Everyone knew she didn't have much.

These days, wherever she goes — the gas station, the supermarket, the corner store to buy cigarettes — she runs into people who knew her son in simpler times. She asks the same thing, over and over.

"You seen Jeff?"

Sometimes the answer is yes. Jeff's been in town since early May, a little more than two months before he was rushed to a hospital after a heroin overdose. Except for brief stints in Florida with other Marlins prospects, Jeff's been in Peabody pretty much his whole life.

"He looks good, don't he?"

You take care of yourself, Noreen.

*

It's hard to know how Jeff Allison is doing. Athletes addicted to OxyContin, like addicts everywhere, are skilled liars. They will routinely and dishonestly blame their use on a doctor who prescribed the drug for chronic pain just to keep them suited up. Brad Nizwantowski had no chronic pain. The same is true for Allison. Brad, twenty-four, says he tried the drug in high school and liked how it made him feel. Allison, who tells *SI* that he did not start using OxyContin regularly until after he finished high school — an assertion that one of his friends challenges — says the drug made him feel "just warm inside, that you could do whatever you want, say whatever you want." (Warmth is a common theme; many users say the high from OxyContin, heroin, methadone, and other opiates is like "being back in the womb.") The hubris associated with gifted athletes makes them particularly susceptible to addiction; they brazenly think they're stronger than the drug's addictive pull. Some come to believe that OC actually improves their performance. For a variety of reasons, OxyContin is particularly popular in and around Boston, although it is also found across the country, often in rural areas, which is why it is sometimes called "hillbilly heroin."

It's work, getting stoned on OxyContin. A single eighty-milligram pill, enough for one person to get high for several hours, costs about $80 at Peabody street prices. To take the drug, the abuser crushes the aspirin-shaped tablet into a fine powder and sniffs it. (It can also be injected.) A full-blown addict will need at least three eighty-milligram tablets a day, at a cost of $240.

An addict is likely to commit crimes on a routine basis to support his habit. Most pharmacies in Peabody have signs posted saying that the store has no stock of OxyContin; when prescribed, the drug is typically delivered to the pharmacy by a private courier. (Still, theft is a regular problem.) Brad Nizwantowski regularly stole cash from his parents and jewelry from his mother, selling the necklaces and watches and rings to pawn-shop managers near Peabody. According to former Peabody High baseball teammate Joel Levine (the son of the Salem school superintendent), who says that he often got stoned with Jeff Allison and who is now in recovery, the chase for the money to get high was the most social part of doing OxyContin. That, and giggling at all the witty things they said at parties when they were high. Jeff Allison was never so funny as he was when the OC was working its magic. But inevitably, things get ugly. An OC addict with no supply gets dope sick: headaches, nausea, diarrhea, itchiness, insomnia, chills. Jeff and Brad experienced all of that.

Even in recovery there are dark days for Brad when he does nothing but sleep. He knows he'll never have his old life back. He's a convicted felon, and his dream of playing professional hockey is dead. All the Nizwantowskis are affected. There are happy moments — the family celebrating the October birthday of the youngest child, Amy, with Chinese food in her University of New Hampshire dorm room — but even those moments are frail. No one knows what will happen next.

The Nizwantowskis and the Allisons have known each other for decades. Brad and Jeff, who's four years younger, have known each other all their lives; they played pond hockey together and pickup games of basketball and football. Jeff had an astonishingly strong arm, and Coach Niz wanted him to be his quarterback at Peabody, but the pitcher was too concerned about a possible football injury. Playing basketball, for some reason, didn't worry him. He was fierce on defense and an excellent rebounder. One of his basketball teammates was Jimmy Leon, the kid he was shooting heroin with on the night last July when he nearly died.

OxyContin and heroin are chemically similar. When an OC addict cannot score his drug of choice, he or she will often turn to heroin, which, if you're near a big city, is easier to find and far cheaper. (Unable to obtain heroin, the drug user might try to get methadone.)

Allison tells *SI* that he takes responsibility for that July night with Leontakianakos. "He came by the house, but I made the decision to go with him," Allison says. They went to a drug house in the nearby town of Lynn. "I was doing OC every day," Allison says. But on that night, unable to get OxyContin, they bought a bag of heroin. "I didn't care about anything," he says. "You just want to get away from your problems."

They shot up in the car and went into a heroin nod. When Leontakianakos noticed that Allison was barely breathing, he rushed him to Union Hospital in Lynn. Allison's mother and sister, Tracy, were called in immediately. Tracy took pictures of medics placing a defibrillator on her brother's chest, to return life to his heart. "If I made it, she wanted me to have pictures of myself like that," Jeff says. "I was basically dead." He spent three days in the hospital. "That was rock bottom for me. There's no more digging after that."

Allison says that was the first time he had used heroin and the last time he used any narcotic drug. He acknowledged that he sometimes smokes pot, but did not want to go into detail with *SI* about his history of using OxyContin. Brad Nizwantowski and Joel Levine, and many other recovering addicts, say that when you are really in recovery, you want to own up to *everything* related to your drug use. Of course, not many recovering addicts are in a position to make tens of millions of dollars playing a game.

Some of the things Jeff Allison tells *SI* do not jibe with Levine's recollections. Allison says he didn't smoke anything in high school and drank only at his senior prom, but Levine says Allison smoked cigarettes and pot regularly and saw him drink often at parties. Though Allison says he never used OxyContin in high school, Levine cites many times and places when he says they got high together on OC during their senior year. Levine regards Allison as a friend and says he's not trying to rat him out. He's trying to fulfill step twelve of his Narcotics Anonymous rehab program: help others. He wants word out about the extreme addictiveness of OxyContin. He knows that the more unlikely the example — why would Jeff Allison, with all his talent and promise, ever risk becoming a drug addict? — the more useful it is as a wake-up call, a public alarm.

There were a few small events in Allison's senior year that didn't help his reputation in professional baseball circles, including a suspension from school for starting a fight. Then came a day in mid-April, when Allison and a group of friends went to Fenway Park to watch a college baseball tournament. A group of pro scouts spotted Allison and approached him. According to two friends who were with him, Allison was stoned. As he talked to the scouts, he kept picking his nose and slurring his words. (Besides slow breathing, fatigue, and abnormal pupil size, the OC high makes the user itchy and unaware of what he is doing.)

Still, the scouts chatted as if there were nothing odd. After all, Jeff Allison was the best high school pitcher in the country, and the baseball men just figured he was arrogant and socially inept, a small price to pay for a wicked eighty-four-mile-per-hour curveball.

The following week Allison was scheduled to pitch a Monday

game. Two dozen scouts, plus the general manager of the Pirates, were expected to attend. But Nizwantowski benched his star pitcher for skipping the Sunday afternoon practice the day before. The coach recalled his Monday conversation with his co-captain like this:

> NIZWANTOWSKI: You know the rule, Jeff. You miss a practice and you don't call, you don't play the next game.
> ALLISON: You better let me play or I'm gonna have my father transfer me right out of here!

(Allison tells *SI* that that confrontation did not happen, that he accepted his benching. When asked why he missed the Sunday practice, he replies, "It was a rainy day. I thought practice was canceled." In fact, the day was bright, sunny, and unusually warm.)

Allison apologized to his teammates for missing the practice. "He loved baseball," says his high school catcher, Brian Garrity. "For him, baseball wasn't about getting to the Show or anything like that. He just loved being on the mound. He was a gamer." Allison's former teammates are consistently generous in their praise of him. Levine says, "Everybody who doesn't know Jeff thinks he's an a——hole. Everybody who does thinks he's a great guy."

One day during his senior year, Allison spoke to a Boston TV station about the Red Sox' aversion to drafting high school pitchers. "Normally, drafting high school pitchers is a risky business," he said, "but I don't think I'm a risky business." He wore number 9, the number Ted Williams famously wore for the Red Sox, and he was making a case for himself to the club he had rooted for all his life.

Noreen proudly shows the tape of that interview. She is sitting in her small house with low ceilings, barely high enough to contain her six-foot-two son. She is burning incense candles and smoking cigarettes and talking nonstop; she has the look and voice of a woman who has never had an easy day in her life. Jeff isn't home. According to his mother he is at his daily meeting with a drug counselor. "There are a lot of things he doesn't want to talk with me about," she says. Her divorce from Jeff's father was bitter, she says. Jeff resents how involved in his life she has always been, and how he always had to rely on her for rides. Money has always been tight. She says, "Kids today don't have enough to do. I just wish they could have the fun we had."

Joel Levine knows that Noreen Allison thought of him as a bad influence on her son. Levine describes getting stoned with Allison in school and before some practices and games. He describes using a blue plastic hall pass to crush the OC tablet in the second-floor bathroom near the school library. Once, according to Levine, after Allison got high without him, the pitcher whispered to him, "I just did a rail in the bathroom."

In his senior year the Peabody Police Department contacted Levine, at Noreen Allison's request, and told him to stop calling the Allison house. The police had heard that the son of the Salem school superintendent and Peabody's most famous ballplayer were using OC, but it was not a priority for them. "We don't counsel kids," one officer says. "We set 'em up and lock 'em up."

While the scouts never suspected Allison of drug use, others did. One day late in Allison's senior year, Bob Russell, a veteran narcotics detective in the Peabody Police Department, received a call from Jeff Berry, an agent at IMG, the sports-marketing firm that represents Derek Jeter, Tiger Woods, and hundreds of other well-known athletes. IMG, as well as its rivals, wanted to represent Allison. According to Russell, Berry, who works out of the IMG Baseball Academy in West Bradenton, Florida, had heard from Russell's son, then a tennis teaching pro in Florida, that Allison might have a drug problem. The agent called the detective.

As Russell recalls the conversation, he asked Berry, "If you sign him, can you make money from him?" Yes, the agent said. "Well then I'd sign him quick," Russell said. "Because he's on our list of things to do." (Asked about the phone conversation, Berry would not comment.) Russell had received one anonymous (and unsubstantiated) call saying that Allison had shaken down a kid to get five or six OC pills from him. It was enough for Russell and his fellow detectives to discuss the matter. "We talked about sitting on him," Russell says.

On the mound Allison was not performing as if he had a drug problem. His stuff all through his senior year was electric. The 2003 amateur draft began in the morning on the first Tuesday in

June, and it was certain that Allison would go in the first round. From what Allison had heard, the Baltimore Orioles might make him the seventh pick. If that didn't happen, Pittsburgh would make him the eighth pick. In the unlikely event that *that* didn't happen, the Cleveland Indians would take him at number eleven. That was the word going around. Allison, following the draft on the Internet from home, was extremely annoyed when the Pirates, who had scouted him so intensively, didn't select him. Nor did the Indians. Then, around 1:30 P.M., came an unexpected call: Florida had made Allison the sixteenth pick. Coach Niz was as surprised as Allison. He couldn't recall having had a single conversation with anyone from the Marlins. No club knew Allison well, but Florida — later named the 2003 Organization of the Year by *Baseball America* — knew him less than others.

Having fallen to the sixteenth pick, Allison wasn't going to get anything like a $2.5 million signing bonus. Still, he was looking at a major payday. IMG, the agency that he and his father had selected to represent him, would make sure of that.

Later that day there was a party for Allison at Extra Innings, a vast, spotless batting cage and baseball practice facility near Peabody where Allison had spent days on end as a kid. School officials were there, and so were Allison's family members, teammates, and coaches, as well as reporters and TV crews. When Allison spoke to reporters, he predicted that he would make the major league All-Star team "in two or three years." A month later he backed off that claim, saying it had just been the "adrenaline talking." After the party, according to Levine, he and Allison slipped out, went into Levine's car, and did a couple of OC rails.

In late June, while IMG and the Marlins were negotiating Allison's signing bonus, team owner Jeffrey Loria invited Allison to watch a Red Sox–Marlins game with him at Fenway. Allison brought along his father and Jimmy Leon. A few weeks later, on July 22, Allison agreed to a $1.85 million signing bonus. His agent of record was Casey Close, the president of IMG's baseball operations, who personally represents Derek Jeter. Allison reported for work in Jupiter, Florida. He was now a professional baseball player.

And, it seemed to some, pretty full of himself. A team executive recalls driving Allison around the club's training site in Jupiter, where he would be playing for the Marlins' rookie-ball team in the Gulf Coast League. Allison made no effort at conversation and, without asking permission, turned on the radio, found a rap station, and started playing the music loudly. The executive said, "What are you doing, man?" Allison was barely that. He was eighteen years old and, except for highly supervised amateur baseball trips, away from Peabody for the first time.

But the Marlins were committed to him. Why wouldn't they be? They had unexpectedly signed the best high school pitcher in the country. Wayne Rosenthal, Florida's major league pitching coach, made an unusual pledge, saying that he would be checking on Allison regularly, keeping an eye on him. The Marlins were expecting Allison to blow right through the minor leagues, just as another strong right-hander, Josh Beckett, had done for them.

The Marlins wanted Allison to go through a weight-training regimen and expected hard work from him. The adjustments were difficult for Allison. Baseball had always come so easily to him.

Allison was living with other Marlins prospects and minor leaguers in a Fairfield Inn off I-95 in Jupiter, in South Florida's flat, chainstore sprawl, which was nothing like Peabody, with its neighborhoods and tight quarters and corner bars. At night Allison hung out with another young pitcher, Greg Bartlett. Bartlett was Allison's opposite. He was a native Californian and the Marlins' twentyeighth-round draft pick out of Phoenix College and had signed for a pittance. Bartlett was nearly two years older than Allison, socially adept, and comfortable around adults. But the two pitchers, the ornery one and the mellow one, bonded. Together, Bartlett and Allison would hit the bars off Indiantown Road that were happy to serve ballplayers even if they were underage.

Bartlett returned to Phoenix in mid-September after his first season in professional baseball. On October 1, just as the Marlins were starting the playoff run that would end with their upset victory over the New York Yankees in the World Series, word came that Bartlett had died of an overdose of methadone. According to Bartlett's mother, Juliana Bridge, her son had no history of drug abuse before leaving Arizona for Florida. She knew that her son and Allison had become good friends. She has a ball Allison signed for her son, and she had heard Greg speak of Allison often. After her son died, she saw Allison's name and telephone number stored in Greg's cell phone. She called Allison to tell him the tragic news and asked him to call back, but he never did. "I never knew why," she says. (Allison did post a message in response to Bartlett's online obituary in which he wrote: "i know your with me and looking down on me, now its time for me to fulfill both of our dreams.")

Tim Cossins, the first-year manager of the Gulf Coast Marlins in 2003, says there were no indications that either Allison or Bartlett had a drug problem. "They were both on the field, ready to work, every morning at 8:15," he says. "Never, not one time, did these kids not perform. I never thought that [drug use] could be going on. They were competitive, focused young athletes." He says that neither ever missed the 11:00 P.M. curfew check.

Shortly before the end of the rookie-ball season the Marlins had sent Allison home for what the club described as rest for his tendinitis. Coach Niz says Allison had never had tendinitis in high school and, because Allison had joined the team with just six weeks left in the season, he'd pitched only briefly in rookie ball, appearing in three games for a total of nine innings, in which he gave up one earned run and struck out eleven. He may not have had tendinitis, but he definitely had a drug problem.

That off-season, back home in Peabody, Allison had money and his own car for the first time in his life. Old teammates and friends suspected that something was seriously amiss with Allison. Brad Nizwantowski even heard about Allison's growing drug use as he sat in a county jail in western Massachusetts. (A guard from Peabody told him.) IMG was able to persuade Allison to come to its Bradenton (Florida) Baseball Academy, hopeful that he would meet with drug counselors there. But Allison's stay was brief.

Back in Peabody, Allison was telling friends that he didn't know if he liked baseball anymore. He had changed. One day he made a rare visit to Extra Innings. One of the owners there, Rob Nash, had been an integral part of Allison's baseball development since age ten. Through high school Allison had worked at Extra Innings whenever he needed spending money. Now he was a professional baseball player with diamond studs in both ears. His flashy new trappings of fame — not just the earrings but also a Cadillac Escalade — clashed heavily with the culture he had grown up in.

"What the hell are you wearing?" Nash asked him.

"Wha'?" Allison said.

"You look like a frickin' idiot," Nash said.

The new baseball season arrived. Last March should have marked the start of the first big league spring training of Allison's professional career. Coach Niz and Terry Lee planned a trip to Jupiter, excited to watch Allison throw heat in his new uniform. But he wasn't there; he was in a halfway house in Lynn. He didn't arrive until April 7, five weeks later than his teammates. When he finally did show up, he told reporters that Bartlett's death had distracted him from tending to his professional obligations. He evaded the question of whether he had a drug problem. "People are saying whatever they want anyhow," he said.

His 2004 stint with the Marlins' organization lasted only a month. By early May he was back in Peabody. On June 13, in a New England Cable News interview, he admitted to having failed a drug test for marijuana and said that the Marlins had fined him $200,000 and, because he had violated the terms of his signing bonus, the team had placed him on the restricted list and stopped making bonus payments to him. (To date, the club has paid him less than a third of his $1.85 million signing bonus.) Allison says he has $200,000 in the bank, but others in Peabody wonder how much he really has left. Cossins, the Marlins' rookie-ball manager, was around Allison again briefly last spring. He says he doesn't know Allison well but that he found him to be "abrasive, very cocky. But it's a false cockiness. His cockiness on the field was warranted. But he's scared as hell off the field."

The police chief in Jupiter says that neither Allison nor Bartlett was ever arrested on any charge while in that town. Whether the Marlins believe that there was any connection between Allison's and Bartlett's drug use is unclear; no one from the team will talk about it. Loria, the Marlins' owner, says through a spokesman that he will not comment about Allison. When others in the organization speak at all about Allison, it is guardedly, yet even so their anger is palpable. In part, of course, that is engendered by Allison's squandered pitching talent and in part by his perceived arrogance. He does little to create goodwill. He makes it easy to forget that you're talking about a kid, a kid with a problem. The kid turned twenty in November.

*

The Marlins have lately taken a hands-off approach in dealing with Allison. Since her son's heroin overdose last July, Noreen Allison says, the only person from the ball club she has heard from is the team doctor, and him only occasionally. None of the baseball people who spoke to *SI* were ready to predict that Allison would become a dominant major league pitcher. There are too many obstacles in his way. "If baseball fits into his life, so be it," says Cossins. "But he's got to get his life healthy first."

Allison says he plans to return to Jupiter for spring training in the new year and get back on the road that leads to the big leagues. "The Marlins want me clean, that's it," he says. "I gotta take one step at a time. Baby steps." He says he was seeing a drug counselor regularly in Brookline, Massachusetts. "My parents fight a lot, and I've got my own issues. I'm immature. I've got an addictive personality. But I don't want to do drugs anymore. I wanna be straight. I wanna play baseball. Self-will is the biggest part of it." He cited the number of days he's been clean. He's looking forward to spring in Florida. In the meantime there's the long, damp Peabody winter. Phil Mitchell and Kevin Houlden, co-owners of Champions, have been dropping by the Allison home now and again, bringing grilled chicken and steak tips for Noreen and her two kids. Everyone in town knows it's been a tough time for them.

You hope, of course, that Jeff Allison is sincere in his resolve. "I don't know," says Brad Nizwantowski. "He's telling you all the right things. But when I call him, he won't talk to me."

Bob Russell, the narcotics detective, has a certain wisdom about Allison and Peabody. "You know how they say it takes a village to raise a child?" he asked one night. "It takes a village to cover up for a kid this much too. At some point everybody knew there was a problem with Jeff Allison. The school people, the teachers, the coaches." He could have added the cops, but he didn't. "But people want to win games. He made people look good. He made the high school look good. He made his summer teams look good. So nobody said anything. It pays not to s—— where you eat."

The Tanners football team wasn't supposed to be any good this year, but it surprised a lot of people, finishing 8–2. Away from the field Coach Niz always had something hanging over his head: a court date for Brad, a family meeting with a therapist, a pile of bills from doctors and lawyers. He'd lose himself in his afternoon practices, his team dinners, his Friday night games. After one win this fall Coach Niz stood at midfield and talked to a few local sportswriters, answering the same questions sportswriters always have, about the bright future of this kid or that. And for a moment all was right in his world.

Brad came to some of the games and practices, helped out where he could. For the first time in years, father and son were doing things together, and sports were returning to Brad's life. Sometimes he'd play late-night "shinny" hockey — wearing nothing but shin guards — at a nearby rink. It had been three years since he lost his hockey scholarship, and for the first time since then he found himself wanting to play again.

Jeff Allison was keeping a low profile. Every so often, though, late on October afternoons, he'd go to a field way behind the school and pitch to his friend Artie Generazzo, his catcher from back in Little League days. At night, on TV, the Red Sox were undoing history and Allison was hanging on every pitch, along with the rest of Red Sox Nation. David Ortiz, with his big bat and big heart, was winning games for the Sox nightly, and at one point Jeff saluted the slugger in an e-mail message to his Peabody buddies:

> fukn Ortiz wut can i say. . . . mvp.

For a while, anyway, something lost had been returned to him.

CHRIS JONES

The Man in the Ice

FROM ESQUIRE

EVEN THE LANDSCAPE has changed in the meantime. Not the biggest things — Saskatoon still rises out of the flats, and a green river still runs through it, and the prairie sky still swallows up the land in the same big hopeful blue. But since Duncan MacPherson went away, the leaves have turned color fourteen times. And the grain elevators that sat on the horizon have been toppled one by one, landmarks gone to tumble and felled like trees.

There's also a statue downtown that he wouldn't recognize, at the corner of First Avenue and Twentieth Street, across from Sears and down from Joe's Lunch. It's a bronze of the badlands hero Gordie Howe, capturing him in his Motor City prime: helmetless, elbows up, and carrying a straight-bladed stick, old school. It was dedicated in 1993, according to the accompanying plaque, "for his outstanding contribution to the sport of hockey." Here in Saskatchewan, when winter blows in and there isn't much light to go by, that's reason enough for a vanishing man to be remembered.

Fewer people remember that MacPherson played hockey the way Howe played hockey, mostly in the corners and in front of the net, elbows up, and carrying a straight-bladed stick. He'd played it tough enough to lose his front teeth and well enough for the New York Islanders to pick him in the first round of the 1984 NHL draft. (He never made it to the big club.) Then, in 1989, he disappeared while traveling in Europe and never made it home.

It took him until last summer to surface. Even the landscape had changed in the meantime. But while the leaves had continued turning and Gordie Howe made the long, slow transition from man to monument, Duncan MacPherson had achieved the impossible. He'd remained forever what he was.

What he was to become was decided when he was just a kid, growing into his big hands and strong chin. He had a gift for delivering open-ice hits, one of the game's lost farm-boy arts, and he was accelerated through hockey's apprentice ranks until he earned a spot on the junior Saskatoon Blades, all possibility and hope. That's where he lost those teeth of his and cut open his knuckles and got stitches in his lip and blew out his ankle and kept right on dreaming. That's why he became a pillar in the Islanders' master plan. He was promise. He was the one who was chosen to be packed off to the proving grounds of the American Hockey League, in Springfield, Massachusetts, where he taped up his wrists to keep them from buckling when gloves got dropped.

Springfield was home to the Indians then, but times have changed, and they're called the Falcons now. For whatever you want to call them, MacPherson cleared out the crease. He also left parts of himself scattered up and down the Eastern Seaboard, his own outstanding contribution to the sport of hockey: ligaments from both his knees, a shoulder cuff, and the blood that ran from a cut across his right eye, courtesy of Kelly Buchberger's skate. It left some kind of scar.

He played on. But for all his heart, he never got closer to the National Hockey League than he did one spring when he was called up to replace the hobbled defenseman Gord Dineen. MacPherson dressed and carved circles into the ice to find his legs before Dineen decided that he could play and that MacPherson could watch from the stands. Sitting there in his suit and tie, he started coming to terms with the inevitable: some fate other than fame awaited him. His dreams weren't as big as they used to be. For the first time in his life, his future was a mystery.

He told his family, almost as an aside, that the CIA had contacted him, hoping to recruit him as a spy — he was big and strong and had a knack for warming up cold shoulders, a nice way about him — but he wasn't ready to leave his old identity behind and become someone new. He could feel, already, that abandoning hockey might make him ache worse than his joints, and before he was able to make firm his inkling to retire at twenty-three, he was offered a job in Scotland, coaching and playing for the Dundee Tigers. He had some gut doubt about it; the team's owner, a Canadian businessman named Ron Dixon, gave him the wrong kind of shivers. But he figured on one last adventure before settling into civilian life.

On August 2, 1989, he took a train from Saskatoon to Edmonton, flew to London, to Frankfurt, and then took another train to Nuremberg, arriving two days after he'd left. He called his family from the home of a longtime friend, George Pesut, who'd landed a roster spot on a team in Germany. One last time he expressed uneasiness about Dixon and Scotland, but he was already a long way from Saskatchewan, and it was too late for him to turn back now.

When Pesut left for training camp on August 7, he tossed his friend the keys to his red Opel Corsa. MacPherson drove south to Fussen, Germany, and overnighted with a former teammate, Roger Kortko, before leaving a little after noon the next day, just for a bit of a wander. He found his way to Innsbruck, Austria, checked into the youth hostel, and on the morning of August 9, he stepped back out into the sunshine.

From that moment on, Duncan MacPherson assumed his usual role as an object of imagination, albeit in other people's nightmares rather than in his own dreams.

It's hard to explain why sometimes it's the little things that last. Duncan MacPherson's parents, Bob and Lynda, live in the same house where they've always lived, on a quiet street in the north end of Saskatoon, not far from the green river. In the garden out front, there's an old length of rusted logging chain that Duncan and his younger brother, Derrick, found as children during a family trip to British Columbia and insisted on dragging home. It's sat there since.

Duncan was supposed to check in here, same as he always did, on August 12, 1989, the date his flight arrived in Scotland — without him, we now know. By the fourteenth, Lynda started to worry, the way mothers always have. On the seventeenth, she finally reached George Pesut. He'd just come home from camp to find his driveway empty and Duncan's hockey bag still in his living room.

"My heart hit the floor," Lynda says now, sitting at her dining room table, a picture of Duncan behind her, a paper trail laid out in front. "And then it was, you know . . ."

She doesn't finish as many sentences as she once did.

The MacPhersons are good people with an enduring love for their boys. Bob was a small-plane pilot; Lynda was a teacher. They both wear glasses, which obscure somewhat the lines around their eyes, the sort that come when sleep makes way for too much thinking. It doesn't take much to push Lynda back into things, pulling away and poring over police reports and photographs. Bob's tried to cultivate a bit more distance from it, losing himself in the building of a log cabin up north, past the height of land, on a rise over the water. He likes it best up there in winter, when the snow falls in perfect blankets and the lake is a smooth white sheet.

Fourteen years ago, staring down a different expanse, the Mac-Phersons first called the bank to find out when Duncan had last cashed a traveler's check. The bank told them that it had been ten days earlier, on August 7, when he'd left George Pesut's in Nuremberg. Hearts hit the floor again. The MacPhersons reported their son missing to the police, who told them that adults who disappear usually mean to. Then, on August 27, after printing two thousand missing posters in German, Italian, and English, they headed for Europe to smoke out Duncan themselves. A search of hotel registries got them to the front door of the youth hostel in Innsbruck, but there the trail grew cold. They drove throughout the Alps, choosing roads at random, putting up posters, and searching for signs. Nothing.

By September 19, the MacPhersons had gone long past desperate. They bypassed the police, went to the offices of the Austrian public television network ORF, and begged the producers to ask viewers to phone in if they'd seen the car. The MacPhersons got a call the next night. For forty-two days, a red Opel Corsa had been sitting in the parking lot at the bottom of Austria's Stubai Glacier, a year-round skiing and snowboarding resort not far from Innsbruck. Employees had been cutting the grass around it.

The MacPhersons, whose continuing hunt had taken them from the television studios to Munich, drove through the night to the glacier that had been so close. While they were checking into a nearby hotel, a man named Walter walked past their rented car, which had one of the missing posters taped in the rear window.

("Pure chance," Bob says of the crossing of paths.) Walter stopped, took a closer look at the photograph, had a rush of recognition, and told the MacPhersons a story, the last new one they'd hear about Duncan for fourteen years.

Walter worked as an instructor at the Stubai Glacier. On the morning of August 9, he gave Duncan, who'd already rented a black Duret snowboard and white boots from the resort, a two-hour lesson. Midway through their session, Walter remembered, Duncan had soaked through his sweater, which Lynda had given him the previous Christmas. He took a break, bought a purple sweatshirt from the gift shop, changed, and hung up his sweater to dry in the resort office before returning to the slopes. He was finding his legs on them. Duncan told Walter that after snowboarding for a while longer, he might hike one of the trails in the mountains that cradle the glacier. It was a beautiful day. They shook hands and said good-bye.

Night fell, and Walter, packing up, saw Duncan's sweater still hanging in the office. Walter assumed that he'd forgotten it and took it home in case Duncan came back for it. He didn't, but Walter kept the sweater anyway, because you never know when someone might turn up out of the blue.

Before GPS and satellite radios and search-and-rescue helicopters, Irish fishermen would head out to sea and be swallowed by the fog. Most of them wore white wool sweaters that had been knitted by their wives or girlfriends. Each had a particular pattern, like a fingerprint, and the women who'd waited too long for their men to come home would walk the rain-swept beaches, now waiting for the sweaters to wash ashore. That's what got them out of bed each morning: when they'd found their man's sweater wet on the sand, they'd found their man, and they could put him and their own hearts to rest.

It wasn't so easy for the MacPhersons. They'd found the artifacts of Duncan's life: the car he drove and the things he carried in it — his passport, his overnight bag, a map to the glacier drawn in someone else's hand — and his sweater. But that, for them, wasn't enough.

"Even though we knew in our hearts that he probably wasn't alive, you always think there's some chance," Bob says now. "That's what made us want to keep going. It's amazing how much you hang on to that thread, the tiniest bit of hope."

Duncan had been the same way, but his destination had been clearer. The resort had told the MacPhersons that Duncan had returned the snowboard and boots, which greatly expanded their search area. It meant, maybe, that Duncan had disappeared on his hike in the mountains, a theory supported by an anonymous eyewitness who said he'd seen a man on the afternoon of August 9 standing alone near a waterfall over the next ridge. In the end, the MacPhersons would take seven separate trips into the Alps and spend more than 250 days walking through the valleys and over the mountains that surround the Stubai Glacier, yearning.

It didn't take nearly as long for their minds to go wandering too, pushed every so often in some new direction by fiction and fate.

In 1994, after the fourth of their fruitless trips, they got a phone call from Canadian Foreign Affairs in Ottawa. A few weeks after Duncan had disappeared, a man had staggered out of the forest near Villach, Austria, not knowing who he was, his past lost to him like some forgotten love. He was held by police and then placed in a hospital, and then he was finally allowed to begin a new life. But five years after the man walked out of the woods, the police were still trying to lift his identity out of the ether.

This is what they knew: the man, who had assumed the first name Mark, which he liked the sound of, and the last name Schöffmann, which was the name of a girl he liked from the hospital, spoke North American English, had been wearing North American jeans, had crowns on his front teeth and surgical scars on his knees, and now, in a belated effort to find out whether he might be the missing Canadian named Duncan MacPherson, had been asked about his abilities on the ice. Did he skate? He did, easily and powerfully, as though he had done it all his life, and through official channels, hopes were raised as far away as Saskatoon.

The MacPhersons hung up the phone and picked it up again, asking yet another former teammate of Duncan's now playing in Europe, Emanuel Viveiros, to drive over and take a look at Mark Schöffmann. In one of those short, very long whiles, Viveiros called back the MacPhersons and spoke with a sag in his voice. Mark Schöffmann was someone's missing someone, but he wasn't Duncan MacPherson, that was for sure.

Another phone call came in 2002, when the Canadian investigative TV program *The Fifth Estate* had begun looking into the buccaneer history of Ron Dixon, who had just been killed in a car accident in Mexico. Did the MacPhersons know that Dixon had a history of shady deals — the Dundee Tigers had been something of a financial mirage after all — and dark connections? And did they ever suspect him in Duncan's disappearance?

Yes. No. Well, not really. Not until then. ("It's amazing where your mind goes," Lynda says.) Until then, Lynda, having stumbled on a newspaper article titled "CIA Looking for a Few Good Spies," had been sifting through her memories of that long-ago conversation in which Duncan had mentioned so casually that the CIA was knocking on his door.

"That sounds exciting," she'd said to him.

"You just don't get it, Mom, do you?" he'd replied. "I'd have to disappear. I couldn't tell anybody what I was or where I was going. Not you. Not Dad. Not anybody. You'd never see or hear from me again."

And they hadn't, until the phone rang once again, at three o'clock in the morning one day last July.

Even the landscape had changed in the meantime. Drip by drip, the Stubai Glacier had re-created itself, advancing and retreating and lifting and folding, all of it so slowly that you might not notice unless you had been gone for a while and come back to it and stared hard into the ice, where this past summer's heat wave had floated a red glove up to the surface. And then a young man behind it.

A skier picking his way down the slopes was the first person to see Duncan in fourteen years, but he was unmistakable. He was still big and strong, still wearing a purple sweatshirt bought from the gift shop, and still had a supposedly returned black Duret snowboard at his side, now long past due.

His dark hair was still thick too. His right eye still carried its scar. His chest was still broad. His digital watch was still tight on his left wrist, and his blue Ocean Pacific wallet was still zipped in the pocket of his bright-yellow jacket. It still contained the SaskTel phone card Duncan had used to call his parents from Nuremberg, his health card, his social-insurance card, and his long-expired international driver's license, for which he'd had his picture taken two days before he left. His birth certificate indicated that he was thirty-seven years old. When they found him, he looked more like he was twenty-three.

He wasn't alone. There was the eighteen-year-old boy who said good-bye to his girlfriend and newborn baby in 1949 and came up for air last summer not long after Duncan did, his blond hair still matted down on his forehead and two wedding rings still in his pack. And there was the German hiker missing since 1971. And several years ago, there were the two climbers who had remained roped together for more than thirty years, their black leather boots still tied tight to their feet, their wooden skis still waxed and strapped to their backs. It's become part of the Alpine summer routine, watching a couple of faces lift out of the melt. Always, the people who have been taken in by these mountains are somehow different from the rest of us, different even from others who have gone missing or died. Different even from the landscape.

The rink where Duncan played for the Saskatoon Blades is gone now, demolished and replaced by a big new arena out past the airport. Boys from across the prairies are drawn to it all the same, playing out their young hearts and holding on to a fantasy almost as old as midwestern life, that they might follow Wendel Clark and Brian Skrudland and Gordie Howe off the farm and onto Long Island or, now, to Phoenix or Anaheim or Nashville or Dallas. They throw themselves against the Red Deer Rebels and the Brandon Wheat Kings, and you can see in their big hopeful blue eyes that they are imagining what it will feel like when they get their chance to go away and carve their own circles into the ice, immortal.

They look an awful lot like he looked, these kids, when he left and when he came home.

You would have needed to know Duncan to see that anything about him was the least bit different, to see that he hadn't just fallen asleep and been dreaming dreams so good that he'd decided not to wake up, just as you would have needed to know the glacier to see the crack in its smooth white sheet, hidden by the glare and a perfect blanket of snow. It swallowed him the way the sky still swallows the land, and then he was buried and frozen in time, probably by a snow-grooming machine and probably alive. Two long, unbroken lines, two histories — a man's and a mountain's — had intersected. And there, in the way that every second of every day for every one of us is some kind of horizon, one of those lines had reached its vanishing point, and hundreds more had begun.

Bob and Lynda MacPherson would spend their days remembering and their nights awake, and they would receive hundreds of letters and cards from strangers and friends, telling them more stories about their son that they'd never heard before. George Pesut would retire from hockey, move back to Canada, name his first son Lucas Duncan, and make his living in the stock market. Roger Kortko would follow him home and become a real estate agent and later sell RVs. Mark Schöffmann would get a job at an architectural firm and look toward the future, because he didn't have a past. Ron Dixon would die in that car crash in Mexico and have all his schemes unravel. Gordie Howe would turn silver, then bronze.

And underneath every last bit of it was Duncan MacPherson, all possibility and hope, just waiting to be discovered for the second time in his life.

Rayna's Second Season

FROM THE BALTIMORE SUN

LONG BEFORE Rayna DuBose became a basketball star — and half a lifetime before the day she got sick, went to the hospital, and almost never came home — she was a dancer. Ballet, to be specific. The soft, poetic music and her long arms and legs formed a natural partnership. Dance was her first love, and as is often the case with first loves, she never forgot what it felt like, to twirl and spin and smirk at the limitations of gravity.

The DuBose family was not rich, but there was money for tutus and ballet slippers, even if Rayna would outgrow them in mere months. At recitals, she towered above the other giggling nine-year-olds, like a redwood in a forest of firs. When it was her turn to whirl across the stage, her thousand-watt smile lit up the auditorium.

My God, her father thought, *my little girl is fearless.*

You've got to get a basketball in that girl's hands, Rayna's pediatrician kept telling her parents.

I don't want to play! she would protest.

Rayna, they don't give out many scholarships to girls wearing tutus.

No! I don't want to play basketball. I want to dance!

Her parents just shook their heads and laughed.

Even then, long before she would trade her toe shoes for high-tops, long before her spinning and soaring would thrill crowds in a gym in Oakland Mills — and even longer before an illness would steal away the game she loved — Rayna DuBose had an unbending will and a bullheaded determination. She was, from the beginning, a force to behold.

They were the worst months of her life, and yet she has almost no memory of those ninety-seven days and nights that began in April

2002 and stretched into July. They run together, overlapping and blurring until they're impossible to retrieve. But maybe the details aren't important. Maybe if you can see her here, sitting on the stairs in her parents' house in Columbia on the day she's finally going back to college, maybe that's enough — a picture that hints at her journey through all that darkness.

It's May 17, 2003, and as her parents load the SUV with boxes, Rayna sits in the foyer, talking quietly on her cell phone. A stuffed blue monkey rests in her lap, and in the monkey's arms is a tiny orange basketball.

When it's time to go, Rayna pulls herself up and steadies herself on legs made of plastic, silicone, titanium, aluminum, and stainless steel. She walks down the driveway and folds her six-foot-three frame into the SUV. Clothes, lamps and light bulbs, CDs, sweatshirts, and food fill the back — and enough pairs of basketball shoes to outfit three teams. She puts her stuffed monkey in there too, next to her extra set of arms.

Those awful months, those weeks when doctors weren't sure she'd ever open her eyes again, are a memory now for her parents. Some details are gone; some, they will never forget. What's important now is *this* moment, their nineteen-year-old daughter on her way back to Virginia Tech, to college life, to independence.

Her coach has walked this road with them, and grown to love Rayna like a daughter. Where Rayna's memory is blank, where her parents' is blurred, the coach's is painfully clear. Piece their memories together, and they not only tell a story but they also raise a question: how much courage does a single step require?

If you're inching along a ledge on an icy mountain peak, or walking a tightrope suspended high above the ground, the answer seems easy. Each step puts your life at risk, so it requires all the courage you can muster in order to stay alive.

But what if you're not risking your life? What if you're trying to get it back?

I think I can play in the boys' league, she said one day.
   I think they'll hurt you, her father said with a grin.
   I ain't worried about getting hurt.

At the first game, the tallest player was the one with a ponytail. She stuck out, and yet she was invisible. None of the boys would pass her the ball. Rayna went home so mad, she burst into tears.

She'd given up ballet for this, stood on the court hour after hour, practicing bank shots. How could all that work pay off if they wouldn't even give her the ball?

She knew exactly what she wanted: to be a star like her brother Quinton. Sixteen years older than Rayna, he had gone off to college on a basketball scholarship. To hear their father tell it, it was watching Quinton play at Providence College — and seeing the crowd erupt in rapture — that lit the fire for Rayna. After all, says Willie DuBose, "there ain't a whole lot of hollering and screaming in ballet."

Night after night, he would come home from work dog-tired, barely able to keep his eyelids upright — and there was Rayna, tugging at his sleeve.

C'mon, Dad, let's go practice.

The next game was more of the same: the boys didn't want to pass to a girl. But a loose ball rolled her way, and with a flick of her wrist, she had her first basket. Minutes later, she had her second. Her last was the game-winner. From then on, the boys were feeding her the ball.

"She started dominating these ten-, eleven-, twelve-year-old boys," Willie recalls, laughing. "Parents were beside themselves. They were saying, 'Damn, this girl is killing my son!'"

Word soon got out, and what do you know? Everyone wanted her on their team. *Can Rayna come play on our travel squad? Can she go to New Orleans for this tournament?* Girls' leagues, boys' leagues — didn't matter.

Fast forward: 1997, Oakland Mills High School in Columbia. At fourteen, Rayna makes the girls' varsity team, mostly because the coach looks at her — six-foot-one and still growing — and dreams of rebounds. At first, the young freshman comes off the bench, just a quiet contributor on a team full of veterans. There is a pecking order coach Teressa Waters wants to uphold, but after a few weeks she sees that it's pointless. The seniors are dropping hints.

Are you going to start Rayna this week? We need her out there.

Oakland Mills begins the season with the modest goal of simply getting to the state tournament, but the more Rayna blossoms, the more the future becomes clear. People start to *believe*. By mid-season, the precocious freshman is grabbing rebounds, hitting jumpers, pushing her opponents aside. Waters can't keep her out of the lineup. She's just too good. By the time the playoffs start, Oakland Mills is in it for one reason only: to win the state title.

State championship game. Oakland Mills is playing against Williamsport, and the whole team is a mess. Nervous, frazzled players are tossing up air balls and flinging passes into the seats. The Oakland Mills fans, ablaze in orange and black, are hushed, as if they are sitting on their hands. The girls haven't played this poorly all year. At halftime, Oakland Mills clings to an 11–10 lead that is even uglier than it looks. In the locker room, Coach Waters is livid, about to peel paint.

Is anyone here going to step up and win this game?

The crowd comes to life as the teams take the court for the second half. But then, more air balls. A year's worth of hard work is getting flushed away as Williamsport pulls ahead. Oakland Mills has never won a state title before in girls' basketball, and the way things look, that drought won't end tonight. Waters stomps her foot and folds her arms, pleading with her team to make some baskets.

But wait a minute — who's that? It's Rayna, grabbing an air ball and turning it into a lay-up. My goodness, she did it again! Oakland Mills has the lead back!

The band is playing, the crowd is pulsing, and Rayna has eight points in eight minutes. Just like her brother, she finds a way to get baskets when the team is about to buckle.

Can the girls hang on? The seconds tick down. Finally, the buzzer goes off and sets every last one of them free. Tears run down their cheeks. The scoreboard reads Oakland Mills 38, Williamsport 31.

When Waters gave her halftime speech, someone was listening. The quiet freshman leads the team with fourteen points.

The following season, the game comes easily for Rayna. She has grown another inch, and with the grace of a dancer, she spins through the lane, between two defenders, and kisses the ball off the glass for a left-handed lay-up.

Halfway up the bleachers are her mom and dad, beaming as their daughter scores twenty-nine points in an upset of rival Mount Hebron. Andrea DuBose is the one talking to everyone, giving out eleven hugs a minute because she's too nervous to watch closely. She worries about Rayna's asthma, worries that she has forgotten her inhaler. Willie? He's the guy with the shaved head, thick mustache, the one rocking back and forth quietly as Rayna brings the ball up. His eyes never leave her, even when she gives up the ball. That's his baby, right there.

The team goes 10–13 for the season, but Rayna averages 16.3 points and 11.7 rebounds. Some nights, she can't be stopped, even by the best teams. She's a star, everyone says. Can't wait to see her next year.

But wait. Who's this new coach? His voice is like a bullhorn, and his icy glare can cut you in half. He takes one look at his star player and scowls.

"He told me I was fat," Rayna recalls. "He went around telling the whole school I weighed two hundred pounds. Not funny."

But after years of praise, isn't this what she needs? Marcus Lewis, a three-sport star for Oakland Mills in the late '80s, decides he's going to coach girls' basketball with a football mentality. No prisoners. No excuses. He figures Rayna has barely tapped her potential. She's lazy. So he runs her.

And runs her.

And runs her.

Demand the ball, he says.

Get in the weight room, he scolds.

If you listen to me, you can dominate.

It drives her crazy — who does he think he is? — but she's too scared not to listen. Her junior year, she averages 18.1 points and 15.1 rebounds and wills Oakland Mills to a 15–9 record. Still, it's not good enough.

Rayna, do you want to play in college? Lewis asks.

Yes. Of course.

Then seek out the best competition. Stop settling for "good enough."

That summer, she walks to the nearby gym and jumps into pickup games. She's not the tallest player anymore. But like so many years ago, she's the only girl on the court, and the men show her no mercy. She dodges elbows and picks herself up when she gets tossed to the floor. Some days, her father wanders over to the gym to watch, and it takes all the restraint he can muster to stay on the sidelines. In his head, he can still hear her tiny voice. He can almost feel the tug on his sleeve.

I think I can play in the boys' league, Dad.
I think they'll hurt you.
I ain't worried about getting hurt.

Virginia Tech feels like a dream: people are friendly, the Blacksburg campus is beautiful, and here she is, moving into the dorm,
starting a new life on a full basketball scholarship. It's August 2001,
and just getting here feels like an accomplishment. The last two
years of high school, there was poetry in her game, especially the
night she dropped forty points on poor Wilde Lake. But academics
was another matter. She spent long, frustrating nights studying to
get her grades up so she could get into the college.

Look out now, Blacksburg. It's Rayna and Monique, friends since
kindergarten. Monique Cook has always been Rayna's oasis from
basketball, the one friend who knows every secret, every word
Rayna's going to say before she says it. Rayna is blunt, and Monique
loves her for it. She says what's on her mind. Together, they observe
only one rule: no talking about basketball. Talk about boys, talk
about freedom, talk about soap operas. Anything but basketball.

"She could be drafted into the NBA, and she wouldn't even tell
me," Monique says.

But there's no denying that basketball will play a huge role at
Tech. When practices start, it feels like nothing — and everything
— has changed. It's the same game, with the same rules, but it's
like playing against boys again. Rayna's graceful spins and effortless
rebounds disappear; older, wiser players bump her out of the way.
She's too timid to push back, and that drives Bonnie Henrickson
crazy.

Not yet forty years old, Henrickson prides herself on coaching
hard-nosed, old-school basketball. Outside the gym, she's as likable
as ice cream. She has Minnesota roots and midwestern charm.
Players don't call her Coach Henrickson; they call her Bonnie. But
on the court, she's a general. *Pain is weakness leaving the body*, it says
on the team's T-shirts. She's one of the hottest young coaches in
the country — already Virginia Tech has had to sweeten her contract twice to keep bigger schools from stealing her away.

Rayna, you're my little ballerina!

Bonnie is yelling, and practice has ground to a halt.

*Don't be such a candy ass! Be physical. Be nasty. There isn't a mean bone
in your body, is there?*

Every day, two hours of running. It feels like boot camp with nets. Rayna's not playing much either. At night, she blows off steam by blowing off homework. The social scene beckons.

Rayna, did you hear about the party the football team is having? See you there, girl!

What the heck. You have to live for the moment. Before long, everyone knows her lyrical name and recognizes her Hollywood smile. *Hey, Rayna! Are you going out tonight? You know you have to be there, right?*

First-semester grades come in: a 1.4 GPA. The next thing you know, Bonnie is laying out the Rayna Rules. No partying, no friends in her dorm room after 10:00 P.M. Every night, a coach will call to make sure she's there alone.

Rayna says she'll go along with it, that she'll get better grades, and for the most part, she does. But she's still sneaky and stubborn in her own way. At night, when the assistant coaches call, Rayna bluffs like a poker player. Monique is there with her, trying not to laugh, as quiet as a hummingbird.

There is one good thing about basketball, though: Rayna's roommate, Erin Gibson, a tall blonde from a tiny Virginia town on the North Carolina border. The two couldn't be more different — black, white, city, country — and yet, they're a perfect match. It's as if Mary J. Blige befriended one of the Dixie Chicks.

They're both power forwards, but instead of causing tension, the situation just becomes a reason to bond. Erin seems even less confident than Rayna on the court, and she's the starter. More than once, Erin sobs on Rayna's shoulder after a bad practice, and in the close quarters of a tiny dorm room, they find strength in each other. They talk about boys, about their families, about the exhibition tour the team will take in two years.

2004. Destination: Australia.

Rayna and Erin can hardly wait. Sometimes at night, they dream of the adventures they'll have on the other side of the world.

The opening act in Rayna's nightmare begins Monday, April 1, 2002. She's on the squat rack inside Merryman Strength Facility. Freshman season is behind her, and now Rayna, Erin, and teammate Fran Recchia — a skinny point guard from Texas who completes this perfect circle of friendship — are beginning the tedium of off-season workouts.

Aren't you guys exhausted? Rayna says, finishing a set of squats. Her T-shirt is soaked with sweat.

Not really, Erin thinks. Not any more than usual. Sounds typical of Rayna, though. She hates squats. Maybe she's just tired from the weekend. She invited Fran home with her for Easter, and on Saturday night, they were up until nearly dawn, dancing at a Baltimore club called Paradox. Monique was there too. They laughed and grooved to house music, flirting and dancing. It was so hot inside, they shared a water bottle, passing it around among friends.

Aren't you guys exhausted? Rayna says again, as they finish lifting weights.

Yeah, I guess, they respond. For an end-of-workout drill, they decide to juggle beanbags, to improve hand-eye coordination. After several awkward minutes, Rayna stops and sits.

I'm really dizzy. I can't do this.

Dizzy? Of course, you're dizzy, Rayna, you're juggling!

Maybe. But it seems like more than that.

In the locker room, Rayna lies down on a couch. Her eyelids feel like dumbbells.

I just need a little nap, and everything will be fine, she says.

Erin and Fran head to the showers. A few minutes later, they return, and Rayna's lost inside a dream. That's weird, Erin thinks. She's never been one for naps.

They leave Rayna to sleep, only to realize later she is too weak to walk to study hall. With their help, Rayna drags herself there, slumping against the wall the entire way. The team's academic adviser, Katie Emmons, arrives to find her crumpled on the floor, arms and legs in a tangled mess. She's sweating like crazy.

Rayna, c'mon. It's eight o'clock. It's time to get going, Emmons says.

First semester, Emmons was always riding Rayna like this, especially after she was put on academic probation. But Emmons's heart softened when, in the second semester, Rayna looked like a candidate for the honor roll. Sometimes she just needed prodding. Like, perhaps, right now.

Rayna, what's up, girl? You can't be sleeping here. Let's get moving.

Katie, Rayna pleads, *I can't get up. I can't.*

Emmons summons Virginia Tech trainer Ron Esteban and Dr. Duane Lagan, a physician in the athletic department. Lagan takes Rayna's pulse, asks about her asthma, then calmly tells someone to call an ambulance. No reason to be alarmed; just want to be safe. Nervous teammates watch Rayna's chest rise and fall as she breathes.

Across town, Bonnie has just returned from the Women's Final Four in San Antonio. She's shaking off jet lag when the phone rings: Rayna is en route to Montgomery Regional Hospital, just up the road, for some tests. She may be dehydrated. Probably nothing serious.

At the hospital, a doctor tells Bonnie that Rayna has a fever. *She's probably coming down with something.* He never says the word flu, but that's the impression Bonnie will remember having.

In Rayna's room, an IV drains into her arm and brings life to her face again. Bonnie calls Rayna's parents to let them know things are fine, and Rayna watches Juan Dixon lead Maryland to a national basketball title on television. At 11:30 P.M., the doctors decide Rayna can leave. Bonnie drops her off at her dorm and says good night. *Get some sleep.*

At 6:30 on Tuesday morning, Erin's alarm wails at them to get out of bed. They have to be at the gym at 7:15 for the team picture. Bonnie is headed out on the road again to do some recruiting, and this morning is the only time everyone can get together. Erin's feet hit the floor, but Rayna's do not.

Erin?

Yeah?

I don't think I can get up. I don't think I can move.

At 6:50, Erin calls Bonnie. There's fear in her voice. *She's like she was yesterday. What should I do?*

Well, Bonnie says, *can she walk? If she can come here, someone can take her to the student health center after we take pictures.*

After a few minutes, Rayna decides that, yes, she can walk to the gym. On the way over, sweat runs down her face. This isn't normal, Erin thinks.

In the locker room, Rayna is too weak to dress herself. Erin and Fran help her into her uniform. When they get to the gym, the photographer fiddles with the lighting, and Rayna, in the back row, struggles to hold up her head. Between each snap of the camera, her chin rests against her chest.

Playfully, the coaches and the photographer tease her. *One more big smile, Rayna. We're not taking the picture until we get one of your real smiles.*

In the weeks and months to come, this is the moment assistant coach Angie Lee will replay in her mind with anguish. She still

won't look at the team picture taken on that day; her copy remains in its bubble-wrap packaging, stuffed in a drawer. But she
doesn't have to see the photo to recall the image that haunts her.
That day, she remembers, the whites of Rayna's eyes were yellow.

In Columbia, the phone rings Tuesday night with the news that
Rayna is back in Montgomery Regional Hospital. She has been sent
there from the student health center for tests, including a spinal
tap. The doctor on the line uses a word that will soon dominate the
DuBoses' lives: meningitis.

According to the federal Centers for Disease Control and Prevention, meningitis is "an infection of the fluid of a person's spinal
cord and the fluid that surrounds the brain." The seriousness of
that infection, however, can differ greatly depending on whether it
is viral or bacterial. Viral meningitis has flulike symptoms that include drowsiness, headache, and fever, and if it is left untreated, a
person will generally recover from it in seven to ten days. Bacterial
meningitis also has flulike symptoms, including drowsiness, headache, and fever, and if it is left untreated, it can kill a person within
hours.

Willie doesn't remember any discussion about exactly what type
of meningitis Rayna might have. He hangs up the phone with the
impression that there is no need to panic, that they can wait and
drive down first thing in the morning.

At 2:00 A.M., the phone rings again. Another doctor.

I'm sorry, he says, *but Rayna has taken a turn for the worse.*

What?

Rayna's white blood cell count is through the roof. It is so high,
doctors think it must be an error. But when the tests are repeated,
the results are the same. Rayna appears to have bacterial meningitis, and her body is shutting down.

We're flying her to Charlottesville. To the University of Virginia Medical Center.

When?

Now. You need to come right away.

What are you saying?

I'm saying she may not make it.

A car flies down the highway. Inside, silence.

Don't talk, don't think, just drive. Three hours to Charlottesville.

Three hours through the rolling hills of Virginia. Three hours to let the imagination run.

Twenty-eight years. Is that how long it has been since they promised they would always be there for each other?

Twenty-eight years of laughing together, praying together, and raising two children. Twenty-eight years of basketball games and Sunday dinners.

In 1973, Andrea Burton was on her lunch break from work at the state library in Norfolk, Virginia, when she met a tall, handsome man standing in line at McDonald's. He made her laugh, and she made him smile. That night, Andrea went home and told her momma she'd met the man she was going to marry.

Andrea had a three-year-old son, Quinton, from a previous relationship, but Willie was always dad. They went to church together, the three of them, and for the first time, the preacher's words moved Willie.

His own father had died when Willie was seven, his mother when he was barely twenty. They were hardworking people, holding down multiple jobs, doing anything they could to give him a step up in the world. But when they passed away, he was all alone. When he and Andrea married in 1979, he had the family he'd long dreamed of.

Willie was selling insurance, but he wasn't making a lot of money. Before long, he made a decision that would change their lives. Purex Corporation, the detergent company, was hiring in Columbia, Maryland.

Andrea didn't want to leave Norfolk until Quinton finished the school year, so they stayed behind while Willie went north and found an apartment. He tossed a mattress on the floor, and that's where he slept until his wife and son joined him.

They'd been in Maryland barely a year when their community realized what Willie and Andrea already knew: Quinton was an artist with a basketball in his hands. In Norfolk, Willie had nailed a backboard and hoop to a pole in their back yard, and from that day forward, Andrea had to drag Quinton inside for dinner. In Columbia, he blossomed into a star, playing on all the best club teams, dribbling as if he had the basketball on a string. Private schools with prestigious alumni began begging Quinton to transfer.

No thanks, the DuBose family said. The neighborhood was safe, they were happy. At sixteen, Quinton was a star at Hammond High School.

When the DuBose team at home learned it was expecting a new member, Quinton started scanning books containing names for babies. His parents had given him the job of naming his sister.

Eighteen years. Is that how long it had been since that October day in 1983 when Rayna arrived? Hardly seems like it now, as Willie and Andrea rush down a dark Virginia highway. Eighteen years of ballet and basketball. Eighteen years of watching with pride as their little girl became a woman.

And now, three hours through the rolling hills of Virginia. Three hours to let the imagination run. Three hours to think the worst while praying for the best.

Wait a minute, are you telling me she's not going to make it?

In Blacksburg, Bonnie Henrickson is on the phone, hearing the impossible: Rayna DuBose is dying. The coach was asleep when the phone rang, but the nurse's words start to sink in.

She's not going to make it.

Go. That's all she can think. No time to grab a bag or ask questions. Just pick up Angie Lee and go. When the assistant coach climbs into Bonnie's car, they begin compiling a mental checklist of the last two days. When did Rayna first start to feel sick? What were her symptoms? How could they have missed the signs?

My God, one of my kids is dying.

Bonnie isn't married, has no children, but every year she sends three or four seniors out into the world and brings in three or four freshmen. Every one of them, all the way down to the last girl on the end of the bench, is family. *My kids.* That's what she calls them. She'd looked into the eyes of so many parents and promised to take care of their daughters. Rayna had been no different.

We love your game, Rayna. But you've got to step it up in school. I know you're smart enough. You can have an outstanding career at Tech. But you've got to work hard. This is the school for you.

Bonnie could be tough. No question about it. She yelled occasionally. All good coaches do. But she gave out hugs too. She loved it when Rayna would stop by her office for no reason at all. Georgia Tech, Providence, George Mason — Bonnie had to battle them all to land Rayna, but it was worth it. She was the kind of ego-free player Bonnie loved. She was already showing flashes of brilliance on the basketball court. It was only a matter of time.

Flying down the highway, the minutes feel like days. The coaches race toward Charlottesville in Bonnie's brand-new Lincoln. From the corner of her eye, Angie peeks at the speedometer. It edges past 100.

What do you mean she's not here?

Bonnie and Angie are frantic. They've barreled into the ER at the University of Virginia Medical Center, and the DuBoses aren't even here yet, and now someone is telling them that Rayna isn't here either.

There were helicopter problems in Blacksburg. The first helicopter couldn't take off, and by the time another one was sent from Roanoke, Rayna's blood pressure had plummeted. She'd had a seizure and couldn't be moved until she was stabilized.

Doctors take Bonnie aside and pepper her with questions: Think hard. What were her symptoms?

She was cranky, she was irritable, she was tired and dehydrated. She just wasn't Rayna.

Willie and Andrea arrive next, at 5:00 A.M., and finally, fifteen minutes later, Rayna's helicopter lands. They can see their daughter for only a moment, as she's being rushed to the emergency room. Running over and over in Andrea's mind is one thought: *She's dying. My daughter is dying.*

Let us do our jobs, the doctors say. *We're doing all we can to stabilize her.* But for several hours, they say little else.

Eventually, there is a diagnosis: Rayna has a particular strain of bacterial meningitis called meningococcal meningitis, which strikes about three thousand Americans every year. The Centers for Disease Control estimate that it is responsible for three hundred deaths a year, and five to fifteen of those who die are college students living in dormitories.

The sun rises, and there is still no news about Rayna's condition. Around 11:00 A.M., a doctor walks into the waiting room. His face is like chiseled stone.

Right now, it does not look good, he says. *Rayna is in a coma. Her brain is swelling, and her kidneys have failed. Her other organs are beginning to shut down. You need to prepare yourself for the possibility that she might die.*

Andrea grabs Bonnie and begins to sob. Over and over, as her tears mix with Bonnie's, Andrea repeats words that make no sense. *I'm sorry. I'm so sorry.*

You're sorry, Bonnie thinks. *I promised to take care of her. I walked into your living room, looked you in the eye, and told you she would be part of our family. My God, I'm the one who's sorry.*

Talk. That's what Andrea wants to do. If she doesn't talk about what's going on, it will make her crazy. She's always been that way. Back in Norfolk, where she sang in the choir at First Baptist Church on Bute Street, family talked about stuff. They talked about faith, they talked about love, and when they had to, they talked about death. Right now, Bonnie and Angie are family.

But what about Willie? See him over there, staring out the window? One minute he's pacing the hallway, bottling up his anger. The next he's near tears, talking quietly to himself.

I can't lose my baby, he repeats, over and over. *Please don't take my baby from me.*

When fear and anger finally give way to exhaustion, the cushions in the waiting room come off the chairs, and together, the four construct a makeshift bed in the middle of the room. Bonnie, Angie, Willie, and Andrea lie down on the floor, holding hands. They can barely keep their eyes open, but no one really sleeps.

Weren't they just saying how lucky they were? Hadn't they just dropped Rayna off at Tech seven months ago and laughed, figuring they were finally in the clear after months of adversity?

When Rayna was a high school senior, Willie was diagnosed with prostate cancer. Andrea had taken a fall that broke both her arms. *What a year,* they joked. *If we can just get through this, we'll be fine.*

Willie's own father knew all about hard times. Willie Sr. was an honest man who did all he could to provide for his family. He spent a lifetime working with his hands, cutting marble and coming home exhausted. He barely had a third-grade education. The only thing he could write was his name. Every week, he proudly signed his paycheck.

He never once saw a doctor, and liver problems took his life when Willie was seven. After he died, money was scarce but Willie's mother, Rosa Lee, managed. Willie would wake up in the morning to find her already gone, off to clean houses, earning money to pay the rent. There was always food on the table. She made sure of that.

Her son didn't know how sick she was until he was older. Cancer. Heart problems. A lot of different things. She tried to keep her ailments to herself, even near the end. Willie had a chance to leave Norfolk, offers to play basketball or football on scholarship. But he stayed home, went to Norfolk State, and worked to earn money for her medical bills.

Now he and Andrea were survivors too. They had jobs they liked — Willie as a supervisor for American Greetings, Andrea with the federal government — money in the bank, and good health. Doctors had caught Willie's cancer early, and he beat it. Andrea had both arms in heavy casts for months, but the bones healed.

They had come through it whole, and they swelled with pride to see their daughter walk across the Blacksburg campus. It was Rayna's turn to go out on her own, to get a shot at her dream. Willie had sent her off into the world knowing he was a lucky man.

Treat them like adults.

That's the best way to break the news to the team, Bonnie decides.

We can't go from "She's going to be fine" to "I'm sorry, but she's gone," she tells her assistant coaches. *We need to get them together right now and tell them it doesn't look good. Don't keep them in the dark.*

The task falls to Bonnie's assistant on campus, Karen Lange. She's so scared, she's shaking after getting off the phone with Bonnie. She writes down what she wants to say and calls the team into the locker room. They know something is going on. Because meningitis can spread so easily, they've all been to the health center for a dose of the drug Cipro as a precaution. Ten seconds into Lange's speech, the whole room is in tears.

Erin sobs on Fran's shoulder. Her mind keeps replaying the last time she saw Rayna, trying to remember what she said when she told her good-bye.

My God, Erin thinks, what about Monique? Does she even know?

Later, Fran fires off an instant message to Monique on her computer. Within minutes, Monique calls Fran, hysterical.

Don't you tell me my best friend is dying. Don't you do that.

What is going on? Hadn't they just been laughing together, pointing out cute guys across the room as they danced well into the morning hours in Baltimore? That was Easter weekend, only three days ago. They were hugging and joking about how hot it was in the club. Sharing the same water bottle.

Why not me? they ask themselves.

Fran and Monique become obsessed with the question, as if the answer will bring them any comfort.

Why not me? Fran asks. *I was with her the whole weekend.*

It doesn't make sense, Monique says. *Every single one of us drank from that bottle after she did.*

Why is Rayna the one fighting for her life?

Each day, each hour, Willie and Andrea DuBose think things can't get any worse. And then they do.

Their daughter, Rayna, a graceful athlete, a college basketball player with a radiant smile, an eighteen-year-old who a week ago had so many possibilities in front of her, is lying in a hospital bed in a coma. For two days, doctors have warned her parents to prepare themselves: she may not live.

Doctors initially gave her an experimental drug called Protein C to fight the infection. But her medical records show they stopped the drug shortly afterward for fear it was causing internal bleeding.

Since her arrival at the hospital around 5:15 A.M. on Wednesday, April 3, 2002, her parents have clung to their faith. They've begged her to keep fighting. But every moment of calm is followed by chaos.

On Thursday, she suffers a heart attack.

Next, her lungs collapse.

Then word comes that, along with her kidneys, her liver is failing.

Doctors are working frantically, trying to save her. In the waiting room, her parents feel helpless. The only thing they can do is pray.

She could be so beautiful with a basketball in her hands.

Her freshman year at Tech, Rayna rarely played for extended stretches. She was frustrated, sick of all the running in practice, tired of being yelled at. She even told her best friend she wished she could quit. But there were nights when all the work seemed worth it.

In January 2002, in the Women's National Invitation Tournament, she had come off the bench toward the end of a lopsided contest against Vermont, and for ten minutes, she recaptured the grace, the poetry, and the muscle that had been missing from her game since high school. She ran the floor, caught passes in traffic, yanked down rebounds, and calmly nailed fast-break jumpers. With just a sliver of playing time, she scored thirteen points, and with every basket, the girls on the bench, the teammates who adored her sense of humor, squealed with joy. Even Bonnie, who had barked at Rayna all season, couldn't resist a smile. She ran the court so hard, with such determination, the muscles in her foot started to cramp. When she was fouled trying to score one last basket, Bonnie called out to the referee to get his attention.

Hey, I think I got one hurt out there, she said. *I think I need to get her out of the game.*

The referee looked back at Rayna, who was standing at the free-throw line grinning, soaking up the polite applause from the crowd and the roars from her teammates.

I think, the referee told Bonnie, *she's going to be fine.*

Finally, Rayna's condition is stable. The swelling in her brain has stopped. She's still in a coma, still not breathing on her own, and may have brain damage. But at least her parents can see her. After a few hours, they ask Bonnie if she'd like to join them in her room. The coach tiptoes in, worried about what she might find.

Tubes run in and out of Rayna's body; machines beep rhythmically as they force her heart to beat and her lungs to breathe. Sitting on the edge of the bed, Bonnie reaches out and touches Rayna's right hand.

It is ice cold.

With her other hand, Bonnie feels Rayna's right arm just below the shoulder.

It is warm.

Inch by inch, she moves her hands toward one another, until they're nearly touching.

Just below the elbow, she stops, her hands inches apart. One touches warm skin, the other cold.

It is the same with Rayna's legs. Just below the knee, her skin is cold.

Her blood pressure is so low that blood isn't circulating to her extremities. Gangrene is setting in. The tissue in her toes and fingers is dying.

There is nothing we can do to stop it, the DuBoses are later told.

Within a week of her hospitalization, Rayna's doctors talk about amputations.

How can one even begin to imagine Willie and Andrea's sorrow? Even if Rayna doesn't have brain damage, what will life be like for someone who was always the best athlete? How do you let go of that person, the one who comes bounding into the house in summertime, who wrestles with her older brother and throws her arms around her mom?

Hours after learning that amputations will almost certainly be necessary, the DuBoses take a walk. As they slip away, Bonnie sneaks back into Rayna's room. It's what she does whenever Willie and Andrea are gone for a few minutes. She talks to Rayna, tells her she loves her. A doctor has said Rayna can't hear, but Bonnie doesn't care. What can it hurt, after all?

When Willie comes back into the room, he is so quiet Bonnie almost doesn't notice him. He takes his daughter's hand, and he speaks. Maybe he's talking to Bonnie; maybe he's just talking out loud. His voice is calm.

I've already started to work it out in my mind how we're going to tell her. I've already started to formulate a plan.

Hours become days and days become weeks.

Bonnie goes home for a change of clothes, and returns the next day. Willie and Andrea know they won't be back at their jobs anytime soon. They check into a hotel but rarely sleep there at the same time. At least one of them is almost always in Rayna's room. There is no comfort zone, just twenty-four-hour vigilance.

The immediate danger is past, but the unknown is terrifying. How much brain damage will she have? Will she recognize them? Several times, doctors lower Rayna's level of sedation to test her mental status, but the pain is so intense, she bolts up in bed, screaming. She snaps in half three bite blocks, placed in her mouth to keep her from biting through her tongue.

Willie wanders the halls and thinks while Andrea works the phones, reassuring family. Every day, a card or a teddy bear arrives in the mail. The DuBoses' family pastor, the Reverend Robert Turner, drives down to Charlottesville to lead them in daily prayers.

Rayna's thirty-four-year-old brother, Quinton, is there too, trying to be strong, yet nearly going to pieces. *That's my baby sister*, he thinks. *I'd do anything. I'd switch places with her if I could.*

He was always the mature one, the old man before his time, Willie often said. But Rayna made her brother, sixteen years her senior, feel like a kid again. Every time he watched her play basketball, he could see a little bit of himself.

And why not? They were close, sharing a passion for basketball, and so much more. He had been given the job of naming her when she was born, and took the job seriously, the same way he approached everything. He went through piles of baby books, trying out dozens of names on his tongue. Only Rayna sounded perfect — like music. In Hebrew, Rayna means "song of the Lord."

She was barely three when Quinton, a star player at Columbia's Hammond High School, went off to college on a basketball scholarship. When the family came to see him play at Providence College, she watched in awe. Sitting in the crowd, listening to it erupt every time Quinton scored, planted a seed that would one day blossom in her.

Summers in their little townhouse in Owen Brown were heaven. He'd toss her in the air, tug her ponytail, and laugh as she tried to squirm away. Even when she got older, and Quinton got married and had a son, they remained close. She'd call him at all hours, just to tease him and tell him she loved him.

Now here he was staring down at her in a hospital bed, wondering if she'd ever walk again.

From a single blink of an eye, hope emerges.

After three weeks, doctors again reduce Rayna's sedation to test her mental status. There's still a tube in her throat, and she can't talk. Her eyes are so red, she's almost unrecognizable. But after a while, she's blinking after every question: once for yes, twice for no.

She recognizes us! She knows who we are! Oh, thank God!

They will never know for certain what saved her from brain damage. But for Willie and Andrea, Protein C — the experimental medicine she was briefly given — will always be "the miracle drug."

When Willie brings Bonnie into the room, she thinks, okay, maybe Rayna recognizes her mom and dad. But she's not going to know who I am. No way.

Rayna, she says, *if you know who I am, stick your tongue out at me.*

Bam. Rayna's tongue shoots out, as if to say, *You mean like this, coach?*

Like the DuBoses, Bonnie is elated. But as she leaves Rayna's room, the coach's smile fades.

Now she's going to know, Bonnie thinks. All her life, she's had a gift. She looked at herself in the mirror and saw an athlete staring back. That's over now.

No one knows what to say. There are days when they try to convince one another that Rayna's hands feel warmer, but in her heart, Bonnie knows they're only trying to avoid the facts.

Rayna can see her hands, black, wrinkled and atrophying from lack of circulation. One day, she motions for a nurse to pull the sheet back. She wants to see her feet. No one can muster the courage to do it.

Rayna won't look her father in the eye. He tries to catch her gaze, but she turns away again and again. It's as if one look from Willie, one sustained moment of contact between father and daughter, will confirm all the fears swirling inside her head.

They squeeze into her room: her parents, her coach, several nurses, a psychiatrist, and the hospital chaplain. They're all here, with Dr. Adam Katz, a plastic surgeon who does most of the talking.

I know you know there's been some damage, the doctor tells Rayna.

She nods her head.

You'll need to have a series of surgeries, and that will allow us to determine how much damage has been done. We'll start with your fingers, and I promise I'll save as much of your arms and legs as possible.

She meets his words with silence. Then, slowly, she speaks, the tube in her throat allowing only a whisper.

Please. Wait. Maybe the blood will start flowing again. Maybe if we just wait, you won't have to amputate.

Dr. Katz does not hesitate. *I'm sorry, Rayna*, he says. *There's just too much damage.*

Again, silence. Then: *Will I walk?*

The best-case scenario, Katz says, *is that we go in and evaluate the damage and you walk out of here on your own. The worst-case scenario is you walk with some assistance.*

Rayna's eyes scan the room until they find her coach at the end of the bed.

Will I play?

In the seconds that pass, Bonnie sees Rayna running down the court, stopping on a dime, and burying a jump shot. The points she has scored, the rebounds — how do I tell her that's all over?

Before Bonnie can answer, Dr. Katz has a reply.

Yes, Rayna, but not at the level you're playing now.

She nods.

Now Bonnie finds words: *Even if you can't play, you'll be a student assistant, Rayna. You'll travel with us, you'll be on the bench, and you'll always be a member of this team. Always.*

Rayna nods, satisfied for the moment.

Later, alone with Bonnie in her room, Rayna wants to talk. She is exhausted, and it is difficult for Bonnie to understand what she is trying to say. Once, twice, three times Rayna tries to speak. Frustrated, her eyes fill with tears.

Okay, Rayna, Bonnie says, *let's do it like charades. Is it a person, place or thing?*

Place.

What place?

Australia, Rayna says. *Can I still go?*

Even when things weren't going well during freshman year, Rayna and her roommate, Erin Gibson, would dream about 2004, how much fun it would be when they traveled with the team to Australia to play in exhibition games. It sounded like an adventure, all the way across the world, and she didn't want to miss it.

It takes a minute for Rayna's words to register with Bonnie.

The team trip in 2004? Can you come to Australia with us?

Rayna nods her head.

Omigod! Of course, you can go, Rayna.

In time, in the weeks and months to come, the real meaning of Rayna's question will resonate with Bonnie: *When can I start living my life again?*

On May 1, 2002, a team of doctors remove Rayna's hands and feet. Seven days later, on May 8, they amputate her limbs: her arms four inches below the elbow, her legs six inches below the knees. She'll have ten operations in all.

Willie and Andrea call family members and close friends, but there are so many people to notify, they can't reach everyone. The next day, the University of Virginia Medical Center releases a statement to the media, saying Rayna has undergone a "bilateral amputation of the upper and lower extremities." It does not elaborate.

Rayna's best friend, her oldest friend, Monique Cook, is driving to work in Columbia when she hears Rayna's name on the radio. She has tried several times to see Rayna, but each time Willie and Andrea have told her the same thing: *Now just isn't a good time.*

Monique has tried to be patient, but she and Rayna have been like sisters, ever since they were in elementary school together. They know every secret, every story, every detail of one another's lives. They even ended up going to the same college, hanging out each week in Rayna's dorm watching soap operas. Monique's been doing her best, trying to be strong ever since Rayna got sick, but it's been hard not seeing her. In her car, taken by surprise, Monique turns up the radio volume.

We regret to bring you this sad news today. Former Oakland Mills basketball player Rayna DuBose, a freshman at Virginia Tech who was stricken with meningitis in April, had to have a bilateral amputation of her upper and lower extremities yesterday.

Screaming. All Monique can hear now is the sound of her own screaming. She pulls her car over to the side of the road.

In Blacksburg, Virginia Tech's assistant coaches break the news to Rayna's teammates. For several hours, her roommate, Erin, is crying so hard, she can barely breathe. She and Rayna were so different, and yet they'd grown so close. Rayna was always making her laugh, encouraging her not to get so down, to not take things so seriously. In Erin's head, she keeps trying to imagine Rayna without hands and feet, but it's impossible.

She can't scratch her nose. She can't sit up because she can't catch herself if she starts to fall. And of course, there is the pain.

Her right arm produces the worst of it. Her initial amputation has left the bone near her elbow exposed. To regenerate healthy tissue, and to fight infection, Dr. Katz decides to cut open a flap in the skin around Rayna's stomach, tuck the arm inside, and sew it up. Eventually, the body will heal what medicine cannot.

But for three weeks, she can barely move. Her father, trying to imagine how much focus this requires, wraps his arm in a towel and fashions a sling. He lies on his hotel bed and stares at the ceiling. After twenty minutes, he damn near goes crazy.

At times, Rayna's pain is accompanied by panic. In the hotel one evening, around midnight, Willie picks up the phone, and all he can hear is his baby girl screaming. Violent, ear-piercing screams that go on and on and never die out. She's a room away from the doctor holding the phone, but to Willie and Andrea, it sounds as if Rayna is inside the receiver.

We can't get her to calm down, the doctor says. *Please come.*

When they arrive, she's thrashing and crying, oblivious to everything except the pain. Willie and Andrea talk with her, pleading with her to breathe, to calm down. But nothing seems to work.

Finally, Willie climbs into his daughter's bed and lies on top of her, holding her still. So still, he can feel her heartbeat.

The minutes creep by. It's impossible to say how many. Eventually, the screaming stops.

There are many bad nights. But none quite like this.

Monique isn't taking no for an answer. Again and again, she calls Willie and Andrea and begs them to let her come to the hospital. *Please,* she says, *she's my best friend in the whole world. I need to see her. I have to see her.*

She's just not ready, Monique, Andrea says. *I'm sorry.*

And so Monique makes a tape: *Hey, Rayna, it's me. It's Monique. I love you and I miss you so much. I want you to know that. These are some of our favorite songs. I can't wait to see you. I just wanted you to hear my voice. I love you!*

A few days later, Monique's cell phone rings. It's Rayna, her voice barely a whisper.

Don't talk, Monique says. *I can hear you breathing, and that's all that matters. I just wanted to say I love you.*

A few days later, Monique is tiptoeing down the hospital hall to Rayna's room with Ivy Baker, another close friend of Rayna's from high school. The visit is awkward at first, but before long, the three of them are laughing, joking, gossiping, and watching *Passions* on TV.

Of course, Rayna's teammates want to see her too. They pepper their coach with questions: *You get to see her, Bonnie. Why can't we?*

It's not that simple, girls, Bonnie tries to explain. *I'm not her buddy. I'm her coach. Yes, your bond with her is so much bigger than basketball, but she's still sorting all that out. Be patient.*

Bonnie tells Willie and Andrea that if Rayna ever wants to see some of her teammates, she'll have them there in a flash. And one day, when Andrea asks Rayna if she's ready, the answer is a surprise: yes.

Erin is away on a trip, and Fran Recchia — the friend who had gone home with Rayna for Easter right before Rayna got sick — is visiting her own family in Texas. But Sarah Hicks, Molly Owings, Emily Lipton, and Crystal Starling are still in Blacksburg for the summer. Bonnie gathers them together, and on the way to Charlottesville, she is blunt: *Be prepared to turn around and come home without seeing her. She might change her mind. You might walk into the hospital, hug her parents, and get right back in the car.*

In the waiting room, the girls practically smother Willie and Andrea, and the DuBoses laugh as they haven't in months. But down the hall, Rayna is crying. She's asking to see Bonnie. Now.

In Rayna's sterile hospital room, Bonnie sits on the edge of the bed. What's going on? she asks. *What's wrong?*

I'm tired, Rayna says, choking back tears.

Anything else wrong?

No. I'm tired.

I know you're tired, Rayna, Bonnie says, *but is there anything else?*

For a moment, the room is quiet.

I'm scared, Rayna says. *I'm scared of how I look.*

Rayna, Bonnie says, *if it were Emily Lipton in this bed, would you care what Emily looked like?*

No, she says, tears running down her cheeks. *I wouldn't care at all.*

They don't care either. They just want to see you and tell you how much they love you.

When her teammates file into the room, Rayna doesn't make eye contact. But with some coaxing, she talks. After a while, someone makes her laugh.

Okay, Bonnie thinks, maybe this is going to be okay.

Even with health insurance coverage, the cost of Rayna's medical care is hundreds of thousands of dollars. And though money is the last thing on Willie and Andrea's mind, in Columbia the community is thinking for them. On June 11, Oakland Mills holds "An Evening for Rayna" at the high school gym.

Throngs of people show up, eager to participate in the walk-athon, the bake sale, the slam-dunk contest. A man who has never met Rayna pays for a $1 hot dog with a $20 bill and tells the cashier to keep the change. The event raises $51,000 — and boosts the DuBoses' spirits too.

Willie and Andrea have driven back to Columbia for the occasion, and Quinton is videotaping the whole thing so Rayna can see it someday. It's the first night both Willie and Andrea have spent away from her since she got sick.

Another evening, Bonnie is keeping Rayna company while her parents are out. Rayna's doctors are worried about depression, and there is talk of having Rayna see a psychologist. Bonnie notes she never seems angry, never lashes out at the world for dealing her this unimaginable twist of fate. I don't know that I could be that strong, the coach thinks. What's going on inside her head? She decides to ask.

Rayna, Bonnie says, *emotionally, where are you right now?*

What do you mean?

I mean, hour after hour you lie in this bed, and I don't know how you do it. Are you angry? Are you mad? Do you sit here and ask why? Because I would if I were you.

As usual, Rayna is silent at first, and her answer, when it comes, is deceptively simple.

No, I'm not mad, Rayna says. *No, I don't sit and wonder.*

Then where are you? Bonnie says. *What are you thinking about?*

School. That's all I think about. Coming back to school.

After ninety-seven days in the hospital, Rayna leaves Charlottesville in an ambulance for Good Samaritan Hospital in Baltimore. It is July 8, 2002. She is in a wheelchair and taking seventeen different medications.

Her kidneys, which doctors initially thought would be damaged beyond repair, are functioning fine now. But she must relearn everything — how to feed herself, brush her teeth, get dressed, and use a bathroom. She can't even push her glasses up when they slide down her nose.

Her new prosthetic arms and legs, the ones custom-fit and made of a soft plastic that looks almost like real flesh, won't be ready for months. For now, she wears arms with hooks on the end that open and close when she rolls her shoulders and puts tension on a cable wired inside a harness on her back.

Twice a week, she has three hours of therapy at the Curtis Hand Center at Union Memorial Hospital in Baltimore. On her first day, her occupational therapist, Dale Eckhaus, exhausts all of her tricks trying to get Rayna to open up. The therapist wants to make these three hours feel like something other than torture, but Rayna responds with one-word answers. She has a wall around her, and there is no getting inside.

Eckhaus doesn't give up easily.

What about bologna sandwiches on white bread? Isn't that your favorite food, Rayna? What if we practiced making bologna sandwiches?

Eckhaus has rehearsed this question, and others like it, in her head at home, late at night. She can't stop thinking about Rayna. Her own daughter is Rayna's age.

So, how about it? This way you won't have to ask your mom for help every time you get hungry.

A tiny smile, a crack in the wall.

Rayna learns how to make a bologna sandwich. Later, she will learn how to brush her teeth. Soon, she is combing her hair, taking off a T-shirt, adjusting her glasses. When she can't do things, she wants to rage; the last thing she wants is help. Her mother, who attends every session in the beginning, tries to adjust Rayna's hat one day, and Rayna is livid.

I want to try to do this myself, she tells anyone who will listen. It's the simple tasks, sometimes, that keep her sane.

Rayna's physical therapist, Mike McMaines, plays the role of the bad cop, the drill sergeant. He makes her sweat and swear, but he also promises that, with some work, she can walk again. First, she must learn how to get from her wheelchair to her bed, and how to overcome fear. With no balance, and no way to catch herself if she leans too much in one direction, she is terrified.

On October 3, her prosthetic legs arrive; her arms show up a few days later. Bonnie has made the trip up from Blacksburg, and everyone is pulsing with nervous energy. How will Rayna react when she tries to take her first steps? What if it doesn't go well?

Wait. There's a problem with her arms. The prostheses are — how do you say this? — Caucasian. Everyone has a good laugh over this mistake, but it's also kind of embarrassing. Eventually, Rayna will get ones that match her skin, but for now, she's stuck with these. Rayna can't stop crossing her new arms, trying to hide them from the world one at a time.

With her father on one side for balance, and McMaines on the other, she stands for the first time. Her legs aren't fitted correctly yet, making her six feet six, about three inches taller than usual. Slowly and deliberately, she puts one foot ahead of the other, arching her back because it feels as if she's going to topple forward.

Sweat drips down her face. For the first time in eight months, she is walking.

At the end of the session, Rayna sits down again, and someone pulls out a basketball. Eckhaus holds it out, and Rayna forms a basket with her new arms. She catches the soft throw and, with a smile, flips the ball back. No one can stop grinning.

As a coach, as a friend, and as a surrogate parent, Bonnie has never been more proud.

My kid.

She's going to be okay, Bonnie thinks. She's going to get her life back, and I'm going to do whatever I can to help her.

Just sixteen days after those tentative first steps, Rayna is back on campus. She's still in a wheelchair, still figuring out how to work her new arms and legs, but this return to Blacksburg is scripted: it's homecoming. Virginia Tech will play Rutgers, and the school wants to use the event to raise money for Rayna's medical bills.

Before the football game, she makes a surprise visit to basketball practice and is mobbed by her teammates. Many of them will never completely let go of the question they asked themselves so many times over the last several months: Why Rayna? Why not me? Even though meningitis can spread like a common cold, even though it can be passed along by coughing, sharing a water bottle, or simply breathing the same air as an infected person, they were spared.

All across campus, people have taped up signs that scream WELCOME BACK RAYNA! in orange and black. At the football game, more than fifty Virginia Tech student-athletes wearing T-shirts with 15 on the back — Rayna's number — ask for donations. They raise $50,000; an anonymous donor later pitches in another $50,000.

The game begins, but in the first quarter, it's called to a stop. Rayna, her parents, and Bonnie drive to the middle of the field in a golf cart, where coach Frank Beamer stands, waiting to hand Rayna a football signed by the team. The crowd of 65,000 gets to its feet and the shouting and clapping is so loud, you can barely hear the announcer on the PA system. When Rayna braces herself on her father's arm and stands up to wave, the cheering grows thunderous.

She puts on a strong face for reporters after the game, speaking publicly for the first time since her illness. "It's a really good feeling to know a lot of people care," she says. "Really, things haven't been that bad."

Her parents let her go dancing with her teammates on this night, and she feels like a college student again.

A month later, when she returns to campus for the women's basketball season opener on November 22, 2002, the wheelchair is gone. She's using crutches with confidence, and when her teammates walk out of the tunnel, onto the floor, she walks with them.

The game begins, and Rayna sits quietly on the bench as Virginia Tech struggles against UNC-Greensboro. In the stands, across the court, her parents try to watch the game, but Willie can't take his eyes off his daughter. During a timeout, Rayna tries to stand up without her crutches, loses her balance, and teeters backward, flopping safely into her seat. Stubborn and undaunted, Rayna cracks a smile, then stands up again. Carefully putting one foot in front of another, she walks over to the huddle, sticks her head in the crowd, and listens as Bonnie talks strategy.

"Did you see that?" Willie says, nudging his wife. "My goodness. She's fearless."

When can I go back to school?

The question, which she whispered before she had even left the hospital, is practically being shouted now. Day after day, Rayna brings it up with her parents. I want to go to classes. *I want to live with Erin and Fran. I want to be in an off-campus apartment. I want to be part of the team again.*

Ready or not, her crutches are cast aside, and there's a steadfast rule in the DuBose household: don't give Rayna any help unless she asks for it.

Sometimes, Willie and Andrea are sitting on the couch when they hear a loud crash upstairs. Andrea's instincts, everything she knows about being a mother, tell her to sprint to Rayna's room. But Willie squeezes his wife's hand, shakes his head. *If she needs help,* he says, *she'll call for us. You know Rayna. It will only make her mad if you go up there.*

When the women's basketball team travels to College Park to play Maryland on December 11, Bonnie invites Rayna to spend the night at the team hotel. She hasn't been away from her parents since she was hospitalized. The DuBoses agree, and spend the night fighting the urge to worry.

In January 2003, Rayna is on a plane, flying with the team to Miami and spending an entire week away from home. Every day, Bonnie is on her cell phone, letting Rayna's parents know she is fine.

In therapy, Rayna is moving so fast that Eckhaus is running out of things for her to do. She's so good with her prosthetic hands, she can pick up potato chips without breaking them. When McMaines asks one day if she wants to try running, she curtly tells him: *Okay, but I've already run.*

When was that? he asks.

The other day, at my house, she says.

Okay. Why did you run?

Well, she says, *I had to go to the bathroom. Bad.*

In late February, the U.S. Basketball Writers Association announces it will award Rayna its Most Courageous Award at the men's Final Four. The organization flies Rayna and her parents to New Orleans for the games and at the April 7 awards banquet, Bonnie stands in front of a room full of sportswriters and tells the story of Rayna DuBose.

The Tech coach's eyes fill with tears and her voice shakes, but her words bring the room to its feet.

"This is the story of a champion," Bonnie says. "A champion of faith, a champion of courage, and now, a champion of her own independence."

She's so much like her father sometimes, it's scary. All those years ago, he was determined to go out on his own, leave Virginia, find happiness for his family. Now Willie DuBose can't help but shake his head. Every day his daughter, still the stubborn ballerina who reluctantly traded her toe shoes for high-tops and held her own on boys' teams, becomes more determined to leave Columbia, to go out on her own again.

Her parents want her to live in a dorm, on the ground floor, in a handicapped-accessible room. But Rayna will have none of it. She's barreling ahead with plans to get an off-campus place with Fran and Erin, logic be damned.

After too many frustrating arguments, she stops seeking her parents' permission and starts telling them what she's going to do. Her scholarship is still good — Bonnie has made certain of that — so she'll get a housing allowance just like her teammates. Why be stuck in some dorm? The way she figures it, she can ride the bus to campus. She already rides one into Baltimore by herself for physical therapy. How is this any different?

Summer school is the compromise. If that goes smoothly, she'll go back in the fall. Bonnie says she can work at the summer Virginia Tech youth basketball camp, and if she likes it, maybe she can work as student assistant for the team during the season. That idea has bounced around in Rayna's head ever since she showed up in the gym at Oakland Mills after her illness, and her old coach, Marcus Lewis, asked her to work with his freshmen. He'd made her promise him one thing: *Don't feel sorry for yourself.* The more she thought about it, the more it became her mantra when everyone else wanted to find someone to blame.

Why don't you sue?

Somebody has to be at fault, right?

She's so sick of hearing those questions. People in Columbia ask them constantly. *You know why I don't?* she answers. *Because I'm moving on with my life. I don't care about any of that. I was vaccinated for meningitis when I came to college. It was just bacteria. It wasn't anyone's fault. I don't have time to worry about that nonsense.*

Rayna enrolls in an online class in human development, thinking maybe she'll choose it as her major. And you know what? She's going to take a full load of classes. Things are going to be just like they were. Aren't they?

Bonnie tells the DuBoses that the coaches are willing to do anything. They'll pick Rayna up and drive her to class if necessary. There are no obstacles Bonnie is unwilling to confront.

But before summer school begins, the coach sits down with Erin and Fran.

I know you think this is going to be fun and great, but it's going to be hard work too, Bonnie tells them.

Rayna's not going to be completely independent every second of the day.

Do you two realize what you're signing on for?

Absolutely, they tell her. *We're scared too. How could we not be? But we'll take care of her.*

Rayna sleeps the entire five-hour drive to Blacksburg. Outside the car window, the Virginia countryside whizzes by. The DuBoses have done this drive many times now, but everyone understands without saying it that this time is different.

Rayna's apartment won't be available for another month, so they arrive at a temporary place where she and Fran will hole up for the summer session. The apartment, previously inhabited by several basketball players, is a mess. Rayna sits in the living room while Willie, Andrea, and assistant coaches Karen Lange and Angie Lee give the place a rigorous scrub-down. It was Angie who stayed with Bonnie and the family those first few days in the hospital. It was Karen who had to break the news to the team that Rayna was sick and might not make it.

A local television crew arrives to interview Rayna about her return to school.

"I'm excited to be back," Rayna says, smiling into the camera on this momentous day, May 17, 2003. "I'm getting on with my life."

She doesn't mention the phantom pain she still deals with sometimes, when it feels like her arms are still there. Her doctors gave her medication for it, but after a while, she stopped taking it. *I'll just deal with it. No way am I going to be on medication for the rest of my life*, she tells her mom.

She doesn't talk about how tired she gets if she has to walk across campus either. She hates bringing that stuff up. She just wants people to treat her the way they always did.

After an hour of mopping floors and scrubbing ceilings, Willie walks outside and leans against the family car. His eyes survey the neighborhood. The apartment is at the bottom of a steep hill, and the bus stop is uphill, a half-mile away.

"I keep looking at this hill and shaking my head," he says. "I don't see how she can do this. She's going to fall down, and we're never even going to hear about it."

The next morning, it's time to say good-bye. Fran is taking a friend back to North Carolina, and Rayna wants to go along for the ride, so they show up early at the hotel where Rayna's parents are staying, dressed in Virginia Tech warm-up gear. Andrea hugs Rayna and Fran in the parking lot, and makes them promise to drive safely. Willie doesn't say much, until he asks Rayna to take a short walk with him. He looks her in the eye and in a low, quiet voice he lets his daughter go one more time.

I want you to be safe. I want you to call us if you need anything. I love you.

There are no tears today. Rayna climbs in on the passenger side, and the car pulls slowly out of the parking lot. Willie's eyes stay fixed on the vehicle until it turns up the street and he can no longer see it. He takes a deep breath and smiles.

"This," he says, "is a day of rejoicing."

It's Monday morning, fifteen minutes before Rayna's first class begins at eight. She steps out of the house wearing white pants, an orange, long-sleeved shirt, brown shoes with the laces untied, and a black Virginia Tech backpack on her shoulders. On the tiny front porch, the sunlight hits her face, and for just a moment, Rayna DuBose could be any college student. Her long brown hair hides much of her face, but it cannot hide the fact that she is alive, she is ready, and she is, without question, beautiful.

On campus, Fran drops her off in front of a gray concrete building with a manicured lawn, and then speeds away to her own class. With careful, measured steps, Rayna walks on legs made of rubber and titanium, and guides them with muscles that were strengthened by hope. She walks slowly to her classroom, opening a heavy wooden door on the way with a hand that is guided by the tension of a thin wire cable.

In the months to come, and the year ahead, so much will change. She'll attend countless basketball practices, rising at absurd hours simply because her teammates are doing it as well. She'll go on road trips, worry her parents because she doesn't call home enough, laugh and party with friends again, and live in her own apartment. She'll pick up a basketball one day, try to shoot a few hoops with her new arms, just to see what it feels like. She'll even say good-bye to Bonnie, who will take a job as head coach at Kansas University.

But all that is in the future. At this moment, Rayna walks alone into a classroom and takes a seat in the very last row. She glances at the other students, most of whom are already in their seats. Many are looking in her direction.

She doesn't mind. In time, they will know her story. She was a ballerina once, then a basketball player. Today she's a student, taking her life back, one delicate step at a time.

Alive and Kicking

FROM TEXAS MONTHLY

"IF RANGERETTES ruled the world, there'd be so much discipline," said Lory Lyon, who was on the lower bunk bed in a dorm room at Kilgore College.

"And respect," added her friend Morgan Duplant, sitting cross-legged on the upper bunk. "The words 'slut' and 'ho' would not exist." "It'd be happy — so joyous," Lory said. "There'd be motivation to be a better person."

As I sat on the floor talking with Lory and Morgan, another girl walked into the room and joined the conversation. "Women would be more ladylike, wearing closed-toe shoes and tights," she said. "And they'd sit properly in public." The girls all nodded in agreement.

Although some might consider the Kilgore Rangerettes an anachronism, dozens of fresh-faced teens from across the state flock to this East Texas junior college every summer to try out for the drill team. Most of them have already been accepted at the school, but some will apply only if they make the squad. This year Lory, who is from Longview, and Morgan, from Beaumont, were among the seventy-eight girls from small towns and big cities who competed for thirty or so coveted spots on the high-kicking squad. Both girls are nineteen-year-old sophomores, with perfect, tanned skin and smooth brown hair. Lory says that Morgan looks like a flamingo, on account of her long, thin limbs; Morgan says that, with her tiny nose and big, round eyes, Lory looks like Cindy Lou Who.

Lory and Morgan had been practicing their kicking and dancing all summer, but they had dreamed of being Rangerettes practically forever: "Since I was three," they told me in unison. Morgan heard about the group from her mother, who was on the team in the midseventies. Lory heard about them from her aunt and her great-aunt, who were both Rangerettes — "Plus my brother was a manager for three years," she said proudly. In high school, Morgan was a cheerleader and a drama student and Lory was on the drill team. Though both had gone to Rangerette summer camp for years, they didn't become friends until last year, when they bonded during the tryouts. When they weren't chosen, they refused to let it get them down, for that is not the Rangerette way. Within seconds of wiping their tears, they decided to go ahead and attend the college, live together that fall in one of the dorms, take dance classes from the Rangerette choreographer, make friends with the Rangerettes, and try out again the next year.

Ever since oil was discovered in Kilgore, the town has produced only one other export: the Rangerettes. As all of them will tell you, they are much more than a precision drill team (although they invented the dancing drill team concept in 1940, thank you very much). "We *have* drill teams because of the Rangerettes," Morgan told me. "They have had only *three* directors, and the uniforms have never changed, and, like, omigod." To the outside world, the group is known for its seemingly effortless hat-brim-touching high kick, which has been performed as far away as Hong Kong and as nearby as the grand opening of the local Brookshire Brothers grocery store. But to the Rangerettes themselves, the organization is more of a military-style finishing school for girls with strong morals, a positive outlook, and the discipline of a drill sergeant. "What scares me is we're picking the future members who will carry on the traditions," a sophomore Rangerette told me. "They will be the ones passing this on."

On Monday morning of the last week in July, Lory, Morgan, and two other hopefuls were sitting around a table in the Kilgore College cafeteria, eating bowls of Cocoa Puffs and reciting the rules they had been given the night before. They were required to wear their hair in a ponytail on top of their heads. They were not allowed to wear makeup except for red lipstick. They had to pin a gigantic name tag on their solid-colored leotards. They could not wear jewelry, needless to say. Unless given permission to speak, they had to answer all questions from their assigned advisers and other sophomore Rangerettes with only "Yes, ma'am. Thank you, Miss Jones [or whatever]." The girls eyed one another across the table, cracking up at their goofy-looking hair fountains and bright-red lip gloss. There were reasons for these rules. "Many girls need to come to a more humble place," director Dana Blair told me. "They have always been the officer and won everything and been the 'it' girl, and if we had all those egos running around, practice would be difficult."

So far, the tryouts were similar in many ways to last year's, Morgan said, chewing her cereal, "only this year it's weird because the sophomores are all our friends." But even though that was true — they had all lived in the same dorm as freshmen — Lory and Morgan were pretty well excluded from the Rangerette fun. The girls have a saying about the organization: "You can't understand it from the outside, and you can't explain it from the inside," and last year Lory and Morgan might as well have been in Alaska.

I walked over to a table of sophomore Rangerettes. A group of a dozen or so stopped talking and looked up at me suspiciously when I asked to sit down. They were all wearing matching baseball shirts with "Rettes" printed on the front and their last names on the back. Their sporty accessories were perfectly color-coordinated, from mod tennies to glittery barrettes. On this particular day, the theme was red, white, and navy blue. The girls live together in the same dorm, eat together, and practice together, leaving one another only on weekends, when they drive back to their hometowns because there isn't much to do in Kilgore, a town of twelve thousand. But wherever they go, they are, first and foremost, Rangerettes. "We're really big on reputation," Hillary Hoffman told me. She and her sisters, Hayley and Cali, who are from Coppell, have the distinction of being the drill team's first triplets. "When you get together at a party, you're still representing the Rangerettes."

Pushing aside her food tray, a sophomore with curly brown hair said that she was having to adjust to her new status as a second-year Rangerette. A freshman, she explained, is constantly bossed around by the sophomores, so that by the time she graduates, she has thoroughly experienced the roles of follower and leader. "It will be weird that the hopefuls can't talk to us from now on," she said, rising from her chair to head to morning practice. "And when we walk into the gym, they all have to greet us by our last names."

A few minutes later, I witnessed that surreal tradition. As the Rangerettes filed into the gym, the hopefuls stopped stretching and beamed panicked, exaggerated smiles at them while raising their right hands high into the air, fingers spread. "Hello, Miss Satterwhite!" they yelled. "Hello, Miss Oden!" "Hello, Miss Coker!" If several sophomores walked in simultaneously, the girls screamed their rapid-fire, unintelligible greetings like superfriendly traders on the floor of the stock exchange.

If the scene sounds mortifying, keep in mind that none of these girls are shy. Several former Rangerettes have gone on to careers in entertainment, as noted by their alumnae organization, Rangerettes Forever, which also funds many of the girls' scholarships. Alice Lon, for example, the longtime Champagne Lady on *The Lawrence Welk Show*, was a Rangerette. Six of the thirty-eight current Dallas Cowboys Cheerleaders are former Rangerettes. And while most of the sophomores I spoke with planned on finishing their degrees at a four-year university and working as accountants, physician's assistants, schoolteachers, and the like, about a quarter of them wanted to become drill team instructors, spreading the word about the Rangerettes so that other girls can grow up like Lory and Morgan, never remembering a time when they didn't know about the organization.

By Monday night, five days before the final results would be announced, nerves had already begun to fray. But grace under pressure is a Rangerette tradition: the group's slogan is "Beauty knows no pain." I had heard stories of girls who kept smiling even after kicking so high they bloodied their noses. I'd heard how Gussie Nell Davis, the Rangerettes' revered and beloved founder — who was never seen wearing anything but stylish suits and four-inch heels — once stomped up to a girl who had fainted on the field and yelled, "I have no time for this! Get up!" That evening, when director Blair announced a surprise evaluation of the dance routine the hopefuls had learned on Sunday, word was out that one stressed-out girl had already packed up and left. Morgan's group of four nailed every move, while Lory's group struggled, panicking in the middle of the routine until one of them remembered a key jump. Throughout the evaluation, however, the girls' expressions remained determinedly cheerful as they strutted and leaped across the floor. Even the one who had mono. Even the one who had slipped and fallen on her behind. Even the one who had thrown up in the middle of the routine.

"All the hard stuff is done," Morgan said on Thursday night. After being weighed in on Sunday, each hopeful had sat down for an interview, during which many of them were asked to describe the ultimate all-American girl (although Lory was asked the more existential question "What makes you Lory?"). On Monday they had suffered through Model Night, when each of them, wearing only a leotard, had to exhibit poise by striding onto an empty stage, turning around to show off her figure, then walking up to a microphone and announcing her name, hometown, and proudest achievement. (The answers ranged from "raising a prize goat" to "organizing an education program for needy children in Indonesia.") On Tuesday night they had sat on the gym floor and eaten pizza while former Rangerettes, some in their seventies, told stories about Gussie Nell Davis, who had once boasted, "By the time I was through with [my girls], they were scared to death to act like heathens." The hopefuls cried when one speaker said that learning a Rangerette's discipline and optimism and perfectionism had guided many women through hard times, "even if it was difficult to understand that not everybody strives for perfection, such as a spouse who is not nearly as ever-so-perfect as you."

At the talent show on Wednesday, Morgan and Lory had performed a jazz routine, which they had paid twin former Rangerettes in Houston $400 to choreograph for them. "It was okay," Lory said, hesitantly. "It was good. Except my adviser said that I kept looking at the ground while I was dancing." Despite her usual optimism, Lory was beginning to seem nervous about her chances. Later that night, in the dorm room, Morgan took a bite out of a peanut butter sandwich and said, "My adviser is so awesome. I love her. She tells me what to do so I can fix it, and she said I've been fixing all these little things." Lory, who was munching on Cheese Nips, just stared blankly at the wall.

One day Morgan told me that her friends from high school thought she was crazy for wanting to be a Rangerette. "You don't understand," she said she told them. "It's tradition." When I mentioned that prancing about in miniskirts and white hats and white boots would be ridiculed in some places these days, she and a few other girls looked baffled. They figure that if someone doesn't understand why they would want to spend their first two years of parentless freedom in the Rangerettes, then that person must have never felt the thrill of being in a world-class drill team and is to be pitied. Besides, Morgan and Lory and the other hopefuls had made their pilgrimage to this little town for a bigger purpose: to become ambassadors for a disappearing way of life. It is a role that clearly strikes a chord. Watching the Rangerettes perform to the school's fight song, a college staffer told me, is an experience so powerful "it will make your hair stand on end."

On Thursday night, before the next day's final tryouts, the hopefuls filed into the auditorium for a "special presentation." Dana Blair walked onstage in front of the silent, ponytailed girls with their perma-grins and said, "You can stop smiling."

"Yes, ma'am. Thank you, Mrs. Blair," they said in unison. Blair announced that there was a special surprise, something that would remind them of why they had been working so hard. A drum roll sounded over the loudspeakers, then, as "The Rangers' Song" played, the Rangerettes marched onto the stage. "I thought *I* was sobbing," Morgan told me later, "then I looked at Lory."

"Sobbing," Lory said.

The hopefuls watched the Rangerettes that night with a heartbreaking eagerness to please, their smiles so fixed their faces twitched. Some of the girls had no backup plan if they didn't make the cut. One of them looked shocked when I asked what she would do if she didn't make it. "Go home, I guess," she said. Lory and Morgan assured me that they would be all right if neither of them made it; Lory would go on to teach elementary school and Morgan would be a Broadway star. But it would not be cool at all if one made it and the other didn't. Explained Morgan, "We wouldn't be on the same level anymore."

Earlier in the summer, I had asked Morgan and Lory to describe what the tryout week's finale is like. "So they bring us all into this auditorium and it's this big thing, right?" Morgan said. "And they bring us all on the stage and we sit down and we're all holding hands and shaking and we're already crying, right?"

"Waaay in advance," Lory said.

"And the Rangerettes are standing there in a line in their uniforms."

"Crying."

"Bawling-crying, because they know who didn't make it," Morgan explained. "And we're crying, and a couple of people say some things, you know, about how everything happens for a reason."

"Blah, blah, blah," said Lory.

"And then finally Mrs. Blair tells us all to bow our heads and say a prayer." Morgan looked at Lory and they each took a deep breath as they relived the moment. "And then a sign drops down" — a board listing the tryout numbers of the new Rangerettes — "and it's *chaos*, with girls *screamin'* and *runnin'* and *jumpin'*."

On Saturday morning at ten, judgment day had finally arrived. No guests were allowed in the building until after the announcement, so the tortured parents waited outside. Inside the auditorium, the line of Rangerettes stood onstage, as stiff as their hats. Their lips trembled and their wet eyes looked far off into the balcony as the hopefuls silently filed in and sat cross-legged on the stage floor in front of them. Lory was far less confident about the outcome than Morgan. At the final tryouts the day before, her foursome had slipped up again and forgotten a good portion of its third routine, to "Son of a Preacher Man." With so much disarray in the group, she had had a tough time remembering the steps. Afterward she had walked proudly off the gym floor, but in the waiting room had collapsed into a pile next to Morgan. Inconsolable, her face red, her lashes and lips blurry with tears, she had held her head between her knees for a long time.

Now it was the moment of truth. Blair stood before the hopefuls and began The Speech. She encouraged the ones who didn't make it to not give up on their dreams, recounting the morning's news report of a surfer who, although she'd lost an arm to a shark attack, was still surfing. The group sniffed and brushed away tears and prayed. Lory was sitting between Morgan and me, and she grabbed our hands and squeezed. Then a Rangerette read a poem called "Freshman Hopeful," and all around us chests heaved as girls sobbed and sweated.

When the sign was lowered, the room fell silent as the girls searched for their numbers. Then everyone let out a high-pitched scream, as if a winning free throw and a car crash had just occurred simultaneously. Lory and Morgan had both made it.

Meanwhile, the anxious parents waiting outside attempted to identify the shrieks inside. There were forty-five girls whose numbers had not appeared on the sign. Some of them hurried through the lobby to the parking lot, their parents hovering silently at their sides. Others lay paralyzed on the stage floor until their moms and dads helped them to their feet and smoothed their hair, hugging them and trying to remove them from the scene gracefully.

Finally, the only ones left were the 2004–2006 Rangerettes. Linking arms and yelling out the drum roll — "*Da* da! *Da* da! Daaaaaaa, *da* da!" — the sophomores surrounded the new members, who stood straight, their faces contorted with pride and emotion. As the group began to sing "The Rangers' Song," most of the new Rangerettes were quiet. But Morgan and Lory sang along, because they knew the words.

MICHAEL ROSENBERG

Why We Must Listen

FROM THE DETROIT FREE PRESS

LAST MONTH, the Detroit Tigers offered Dominican pitcher Carlos Perez a contract. He did not accept. The Tigers then withdrew their proposal.

Just another athlete-team negotiation.

Except that on three occasions, women have told authorities that Perez raped them.

"I know that he's had some problems," said Tigers president Dave Dombrowski. "We didn't even get to that point to where we had to check."

The incidents were separate. The women have never met. Perez has never been convicted; in fact, he has never gone to trial. He has maintained his innocence in all three incidents, saying the accusations are "lies."

But to at least two of the alleged victims, these cases show something else: the difficulty of a rape victim going up against a sports organization, an athlete, and the criminal justice system.

Seemingly every week, another athlete is accused of sexual assault. In our 24/7 media environment, these stories are like the sun bursting through the clouds: both blinding and fleeting.

This is the story of one athlete, the women who accused him, and the repercussions for all of them. Two of the women will speak on the record. The other will be quoted from police transcripts. Perez declined an interview request through his attorney, but one of the women filed a civil suit, and he gave a deposition for that. He will be quoted from that deposition.

This is also the story of how the system reacts. And it is a story to think about the next time an athlete is accused of sexual assault, and it flashes on our TVs.

We hear the accusation. We question the motives of the alleged victim, which we don't do with other crimes. We question the accuser more than we question the accused.

Team officials instinctively defend the player. Expensive attorneys disparage the accuser, saying the allegations are false. Sometimes the allegations are indeed false.

We decide, almost instantly, whom we believe.

Teammates and many fans defend the player, pointing out that consensual sex is readily available for pro athletes, so why would an athlete rape somebody? We don't give much thought to the counterargument: because sex is so readily available, some athletes feel entitled to it, regardless of the woman's wishes.

The woman has only her story. The police might believe her, as they did in all three cases with Carlos Perez. But oftentimes, that is not enough for a conviction or even a trial.

And then the player, media, and culture move along to the next sunburst, often leaving the alleged victim behind.

"I wanted to just crawl under a bed and hide," said Amy McQuillin, one of Perez's alleged victims. "My father really wanted me to report it immediately. I had people that I knew, that I had worked with in the media . . . It was just an absolute nightmare, the thought of it.

"You can't imagine someone is out there doing this on a regular basis and they're getting away with it continually. I really feel it's a systemic problem."

In the case of Carlos Perez, the women's accusations are similar, and their stories follow a familiar downward spiral.

The first time Perez was accused was in 1995, when he was an All-Star pitcher with the Montreal Expos. He was arrested on a road trip to Atlanta.

The case remained open for almost five years. Finally, in June 2000, the district attorney in Fulton County, Georgia, dropped the case — at the victim's request, said district attorney spokesman Erik Friedly.

But the accuser, Mandy Bernard, told the *Free Press* that she never asked for the case to be dropped. By all accounts, Bernard made it clear at the beginning that she wanted to press charges, and she assumed it would go to trial. For a year, she felt like she was trying to keep in contact with the police more than they were trying to keep in contact with her.

When the DA finally approached her, she had given up on the case. She didn't even respond.

"If they had come to me a month after, or even six months after, I would have gone after it," Bernard said. "For those four years, I was just kind of left wondering, 'I wonder what happened?'"

In 1999, Perez was investigated for two alleged rapes in Vero Beach, Florida. One of the women asked police to drop the investigation because she did not want to go through a grueling legal process. In the other case, the state attorney believed the alleged victim, McQuillin, but decided the chances of a conviction were too slim to merit a trial.

The *Free Press* generally does not publish the names of possible sexual-assault victims without their consent; Bernard and McQuillin agreed to have their names used.

McQuillin has a civil suit pending against Perez. In a deposition for that suit, he said he had consensual sex with Bernard and did not have sex with McQuillin or the other Florida woman at all.

Regardless of the outcome of the civil suit, the criminal justice system has run its course. In the eyes of the law, Carlos Perez is, was, and will remain an innocent man.

But soon, other athletes will be accused of similar crimes. And in an instant, we will react to the sunburst.

All of us.

"What goes through my mind?" Bernard said. "'That poor girl.' Honestly, that's what goes through my mind. I don't know what's worse: the actual incident that happens or the media and what happens afterward.

"It's more so what happens afterward that I feel sorry for."

An Incident in Atlanta

On the morning of September 23, 1995, Atlanta police detective C. A. Povilaitis arrived at the Atlanta Marriott Marquis to investigate a suspected sexual assault. He recently described the case as "very strong."

The suspect: Montreal Expos All-Star pitcher Carlos Perez.

The suspected victim: twenty-year-old Atlanta resident Mandy Bernard.

The allegation: Perez forced Bernard to have vaginal, oral, and anal sex.

The evidence on the police report: bruises throughout her body, her pantyhose in his room. Police took more than ninety photos of Bernard. She went to a hospital, where physical evidence was taken.

In an interview with the *Free Press*, Bernard repeated the story she told Povilaitis that night:

She had met Perez through a mutual friend at the Tongue and Groove nightclub in the upscale Buckhead neighborhood of Atlanta. They danced, and he bought her a drink. He asked for her phone number; she agreed to give it to him. He pulled out a DO NOT DISTURB doorknob sign for her to write on, which she thought was "odd." She wrote her phone number on it.

She was supposed to meet several friends outside the club at closing time, but they didn't show.

Perez offered to get her a cab. Bernard said okay. When he hailed one, she got in, and to her surprise, he joined her. She told the driver where she lived. Perez leaned forward and whispered something to the driver. The driver drove toward the Marriott, in the opposite direction of her house.

Bernard protested; she was a single mother and had to go home to her three-month-old son. Perez said he wanted to go back to his hotel room to give her something because they wouldn't see each other again for a while. She did not want to go. As they argued, the driver kept going to the hotel.

Perez held her arm firmly as they walked toward the elevator.

"I started getting a little concerned about the situation," Bernard said, "but not to where I could ever in my wildest dreams imagine that what was about to happen would happen."

When they got to his room, he walked over to a radio and turned it on. He started taking off his clothes.

She immediately tried to leave, but he grabbed her and threw her on his bed.

He then forced her to have vaginal, oral, and anal sex.

"I was like, 'Get off me! Stop!'" Bernard said. "I was trying to push him away. That's when I started yelling and crying.

"He put a pillow over my head. At that point, I really was just fearful for my life. I couldn't breathe. He was putting his hand over my mouth and on top of that had a pillow over my head. I just kind of gave up. The more I was fighting back, the worse and worse it was getting. I just kind of gave in."

Bernard said that when Perez finished the assault, he went into the bathroom for a quick shower. Bernard, crying and shocked, reached for the phone and called her friends. He came out of the bathroom and pushed her out of the room.

Friedly, the district attorney's spokesman, said the case file was missing. The *Free Press* obtained a copy of the police report through Bernard, who had requested a copy.

When Perez was deposed for McQuillin's civil trial, he told his version of the story, in English and in his native Spanish through an interpreter. As with Bernard's version, it starts with dancing and drinks at the Tongue and Groove.

"'Listen, I'm leaving,'" he recalled telling Bernard. "'I don't know if you want to hang out for a while.' She said, 'No problem, let's go.' We went together. So we take a taxi, and the taxi try to drop me in the back door from the hotel.

"I said, 'No, no, no. Let's go. Let's drop you in the front and just walk together.' I walk first, she walking right behind me. I never grab her hands.

"And nothing, we have sex. And then she — first she told me going to stay . . . She leave in the morning . . . And at two, three hours later in the morning she leave, people knock on my door like crazy. I was thinking (it was) one of my teammates, we going to go shopping, buying shoes and stuff."

Instead, it was the cops.

"They arrested me, you know," Perez said. "I was in jail for — I think it was two days. And then that was so funny. And then . . . they find out she was lying and everything. I feel bad that was myself."

He also said, "It was knocked down, they got rid of it because it was all a lie."

Not so, according to the district attorney.

Povilaitis, the detective on the scene, said he thought the case would be prosecuted.

"I believe that it was very strong," Povilaitis said. "Her statements never contradicted any other statement she had given me. There were definite signs of bruising and a struggle. We did take photos. There was an article of her clothing in a trash can in his room."

Two days after the arrest, Bernard testified at a preliminary hearing. She recounted the day of her testimony: To her left were a slew of news cameras. To her right was Carlos Perez, a man she said had raped her less than seventy-two hours earlier. In front of her was Perez's attorney, Guy Davis, peppering her with questions.

Afterward, Expos general manager Kevin Malone defended Perez.

"Everybody knows he's free-spirited," Malone told reporters, "but nobody would say he's mean or belligerent. Nobody can believe he would do that."

Perez was released on $50,000 bond. Davis told the media Perez was being set up, possibly for money. In a recent interview, he said he thought that was Bernard's motive all along, even though she never filed a civil suit. And he said the sex was obviously consensual.

Otherwise, why would she write her phone number on the DO NOT DISTURB sign in his room?

If Bernard requested an end to the case, it was news to him, Davis said. As far as he was concerned, the investigation was dropped because the case was weak.

"All of her story was incredible," he said. "I don't know what got the woman angry, or if she had lawsuits in mind from the beginning. Her story just didn't check out."

What about the photographs of her bruises?

"I don't recall that," Davis said. "Even if there was, the lovemaking might have got a little rough. Who knows?"

Bernard said she spent years wondering when the case would develop.

"I waited, waited, waited, waited, didn't hear anything," she said. "My family is all freaking out. I talked to Povilaitis several times over the next few months."

Povilaitis moved to the homicide division (and eventually to the Chatham County, Georgia, police department). Bernard said she called the police numerous times and was "given the run-around."

She finally decided to move on. She admits that as she looks back on it, she wished she had been more aggressive.

"I didn't want the charges dropped," Bernard said. "I have to be honest and say I wasn't actively pursuing it either."

Years after the incident — apparently in the late spring of 2000 — Bernard said she got a call from her father, Jim. Two men had shown up at his door and told him they needed an answer from Mandy Bernard.

Bernard did not call the district attorney. She did not want to relive an incident from almost five years earlier. Her son, three months old at the time of the incident, was now entering kindergarten. She was no longer determined to seek a trial.

Why did it take almost five years to reach a conclusion to the case?

On February 2, 1996, the *Montreal Gazette* quoted assistant district attorney Charles Hadaway as saying he was "looking toward having something one way or another" by February 16, 1996.

On April 14, 1997, the *Denver Post* reported that the district attorney still had not made a decision. Almost nineteen months had passed since Perez's arrest.

"The only time I've ever had to wait that long was when I knew the suspect was out of the country and I couldn't get my hands on them," Povilaitis said.

Perez did not pitch for Montreal in 1996 because of shoulder trouble, but from 1997 to 2000, he pitched for the Expos and Los Angeles Dodgers. The district attorney could have gone to Perez whenever he was in the United States if he wanted.

There was no need to go far. From 1997 until the case was dismissed, Perez's teams played twenty-five games in Atlanta.

What happened?

"My strong suspicion is that this case was one of the literally thousands of cases that were part of the backlog that this administration inherited" when it took office in 1997, Friedly said. "It took us a long time to really catch up and move forward. We had to clear out roughly fourteen thousand old cases."

An Accusation in Florida

Spring training, 1999. The Fulton County district attorney's office was supposedly in its fourth year of deciding whether to press charges against Carlos Perez. The police in Vero Beach, Florida, the spring training home of the Dodgers, were about to conduct their own investigations.

Word had filtered through the Dodgers organization that a woman said Perez had raped her. Somebody alerted Major League Baseball's security team, which then contacted the Vero Beach police. Vero Beach detective Keith Touchberry called the alleged victim.

The woman could not be reached by the *Free Press*. But according to police department transcripts, this is what she told Touchberry:

She had been living temporarily with a friend, Dodgers pitcher Pedro Borbon, and fellow pitcher Carlos Perez. She said Perez had made numerous advances, which made her uncomfortable.

"I was afraid Carlos was gonna do something to me," she told Touchberry. "Pedro said he wouldn't, because him and Pedro were such good friends . . . so when Carlos kept harassing me the next two days I thought I would get it on tape and let Pedro see for himself, 'cause he doesn't believe anything."

The woman told Touchberry that she hid a tape recorder in her bag. On March 31, 1999, as she did laundry in the home where Perez and Borbon lived, Perez arrived home and came on to her. She then went into the kitchen. Her bag, and the tape recorder, remained in the laundry room.

"That's when he took my car keys from me and that's when he took me into his bedroom," she told Touchberry. "I said I didn't need my keys, that I could walk, and he said that I could not go anywhere and he'd kill me there, and that's about where it just got out of control."

The phone rang. Perez answered. It was somebody who was supposed to meet him. He told the caller to wait an hour.

"I think we were in the kitchen discussing this for like, probably ten to fifteen minutes," the woman said. "I was like, 'Carlos, you don't wanna do this. You know, this is stupid.' . . . He kept saying that he wanted to have sex with me.

"I was backed up against the counter . . . and he had a hand on either side of me, so, I mean, there was no way that he was gonna let me anywhere . . . He picked me up and took me into the bedroom, carried me in there . . . against my will . . . I was like, hanging onto the door jamb as he was carrying me from the kitchen into the bedroom . . .

"It was absolutely foolish of me to think that there, you know, to even attempt, but . . . I did make some attempt. I was crying and saying, 'Please don't do this, no, no no,' and he, uh, pushed up, well . . . I don't wanna give details over the telephone.

"From there he proceeded to perform sexual acts against my will. Put it that way."

The woman told Touchberry she did not want to press charges. She had been molested before, when she was a patient at a hospital and a hospital employee attacked her.

The man went to jail for that attack, but she did not want to go through another court ordeal.

"I'm not committing that I want that kind of nightmare in my life again," she told Touchberry during one of their phone conversations.

Touchberry said he understood.

But the woman also had a request.

"Will you do me a favor?" she asked. "Will you try and find that Amy McQuillin girl?"

Another Inquiry in Florida

The cops soon tracked down Amy McQuillin. The other woman had heard that Perez had raped McQuillin. McQuillin told police she had not gone to them because she was worried nobody would believe her. She says now that she was fearful of the media coverage that would accompany an accusation; in the early 1990s, she was a public relations assistant for Major League Baseball and saw how alleged victims were perceived.

She knew how she had reacted.

"I was on the other side of the fence," McQuillin said. "If somebody had said something like this to me years ago, I would have said, 'They're after his money.' I was the last person I thought this would happen to."

Police pressed for her help. After initial reservations, she told them her story:

On the night of March 24, 1999, McQuillin was introduced to Perez through a mutual friend, former major leaguer Gilberto Reyes. They spent an hour or more talking at her family's vacation home in Vero Beach. Her parents were there.

Perez was going to take Reyes home in his Mercedes. He offered to take McQuillin for a ride.

"We were going to drive around the block, drop Gil off, and bring me to my parents' house," McQuillin said. "He didn't do that. He brought me to his house."

He said he needed to change his clothes. She waited in the living room. He called her into the bedroom. He began to kiss her, then said, "I'm going to own you," and pushed her back onto the bed.

Perez started to perform oral sex on her; she tried to get up, but he would not let her.

Then he shoved a pillow over her neck and face and forced her to have vaginal sex.

After he was through, he said, "That was just like pitching another ball game." McQuillin was bleeding.

In his deposition for McQuillin's civil suit, Perez was asked about both alleged attacks in Florida.

He said he never had sex with either woman.

He said the first woman in Florida never accused him of assault and battery. ("No, I never hear anything from that lady.") He said she never accused him of rape or making illicit advances toward her.

But Borbon, in his own deposition, said he confronted Perez about the woman's accusation. And Perez admitted that Borbon confronted him.

Perez said he avoided her whenever possible.

"When that lady was there, I left the house," Perez said in his deposition. "And always I was trying to get away from her because she was always trying to get close to me . . . You know, I don't know why she do it."

As for McQuillin?

He said they kissed in his car. When he got to his house, he changed his clothes and they left.

Perez was married at the time of his deposition. He testified he had not told his wife about the accusations or the civil suit.

Unlike the other accuser in Florida, McQuillin wanted charges pressed against Perez. The state attorney decided against it. McQuillin said she was not notified of the decision until she contacted authorities three months later.

"They found she wasn't credible," said Charles A. Sullivan Sr., Perez's attorney in Florida.

Vero Beach detective Kyle King disputes that. He said the investigation was closed because prosecutors were skeptical of their chances in court — there was limited physical evidence and significant time had elapsed since the incident. But King said he saw McQuillin as a "victim."

"I believed she was telling the truth," King said. "I don't have any reason to believe it didn't happen exactly the way she said it did. She was very candid. She did not try to alter facts that made the case more difficult to prove.

"She laid out exactly what happened — to the detriment of the case, in some regard, because she was so absolutely honest, it actually hurt the case."

The Epilogue

While the investigations were being conducted — and after they were completed — Carlos Perez was free to continue his major league career.

On July 16, 1999, he repeatedly bashed a water cooler in the Dodgers' dugout after a poor performance.

On March 11, 2000, he was arrested on a charge of driving under the influence in Vero Beach.

On March 26, 2001, he went on an expletive-laced rant against Dodgers management.

And on July 2, 2000, he allegedly shook flight attendant Sandra Komine violently on the team plane. She sued him.

"A stewardess accusing me of something," Perez said in his deposition. "It's a lie, that I pulled her hair."

Perez settled the suit for $150,000, according to Komine's attorney, Bruce Brusavich.

Mandy Bernard's rape accusation, a major news story at the time, is barely remembered by anybody but her.

The other two accusations never saw daylight. Just two more cases of "he said/she said."

All told, that makes this a story of "he said/she said/she said/she said."

Three women. They never knew one another.

Three separate incidents. Three accusations of rape against the same man.

"I don't find it unusual at all," said Davis, Perez's attorney in Atlanta. "I'll tell you one thing: black athletes are particularly susceptible to these allegations, particularly when white women are involved.

"Some of these folks don't seem to understand they are dealing with athletes. They are generally large and strong people. And (the women) get more than they bargained for. And I truly believe there are a large percentage of women that target black athletes, particularly white women — as was the case in Atlanta."

It should be obvious from those comments that Davis did not represent Perez in the Florida incidents. For one thing, Perez denies having sex with either woman in Florida; it is hard to argue that there was both no sex and rough sex.

And it is hard to argue that the women in Florida were after Perez's money from the beginning, since neither woman even went to the police. The police, upon hearing the accusations, went to them.

McQuillin eventually filed a civil suit, but the other woman has not pursued any criminal or civil action.

"There is probably no ballplayer alive who hasn't had this happen two or three times," said Sullivan, Perez's Florida attorney.

McQuillin, he said, "has just made up a story, as far as we're concerned. She's suing for money.

"The other woman in Florida — I don't know anything about that case. She herself said she didn't want to make any claim against him and it was all a misunderstanding."

A misunderstanding.

She said he forced her to have sex. He said they never had sex at all.

How could there be a misunderstanding?

Carlos Perez, thirty-three, is pitching in the Dominican Republic, with hopes of resuming his major league career.

Mandy Bernard, twenty-nine, works in accounting in Atlanta. She is happily married to a computer programmer. Her son, an infant when she met Perez, is now in the fourth grade.

"I'm past the point of crying and nightmares and being all freaked out now," Bernard said. "I'm pissed off. And I'm pissed off at myself for not following through."

Amy McQuillin, thirty-eight, is a copywriter and Web marketing specialist in Miami. She is taking paralegal courses and has contemplated law school. She also works with children who have been placed in the care of the state.

McQuillin spends much of her free time working on her civil suit, the last vestige of the women's accusations against Carlos Perez.

"I'm doing what I'm doing because I know it's not just me," McQuillin said. "I have a responsibility not to keep my mouth shut. People say it's not the brightest move. I'm at the point where I just don't care anymore. Something in my gut feeling says, 'You've got to say what happened.'"

TOM VERDUCCI

Sportsmen of the Year

FROM SPORTS ILLUSTRATED

THE CANCER would have killed most men long ago, but not George Sumner. The Waltham, Massachusetts, native had served three years aboard the USS *Arkansas* in World War II, raised six kids with a hell of a lot more love than the money that came from fixing oil burners, and watched from his favorite leather chair in front of the television — except for the handful of times he had the money to buy bleacher seats at Fenway — his Boston Red Sox, who had found a way not to win the World Series in every one of the seventy-nine years of his life. George Sumner knew something about persistence.

The doctors and his family thought they had lost George last Christmas Day, more than two years after the diagnosis. Somehow George pulled through. And soon, though still sick and racked by the chemo, the radiation, and the trips in and out of hospitals for weeks at a time, George was saying, "You know what? With Pedro and Schilling we've got a pretty good staff this year. Please let this be the year."

On the night of October 13, 2004, George Sumner knew he was running out of persistence. The TV in his room at Newton-Wellesley Hospital was showing Pedro Martinez and the Red Sox losing to the New York Yankees in game two of the American League Championship Series — this after Boston had lost game one behind Curt Schilling. During commercial breaks Sumner talked with his daughter Leah about what to do with his personal possessions. Only a few days earlier his wife, Jeanne, had told him, "If the pain is too much, George, it's okay if you want to go."

But Leah knew how much George loved the Red Sox, saw how closely he still watched their games, and understood that her father, ever quick with a smile or a joke, was up to something.

"Dad, you're waiting around to see if they go to the World Series, aren't you?" she said. "You really want to see them win it, right?"

A sparkle flickered in the sick man's eyes and a smile creased his lips.

"Don't tell your mother," he whispered.

At that moment, thirty miles away in Weymouth, Massachusetts, Jaime Andrews stewed about the Red Sox losing again but found some relief in knowing that he might be spared the conflict he had feared for almost nine months. His wife, Alice, was due to give birth on October 27. Game four of the World Series was scheduled for that night. Jaime was the kind of tortured fan who could not watch when the Red Sox were protecting a lead late in the game, because of a chronic, aching certainty that his team would blow it again.

Alice was not happy that Jaime worried at all about the possible conflict between the birth and the Sox. She threatened to bar him from the delivery room if Boston was playing that night. "Pathetic," she called his obsession with his team.

"It's not my fault," Jaime would plead, and then fall on the DNA defense. "It was passed down through generations, from my grandfather to my mother to me."

Oh, well, Jaimie thought as he watched the Red Sox lose game two, *at least now I won't have to worry about my team in the World Series when my baby is born.*

Dear Red Sox:

    My boyfriend is a lifelong Red Sox fan. He told me we'll get married when the Red Sox win the World Series . . . I watched every pitch of the playoffs.

                — SIGNED BY A BRIDE-TO-BE

The most emotionally powerful words in the English language are monosyllabic: love, hate, born, live, die, sex, kill, laugh, cry, want, need, give, take, Sawx.

The Boston Red Sox are, of course, a civic religion in New England. As grounds crew workers tended to the Fenway Park field last summer after a night game, one of them found a white plastic bottle of holy water in the outfield grass. There was a handwritten message on the side: GO SOX. The team's 2003 highlight film, punctuated by the crescendo of the walk-off home run by the Yankees' Aaron Boone in ALCS game seven, was christened, *Still, We Believe.*

"We took the wording straight out of the Catholic canon," club president Larry Lucchino says. "It's not *We Still Believe.* Our working slogan for next year is *It's More than Baseball. It's the Red Sox.*"

Rooting for the Red Sox is, as evident daily in the obituary pages, a life's definitive calling. Every day all over New England, and sometimes beyond, death notices include age, occupation, parish, and allegiance to the Sox. Charles F. Brazeau, born in North Adams, Massachusetts, and an Army vet who was awarded a Purple Heart in World War II, lived his entire eighty-five years without seeing the Red Sox win a world championship, though barely so. When he passed on in Amarillo, Texas, just two days before Boston won the 2004 World Series, the *Amarillo Globe News* eulogized him as a man who "loved the Red Sox and cheap beer."

Rest in peace.

What the Red Sox mean to their faithful — and larger still, what sport at its best means to American culture — never was more evident than at precisely 11:40 EDT on the night of October 27. At that moment in St. Louis, Red Sox closer Keith Foulke, upon fielding a ground ball, threw to first baseman Doug Mientkiewicz for the final out of the World Series — and the first Red Sox world championship since 1918. And then all hell didn't just break loose. It pretty much froze over.

All over New England, church bells clanged. Grown men wept. Poets whooped. Convicts cheered. Children rushed into the streets. Horns honked. Champagne corks popped. Strangers hugged.

Virginia Muise, 111, and Fred Hale, 113, smiled. Both Virginia, who kept a Red Sox cap beside her nightstand in New Hampshire, and Fred, who lived in Maine until moving to Syracuse, New York, at 109, were Red Sox fans who, curse be damned, were born *before Babe Ruth himself.* Virginia was the oldest person in New England. Fred was the oldest man in the world. Within three weeks after they had watched the Sox win the Series, both of them passed away.

They died happy.

*

Dear Red Sox:
Can you get married on the mound in, say, November at Fenway?

On its most basic level, sport satisfies man's urge to challenge his physical being. And sometimes, if performed well enough, it inspires others in their own pursuits. And then, very rarely, it changes the social and cultural history of America; it changes *lives*. The 2004 Boston Red Sox are such a perfect storm.

The Red Sox are *SI*'s Sportsmen of the Year, an honor they may have won even if the magnitude of their unprecedented athletic achievement was all that had been considered. Three outs from being swept in the ALCS, they won eight consecutive games, the last six without ever trailing. Their place in the sporting pantheon is fixed; the Saint Jude of sports, patron saint of lost athletic causes, their spirit will be summoned at the bleakest of moments.

"It is the story of hope and faith rewarded," says Red Sox executive vice president Charles Steinberg. "You really believe that this is the story they're going to teach seven-year-olds fifty years from now. When they say, 'Naw, I can't do this,' you can say, 'Ah, yes you can. The obstacle was much greater for these twenty-five men, and they overcame. So can you.'"

What makes them undeniably, unforgettably Sportsmen, however, is that their achievement transcended the ballpark like that of no other professional sports team. The 1955 Brooklyn Dodgers were the coda to a sweet, special time and place in Americana. The 1968 Detroit Tigers gave needed joy to a city teeming with anger and strife. The 2001 Yankees provided a gathering place, even as a diversion, for a grieving, wounded city. The 2004 Red Sox made an even deeper impact because this championship was lifetimes in the making.

This Boston team connected generations, for the first time, with joy instead of disappointment as the emotional mortar. This team changed the way a people, raised to expect the worst, would think of themselves and the future. And the impact, like all things in that great, wide community called Red Sox Nation, resounded from cradle to grave.

On the morning after the Red Sox won the World Series, Sergeant Paul Barnicle, a detective with the Boston police and brother of *Boston Herald* columnist Mike Barnicle, left his shift at six, purchased a single red rose at the city's flower market, drove forty-two miles to a cemetery in Fitchburg, Massachusetts, and placed the rose on the headstone of his mother and father, among the many who had not lived long enough to see it.

Five days later, Roger Altman, former deputy treasury secretary in the Clinton administration, who was born and raised in Brookline, Massachusetts, flew from New York City to Boston carrying a laminated front page of the October 28 *New York Times* (headline: "Red Sox Erase 86 Years of Futility in Four Games"). He drove to the gravesite of his mother, who had died in November 2003 at age ninety-five, dug a shallow trench, and buried the front page there.

Such pilgrimages to the deceased, common after the Red Sox conquered the Yankees in the ALCS, were repeated throughout the graveyards of New England. The totems changed, but the sentiments remained the same. At Mount Auburn Cemetery in Cambridge, for instance, gravestones were decorated with Red Sox pennants, hats, jerseys, baseballs, license plates, and a hand-painted pumpkin.

So widespread was the remembrance of the deceased that several people, including Neil Van Zile Jr. of Westmoreland, New Hampshire, beseeched the ball club to issue a permanent, weatherproof official Red Sox grave marker for dearly departed fans, similar to the metal markers the federal government provides for veterans. (Team president Lucchino says he's going to look into it, though Major League Baseball Properties would have to license it.) Van Zile's mother, Helen, a Sox fan who kept score during games and took her son to game two of the 1967 World Series, died in 1995 at seventy-two.

"There are thousands of people who would want it," Van Zile says. "My mom didn't get to see it. There isn't anything else I can do for her."

One day last year Van Zile was walking through a cemetery in Chesterfield, New Hampshire, when the inscription on a grave stopped him. BLOUIN was the family name chiseled into the marble. Beneath that it said NAPOLEON A. 1926–1986. At the bottom, nearest to the ground, was the kicker of a lifetime.

DARN THOSE RED SOX.

*

Dear Red Sox:

Thanks for the motivation.

—JOSUE RODAS, MARINE, 6TH MOTOR TRANSPORT COMPANY, IRAQ

Like snowflakes in a blizzard came the e-mails. More than ten thousand of them flew into the Red Sox server in the first ten days after Boston won the World Series. No two exactly alike. They came from New England, but they also came from Japan, Italy, Pakistan, and at least eleven other countries. The New England town hall of the twenty-first century was electronic.

There were thank-you letters. There were love letters. The letters were worded as if they were written to family members, and indeed the Red Sox were, in their own unkempt, scruffy, irreverent way, a likable, familial bunch. How could the faithful not love a band of characters self-deprecatingly self-dubbed the "idiots"?

DH David Ortiz, who slammed three walk-off postseason hits, was the Big Papi of the lineup and the clubhouse, with his outsized grin as much a signature of this team as his bat. Left fielder Manny Ramirez hit like a machine but played the game with a sandlot smile plastered on his mug, even when taking pratfalls in the outfield. Long-locked center fielder Johnny Damon made women swoon and men cheer and, with his Nazarene look, prompted a T-shirt and bumper sticker bonanza (WWJDD: WHAT WOULD JOHNNY DAMON DO? and HONK IF YOU LOVE JOHNNY).

First baseman Kevin Millar, with his Honest Abe beard and goofball personality, had the discipline to draw the walk off Yankees closer Mariano Rivera that began Boston's comeback in the ninth inning of ALCS game four. Right-hander Derek Lowe, another shaggy eccentric, became the first pitcher to win the clinching game of three postseason series in one October. Foulke, third baseman Bill Mueller, catcher Jason Varitek, and right fielder Trot Nixon — the club's longest-tenured player, known for his pine-tar-encrusted batting helmet — provided gritty ballast.

The love came in e-mails that brought word from soldiers in Iraq with Red Sox patches on their uniforms or Red Sox camouflage hats, the symbols of a nation within a nation. The cannon cockers of the Third Battalion Eleventh Marine Regiment built a mini Fenway Park at Camp Ramadi. Soldiers awoke at 3:00 A.M. to watch the Sox on a conference-room TV at Camp Liberty in Baghdad, the games ending just in time for the troops to fall in and receive their daily battle briefing.

A woman wrote of visiting an ancient temple in Tokyo and finding this message inscribed on a prayer block: MAY THE RED SOX PLAY ALWAYS AT FENWAY PARK, AND MAY THEY WIN THE WORLD SERIES IN MY LIFETIME.

Besides the e-mails there were boxes upon boxes of letters, photographs, postcards, school projects, and drawings that continue to cover what little floor space is left in the Red Sox offices. Mostly the missives convey profound gratitude.

"Thank you," wrote Maryam Farzeneh, a Boston University graduate student from Iran, "for being another reason for me and my boyfriend to connect and love each other. He is a Red Sox fan and moved to Ohio two years ago. There were countless nights that I kept the phone next to the radio so that we could listen to the game together."

Maryam had never seen a baseball game before 1998. She knew how obsessed people back home were about soccer teams. "Although I should admit," she wrote, "that is nothing like the relationship between the Red Sox and the fans in New England."

Dear Red Sox:
   Your first round of drinks is free.

                         — THE LOOSE MOOSE SALOON, GRAY, MAINE

Nightfall, and the little girl lies on her back in the rear seat of a sedan as it chugs homeward to Hartford. She watches the stars twinkle in between the wooden telephone poles that rhythmically interrupt her view of the summer sky. And there is the familiar company of a gravelly voice on the car radio providing play-by-play of Red Sox baseball. The great Ted Williams, her mother's favorite, is batting.

Roberta Rogers closes her eyes, and she is that little girl again, and the world is just as perfect and as full of wonder and possibilities as it was on those warm summer nights growing up in postwar New England.

"I laugh when I think about it," she says. "There is nothing wrong with the memory. Nothing."

Once every summer her parents took her and her brother, Nathaniel, to Boston to stay at the Kenmore Hotel and watch the

Red Sox at Fenway. Nathaniel liked to operate the safety gates of the hotel elevator, often letting on and off the visiting ballplayers who stayed at the Kenmore.

"Look," Kathryn Stoddard, their mother, said quietly one day as a well-dressed gentleman stepped off the lift. "That's Joe Di-Maggio."

Kathryn, of course, so despised the Yankees that she never called them just the *Yankees*. They were always the *Damnyankees*, as if it were one word.

"We didn't have much money," Roberta says. "We didn't take vacations, didn't go to the beach. That was it. We went to the Kenmore, and we watched the Red Sox at Fenway. I still have the images . . . the crowds, the stadium, the sounds, the feel of the cement under my feet, passing hot dogs down the row, the big green wall, the Citgo sign — it was green back then — coming into view as we drove into Boston, telling us we were almost there . . ."

Roberta lives in New Market, Virginia, now, her mother nearby in a retirement facility. Kathryn is ninety-five years old and still takes the measure of people by their rooting interest in baseball.

"Acceptable if they root for the Sox, suspect if they don't, and if a Damnyankee fan, hardly worth mentioning," Roberta says.

On October 27, two outs in the bottom of the ninth, Boston winning 3–0, Roberta paced in her living room, her eyes turned away from the TV.

"Oh, Bill," she said to her husband, "they can still be the Red Sox! They can still lose this game!"

It was not without good reason that her mother had called them the Red Flops all these years.

"And then I heard the roar," Roberta says.

This time they really did it. They really won. She called her children and called "everybody I could think of." It was too late to ring Kathryn, she figured. Kathryn's eyesight and hearing are failing, and she was surely sleeping at such a late hour.

So Roberta went to see Kathryn first thing the next morning.

"Mom, guess what? I've got the best news!" Roberta said. "They won! The Red Sox won!"

Kathryn's face lit up with a big smile, and she lifted both fists in triumph. And then the mother and daughter laughed and laughed. Just like little girls.

*

Dear Red Sox:

I really want to surprise my whole school and the principal.
— MAINE HIGH SCHOOL STUDENT, ASKING THAT THE ENTIRE TEAM
VISIT HIS SCHOOL

"Is that what I think it is?"

The conductor on the 11:15 A.M. Acela out of Boston to New York, Larry Solomon, had recognized Charles Steinberg and noted the size of the case he was carrying.

"Yes," the Red Sox VP replied. "Would you like to see it?"

Steinberg opened the case and revealed the gleaming gold Commissioner's Trophy, the Red Sox world championship trophy. Solomon, who had survived leukemia and rooting for the Sox, fought back tears.

The Red Sox are taking the trophy on tour to their fans. On this day it was off to New York City and a convocation of the Benevolent Loyal Order of the Honorable Ancient Redsox Diehard Sufferers, aka the BLOHARDS.

"I've only cried twice in my life," Richard Welch, sixty-four and a BLOHARD, said that night. "Once when the Vietnam War ended. And two weeks ago when the Red Sox won the World Series."

Everywhere the trophy goes someone weeps at the sight of it. Everyone wants to touch it, like Thomas probing the wounds of the risen Jesus. Touching is encouraged.

"Their emotional buckets have filled all these years," Steinberg says, "and the trophy overflows them. It's an intense, cathartic experience."

Why? Why should the bond between a people and their baseball team be so intense? Fenway Park is a part of it, offering a physical continuum to the bond, not only because Papi can stand in the same batter's box as Teddy Ballgame, but also because a son might sit in the same wooden-slat seat as his father.

"We do have our tragic history," says the poet Donald Hall, a Vermonter who lives in the house where his great-grandfather once lived.

The Sox specialized not, like the Chicago Cubs, in woebegone, hopeless baseball, but in an agonizing, painful kind. Indeed, hope was at the very breakable heart of their cruelty. From the 1967 Impossible Dream team until last season, the Red Sox had fielded thirty-one winning teams in thirty-seven years, nine of which reached the postseason. They were good enough to make it hurt.

"It's probably the desperately cruel winters we endure in New England," Mike Barnicle offers as an explanation. "When the Red Sox reappear, that's the season when the sun is back and warmth returns and we associate them with that.

"Also, a lot has to do with how the area is more stable in terms of demographics than most places. People don't move from New England. They stay here. And others come to college here and get infected with Red Sox fever. They get it at the age of eighteen and carry it with them when they go out into the world."

If you are born north of Hartford, there is no other big league baseball team for which to root, just as it has been since the Braves left Boston for Milwaukee in 1953. It is a birthright to which you quickly learn the oral history. The Babe, Denny Galehouse, Johnny Pesky, Bucky Dent, Bill Buckner, and Aaron Boone are beads on a string, an antirosary committed to memory by every son and daughter of the Nation.

"I've known nothing different in my life," says David Nathan, thirty-four, who, like his brother Marc, thirty-seven, learned at the hand of his father, Leslie, sixty-eight, who learned at the hand of his father, Morris, ninety-six. "It's so hard to put into words. I was sixteen in 1986 sitting in the living room when the ball went through Buckner's legs. We all had champagne ready, and you just sit back and watch it in disbelief.

"I was at game seven last year and brought my wife. I said, 'You need to experience it.' The Sox were up 5–2, and my wife said to me, 'They've got this in the bag.' I said, 'No, they don't. I'm telling you, they don't until the last out.'

"I used to look at my dad and not understand why he cried when they lost or cried when they won. Now I understand."

At 11:40 on the night of October 27, David Nathan held a bottle of champagne in one hand and a telephone in the other, his father on the other end of the line. David screamed so loud that he woke up his four-year-old son, Jack, the fourth-generation Nathan who, along with Marc's four-year-old daughter, Jessica, will know a whole new world of Sox fandom. The string of beads is broken.

David's wife recorded the moment with a video camera. Two

weeks later David would sit and write it all down in a long e-mail, expressing his thanks to Red Sox owner John Henry.

"As my father said to me the next day," David wrote, "he felt like a burden was finally lifted off of his shoulders after all these years."

He read the e-mail to his father over the telephone. It ended, "Thanks again and long live Red Sox Nation." David could hear his father sobbing on the other end.

"It's nice to know after all these years," Leslie said, "something of mine has rubbed off on you."

Dear Red Sox:
    I obviously didn't know what I was talking about.
    — FAN APOLOGIZING FOR HIS MANY PREVIOUS E-MAILS, ESPECIALLY
THE ONE AFTER GAME THREE OF THE ALCS, IN WHICH HE VERY COL-
ORFULLY EXPRESSED HIS DISGUST FOR THE TEAM AND THE PEOPLE
RUNNING IT

It was one minute after midnight on October 20, and Jared Dolphin, thirty, had just assumed his guard post on the overnight shift at the Corrigan-Radgowski correctional facility in Montville, Connecticut, a Level IV security prison, one level below the maximum. The inmate in the cell nearest him was ten years into a 180-year sentence for killing his girlfriend's entire family, including the dog.

Some of the inmates wore makeshift Red Sox "caps" — a commissary bandanna or handkerchief festooned with a hand-drawn iconic "B." Technically they were considered contraband, but the rules were bent when it came to rooting for the Red Sox in October. A few inmates watched ALCS game seven on twelve-inch portable televisions they had purchased in the prison for $200. Most leaned their faces against the little window of their cell door to catch the game on the cell block television. Others saw only the reflection of the TV on the window of another cell door.

A Sox fan himself, Dolphin watched as Alan Embree retired the Yankees' Ruben Sierra on a ground ball to end the greatest comeback in sports history. Dolphin started to cry.

"Suddenly the block erupted," Dolphin wrote in an e-mail. "I bristled immediately and instinctively my hand reached for my flashlight. It was pandemonium — whistling, shouting, pounding on sinks, doors, bunks, anything cons could find. This was against every housing rule in the book, so I jumped up, ready to lay down the law.

"But as I stood there looking around the block I felt something else. I felt hope. Here I was, less than ten feet away from guys that will never see the outside of prison ever again in their lives. The guy in the cell to my immediate left had 180 years. He wasn't going anywhere anytime soon. But as I watched him scream, holler, and pound on the door I realized he and I had something in common. That night hope beamed into his life as well. As Red Sox fans we had watched the impossible happen, and if that dream could come true why couldn't others.

"Instead of marching around the block trying to restore order I put my flashlight down and clapped. My applause joined the ruckus they were making and for five minutes it didn't stop. I applauded until my hands hurt. I was applauding the possibilities for the future."

Dear Red Sox:
    Any player who speaks Latin.
    — REQUEST FOR A RED SOX PLAYER TO VISIT THE LATIN CLASS AT A
MIDDLE SCHOOL IN NEWTON, MASSACHUSETTS

On the day after Christmas 2003, Gregory Miller, thirty-eight, of Foxboro, Massachusetts, an enthusiastic sports fan, especially when it came to the Sox, dropped dead of an aneurysm. He left behind a wife, Sharon, six-year-old twin boys, and an eighteen-month-old daughter. Sharon fell into unspeakable sadness and loneliness.

And then came October and the Red Sox.

Sharon, not much more than a casual fan before then, grew enthralled with the team's playoff run. She called her mother, Carolyn Bailey, in Walpole, as many as fifteen times during the course of a game to complain, exult, worry, commiserate, and celebrate. She even made jokes.

"My eyes need toothpicks to stay open," Sharon would say during the run of late games. "More Visine. I need more Visine."

Carolyn laughed, and her heart leaped to see her daughter joyful again. She had not seen or heard her like this since Gregory died.

"It was the first time she started to smile and laugh again," Carolyn says. "The Red Sox gave her something to look forward to every day. They became like part of the family."

The day after the Red Sox won the World Series, Carolyn wrote a letter to the team. In it she said of her daughter, "The Red Sox became her medicine on the road back from this tragedy. On behalf of my entire family — thank you from the bottom of our hearts."

Leah Storey of Tilton, New Hampshire, composed her own letter of thanks to the Red Sox. Her father had died exactly one year before the Red Sox won the World Series. Then her twenty-six-year-old brother, Ethan, died of an accidental drug overdose only hours after enthusiastically watching the Red Sox win ALCS game five. When the Red Sox won the World Series, Ethan's friends and family rushed outside the Storey house, yelled for joy, popped open a bottle of Dom Perignon, and gazed up in wonder at a lunar eclipse, and beyond.

"To us, with the memory of Ethan's happy night fresh in our minds, those games took on new meaning," Leah wrote of Boston's run to the championship. "Almost as if they were being played in his honor. Thank you for not letting him down. I can't express enough the comfort we derived from watching you play night after night. It didn't erase the pain, but it helped."

Dear Red Sox:
    I would even volunteer my time to clean up, do the dishes, whatever.
    — FAN ASKING THAT THE SOX HOST AN EVENT WHERE PLAYERS GREET FANS EIGHTY AND OLDER

On October 25 the Sox were two victories away from winning the World Series when doctors sent George Sumner home to his Waltham house to die. There was nothing more they could do for him. At home, though, George's stomach began to fill with fluid, and he was rushed back to the hospital. The doctors did what they could. They said he was in such bad shape that they were uncertain if he could survive the ride back home.

Suddenly, his eyes still closed, George pointed to a corner of the room, as if someone was there, and said, "Nope, not yet."

And then George went back home to Waltham. Leah knew that every day and every game were precious. She prayed hard for a sweep.

On the morning of game four, which stood to be the highlight of Jaime Andrews's life as a "pathetic," obsessed Red Sox fan, his wife, Alice, went into labor. Here it was: the conflict Jaime had feared all summer. At 2:30 P.M. he took her into South Shore Hospital, where they were greeted by nurses wearing Red Sox jerseys over their scrubs.

At 8:25 P.M., Alice was in the delivery room. There was a TV in the room. The game in St. Louis was about to begin.

"Turn on the game."

It was Alice who wanted the TV on. Damon, the leadoff hitter, stepped into the batter's box.

"Johnny Damon!" Alice exclaimed. "He'll hit a home run."

And Damon, his long brown locks flowing out the back of his batting helmet, did just that.

The Red Sox led, 3–0, in the bottom of the fifth inning when the Cardinals put a runner on third base with one out. Jaime could not stand the anxiety. His head hurt. He was having difficulty breathing. He broke out in hives. It was too much to take. He asked Alice to turn off the television. Alice insisted they watch until the end of the inning. They saw Lowe pitch out of the jam. Jaime nervously clicked off the TV.

At home in Waltham, George Sumner slipped in and out of sleep. His eyes were alert when the game was on, but when an inning ended he would say in a whisper, which was all he could muster, "Wake me up when the game comes back on." Each time no one could be certain if he would open his eyes again.

The Red Sox held their 3–0 lead, and the TV remained off in the delivery room of South Shore Hospital. At 11:27 P.M. Alice gave birth to a beautiful boy. Jaime noticed that the baby had unusually long hair down the back of his neck. The nurses cleaned and measured the boy. Jaime was still nervous.

"Can I check the TV for the final score?" he asked Alice.

"Sure," she said.

It was 11:40 P.M. The Red Sox were jumping upon one another in the middle of the diamond. They were world champions.

George Sumner had waited a lifetime to see this — seventy-nine years, to be exact, the last three while fighting cancer. He drew upon whatever strength was left in his body and in the loudest whisper that was possible he said, "Yippee!"

And then he closed his eyes and went to sleep.

"It was probably the last real conscious moment he ever had," Leah says.

George opened his eyes one last time the next day. When he did he saw that he was surrounded by his extended family. He said, "Hi," and went back to sleep for the final time.

George Sumner, avid Red Sox fan, passed away at 2:30 A.M. on October 29. He was laid to rest with full military honors on November 2.

On the day that George Sumner died, Alice and Jaime Andrews took home a healthy baby boy. They named him Damon.

Dear Red Sox:
  Thank you, 2004 World Series Champs, Boston Red Sox. It was worth the wait.
  — CLOSING LINES OF THE OBITUARY FOR CYNTHIA MARIE RILEY-RUBINO IN A HAMDEN, CONNECTICUT, NEWSPAPER, SENT TO THE TEAM BY ANOTHER FAN

Ballplayers are not social scientists or cultural historians. Quite to the contrary, they create an insular fortress in which all considerations beyond the game itself are feared to carry the poison of what are known generically as "distractions."

The Red Sox are not from Boston; they come from all corners of the United States and Latin America, and flew to their real homes immediately after a huge, cathartic parade on October 30, during which normal life in New England was basically TiVoed for three hours. ("Three and a half million people there *and* a 33 rating on TV!" marveled Steinberg.)

There is an awful imbalance to our relationship with athletes, as if we are looking through a one-way mirror. We know them, love them, dress like them, and somehow believe our actions, however trivial, alter the outcome of theirs, all while they know only that we are there but cannot really see us.

Howard Frank Mosher of Vermont was in northern Maine in the summer of '03 for a book-signing, during which he discussed his upcoming novel, *Waiting for Teddy Williams*, a fanciful tale in which the Red Sox (can you imagine?) win the Series; he heard a small group of people singing in the back of the bookstore. It sounded like, *Johnny Angel, how I love him* . . .

As Mosher drew closer he realized they were singing, *Johnny Damon, how I love him* . . . What was going on? he wondered.

"We're performing an incantation," one of the men said. "Damon has been in a slump. We think it's working. He was 4-for-5 last night."

Crazy. How could Damon know this? How could any Boston player know that the Reverend William Bourke, an avid Sox fan who died in his native Rhode Island before game two of the World Series, was buried the day after Boston won it all, with a commemorative Sox baseball and that morning's paper tucked into his casket?

How could Pedro Martinez know that on the morning of World Series game two, Dianne Connolly, her three-year-old son, Patrick, and the rest of the congregation of St. Francis of Assisi parish in Litchfield, New Hampshire, heard the choir sing a prayer for the Red Sox after the recessional? "Our Father, who art in Fenway," the singers began. They continued, "Give us this day our perfect Pedro; and forgive those, like Bill Buckner; and lead us not into depression . . ."

How could Curt Schilling know that Laura Deforge, eighty-four, of Winooski, Vermont, who watched every Red Sox game on TV — many of them *twice* — turned the ALCS around when she found a lucky, thirty-year-old Red Sox hat in her closet after game three? Laura wore it everywhere for the next eleven days, including to bingo. (And she's still wearing it.)

"I've only been here a year," Schilling says, "and it's humbling to be a part of the relationship between Red Sox Nation and this team. I can't understand it all. I can't. All I can do is thank God that He blessed me with the skills that can have an impact on people's lives in some positive way."

The lives of these players are forever changed as professionals. Backup catcher Doug Mirabelli, for instance, will be a celebrity thirty years from now if he shows up anywhere from Woonsocket to Winooski. The '04 Red Sox have a sheen that will never fade or be surpassed.

The real resonance to this championship, however, is that it changed so many of the people on the other side of the one-way glass, poets and convicts, fathers and sons, mothers and daughters, the dying and the newborn.

The dawn that broke over New England on October 28, the first in the life of little Damon Andrews, was unlike any other seen in three generations. Here began the birth of a new Red Sox Nation, sons no longer bearing the scars and dread of their fathers and grandfathers. It felt as clean and fresh as New Year's Day.

Damon's first dawn also was the last in the fully lived life of George Sumner.

"I walked into work that day," Leah Sumner says, "and I had tears in my eyes. People were saying, 'Did he see it? Did he see it? Please tell me your dad saw it.' You don't understand how much comfort it gave my brothers and sisters. It would have been that much sadder if he didn't get to see it.

"It was like a blessing. One lady told me he lived and died by the hand of God. I'm not religious, but he was blessed. If he was sitting here, he would agree there was something stronger there.

"It was the best year, and it was the worst year. It was an unbelievable year. I will tell my children and make sure they tell their children."

The story they will tell is not just the story of George Sumner. It is not just the story of the 2004 Boston Red Sox. It is the story of the bond between a nation of fans and its beloved team.

"It's not even relief," Leah says. "No, it's like we were a part of it. It's not like they did it for themselves or for money or for fame, but like they did it for us.

"It's bigger than money. It's bigger than fame. It's who we are. It's like I tell people. There are three things you must know about me. I love my family. I love blues music. And I love baseball."

Spectacular — but Sad

FROM THE PROVIDENCE JOURNAL

P. T. BARNUM, WHO SAID, "There's a sucker born every minute," once had an act where two midgets named Tom Thumb and
Lavinia Warren were on display.

This was in Bridgeport, Connecticut, Barnum's hometown, and
as the crowds flocked to see what was billed as the smallest couple
in the world, there was only one problem. People simply stopped
and stared too long, thus creating long lines.

What to do?

So Barnum, according to the book *Chase the Game*, put a sign over
the couple's head. It said, SEE THE EGRESS, with an arrow. The
crowd followed the arrow, only to see another sign leading them to
the EGRESS, then another that said, APPROACHING EGRESS. To
one last sign that said, AT LAST, THE EGRESS.

At which point the people went through a door that led them to
the street, "egress" being from the Latin word for exit.

I was thinking of that yesterday at the Convention Center, at
something called "The Sox Spectacular," where a handful of Sox
players — highlighted by Manny Ramirez and Johnny Damon —
were on display.

For a price.

Or how does $175 for a signed ball sound? Or $250 for so-called
premium items?

After you pay the $20 entrance fee, of course.

This way to the Egress.

The obvious question is why do men who make millions charge
big appearance fees to meet their fans? Why do men with rich and

famous lifestyles feel the need to gouge the very fans whose allegiance ultimately pays for their lifestyles?

The simple answer?

Because they can.

The other answer?

Good ol' American commerce, I suppose. What the market will
bear.

And there's no question there's a market. By all accounts Red
Sox memorabilia is all but jumping off the shelves, as everyone
wants to feel a connection to this team that won its first World
Series title in eighty-six years. There's also a huge memorabilia
business out there, one that's independent of the Sox winning
the World Series. Combine the two and you have "The Sox Spectacular."

Just don't forget to bring your wallet.

And yet there was something sad about yesterday's show.

Like the woman who said she couldn't afford to get Johnny
Damon's autograph for $175 and had to settle for Doug Mira-
belli's, which went for only $30.

Like the woman with two little kids in Manny jerseys who had
forked over something like $460 for his autograph, and was still
waiting at 2:15 even though Manny was supposed to have been
there at one o'clock.

Like the innumerable people who had to stand behind the cor-
doned-off autograph area, nearly fifty yards away from where the
players signed, if they didn't spring for the autograph fee.

For these are the people who make the Red Sox such a phenom-
enon, the ones who give their hearts to it, make these players the
stars they are. It's the fans who made the Sox finally winning a
world title such a wonderful story, the ones who are there year after
year as the players come and go. The fans, and their long-suffering
wait, who became almost as much a part of the story as the players
themselves.

And yet yesterday the only thing that seemed to matter was how
much? How much for Manny? How much for Damon?

How much?

As if even affection comes with a price tag.

You could see that with Damon's appearance.

He came out to cheers, even if the size of the crowd shortly after one o'clock was only a few hundred people, far less than what I'd been led to believe. He sat down to sign, and the people who had bought the autograph ticket started going through the roped-off funnel that led to Damon, like parishioners on their way to Lourdes.

The others stood behind the barricade. They waved. They took pictures. Occasionally, they yelled out to Damon. In the end, though, it all seemed about as intimate as trying to find a date on the Internet.

And when Damon was finally finished, he stood up, waved a few times, and disappeared through the curtain.

Couldn't he have walked along the perimeter and shaken some hands? Couldn't he have done *something* to acknowledge the people not in the autograph area before vanishing through the looking glass?

Guess not.

And maybe it doesn't matter. Certainly it doesn't when you are twelve and your name is Aaron Granoff and you and your friend are here because you pleaded with your mother to take you.

But then, you're twelve.

And I know that no one's putting a gun to anyone's head to pay for an autograph. And I know you can make a case that the players are simply trying to cash in on a business in which someone is always trying to rip off their signatures. But take away Bronson Arroyo and these are the same players who couldn't find the time to come here when the Red Sox brought the World Series trophy to the State House lawn, back when there was no appearance fee.

So when I left the Convention Center yesterday I wanted to take a shower, anything to wash away the slime of naked commerce. To wash away the sight of overpaid players, who should get down on their knees and kiss the feet of the fans, instead of charging people who adore them too much. And the people who want to give someone who makes $20 million a year $195 for his autograph?

This way to the Egress.

Biographical Notes

Notable Sports Writing of 2004

Biographical Notes

MICHAEL BAMBERGER is a senior writer for *Sports Illustrated*. Before joining *SI*, he was a reporter for the *Philadelphia Inquirer*. This is his third appearance in *The Best American Sports Writing*.

PAM BELLUCK is the New England bureau chief for the *New York Times*. A graduate of Princeton and winner of a Fulbright Scholarship, she got her start in journalism as a freelance correspondent in the Philippines for the *San Francisco Chronicle*. She subsequently worked for the *Atlanta Journal-Constitution* and the *Philadelphia Inquirer*. During her ten years at the *New York Times* she has covered stories ranging from the Oklahoma City bombing to the New York City school system to the struggles families face when making end-of-life decisions. She has also worked on several investigative projects. From 1997 until late 2001, she was the paper's Midwest bureau chief, writing on everything from inner-city housing to Indian reservations. Since then, she has been based in Boston, where she is responsible for covering the region and has led the paper's national coverage of issues like the clergy sexual abuse crisis and the controversy over same-sex marriage.

IRA BERKOW has been a sports columnist and feature writer for the *New York Times* for the past twenty-four years. He shared a Pulitzer Prize for national reporting at the *Times* and was a finalist for the Pulitzer for commentary. He has appeared several times in *The Best American Sports Writing*, as well as in *The Best American Sports Writing of the Century*.

JOHN BRANT has been a senior writer and writer at large for *Runner's World* since 1985 and a contributing editor for *Outside* since 1992. He has contributed features to *Rolling Stone*, the *New York Times Magazine*, *National*

Geographic Adventure, Travel and Leisure, SI Women, Inc., Worth, and many other publications. A book-length version of "Duel in the Sun" will be published in late 2005 or early 2006.

STEVE COLL started his career at the *Washington Post* in 1985. Initially a staff writer for the paper's style section, he went on to serve as the *Post's* New York financial correspondent, the South Asia bureau chief, editor of the *Washington Post Magazine,* and managing editor. Coll was awarded the Pulitzer Prize for explanatory journalism in 1990 for his piece (co-written with David A. Vise) on the Securities and Exchange Commission and the Livingston Award in 1992 for outstanding international journalism. He is the author of several books, including *The Deal of the Century, Eagle on the Street* (with David A. Vise), *On the Grand Trunk Road, The Taking of Getty Oil,* and *Ghost Wars: The Secret History of the CIA, Afghanistan, and Bin Laden, from the Soviet Invasion to September 10, 2001.*

DAVID DIBENEDETTO is the editor of *Salt Water Sportsman* magazine and the author of *On the Run: An Angler's Journey Down the Striper Coast.* He has written for numerous publications, including *Rolling Stone, Men's Journal,* and *Field and Stream.*

MARK FAINARU-WADA is an investigative reporter for the *San Francisco Chronicle.* He and his colleague Lance Williams were honored with George Polk, Edgar A. Poe, Associated Press Sports Editors, and Dick Schaap Excellence in Sports Journalism national awards for their coverage of the BALCO steroids scandal. Fainaru-Wada is a graduate of Northwestern University.

SEAN FLYNN is a frequent contributor to *Esquire* and many other publications. His *Esquire* article "The Perfect Fire" won the National Magazine Award and was later expanded into the book *3000 Degrees.* He is also the author of *Boston DA,* an account of life inside a big-city district attorney's office.

MICHAEL HALL has written for the *Austin Chronicle,* the *Austin American-Statesman, Trouser Press, Blender,* and *Men's Journal.* Since 1997 he has been a senior editor at *Texas Monthly;* his December 2003 story "Death Isn't Fair" was nominated for a National Magazine Award. Hall is an accomplished songwriter and musician and has recorded numerous albums, both with various bands (Wild Seeds, Setters, Woodpeckers) and on his own. He lives in Austin with his wife Liz, son Jackson, and stepdaughter Natalie.

TRAVIS HANEY wrote for the *Anderson* (South Carolina) *Independent-Mail* and the *Augusta Chronicle* before joining Morris News Service in Atlanta in March 2005 to cover Major League Baseball. He graduated from the University of Tennessee in 2003.

CHRIS JONES, winner of the 2005 National Magazine Award in feature writing, is a writer at large at *Esquire.* He lives in Ottawa.

PAT JORDAN has been a freelance writer for forty years. He lives and works in Fort Lauderdale, Florida, with his wife, Susan, six dogs, and a bird. He has written thirteen books, among them *A False Spring*, a memoir that *Time* magazine called the best book ever written about sport. *A False Spring* and his other memoir, *A Nice Tuesday*, will be reprinted this fall by the University of Nebraska Press. He is also the author of hundreds of magazine stories for such publications as the *New York Times, Playboy, The New Yorker,* the *Atlantic Monthly,* and *Harper's.*

MARK KRAM, JR. has previously appeared in *The Best American Sports Writing* in 1994, 2002, and 2003. A sportswriter for the *Philadelphia Daily News* since 1987, he previously worked for the *Detroit Free Press* and the *Baltimore News American.* He is also a contributing writer for *Philadelphia* magazine. Kram lives in Haddonfield, New Jersey, with his wife and two daughters.

MICHAEL LEWIS is the author of several bestselling books, including *Liar's Poker* and *Moneyball.* Lewis has served as editor and columnist for the British weekly *The Spectator* and as senior editor and campaign correspondent of *The New Republic.* He has filmed and narrated short pieces for ABC-TV's *Nightline,* hosted a series on presidential politics for National Public Radio, and served as a visiting fellow at the University of California at Berkeley. He holds a BA degree from Princeton and a master's in economics from the London School of Economics.

THOMAS MCGUANE lives in Sweet Grass County, Montana. He is the author of eight novels and a collection of stories, as well as two collections of essays, including *The Longest Silence: A Life in Fishing.*

ANDREW MILLER spends most workdays on his primary freelance focus, music, by reviewing records and interviewing bands, but baseball remains an equally consuming passion. His work has appeared in *Alternative Press, Rolling Stone,* the *Dallas Observer, The Pitch,* and more than a dozen other publications. He lives in Kansas City, where he roots for the Royals with unrelenting optimism.

BILL PLASCHKE, a native of Louisville, Kentucky, has been a sports columnist with the *Los Angeles Times* since 1996. He has been named National Sports Columnist of the Year by a variety of organizations, including the Associated Press, Sigma Delta Chi, and National Headliners;

nominated for a Pulitzer Prize; and named Man of the Year by the Los Angeles chapter of Big Brothers/Big Sisters for his longtime involvement in that organization as a Big Brother. A regular panelist on the ESPN daily talk show *Around the Horn,* he has also published a collection of his columns entitled *Plaschke: Good Sports, Spoil Sports, Foul Balls, and Odd Balls.* Plaschke and his wife, Lisa Jacobs, have three children: Tessa, Willie, and Mary Clare.

BILL REYNOLDS is a sports columnist at the *Providence Journal.* He has written eight books, including *Fall River Dreams, Glory Days,* and the best-selling *Success Is a Choice,* with Rick Pitino. His latest book is *Cousy: His Life, Career, and the Birth of Big-Time Basketball.*

LINDA ROBERTSON is a columnist and feature writer at the *Miami Herald.* Originally from Midland, Michigan, she was once Miami's fastest prep miler, later graduated from the University of North Carolina, and now lives in Coral Gables with her husband Andres Viglucci and children Nicolas, Natalie, and Sofia. She is a former president of the Association for Women in Sports Media. This is her fifth appearance in *The Best American Sports Writing.*

MICHAEL ROSENBERG is a columnist for the *Detroit Free Press,* where he has worked since 1999. He has also worked for the *Washington Post,* the *Chicago Tribune,* the *Philadelphia Inquirer,* and the *Sacramento Bee.* He lives in Michigan with his wife Erin.

RICHARD SANDOMIR has been the sports television and business writer for the *New York Times* since 1991; he previously worked for *Newsday, Sports Inc., Financial World,* and the *Stamford Advocate.* His work has appeared in *Sports Illustrated, Sport, Manhattan Inc.,* the *Los Angeles Times,* the *Washington Post,* and *Inside Media.* He is the author or coauthor of four books, including *Bald Like Me* and *Friendly Persuasion,* with Bob Woolf, about the art of negotiating.

DAVID SHIELDS is the author of eight books of fiction and nonfiction, including *Black Planet: Facing Race During an NBA Season,* and a finalist for the National Book Critics Circle Award in criticism and the PEN USA Award in creative nonfiction. His book *Remote: Reflections on Life in the Shadow of Celebrity* won a PEN/Revson Foundation Fellowship, and *Dead Languages: A Novel* received the Governor's Writers Award. He has also received a Guggenheim Fellowship and two National Endowment for the Arts Fellowships. His essays and stories have appeared in the *New York Times Magazine, Harper's,* the *Yale Review,* the *Village Voice,* Salon.com, *Slate, McSweeney's,* the *Utne Reader,* and dozens of other publications.

GARY SMITH is a senior writer at *Sports Illustrated* and past winner of a National Magazine Award for feature writing. The author of *Beyond the Game: The Collected Sports Writing of Gary Smith*, he has appeared in *The Best American Sports Writing* a record ten times.

WRIGHT THOMPSON is the sports enterprise reporter for the *Kansas City Star*. A native of Clarksdale, Mississippi, he is the son of Walter and Mary Thompson. He dedicates his story to his father, who passed away in 2004 after a lengthy battle with cancer.

KEVIN VAN VALKENBURG is a graduate of the University of Montana, where he briefly played college football. He lives in Baltimore and has worked as a reporter for the *Baltimore Sun* since 2000.

TOM VERDUCCI spent ten years as a sports reporter for *Newsday*, serving as its national baseball columnist from 1990 to 1993, before joining *Sports Illustrated* as a senior writer. Born in East Orange, New Jersey, and raised in Glen Ridge, New Jersey, he received a BA in journalism in 1982.

KATY VINE, a staff writer at *Texas Monthly*, has contributed to the *Oxford American*, *This American Life*, and the *Texas Observer*. She lives in Austin.

L. JON WERTHEIM has been a senior writer for *Sports Illustrated* since 1997, covering tennis, sports business issues, and the NBA. He received a law degree from the University of Pennsylvania and joined *SI* immediately after passing both the New Jersey and New York bar exams. Before law school, he was the assistant editor at *Rip City*, a Portland Trail Blazers fan magazine. He received his BA degree from Yale in 1993.

MARK ZEIGLER joined the *San Diego Union* after graduating from Stanford in 1985 with a degree in classical studies. When the *Union* merged with the *San Diego Tribune* in 1992, Ziegler remained on staff, where he now writes about soccer, the Olympics, drug use in sports, and other issues. He lives in San Diego and coaches varsity high school basketball.

Notable Sports Writing of 2004

SELECTED BY GLENN STOUT

RICK BASS
The Old Bull. *Field and Stream,*
December 2004
ROB BIERTEMPFEL
Fayette Native Took Painful Track to
Fame. *Tribune-Review,* July 24, 2004
JOHN BILLMAN
BadAss Brother Truckers. *Skiing,*
October 2004
BARRY BLITT
Let Us Now Praise Crazy Mofos.
Outside, June 2004

DIRK CHATELAIN
All the King's Children. *Omaha World
Herald,* December 17, 2004
GREG CHILD
The Color of Darkness. *Outside,* June
2004
KEVIN CONLEY
Be Like Dee. *The New Yorker,* March 8,
2004
KAREN CROUSE
Strokes of Sorrow. *Palm Beach Post,*
July 4, 2004

BONNIE DESIMONE
Covering Tour Can Be a Fog, Yet
Fantastic. *Chicago Tribune,* June 30,
2004

WAYNE DREHS
Touched by Fate. *ESPN.com,* May 20,
2004
CHRIS DUFRESNE
Pitch Counts? Set-up Men? Six-
Inning Quality Starts? *Los Angeles
Times,* June 13, 2004
CHARLES DUHIGG
See You Later? *Los Angeles Times,* June
29, 2004

DAVID FERRELL
With a Great Divide, Lakers Season
Hasn't Really Come Together. *Los
Angeles Times,* May 8, 2004
BILL FIELDS
The Rarest Bird. *Golf World,* April 2,
2004
JONATHAN SAFRAN FOER
Kingpong. *Details,* September 2004
STEVE FRIEDMAN
Lost and Found. *Runner's World,* July
2004
Me and My Bike: A Love Story.
Bicycling, September 2004

JERRY GARRETT
Angela Does NASCAR. *Car and Driver,*
December 2004

THE B·E·S·T AMERICAN SERIES®

THE BEST AMERICAN SHORT STORIES® 2005

Michael Chabon, guest editor, Katrina Kenison, series editor. "Story for story, readers can't beat the *Best American Short Stories* series" (*Chicago Tribune*). This year's most beloved short fiction anthology is edited by the Pulitzer Prize–winning novelist Michael Chabon and features stories by Tom Perrotta, Alice Munro, Edward P. Jones, Joyce Carol Oates, and Thomas McGuane, among others.

0-618-42705-8 PA $14.00 / 0-618-42349-4 CL $27.50

THE BEST AMERICAN ESSAYS® 2005

Susan Orlean, guest editor, Robert Atwan, series editor. Since 1986, *The Best American Essays* has gathered the best nonfiction writing of the year and established itself as the premier anthology of its kind. Edited by the best-selling writer Susan Orlean, this year's volume features writing by Roger Angell, Jonathan Franzen, David Sedaris, Andrea Barrett, and others.

0-618-35713-0 PA $14.00 / 0-618-35712-2 CL $27.50

THE BEST AMERICAN MYSTERY STORIES™ 2005

Joyce Carol Oates, guest editor, Otto Penzler, series editor. This perennially popular anthology is sure to appeal to crime fiction fans of every variety. This year's volume is edited by the National Book Award winner Joyce Carol Oates and offers stories by Scott Turow, Dennis Lehane, Louise Erdrich, George V. Higgins, and others.

0-618-51745-6 PA $14.00 / 0-618-51744-8 CL $27.50

THE BEST AMERICAN SPORTS WRITING™ 2005

Mike Lupica, guest editor, Glenn Stout, series editor. "An ongoing centerpiece for all sports collections" (*Booklist*), this series has garnered wide acclaim for its extraordinary sports writing and topnotch editors. Mike Lupica, the *New York Daily News* columnist and best-selling author, continues that tradition with pieces by Michael Lewis, Gary Smith, Bill Plaschke, Pat Jordan, L. Jon Wertheim, and others.

0-618-47020-4 PA $14.00 / 0-618-47019-0 CL $27.50

THE BEST AMERICAN TRAVEL WRITING 2005

Jamaica Kincaid, guest editor, Jason Wilson, series editor. Edited by the renowned novelist and travel writer Jamaica Kincaid, *The Best American Travel Writing 2005* captures the traveler's wandering spirit and ever-present quest for adventure. Giving new life to armchair journeys this year are Tom Bissell, Ian Frazier, Simon Winchester, John McPhee, and many others.

0-618-36952-X PA $14.00 / 0-618-36951-1 CL $27.50

THE B·E·S·T AMERICAN SERIES®

THE BEST AMERICAN SCIENCE AND NATURE WRITING 2005

Jonathan Weiner, guest editor, Tim Folger, series editor. This year's edition presents another "eclectic, provocative collection" (*Entertainment Weekly*). Edited by Jonathan Weiner, the author of *The Beak of the Finch* and *Time, Love, Memory*, it features work by Oliver Sacks, Natalie Angier, Malcolm Gladwell, Sherwin B. Nuland, and others.

0-618-27343-3 PA $14.00 / 0-618-27341-7 CL $27.50

THE BEST AMERICAN RECIPES 2005–2006

Edited by Fran McCullough and Molly Stevens. "Give this book to any cook who is looking for the newest, latest recipes and the stories behind them" (*Chicago Tribune*). Offering the very best of what America is cooking, as well as the latest trends, time-saving tips, and techniques, this year's edition includes a foreword by celebrated chef Mario Batali.

0-618-57478-6 CL $26.00

THE BEST AMERICAN NONREQUIRED READING 2005

Edited by Dave Eggers, Introduction by Beck. In this genre-busting volume, bestselling author Dave Eggers draws the finest, most interesting, and least expected fiction, nonfiction, humor, alternative comics, and more from publications large, small, and on-line. With an introduction by the Grammy Award–winning musician Beck, this year's volume features writing by Jhumpa Lahiri, George Saunders, Aimee Bender, Stephen Elliott, and others.

0-618-57048-9 PA $14.00 / 0-618-57047-0 CL $27.50

THE BEST AMERICAN SPIRITUAL WRITING 2005

Edited by Philip Zaleski, Introduction by Barry Lopez. Featuring an introduction by the National Book Award winner Barry Lopez, *The Best American Spiritual Writing 2005* brings the year's finest writing about faith and spirituality to all readers. This year's volume gathers pieces from diverse faiths and denominations and includes writing by Natalie Goldberg, Harvey Cox, W. S. Merwin, Patricia Hampl, and others.

0-618-58643-1 PA $14.00 / 0-618-58642-3 CL $27.50

HOUGHTON MIFFLIN COMPANY www.houghtonmifflinbooks.com